THE INVISIBLE SOLDIER

THE INVISIBLE SOLDIER

The Experience of the Black Soldier, World War II

Compiled and Edited by Mary Penick Motley
with a Foreword by Colonel Howard Donovan Queen, USA (Ret.)

Wayne State University Press, Detroit, 1975

Library of Congress Cataloging in Publication Data
Main entry under title:

The Invisible soldier.

Bibliography: p.
Includes index.
1. World War, 1939–1945–Afro-Americans–Sources.
2. Afro-Americans–Interviews. 3. Afro-Americans–
History–1877–1964–Sources. 4. United States–Race
question. I. Motley, Mary Penick, 1920–
D810.N4I58   940.54 03   75-29420
ISBN 0-8143-1550-X

The opinions expressed in the oral histories compiled in this
book are those of the informants and do not reflect an editorial policy
of the publisher.
Grateful acknowledgment is made to the following for
financial assistance in the publication of this volume: Mr. Ernest
Goodman; Move Detroit Forward Committee; Mrs. Mary A. Hamilton; Dr.
Marjorie Peebles Meyers.

This book is dedicated:

to Colonel Howard Donovan Queen (Ret.).

To all black men who have served
in the armed forces of the United States.

And particularly to the black
soldiers of World War II who endured and persevered far above and
beyond the call of duty.

Gentlemen, I salute you!

CONTENTS

ILLUSTRATIONS AND MAPS

Illustrations 1–13 follow p. 31 in text.

Illustrations 14–26 and Maps follow p. 135 in text.

Maps

1. Scattered training camps for elements of the 92nd Infantry Division preceding 1943 transfer to Fort Huachuca, Arizona.
2. Fortified town of Massa and Other Objectives of Allied Troops before and after Cinquale Canal Crossing, February 5–8, 1945.
3. Serchio Valley Sector, Italy, Fall-Winter, 1944–45.
4. Towns in France and Belgium; Long-Range Escort Missions of the 332nd Fighter Group.

Each man interviewed is introduced with the rank held at the time he left the armed services for civilian life.

Usage of the 1970s indicates *black* as the preferred term for people of Afro-American descent, in both scholarly and popular works. I have made no attempt to force consistency upon the oral histories here presented. The reader will find *colored, Afro-American, Negro,* and *black*, according to the preference of the informants. Acronyms and abbreviations, as well as some slang terms, are explained in the glossary.

The most frequently quoted source of background information is Ulysses Lee, *The United States Army in World War II: Special Studies: The Employment of Negro Troops*, Washington: Office of the Chief of Military History, 1966. Parenthetical page references in the text are to this source. Full publishing information for all sources briefly cited in the notes will be found in the bibliography.

FOREWORD

It gives me a great deal of pleasure to be a part of the book *The Invisible Soldier* because the Afro-American soldier has been studiously neglected in the chronicles of America's wars. As a Regular Army man, having retired after thirty-nine years of service in the United States Army, I have bitterly resented the civilian notion that Negroes cannot cut it as fighting men; such ideas come from ignorance of the facts.

I am glad *The Invisible Soldier* concentrates upon the Afro-American GI of World War II; it is most fitting. Prejudice and segregation grew rapidly in the armed forces with the turn of the century* and the malignancy of racism reached such outrageous proportions during our war against fascism it bordered on insanity.

Just as the seeds of World War II are to be found in World War I the seeds for the most flagrant racism Negro soldiers would ever encounter took root in World War I. It is therefore essential that the reader of this book have a rudimentary knowledge of the Negro soldier during World War I.

For Negro America World War I was a traumatic experience. The treatment of Negro officers was shameful. Negro soldiers were repeatedly humiliated. Both officers and soldiers trained for combat were forced into labor battalions or assigned menial chores. Throughout the war there were ugly conflicts between Negro and white soldiers, and Negro soldiers and white civilians.

Especially galling was the prejudicial attitude of the Wilson administration. When the war broke out, Colonel Charles Young, the highest-ranking Negro officer in the country, was ordered to Letterman General Hospital in California and retired for high blood pressure. To dramatize his physical

*See Marvin E. Fletcher, *The Black Soldier and Officer in the United States Army, 1891–1917*, for a detailed account of the circumstances from which this situation developed. M.P.M.

fitness, the colonel rode his old horse, Charlie, from Xenia, Ohio, to Washington, D. C., but he was never returned to duty. The removal of Colonel Young was a bitter blow to America's Negroes and an indication of things to come.

It is not generally known that Colonel Young established the first training school for Negro officers at Fort Huachuca, Arizona, in the early part of 1917. Fifteen of us passed the officers' examination only to be told we would not be commissioned and that we were to report to Fort Des Moines not later than June 1917.

One has little difficulty recalling incidents of stateside mistreatment of Negro soldiers in the Great War. In August 1917, a race riot between the white citizens of Houston, Texas, and the 24th Infantry Regiment, a Regular Army regiment, occurred. It was the result of insults and abuse heaped upon the members of the 24th by the white citizenry. Two Negroes and seventeen whites were killed in the ensuing battle. This happened at the time 1,200 Negroes were in training at the 17th Provisional Training Unit at Fort Des Moines. Several noncommissioned officers of the 24th were selected to return to their regiment and aid in indicting those accused of participating in the riot.

Major General Chamberlain, Inspector General, United States Army, came to Fort Des Moines and in the presence of the 1,200 men announced, "If you know anything about the matter [Houston] you'd better start talking now because there is going to be a big hanging"; this before the General Court-martial members had been appointed to try the case! Thirteen soldiers were hanged and a large number were sent to prison for life.

A second Houston was barely averted a few weeks later in South Carolina. The 15th National Guard Unit from New York City, later designated the 369th Infantry Regiment, was sent to Spartansburg, South Carolina, for training. Colonel Haywood, the commanding officer, was white; but like all Negro National Guard units it had a predominance of Negro officers and an all-Negro personnel.

The white citizens of Spartansburg resented these black Yankees. One night Noble Sissle, who later became a world famous band leader, was kicked bodily out of a white hotel for daring to purchase a newspaper in the lobby. The next night members of the 15th marched on Spartansburg. Colonel Haywood succeeded in intercepting his men and persuaded them to return to camp. He went to Washington in person and asked that his unit be removed from Spartansburg and not be placed in similar environs. The request was complied with at once; the 369th became the first black combat regiment to go overseas; that it was totally untrained for military action was irrevelant.

I was no longer at Fort Des Moines when the 369th was rushed overseas. I had been assigned to the 368th Infantry Regiment, 92nd Division, Camp Mead, Maryland; my rank was captain. At Camp Mead all Negro artillery and engineering officers were relieved of their commands and made infantry officers. The reason: Negro officers could not possibly be intelligent enough to hold these positions, particularly in the engineers.

Major General C. C. Ballou, commander of the 92nd Division, made it a point after every critique following a field problem to say, "The white man made the 92nd Division and the white man can break the 92nd Division. You people constitute only ten percent of the population of the United States."

We sailed from our POE aboard the USS *George Washington* under totally segregated conditions. We hoped for some respite on foreign soil, but once in France our troubles really began. American authorities spent considerable time watching Negro soldiers and French women. Brigadier General James B. Irwin issued an order which forbade Negro soldiers speaking to French women. American MPs would arrest soldiers of color caught disobeying this order. The whole anti-Negro campaign reached its height, rather its depth, with an order from General Pershing's headquarters 7 August 1918:

> *TO THE FRENCH MILITARY MISSION STATIONED*
> *WITH THE AMERICAN ARMY*
> Secret Information Concerning Black American Troops

We must prevent the rise of any pronounced degree of intimacy between French officers and black officers. We may be courteous and amiable with the last but we cannot deal with them on the same plane as white American officers without deeply wounding the latter. We must not eat with them, must not shake hands with them, seek to talk to them or to meet with them outside the requirements of military service. We must not commend too highly these troops particularly in front of white Americans. Make a point of keeping the native cantonment from spoiling the Negro. White Americans become very incensed at any particular expression of intimacy between white women and black men.

Racial prejudice supported by Pershing's directive was the reason Private Henry Johnson and Sergeant William Butler of the 369th Infantry Regiment were not given the Congressional Medal of Honor. Both men were awarded the *Croix de Guerre* with Palm by the French.* Butler did receive the

---

*The citation of Private Henry Johnson, Company C, 369th Infantry Regiment, by order of General Gouraud, reads: "While serving on double night sentry duty, having been attacked by a group of a dozen Germans, he put one of the group out of commission with a gun shot and seriously wounded two others with knife blows. Although having received three wounds from a revolver and hand grenade in the beginning of the confrontation he went to the aid of his wounded companion who was being captured by the enemy and continued the struggle until the Germans were put to flight. He gave a magnificent example of courage and energy. . . ."

The citation of Sergeant William Butler, Company L of the same regiment, by order of Marshal Pétain, December 8, 1918, reads: " . . . Under-officer giving to his men a constant example of courage. August 11, 1918, a sudden attack was being made by the regiment and he rushed to guide their undertaking. August 18, he counter-attacked a

Distinguished Service Cross but Johnson was ignored by his country. I think Colonel Young's statement, "The sole intent of the white man during World War I was to discourage and discredit Negro leadership," was accurate then and applied equally in World War II.

Contrary to popular opinion the Negro combat soldier in World War I brought shame neither to his people nor his uniform. General Goybet, of the French army, in his farewell speech to the Afro-American soldiers of the 371st and 372nd Infantry regiments that had been brigaded with his division, the 15th (Red Hand) Division said:

> For seven months we have lived as brothers-at-arms, partaking in the same activities, sharing the same dangers, and the same hardships.
> Never will the Red Hand forget the indomitable dash, the heroic rush of the American regiments up the Observatory Ridge and into the Plains of Monthois. The most powerful defenses, the most strongly organized machine gun nests, the heaviest artillery barrage, nothing could stop them. These crack regiments overcame every obstacle with a complete contempt for danger; through their steadfast devotion the Red Hand Division, for nine whole days of severe struggle was constantly leading the way for the victorious advance of the 4th Army.

Upon arriving in France the men of the 369th Infantry Regiment were put to work constructing a railroad yard and stevedoring. When this regiment was transferred to the French high command they were trained for combat by the French, using French helmets and weapons. For the 191 days they were on the front line the 369th never lost an inch of ground nor one man as a prisoner of war. The German's called them "hell fighters." The commanding officer of the 369th was awarded Frances's highest decoration, the Legion of Honor.

General Pershing, addressing the men of the 92nd Division at Le Mans, 28 January 1919, said, "I want you officers and soldiers to know that your division stands second to none in the record you have made since your arrival in France." These are strange words indeed, for the 92nd Division spent a goodly portion of its time as labor battalions, thanks to the same General Pershing. Pershing had no excuse for doubting the fighting ability of Negro soldiers since his nickname "Black Jack" and his reputation as a soldier had come from commanding the renowned black 10th Cavalry.

The 369th, 370th, 371st, and 372nd all-Negro Infantry regiments brigaded with the French Army were not misused as were the regiments of the 92nd Division. They were trained by the French for combat, and that is the

---

group of 25 Germans who were leading away his wounded officer and four men whom he rescued while killing four of the enemy. . . ."

(Citations courtesy of Brigadier General E. de Grasset, French Military Attaché, Washington, D.C., translated by Irene Graves.)

role they played. The result was these four regiments sustained a large number of battlefield casualties, which was not true of the 92nd Division. It should be noted that the 370th was originally the old 8th Illinois National Guard Unit, commanded by Colonel Franklin A. Denison, a Negro, and had all Negro officers. There is every reason to believe that the 93rd Division never became a reality in World War I because it would have included the 369th and the 370th; the 370th was completely Negro with a Negro colonel, and the 369th's officer roster was almost entirely colored. There were just too many Negro officers above the rank of lieutenant to make a 93rd Division palatable.

One of the great ironies of the war concerned the four Negro Regular Army regiments that had already earned outstanding reputations on many battlefields: the 9th and 10th Cavalry and the 24th and 25th Infantry regiments. These units were assigned to positions within the United States or its territories while draftees were chosen to do the fighting. These four outfits, professional by reputation and experience, had fought Indians, Spaniards, Filipinos, and Mexicans but were not allowed to fight the Teutonic Germans.

Colonel James Moss, commanding officer of the 367th, which had done an outstanding job at the Battle of Metz, 10 November 1918, saving the white 56th from annihilation, wrote a regimental book on the 367th, stating in the introduction:

> Having been born and bred in Louisiana, and having served eighteen of my twenty-one years in the army with colored troops, what I say is based on experience.
> If properly trained and instructed, the colored man makes as good a soldier the world has ever seen. The history of the Negro in all of our wars, including the Indian Campaign, shows this. He is by nature of a happy disposition; he is responsive and tractable; he is amenable to discipline, he takes pride in his uniform; he has faith and confidence in his leader, he possesses physical courage—all of which are valuable military assets.
> Make the colored man feel you have faith in him. Be strict with him but treat him fairly and justly making him realize that in your dealings with him he will always be given a square deal. Commend him when he does well and punish him when he is refractory—that is to say let him know he will always know that he will get what is coming to him be it reward or punishment.
> In other words, treat and handle the colored man as you would any other human being out of whom you would make a soldier, and you will have as good a soldier as history has every known [Quoted in Emmett Scott, *The American Negro in the World War*, p. 194.]

The sentiments of Colonel Moss, a military expert of world fame, and a handful of officers of similar thinking, such as Colonel William Haywood, were given no consideration as a number of years were spent on studying the role of the black soldier in future wars. A committee of field grade officers, many of whom would play major roles in World War II, produced a brief which explained the black man as a soldier for future commanders of black troops, stating:

> As an individual the negro is docile, tractable, lighthearted, carefree, and good-natured. If unjustly treated he is likely to become surly and stubborn, though this is usually a temporary phase. He is careless, shiftless, irresponsible and secretive. He resents censure and is best handled with praise and by ridicule. He is immoral, untruthful, and his sense of right doing is relatively inferior. Crimes and convictions involving moral turpitude are nearly five to one as compared to convictions of whites on similar charges.
>
> On the other hand the negro is cheerful, loyal, and uncomplaining if reasonably well fed. He has a musical nature and a remarkable sense of rhythm. His art is primitive. He is religious. With proper direction in mass, Negroes are industrious. . . . Their emotions are unstable and their reactions uncertain. Bad leadership . . . is easy to communicate to them. [Lee, p. 45.]

This simple-minded summation of a whole people would be the guideline for white officers under whom Negro soldiers would be captive subjects during World War II.

Colonel Howard Donovan Queen, Ret.*

---

*Biographical Note: Howard Donovan Queen was born 18 November 1894, the son of Sergeant Richard Queen, Troop F, 10th Cavalry, a fifteen-year veteran of the Indian campaign. Following his father's footsteps, young Queen enlisted in the United States Army 13 April 1911 and became a member of Troop K, 10th Cavalry. In 1916 as Corporal Queen he was one of the few survivors of the massacre at Carrizel during the punitive expedition against Pancho Villa in Mexico. During World War I he was a captain with the 368th Infantry Regiment, 92nd Division. In World War II he was commanding officer of the all-black 366th Infantry Regiment.

PREFACE

This book records personal experiences of black American soldiers during World War II, collected in 1971–72 from taped interviews and letters. I have two reasons for compiling it. First: until very recently, popular history texts have made very little, if any, mention of the black soldiers in America's wars, as if the black disappeared during wartime only to reappear when the smoke cleared away. The second reason is contingent on the first: many young blacks today insist there is no black history before 1965 (why this should be the date of its inception I do not know, nor do they when one demands a clear explanation) and that all before this date is somehow tainted with slavery and "tomism." Middle-aged and older black veterans of America's wars, who bear the brunt of this attitude, know better.

To ignore the place of the black soldier in his country's history is to deny him and his people part of their heritage as Americans, a heritage antedating the American Revolution. The heroism of black soldiers in America's wars is attested by the records of the highest decorations awarded to American fighting men. Twenty black soldiers won the Congressional Medal of Honor during the Civil War. (It was during that war that the Medal of Honor came into existence.) Twenty blacks won the medal during the Indian campaign from 1866 to 1890. Eight won the Congressional Medal during the Spanish-American War of 1898. No black soldier was awarded the medal during World Wars I and II; however, sixteen won it in the Korean and Viet Nam wars.* The disappearance of blacks from the Medal of Honor list for fifty-two years would be more than adequate motivation for study, and indeed it supplied impetus to mine.

To date, the most extensive treatment of the part played by black

---

*Medal of Honor List supplied by the Library of Congress; Irwin Lee, *Negro Medal of Honor Men* (New York: Dodd, Mead & Co., 1966); *Medal of Honor Men* (Washington, D.C.: USGPO, 1973).

17

soldiers in World War II is Ulysses Lee's *The Employment of Negro Troops* (1966), eighth volume of the subseries of special studies published in the multivolume *The United States Army in World War II* under the aegis of the Office of the Chief of Military History. This work is of primary value to the student and to the research worker. I have depended upon it for place names, dates, names of military units, maps, etc. Even a cursory examination reveals its unsuitability for use by the general reader: its ponderous size (740 pages) and a text set in double columns to accommodate exhaustive documentation are enough to make it discourage all but the most serious, determined, and qualified readers. The condensation of extended research into one volume compounds its difficulty.

Lee's work is not intended for use by the general public (it is available through the Superintendent of Documents, United States Government Printing Office); furthermore, since it was planned as a volume in a series that would "present a comprehensive account of the activities of the Military Establishment during World War II" (p. ii) it is, in one sense, a view from the top.

An orientation "from the top" strikes the reader with the first sentence of the foreword by Brigadier General Hal Pattison, Chief of Military History: "The principal problem in the employment of Negro Americans as soldiers in World War II was that the civilian backgrounds of Negroes made them generally less well prepared than white Americans to become soldiers or leaders of men" (p. vii).

This statement implies a military-establishment assumption which, if policies were based upon it, would result in data to "justify" it. Its validity as a conclusion—if indeed it was a conclusion based on evidence—would depend on the amount and kind of evidence supporting it. Recent scholarship shows that the assumption was unjustified and the conclusion invalid. But it takes time for false images to be replaced by more accurate ones in the public mind. It is long past time, I believe, to utilize the still-living sources of evidence as well as the archives. Oral accounts of World War II, by black soldiers and junior officers, are an available source of evidence that has been neglected for almost thirty years. Along with scholarly studies based on primary materials from the war years, they can help to replace myth with knowledge about black Americans during World War II.

Gathering material from government agencies to document my study was often difficult. Information sought from the St. Louis Bureau of Military Records became "unprivileged" only after I appealed to my congressman, Charles Diggs, Jr.; to Rear Admiral Samuel Gravely, U.S. Navy; and to Major General Daniel ("Chappie") James (332nd Fighter Group). Earlier, the Bureau had informed me that two black Distinguished Service Cross winners had never served in the armed forces. On my insistence, the Bureau eventually discovered the records of these two men and sent copies of their citations. I received one unforgettable response from a government agency to my request for casualty lists for blacks in World Wars I and II: "We do not keep records of casualties or citations for World War I and II on an ethnic basis." My interviewees and I were astonished; neither they nor I could understand how segregated armies could produce integrated casualty and citation lists.

With the help of Congressman Diggs I eventually received casualty lists for the 92nd Division in World Wars I and II. Although I received a list of casualties for the 93rd Division, World War II, I was thwarted in my effort to obtain such a list for certain black regiments. I was informed that casualty records were kept on divisions only. Most whites belonged to divisions, most blacks to smaller units that were temporarily attached to a division for a specific purpose.

Another difficulty encountered was to secure the cooperation of the ex-servicemen approached. Some had told their stories before; as nothing had come of it they felt exploited, and rightly so. Others could not bring themselves to relive the days they had spent in the service. Several, although agreeing that such a book should be written and that as yet no man had come forth to do it, could not bring themselves to discuss their wartime experiences with a woman. Several who eventually granted my request for information said that their only reason for doing so was that I was perhaps right in believing that the public in general and the younger generation in particular should know what happened to black men—because they were black—in the United States armed forces during World War II.

As to the accuracy of the interviews, none of the men I talked with pretends to have total recall. Close to thirty years have passed since the events described, and time inevitably blurs outlines and erases details. Fortunately, some of the men had kept letters and diaries from the war years which became part of the taped interviews. Exact personal names and places were the details most likely to be forgotten. Lee's history was indispensable in transcribing and checking place names. Maps and gazetteers, a more obvious source of help, were of limited use in that some towns and villages are too small to be considered mapworthy by cartographers and were listed in no gazetteer at my disposal. Hamlets obliterated by military action appear in no recent gazetteer. The headnotes to the chapters and individual interviews indicate the location of these, where possible, by reference to a neighboring large town or city.

Occasionally accounts conflict. I have noted discrepancies but have not always been able to resolve them. My essential purpose is to preserve each man's perspective upon the events affecting him. Occasionally, one man's recollection pieces out, or explains, something incomplete or unexplained in another's. The reader will notice this particularly in chapter 5, where one man's contribution suggests an answer to a hitherto unanswered question about an event during the Italian phase of the war.

My book does not pretend to be a scientific sampling of opinions.

Even were this my purpose, the universe from which such a sampling would come no longer exists to be sampled. Although several interviews represent friends and acquaintances in Detroit, whom I knew during the war years, I was not acquainted with most of the men included here before the beginning of my project. Charles Hill, Jr., was a childhood friend; I had not known that Herbert Barland, whom I met in postwar years, had been a fighter pilot. Each man interviewed or heard from gave me names of others to contact. (I had yet to meet one man who has contributed inestimably to this book, Colonel Howard Donovan Queen of the United States Army (ret.).) At the suggestion of Edward Brooke (366th Infantry Regiment, World War II), to whom I wrote for information, and the Honorable Judge Wade McCree, a Detroiter, I wrote to Colonel Queen and thereby uncovered a wealth of information. Colonel Queen not only contributed a foreword to the book, but provided a personal account of his war experience as commanding officer of the 366th Infantry Regiment, along with statements and evaluations that I have used throughout the course of the book, especially in the introduction to chapters 1 and 5.

Since the book is a compilation of oral histories, I have avoided a topical arrangement that would break up individual accounts. Each man's stateside experiences are personal equipment or burden that he carried overseas with him, an integral part of what he has to say. To orient the reader I have, however, made use of groupings that the study of my material suggested.

Men from unrelated units, but with a similar thread of experience and reaction, are grouped together in the first chapter, which includes accounts emphasizing how the black soldier, part of a national war effort, found himself confronted by an array of local attitudes and customs, in the training camp to which he was sent, in the surrounding community, on maneuvers, and overseas. In this chapter patterns of experience take shape, to reappear throughout the book.

Men of the 93rd Infantry Division are grouped within the chapter "Servicemen in the Pacific and the Far East," which also includes interviews with a few men who served in the U.S. Navy, and accounts of war experiences by men who drove the Ledo Road in the China-Burma-India theater of war. I have combined the accounts of the 761st Tank Battalion and the 614th Tank Destroyer Battalion within a chapter on men in the armored forces and have placed with them interviews of two field artillery men who served in the same campaigns as did the tankers, and an interview with a driver of the "Red Ball Express," which supplied the men of the armored forces in France, 1944–45. Interviews with men of the 332nd Fighter Group appear within one chapter. Interviews with men of the all-black 92nd Infantry Division form the final chapter. Since the 366th Infantry Regiment was attached to that division in the late fall of 1944 for combat service, interviews with members of the 366th are integral to that chapter.

A short introduction precedes each chapter, and headnotes are provided to orient the reader as well as to provide continuity. Since I had more than sixty informants, sometimes only one from a given unit, space would preclude a background for them all. Even without space limitations, complete backgrounds would often be impossible because information from official sources is unavailable. Histories of small units such as regiments and battalions are not kept by the government but are the responsibility of the individual unit. Two black combat units—the 761st Tank and the 614th Tank Destroyer battalions—kept detailed battalion histories which I found invaluable in preparing the introduction to chapter 3. Not all service units had experiences as dramatic as those of the Red Ball Express and of drivers on the Ledo Road; men in service units were not impelled to write histories of the roads they built, the latrines they dug, or the laundry they washed. Some of the interviews here are the only available history for a unit.

Space limitations dictated some condensation or omission. References to the Korean War have been shortened, and the interviews of several informants were omitted.

In the writing of this book there are so many to thank for so much. First, I wish to express my gratitude to all of the men whose favorable response to my request for an interview made this book possible. There were sixty-four altogether; their names appear in the list of contributors preceding the index. In their honesty and openness, they have trusted in my not misquoting or misinterpreting what they told me, and I hope their approval of the text will justify their trust.

In addition to granting an interview, Christopher Sturkey assisted me with names of men to contact, incidents to include, and gave me a thorough lesson in the workings of a tank destroyer battalion. The cooperation of Horace Evans, Horace Jones, and Edward Donald was total in their patient response to my repeated requests for details about tanks. Hondon Hargrove, Floyd Jones, and Howard Tandy were my field artillery experts. Alexander Jefferson, Henry Peoples, and Charles Hill, Jr., were always courteous and informative about planes in general and combat flying in particular.

I am deeply indebted to the Honorable Judge Wade McCree, Jr., for his invaluable assistance with the 92nd Infantry Division and the 366th Infantry Regiment. He also made contacts for me and gave me an unforgettable lesson in the geography of the Po Valley. Judge McCree also suggested the title for my book.

Harry Duplessis, Chico Hollander, Robert Pitts, Christopher Sturkey, and Horace Evans entrusted scrapbooks and battalion histories to me which were invaluable in checking dates and places.

The staff of the Purdy Memorial Library, Wayne State University, were unfailingly courteous and helpful. Donald Ewing, reference librarian, located books for me concerning the battles and campaigns mentioned in the interviews. George Masterton, reference librarian, verified names of military units; and Paul Anderson, research assistant at the archives, verified place names which were difficult to transcribe from the tapes.

Ralph Jones kindly furnished the group photographs of the 332nd Fighter Group; Ivan Harrison furnished those of the 761st Tank Battalion and the 969th Field Artillery Battalion. These photographs were made by the U.S. Signal Corps. Colonel Queen provided the photographs of the 366th Infantry Regiment. Individual photographs of men of the 332nd came from the scrapbook of Robert Pitts. The photograph of Charles L. Thomas was lent by his family.

Alexander Jefferson was my cartographer; Hondon Hargrove supplied the geographical positions of the 92nd Division's front. Alfred McKenzie furnished documents relating to the court-martial of 101 air force officers, mentioned in Richard Jennings's interview.

Brigadier General E. de Grasset, French military attaché, Washington, D.C., secured the World War I citations of Henry Johnson and William Butler and sent information about black regiments brigaded with the French during World War I. The citations were translated by Irene Graves. The Bureau of Military Records, St. Louis, furnished citations for World War II.

A special thanks goes to Colonel Queen, my "anchor man." It was comforting and helpful to have a Regular Army man, who had kept fairly complete records and journals of his long years in the service, to call upon for even the smallest detail. I wish also to acknowledge the help and cooperation of two other officers in World War I: Dr. De Haven Hinkson, highest-ranking Negro medical officer (lieutenant colonel) and Earl Dickerson (2nd lieutenant).

Finally, I wish to thank Richard R. Kinney, associate director, and Barbara C. Woodward, chief editor, Wayne State University Press for their encouragement, advice, and professional assistance which helped to expedite the publication of this book.

INTRODUCTION

In the government-sponsored *United States Army in World War II*, one volume of a subseries is devoted to the part played by black soldiers in the armed forces. Begun by Ulysses Lee of Howard University, but completed by other hands, it is entitled *The Employment of Negro Troops*. An unobtrusive but significant phrase forms part of the opening sentence of Lee's third chapter.

> As the conflict which was to become World War II approached, Negroes asked with increasing frequency for the opportunity that *they believed to be* rightfully theirs in the first place: the opportunity to participate in the defense of their country in the same manner and on the same basis and in the same services as other Americans. [P. 51, emphasis added]

How and why the phrase stands as "they believed to be" instead of "was" piques a present-day reader's curiosity. In any event, the phrase chosen symbolizes the situation in 1940 of the men whose war experiences form this book: the situation of sufferance rather than acceptance by America's dominant majority.

The relationship between arms-bearing and full citizenship for black Americans had been summed up, after the Civil War, by Frederick Douglass, abolitionist leader and former slave: "The Negro had been a citizen three times in the history of the government, in 1776, 1812, and 1865, and in the time of trouble the Negro was a citizen and in time of peace he was an alien."[1] In the long, honorable, but sparsely mentioned history of the black American's participation in this right of citizenship, the first years were ones in which his invisibility could be understood on practical grounds, were he a slave escaped to the free states. A professional historian might be able to name the first two black regiments serving the Union army during the Civil War—the 54th Massachusetts (free blacks) and the 1st South Carolina (ex-slave). The general public is no more familiar with them than with the four black Regular Army

23

regiments formed in 1866, the 24th and 25th Infantry, and the 9th and 10th Cavalry. As part of the punitive expedition against Pancho Villa in 1913, the 10th may receive notice for its association with the expedition's leader, Lieutenant General John J. Pershing. His nickname of "Black Jack" still clung to him as commander of the American Expeditionary Forces during World War I.

With the national preparation for that war, another opportunity seemed imminent for the black American to exercise the full right and obligation of citizenship. Despite the personal, social, and economic inequities still afflicting blacks in the second decade of the twentieth century, their leaders urged them to close ranks behind the war effort, and the number of black servicemen eventually enrolled in the armed forces shows that they did.[2] But the prevailing impression of the black soldier in World War I consists far more of his problems and failures than of his contributions.

Colonel Queen's foreword to this book describes the indignities suffered by black regiments serving in France. The experience of black American citizen soldiers reads like a prophecy of the 1940s: blacks were used mostly as service troops in stevedoring and general labor. Staff assumed that white southern officers "understood" blacks. White officers of the segregated 92nd Division (which had been trained at scattered locations throughout the United States) remarked on the unsuitability of black soldiers as combat troops and voiced assumptions of natural inferiority and cowardice. Back home, fighting between black soldiers and white civilians occurred frequently and violently enough to be noticed in the press, and officials of southern states begged to have training camps removed from their neighborhoods.[3]

Except for those in American regiments brigaded with the French army, which was under no compunction to observe southern racial etiquette, the black serviceman cannot be said to have enjoyed anything remotely resembling full and equal citizenship during this period. Indeed, his experience often led him to believe that his inability to exercise it was the result of deliberate intent.[4] Nor was his war contribution to be rewarded by full citizenship in the years immediately following the end of the war, as the statistics of lynchings indicate.[5] The black merely resumed his status as an alien in white America between wars.

As the 1930s drew to a close and the inevitability of war with the Axis powers became evident to President Franklin D. Roosevelt and his advisers, the question again arose of the part to be played by black Americans in the citizen army to be formed. Although it is inaccurate to say that the military establishment was a microcosm of the larger society, anyone who studies the years just preceding World War II is aware of at least one important parallel: resistance to accepting black Americans in both the military and the industrial defense of the nation. As the civilian society between wars had found it hard to make any place for a black except as the performer of humble services, the United States Navy admitted a black enlistee only as a servant to officers or as a waiter at table. Neither the U.S. Army Air Corps nor the Marines could find a niche where he might fit; both rejected blacks during those years.[6]

In the interval between wars, black participation in the Regular Army had shrunk; "black Americans could enlist only in the few vacancies of the four Regular Army units, and the strength of these was drastically reduced in the 1920's and 1930's."[7] Since the United States Army policy statement of October 1940 would permit the assignment of black officers to units of the National Guard only, restricting them from Regular Army units, only a few were needed. Following the government's decision to employ black manpower on a proportional basis but in segregated units, most black outfits were necessarily staffed with white officers. At the beginning of hostilities, it seemed as if the unsatisfactory patterns of World War I were to be repeated.[8]

Douglass's nineteenth-century observation about arms-bearing and citizenship applied also in the twentieth: the black community knew very well that the refusal of the service branches to accept black recruits was part of a deliberate effort to prevent the exercise of rights of citizenship. If they were ever to be full-fledged citizens, black Americans had constantly to demand full participation in the war effort. To return once more to Douglass, "Power concedes nothing without a demand. It never did and it never will."[9]

Records of congressional hearings concerning proposed amendments to the 1940 Selective Service Act show unmistakably that both the House and the Senate resisted full and equitable training and opportunities for blacks in the armed forces. It is all too easy, from the perspective of the seventies, to laugh condescendingly at congressmen and senators who seemed veritably obsessed with maintaining the social customs of the southern states; but their kind of thinking yielded the segregated army, navy, and air force of World War II, along with the inefficency that dogged segregation at every move.[10]

During the war years, those who saw both the inequality and the inefficiency lacked the clout to eliminate it. The superior performance of some combat units hastily integrated in emergencies was duly noted at Allied headquarters; nonetheless, the units were dissolved at the war's end. Except for air corps cadets, all officer candidates attended integrated classes. The services previously excluding black enlistees eventually made plans to accept them; by the last year of the war one of the men interviewed in this book reported actually having seen several black navy officers.[11] The story of armed forces integration belongs to the years following World War II. Officially established by President Harry S. Truman's Executive Order 8891, 26 July 1948, it was stubbornly resisted, especially by the army, and cannot be described as accomplished until the end of 1954.[12]

Refusal by the military establishment to accept the black's full participation in his country's defense was matched by industry's refusal to include him fully in its defense plans. A spokesman for the aviation industry openly said as much:

> While we are in complete sympathy with the Negro, it is against company policy to employ them as aircraft workers or mechanics . . . regardless of their training. . . . There will be some jobs as janitors for Negroes.
> President, North American Aviation Co. [13]

A response to discrimination in the armed forces and in defense employment came in the black March on Washington Movement (MOWM), led by A. Philip Randoph, president of the Brotherhood of Sleeping Car Porters. The urgency of events overseas and the pressures from MOWM's threat of angry unemployed black thousands marching into the capital resulted in Executive Order 8802, establishing the Fair Employment Practices Commission (FEPC) in June 1941.[14] But a labor report made in the spring of 1942 indicated that less than three percent of workers employed in the war effort were black.[15]

     The facts underlying that statistic were dynamite. The depression of the 1930s had been hard on both black and white Americans, but with discriminatory hiring practices the black American climbed out of the well more slowly than the white worker. In a city like Detroit, this state of affairs was made explosive by the influx of workers pouring into the city. The fifty thousand southern blacks who moved into the metropolitan area between 1940 and 1943 were far outnumbered by the five hundred thousand southern whites who also moved in.[16] Already overcrowded black neighborhoods had to absorb black newcomers as whites resisted black attempts to improve their living situations by moving to better surroundings. An incident that occurred in Detroit a year before the 1943 explosion bears mention here because it involved a civic leader whose actions and reputation later affected the fortunes of two men interviewed for this book.

     The Detroit Housing Commission planned some minimal relief to the overcrowding through the 200-family Sojourner Truth Homes, to be built with federal assistance in a part of the city then exclusively occupied by whites. Notices of the project, encouraging black Detroiters to register for occupancy, had appeared October 1941. At some point between October and January 1942, white residents heard of the plans to move blacks into their neighborhood and registered "a howl that could be heard all the way to Washington." Black citizens, now informed that there were no vacancies, appealed for help to the Reverend Charles A. Hill, a local black minister with a long record of interest in workers and their problems. He helped them to organize a protest. On one of his many trips to Washington he turned down a $25,000 bribe to desist.[17]

     For several months the federal government and the mayor of Detroit vacillated. It was announced that applicants of both races would be admitted to the project; then a plan was proposed to designate the project for white residents and to move the name "Sojourner Truth" to another housing project planned for black occupants in another neighborhood. On 28 February blacks and whites angrily confronted one another as word came from the mayor that a plan to move blacks into the project was "postponed until further notice." On the same day the *Detroit Free Press* headlined an article, "Housing Row Laid to Reds." By 10 March the *Free Press* reported the Attorney General as considering an investigation to determine if a conspiracy existed to prevent blacks from occupying a federal housing project. Still, the prospective occupants could not move in, and patience was wearing thin. At one point, Hill addressed an angry mob of blacks intending to occupy the project by force. He calmed them by promising to extract from City Hall a commitment as to a date when they could move in. On 30 April, 1,750 National Guardsmen, state troopers, and Detroit police were on hand to escort the prospective residents to their homes.[18]

Hill continued to press constantly for an end to segregation and discrimination. He was the first black candidate to run for Detroit Common Council (1945), and he was an active local leader in the Progressive party, supporting Henry Wallace for president in 1948. For his activism he encountered harassment by the House Un-American Activities Committee; guilt-by-association infected his son and his daughter's husband, both career army officers (Roger Walden, chapter 1; Charles A. Hill, Jr., chapter 4).

The Sojourner Truth incident pointed to the need for swift and decisive action, which was not filled. In the following year Detroit had a major outbreak of racial violence taking the lives of twenty-five blacks and nine whites.[19]

Frustration, cynicism, despair, and occasionally hope are words that describe the mood of black Americans on the home front in World War II, and it has been said that although a job was of first importance to the black civilian, he felt the soldier's hardships more keenly than his own.[20] The black newspapers, their combined circulation now more than a million, gave a voice to both the frustration and the hope as they pressed constantly for fairness both to workers and to soldiers.[21] Some of the interviews refer to effects of this pressure, actual or presumed. Stories of the hardships of black soldiers did not find their way into the columns of white newspapers, but appeared only in the learned journals and in liberal weeklies like the *Nation* and the *New Republic.* Genteel conservatives like the *Atlantic* contented themselves with lecturing the black press on divisiveness, entirely overlooking the quite unrevolutionary aims supporting the editorial rhetoric of the *Pittsburgh Courier*, for example. To the federal government, the press was cause rather than symptom of dissatisfaction and unrest. Black newspapers were banned from military posts until 1943; some publishers found it hard to purchase newsprint;

others were actually accused of sedition, although nothing came of the accusations.[22]

Against such a background, the reader of this book may find it hard to understand a draftee's statement that he encountered discrimination and segregation for the first time in the army, or to picture the soldier's lot as more miserable than the black civilian's.

Most of the men interviewed in this book grew up in Detroit, Chicago, Cincinnati, Cleveland, or other midwestern cities and towns. Some of them were the children of southern-born parents, who were among those accounting for the 611 percent increase in the black population of Detroit between 1916 and 1919. [23] As boys, future black soldiers played on crowded streets in Detroit, more than likely in the thirty-block section known as Paradise Valley, the center of black life, business, and entertainment.

Yet the black child's life in Detroit was partially integrated through the school. Small, white-owned shops dotted the black neighborhoods. The Syrian, Armenian, or Jewish shopowners often lived above their shops, and their children attended the neighborhood schools. Classroom and athletic fields were integrated, although black students experienced complete social isolation. Detroit had many all-white schools during those years, but no all-black ones.

For a fortunate few wage-earners a good life was possible in Detroit in the years just before the war, despite segregation and limits on the kinds of jobs they would be hired for. Some took a pragmatic view: working at the Ford plant, a man could earn a living that enabled him to buy a house and raise a family. In the era of the overeducated redcap, higher education produced few economic rewards. The friends of a man whose interview appears in chapter 4 thought he was mad to attend the University of Michigan to seek a degree in aeronautical engineering, sensing that job discrimination would prevent his technical skills being used. (And, for the time being, they were right, as his interview shows.)

In some of the interviews, resentment at being treated unfairly in civilian life surfaces as a man reflects on his past from a now heightened awareness. More common is the response of man who said, in describing his youth, "In my home town, Detroit, I guess I was too stupid to know about segregation, or at least I didn't think about it. We had the Valley and our places. I knew we didn't go to the white bars but this was no big thing in my life so it didn't bother me too much." Although the white restaurant-owner posted "Prices subject to change without notice" above the cash register and the usher at the theater announced, "balcony upstairs to the right," such illegalities could be confronted and often were. Legal safeguards existed to protect one's minimal civil rights, and as a last resort there was always the NAACP to turn to.[24]

By contrast, segregation in the army was not a sleazy aspect of life to be avoided or accommodated, but a policy to be enforced by one's military superiors. The black soldier lived in a segregated area of camp because of army regulations. He could not eat at certain specified locations or enjoy recreation at others because of regulations. He could not buy shoes at a certain location because of regulations. He could live for a year in a segregated camp, less than a mile from his best friend in the same camp, and not see that friend because of regulations affecting his off-duty hours. Under pain of disciplinary action he had to swallow daily insults. And what rankled most was not having to risk his life for a country that disowned him in many ways, but having to *see* that classification by race took precedence over the state of war between Germany and the United States of America.

The white war veteran who reads the interviews will be puzzled by the black soldier's unawareness of the white soldier's disenchantment with the army. White GIs, for example, can recall that "off-limits" signs prevented their ever getting to know the native villagers in Guam, and that their privileged captain was just another civilian whose shoulder bars required a salute, obedience, and the use of "sir" in responding to a command. Humiliation of the white private by the Regular Army white noncom was hardly unusual. But the black soldier could not know that these experiences were shared, and here surely is the measure of his isolation.

The Publisher

Notes

See the bibliography for complete information on sources briefly cited here.

1. Quoted by Herbert Garfinkel, "Negroes in the Defense Emergency," in *Blacks in White America Since 1865*, ed. Robert C. Twombly, p. 51.

2. Lee (p. 5) estimates 404,348 blacks in the service during World War I, including commissioned officers, field clerks, and army nurses. Richard M. Dalfiume, *Desegregation in the Armed Forces*, quotes (p. 11) the W. E. B. DuBois editorial urging black Americans to support the war effort. The oft-quoted "Close Ranks" appeared in *Crisis*, July 1918.

3. See the discussion of contemporary views in Lee, pp. 13–20; Dalfiume, pp. 16–18, on the extent of racism during World War I.

4. "The Experience of black soldiers in World War I seemed to confirm the popular belief held among the Negro community that there was a conspiracy to discredit their service. . . . When World War II began, those leading the protest against discrimination and segregation were former Negro officers and soldiers" (Dalfiume, p. 21).

5. C. Eric Lincoln states that 28 blacks were *burned to death* in lynchings between 1918 and 1923. "The Black Muslims as a Protest Movement," in *Assuring Freedom to the Free*, ed. Arnold M. Rose, p. 227.

6. Lee, Chapter 2, "Peacetime Practices and Plans," pp. 22–50, esp. p. 47 on Air Corps policy; on the Marines, Dalfiume, p. 26.
7. Dalfiume, p. 26.
8. A curious fact is that the Michigan legislature had in 1940 appropriated funds to finance an integrated National Guard unit, but the War Department indicated it would not recognize the unit if formed. Dalfiume, p. 35, quoting a letter from Charles C. Diggs to Stephen Early 1 July 1940. The policy of assigning black officers to segregated National Guard units was one way of insuring that a white officer would never be outranked by a black. The modified game of musical chairs played when black officers were assigned to units of the newly formed all-black divisions is described in the interviews below.
9. Quoted in Broadus N. Butler, "The City of Detroit and the Emancipation Proclamations," in *Assuring Freedom to the Free*, p. 91.
10. See Lee, pp. 72–73: the testimony of Rayford W. Logan of Howard University, appearing before the House Committee on Military Affairs as chairman of the civilian Committee on Participation of Negroes in the National Defense Program to plead for no-discrimination in the selection and training of men for the armed forces; the fears expressed by the two senators from Louisiana; and the scolding administered by Senator Tom Connally of Texas to Senator Robert F. Wagner of New York for proposing specific mention of aviation units and for wanting to make mandatory the selection of men without regard to race, creed, or color. Connally assumes the stance of the southerner who understands "the colored people" (p. 73).
11. See chap. 3, below, for volunteer units after the Battle of the Bulge; on officer candidate schools, Dalfiume, p. 65. For a summary of changes in policy, Lee Finkle, "The Conservative Aims of Militant Rhetoric," *Journal of American History*, 60 (1973): 699.
12. Dalfiume, p. 171, for the text of the executive order; p. 220 for the terminal date. See chaps. 7–10 for resistance to the order. One of the holdouts was General Edward M. Almond, commander of the 92nd Infantry Division during World War II (see intro. to chap. 5 below), a member of General Douglas MacArthur's staff in Tokyo, during the Korean War. Finding that the 2nd Division in Korea had been integrated out of necessity for replacements, he ordered its re-segregation. Leo Bogart, intro. to *Social Research and the Desegregation of the U.S. Army*, p. 20.
13. Quoted by Garfinkel, "Negroes in the Defense Emergency," p. 51.
14. According to Dalfiume's analysis, Roosevelt's canny observation of favorable responses in the black press concerning his willingness to grant less than MOWM demanded led to the "shrewd victory of a politically wise president over the demands of a militant minority" (pp. 116–20; quotation from p. 120).
15. Finkle, "Conservative Aims of Militant Rhetoric," p. 700.
16. Harvard Sitkoff, "The Detroit Race Riot of 1943," in *Blacks in White America Since 1865*, ed. R. C. Twombly, p. 317. Sitkoff uses the phrase "Arsenal of Democracy," which would include more than the central city.
17. Mary P. Motley, "Charles Andrew Hill" (unpublished), drawing upon interviews with Georgia Hill, and the *Detroit Free Press*, 30 Oct. 1941.
18. Motley, "Charles Andrew Hill," drawing upon the *Detroit Free Press*, 23 and 30 Jan. 1942; 4, 6, and 28 Feb. 1942; 2 and 10 Mar. 1942; 16 and 30 Apr. 1942.
19. Sitkoff gives a detailed account in "The Detroit Race Riot of 1943," pp. 315–32. He notes (p. 317) that riots occurred also in Los Angeles; Beaumont, Texas; and Mobile, Ala. The Social Science Institute at Fisk University counted 242 battles in 47 cities. Sitkoff, "Racial Militancy and Interracial Violence in the Second World War," *Journal of American History*, 58 (1971): 671. Mrs. Motley's records indicate a total of 68 deaths in the 1943 Detroit riot, 34 on each side.
20. "In many respects the discriminatory practices against Negroes which characterized the military programs of the defense and later war periods cut deeper into Negro feelings than did employment discrimination" (Garfinkel, "Negroes in the Defense Emergency," p. 298).

21. Finkle, "Conservative Aims of Militant Rhetoric," pp. 695–96. See also Finkle's description of the *Pittsburgh Courier*'s campaigns against "military taxation without representation" (p. 693). The *Chicago Defender* adopted as its wartime slogan, "Remember Pearl Harbor and Sikeston, Too," a reference to the lynching of Theo Wright, Sikeston, Mo., a few weeks after Pearl Harbor (Dalfiume, p. 112). Finkle notes that although the black press supported Randolph wholeheartedly in MOWM, they abandoned him when he contemplated a Gandhi-inspired civil disobedience program three years later ("Conservative Aims of Militant Rhetoric," p. 711).

22. Dalfiume, p. 124.

23. Dates and percentages are from Allan H. Spear, "From South Side to North Side," in *Blacks in White America Since 1865*, p. 179. Information about Detroit life before 1940 in this and the following paragraph is from the personal records of Mary P. Motley.

24. *Legislative Manual for the State of Michigan for the Year 1881* records an 1870 amendment to the state constitution of 1850, striking the word "white" from the qualifications for electors in Michigan. Public Act No. 328 (1931) guaranteed "equal accommodations" to all persons regardless of race. Public Act No. 117 (1937), the Diggs-Hailwood-Dunckel-Palmer amendment, extended the meaning of the word "accommodations" to include elevators, escalators, billiard parlors, hotels, stores, etc. (Source: *Michigan Compiled Laws*, Annotated.)

1. Corporal Howard Donovan Queen, Troop K, U.S. Cavalry, photographed at Fort Huachuca, Arizona, April 1915.

2. Sergeant Lester Duane Simons, 94th Engineer Battalion, who met his enemy in Arkansas. (See chapter 1.)

3. Corporal Douglas Tibbs, 9th Cavalry Regiment, 1942. *U.S. Army Signal Corps photo*.

4. Personnel section, 9th Cavalry Regiment, Fort Clark, Texas, 1943. (Corporal Tibbs is seated second row at left.)

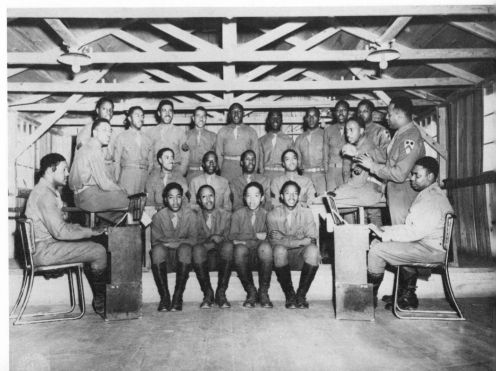

5. View from right of turret area, Sherman tank. Tank commander Sergeant Harold Gary. *U.S. Army Signal Corps photo.*

6. 761st in Sherman tanks, medium M48, crossing the Moselle River at Moyenvic, France, 1944. *U.S. Army Signal Corps photo.*

7. Sergeant Moses Ballard, 761st Tank Battalion, photographed with Paul Robeson at Hitler's Berchtesgaden, Austria, 1945.

8. The late State Senator Richard Carter of Illinois (left) and Lieutenant Colonel (ret.) Ivan Harrison, 761st Tank Battalion, at the opening ceremonies of the new Patton Museum, Fort Knox, Ky., 11 November 1972. *U.S. Army photo by SP4 Daniel Hager, Photo Br, A-V Sys Div, DC-E. Used by permission.*

9. Reunion of the Detroit chapter, 761st Tank Battalion, 1951. Top row, left to right: James Corbin, Edward Donald, Wilbur Johnson, Wendell Johnson, Horace Jones, James London, and Henry Mills. Below, left to right: Robert Kitchin, Roosevelt Haynes, James Hawkins, Leonard Holland, Horace Evans, Robert Lewis, and William Caldwell. *Photo by Addie Lawson and Earl Fowler, Top Hat Studio, Detroit.*

10. David Williams (captain, 761st Tank Battalion), and the late State Senator Carter (right) photographed at the 1967 reunion of the Detroit chapter, 761st Tank Battalion, with Mrs. Norma Rodriguez, daughter of Dr. Anderson, battalion physician.

11. Personnel of the 969th Field Artillery Battalion in action during World War II. *U.S. Army Signal Corps photo.*

12. Captain Charles L. Thomas, 614th Tank Destroyer Battalion, who won the DSC for heroism at the battle of Climbach, France, in 1944. *Photo by Hy-Lite, Detroit.*

13. Lieutenant Christopher Sturkey, 614th Tank Destroyer Battalion, awarded the Silver Star and a battlefield commission for gallantry in action, November 1944.

Chapter 1

The Wrong War in the Wrong Century

The situation facing the young black draftee in 1940, with the passage of the Selective Service Act, is graphically described by Colonel Howard Donovan Queen, a black officer in the Regular Army, stationed at Fort Benning, Georgia, at the time:

World War I [had been] one big racial problem for the Negro soldier. World War II was a racial nightmare. . . .

Before being transferred to the 366th [Infantry Regiment] I was stationed at Fort Benning, Georgia. The racial policies at the fort were certainly not going to build morale or patriotism in young Negro draftees. Knowing that Fort Benning was the rule rather than the exception, I was not surprised at the riotous conditions which repeatedly prevailed at many army posts once inductees began to come into the army in large numbers.

In 1941 Negro officers could not attend the officers' club at Fort Benning or the main theater on the post. A black enlisted man was shot by a white MP for talking back to a white telephone operator. Colored soldiers of the 24th Infantry Regiment were tried by a court-martial at Benning after they had been convicted by a civilian court in Columbus, Georgia, for an offense. This constituted double jeopardy but nothing was done about it. A colored lieutenant was brutally beaten by the civilian police in Columbus. He was disfigured for life by the terrible gashes in his face. No action was taken by the military for this cruel act against one of their own.

Negro regulars had chosen the army, and they had to be pushed hard before they fought back because they knew they would receive the full vindictiveness of local and federal authority. However, when they did go on a rampage they did not play, as the Houston Incident will attest to. Negro draftees and volunteers in World War II were much more prone to react swfitly. They felt dying stateside was just as good, if not preferable, to dying on foreign soil. Moreover, they didn't give a damn about a military career. It boiled down to this: all they had to lose was their lives.

Few civilians are aware of the number of racially violent incidents that took place on army reservations or in small southern towns. Let us not overlook some of the northern camps. Fort Dix and the white *civilians of New Jersey were no better than those in the deep south. One of the worst riots between black and white soldiers occurred at Camp Shenango, Pennsylvania. Pennsylvania until very recent years would not accept Negroes in their National Guard.*

Negro soldiers were sent to prison for inciting to riot, riot, and mutiny. It would be interesting to know how many, if any, white soldiers involved in racial disturbances were tried, convicted, and sentenced. There was also the old custom of shipping out Negro troops that were troublesome, trained or not. However, let it be noted that all of this arbitrary and hard-line discipline, on the part of the military, failed to keep the pot from boiling over regularly. The Negro soldier's first taste of warfare in World War II was on army posts right here in his own country. This in its turn caused considerable confusion in the minds of the draftees as to who the enemy really was.*

To this professional assessment of the situation, the following succinct comment, drawn from one of the interviews, may be added: "The medal for the southern field of operations was the only ribbon in the army that came in two parts: one black and the other white and you couldn't put them together."**

Of the men whose interviews appear in this chapter, Sergeant Eugene Gaillard was among the first to be drafted, ten months before Pearl Harbor. He and Staff Sergeant Lester Duane Simons, whose interview follows his, were both inducted in February 1941 and assigned to separate companies of the same battalion, the 94th Engineers. Both eventually saw overseas service as combat engineers, helping to restore the railroads in the Volturno River and Naples areas in Italy in 1943. As Gaillard's interview shows, the first battle theater in which the 94th met the enemy was the United States and the first enemies confronted were not Germans or Japanese soldiers but American citizens in Arkansas, 14 August 1941. (The interested reader should also refer to Lee, pp. 352–55, for an analysis of the local situation preceding and following that day.)

Eugene Gaillard: "February 17, 1941, was the day that my number came up in the draft and I was wedded to the United States Army for better or for worse. Candidly speaking, this is one partnership that did not seem to have a

---

*This quotation is contained in a personal communication from Col. H. D. Queen. With reference to Camp Shenango incident 14 July 1943, see Lee, p. 374. I was refused an interview with a veteran who had been involved in the incident on the grounds that he could not bear to discuss his experience.

**See the interview with Ambrose B. Nutt, chapter 4. Technical Sergeant Edmon Jennings, Medical Corps, said, "My commanding officer's views are covered by his brilliant observation, 'After all we have to respect states rights.' I thought about the Civil War and felt he was in the wrong war in the wrong century."

better side; these many years later have not changed my negative thoughts on my time spent in the armed forces of my country.

"After induction in Detroit I was sent to Fort Custer, Michigan, where I was attached to the 94th Engineers. I had had about three months of training when the 94th was sent to Murfreesboro, Tennessee, for maneuvers. We left in May and I am happy to say we returned to Custer in July, although it seemed then that we had spent years in Tennessee acting as a service unit to the 5th Division.

"The 94th had hardly breathed deeply of the free northern air when we were sent to Arkansas for more maneuvers with the 5th Division. If Tennessee was south, Arkansas was south of hell, sin, and damnation. Here we encountered all kinds of discrimination and the infamous, but oh so real, southern hostility and brutality with a capital *B*.

"The 94th was made up of northern Negroes; even our officers, for the most part white, were from the north. Arkansas, with its antebellum mentality, proved to be a nightmare that the men of the 94th Engineers would never forget. Our unsought enemies were the state police, local police, MPs, with the vicious white civilian population lurking in the background.

"Things got so bad down there the army sent General Lear down to speak to us. If we had any misconceived idea that the government had come to rescue us we soon learned it was a poorly blown soap-bubble that burst in our faces. The general promptly relieved Colonel Herman, our commanding officer, saying he couldn't control his men. He then spoke to the officers and I suspect he chewed their butts up. The enlisted men were called to a formation and he let us have it. I will never forget his words, 'You are a disgrace to your race to come down here and try to change the rules of the south.'

"That we were being harassed and mistreated, an understatement, was of no importance to General Lear. His words and attitude did not help nor the notoriety of what we were supposed to have done, which haunted us all the way to Louisiana. We were tormented and abused along our entire route until our return to Custer in the fall of the year.

"I have to this day been unable to figure out what we did that brought such a reprimand down upon our heads. We hadn't murdered anyone, robbed or mugged anyone, and the doubtful chastity of the redneck women was certainly intact. The local yokels who were always after our men, sending them back bruised and battered, won every encounter but one. I heard that a couple of the city cops got clobbered when they made the mistake of wading into a group of our men and swinging their clubs. I learned from the colored population that the whites down there believed we had come down there to take over the South. I would no more put any credence in that than in the fairy tale of the cow jumping over the moon. Besides, just what those poor, anemic, ignorant, illiterate Arkansas crackers had for anyone to take escapes me.

"I reiterate, we did not instigate or start anything. We did try to stand up and defend ourselves, though we were strictly at a disadvantage. Even on guard duty our guns had no ammunition in them. We had no protection whatsoever, neither from good old Uncle Sam, nor from our officers who were not in much better shape than we were; nor could we protect ourselves in the true sense of the word.

"Our trouble started while we were at Camp Robinson, near Little Rock. The night before we left Camp Robinson some of our men went to town on passes. They entered a liquor store to make some purchases and were refused service. White soldiers in there insisted that our men be served, saying that they all came from the same place and, 'You serve them or take ours back.' The proprietor obliged, then sneaked off to call the police. The police were surly and insulting, so the guys turned their car over and burned it. They returned to camp thinking that was that. How wrong they were! After we pulled out of camp the following morning we were rocked, called obscenities, given the full treatment all the way to Gurdon, Arkansas. This town was immediately put off limits to the 94th.

"The colored population of the little nearby town of Hope, invited us to a dance. Arriving about 5:00 P.M., we entered a little store-front hall. The band, of which I was a member, set up and began to play. We had just finished our first number when in walked the state police. Wasting no words, they started in with their night sticks—male, female, it made no difference. They drove all of the civilians out and ordered us back to camp.

"Around the 14th of August we were hiking from our encampment at Gurdon to a new area further away. We had been marching about two hours when we were stopped by the state police and MPs. They approached the officer leading us. One of them said, 'You officers get those niggahs off the road. Yes, I mean you, niggah lover.' One of the officers didn't move fast enough and a deputy walked over and hit him on the side of his head, knocking off his glasses. Lieutenant Curry retaliated with a few well-thrown punches, which I regret to say did not help his situation. They almost beat him to death.

"I was in the front line of the march and a deputy stuck a sub-Thompson machine gun under my nose and told me, 'Get the hell up in the rough, niggah, I mean you.' I rolled down fast into the gully, which was full of water. We had to walk either in the ditch or in the brush behind the ditch, being forbidden to put our black feet on the white man's highway.

"A large number of the enlisted men and NCOs went AWOL, heading north. I didn't go because I figured the greatest safety, such as it was, was with the largest number; the majority stayed. I just couldn't see myself caught out in some lonely Godforsaken place with just a few of the fellows. Those crackers were making our lives a living hell with a whole battalion so what chance would a small group of men have? Nevertheless, some of the men took off. You will have to talk to one of them to find out about their nightmare of being hunted down. Only a handful made it back to Custer.

In July 1942, sometime after our southern trek, the 94th Engineers was made into a general service regiment, and we were sent to our POE, Fort Dix, New Jersey. Just before our arrival, Dix had had a riot. This was easy to understand, for in short order we learned we might as well have been in the heart of Dixie. There were a series of incidents. They didn't want black soldiers to come to the PX when whites were there, so set certain hours for us. One night in front of the show one of the men, Private Woods, was shot to death. He was killed because he got in front of another soldier in the line. A white MP ordered him out of the line and when Woods wouldn't move he shot him in the stomach. Woods died shortly afterwards that night. There were plenty of witnesses to the act willing to testify, but nothing was done about it.

In March 1943 we shipped out, and my group landed in Casablanca. I say "my group" because just before sending us out they broke us up into three separate units saying we were troublemakers, and sent us in three different directions. They filled the vacancies caused by this sudden shifting with eighteen-year-old kids. They also broke up the band, which they later regretted—no entertainment when unoccupied and bored.

"Our job in Morocco was guarding POWs, building prison compounds, and working at the depot where they were assembling trucks. We had no problems with the prisoners; they were very courteous, very nice.*

"My group, in October '43, was sent to Oran and from there to Naples, Italy. We went immediately from there to the Volturno River, where fighting was going on. Upon our arrival there we reverted to being what we had originally been trained for, combat engineers. Whatever they decided needed to be done in the way of labor, that was our assignment. We put a bridge across the Volturno while under fire from the 'screaming meemies' and the deadly German 88mm field piece. When this was completed we were returned to Naples and put to work restoring the railroad service from Naples to Rome so supplies could go via rail to supply the 5th Army. From Rome we repaired the railroad as far as Florence.

"I didn't get any further than Querceta. There I was struck by fragments from a booby-trapped bazooka. Hospitalized temporarily in Italy, I was soon returned to the United States. On May 17, 1945, I was discharged from Billings General Hospital and from the army in Indiana.

"A meaningful experience? Oh yes, it was that. I met or I should say I came in contact with some of the meanest white people the good Lord ever

---

*For an explanation of this remark, see Index under the entry Prisoners of War, German.

created. And for my country that disavowed me I got some metal in my body and lost an eye. Oh yes, it was meaningful!"

Sergeant Lester Duane Simons of the 94th Engineers was living in Ann Arbor, Michigan, at the time he was drafted. A recent graduate of Ann Arbor High School, where he was a letter man on the varsity swimming team, with all it implies in the way of acceptance and popularity with his fellow students both black and white, he was totally unprepared for his army experience in the south.

Duane Simons: "I have no particular reason for wanting to remember the day I entered the army in 1941. I remember my ratings since they ran regularly from buck private to staff sergeant. Every time I made sergeant it seemed to coincide with my AWOL itch and down the ladder I'd go again.

"When I joined the 94th Engineers at Fort Custer it was just a starting company. I was 'lucky' enough to get in on the beginning of this new outfit. Its black NCOs were all regulars from Fort Bragg. They had army routine down to a fine art and were a nice bunch of guys. Under their guidance the 94th began to shape up and I worked up to staff sergeant. Who knows, if things had continued as they were during this period I might have been a good soldier and liked the army? But then, nothing is as it seems.

"At Custer everything was fairly smooth. The segregated set-up was a new experience but it was not total segregation and on pass or furlough I could go home, so I took it in stride. One thing I noticed was that something was always wrong whenever the camp was visited by inspecting generals. Trivial things caused a lot of commotion. An example would be a green private saluting with a cigarette in his mouth. Let's face it, we didn't see generals every day and the new fellows had never seen one. Such things were chalked up against the unit as inefficiency. I later learned black outfits were consistently low in efficiency.

There were no racial incidents at Custer that I know of. The army was new in the area and was trying to muster men into all branches of the service, 'they' said (meaning those in charge of Custer). However, no matter what a colored fellow signed up for as a preference he ended up in the quartermasters or engineers; all other units were closed to us at that time.

"Our officers were white with the exception of two warrant officers, Rice and Johnson, and our chaplain. The white officers' attitudes were a lot like those of the soldiers: we are here, let's make the best of it. Occasionally we would get a West Pointer. He would inevitably be a 'by-the-book' man and that would cause problems, for draftees were simply not regular army men. I wonder if that ever occurred to anyone at West Point.

"I was at Custer about nine months when we were shipped out to Murfreesboro, Tennessee, for maneuvers. We were the first colored troops sent south since World War I, I was told. None of us had ever been south therefore had no idea of the problems we would encounter, particularly with the Tennessee State Police. They just didn't want 'niggers' walking on their highways, in their areas, in their towns, or on the sidewalk, and they were not going to tolerate it. Even the colored people closed their doors and pulled down their shades because they were afraid of retaliation against them. They had been warned against fraternizing, so it was some time before we were able to make any social contact with them.

"I would like to state here that in my opinion there were three kinds of GIs: neutral, scared, and didn't-give-a-damn. I think I touched all three bases at one time or another. I ended up not giving a tinker's damn, period, thanks to the army.

"The Tennessee State Police really worked some of our guys over unmercifully. I was with my friend David Hughbanks when they really did him up. Yes, I stood by and watched. Two fists are no match for billy clubs, 45s, and rifles; ask any man who has been there. David and I returned to camp and reported to the officer in charge what had happened. There was nothing to do, he was sorry to inform us. Our white officers were also being discriminated against. They were not allowed to stay in the downtown hotels and were completely ostracized socially. Their problem was that they were considered traitors by the Tennessee crackers because their troops were black.

"We obviously didn't enjoy our stay in Murfreesboro, but little did we know that on the next maneuvers in Arkansas, Tennessee would appear to have been a congenial picnic.

"Little Rock, Arkansas, that's where the 94th's trial by fire began. We were encamped at Camp Robinson near Little Rock. On our first passes we sought the usual fare: booze and babes. No one had told us this was off limits to us as we boarded the bus for an evening of fun. I guess we were too dumb to know Arkansas qualified as a deep southern state. We paid dearly for our ignorance of this historical fact.

"When the bus let us off in the black belt we started walking to the main drag in the area. We came to a barricaded street, with a posted sign declaring it off limits. As we looked down the street we could see the lights and hear the music so we said 'To hell with the sign' and down the street we went; there were about forty of us. Breaking up into smaller groups we spread out through four or five bars. Police went into one of the bars and started pushing the guys around. That was a mistake because the fellows laid them out with a few well directed punches. The word spread and we all split for camp.

"Our entire group departed early the next morning but the words 'police-beaters' preceded us wherever we landed. Would you believe that politically those crackers were so powerful that they called the tune and everyone jumped, meaning the United States government? Federal power was a big joke below the Mason-Dixon line. White officers who tried to buck the system were busted and moved, those from captain down. Don't you ever think those crackers were above putting their hands on a white army officer; they weren't and they did. You can imagine where this left the colored NCOs and the enlisted men.

"When we arrived at Pine Bluff, the colored college there gave a party for some of us. Our major decided we could not attend. I think he was afraid something would happen and he would get a demerit. Fortunately for us there was a colored colonel—I believe he was on the campus, but he was an army man; he ordered our major to rescind his order so we attended the dance and had a good time.

"On maneuvers we were in a wooded area. We had rifles but no ammunition, not even bayonets. Our officers had their 45s, and that was all the protection we had in an area that was getting more hostile every minute. It was decided that we would move about twenty miles down the road. As we marched along counting cadence, to our new destination, a group of mounted farmers came out of nowhere, or so it seemed. Their spokesman told our lieutenant to 'Get those god-damned niggers off of the white highway and march 'em in the ditch.' The ditch he spoke of had several inches of water in it; water mocassins' playground. Our lieutenant objected and told them if they weren't careful the area would be placed under martial law (which should have been done in the beginning). The rednecks rode him down with their horses, then pistol-whipped him—one of their own color! The lieutenant was later given a medical discharge because of this beating; they damned near killed him.

"While this was happening a truckload of white MPs, who were armed, sat in their truck and offered no assistance to this white officer. More horse-riding dirt farmers were coming; we could see them in the distance burning our one truck with our supplies. A company was on a parallel road about five miles over and they too were set upon by these male witches on their broomsticks.

"About thirty to forty of our guys took the packs off their backs and were gone. When I heard about this I turned my platoon over to the next sergeant and told him I was heading back to Fort Custer. He said he was going back north also. It ended up with four sergeants, two corporals, and a private leaving for God's country.

"We moved out and headed for the first bus or train station. It turned out to be a train station at Arkadelphia some forty-one miles away. We had stopped in a nearby colored settlement to try and secure some food and we were told the word was out, anyone helping any colored soldier would be in serious trouble. It turned out that over two hundred men had left for Fort Custer.

"Night had set in before we reached Arkadelphia, and I had managed to pick up a nail in my boot. Every time I tried to stop and get it out we could hear our pursuers on their goddamn horses crashing through the brush. This coupled with the prodding of a rattlesnake's warning kept us moving forward as fast as we could and still breathe. When I pulled off my boot in Arkadelphia my sock was soaked with blood.

"When the train finally pulled into the Arkadelphia station, soldiers appeared from everywhere and began to climb aboard. The conductor was pleading with them to get off, at least those in the blinds between coaches. I dropped off on the other side and climbed into an empty boxcar. Four other guys followed me, including my buddy, James Humphries. The train started and was struggling to pull a grade. Finally when it got to the top, there waiting was a load of MPs. They got quite a haul.

"We had a lot of luck for guys who had never ridden the rails before. We managed to get within the vicinity of Poplar Bluffs on one train before the conductor spotted us. We jumped off and when we picked ourselves up we were in the hills. Eventually we made it to Bismarck, Missouri. Here it was my turn to have the conductor chase me so the guys could get on. When the warning whistle blew I would cut back for the train and hop on. Just as the engineer sounded the highball signal and I was heading back leaving the conductor like he was standing still, a deputy sheriff stepped between me and the train with a drawn gun. The train was moving out and I felt like I had been shot and was dying.

"There were white soldiers aboard who were going to some hospital. They kicked at the deputy, begged, pleaded, tried to pull me on the train. In spite of their attempts all I could do was stand there and watch the train leaving with my friends aboard, but very much aware of the gun leveled at me at all times. When the train was finally out of my sight, I never felt so alone in my life.

"The deputy finally spoke, 'Nigger, if you're here at sunset,' he pointed to a tree, 'we'll hang you right there. Same place we hung another nigger 'bout fifteen years ago.' He didn't say for what and I didn't ask. Being part chicken under certain circumstances and fleet of foot, I took off.

"After putting a lot of distance between me and the hanging tree, I stopped at a gas station and asked if I might wash up. The attendant pointed and said, 'Over there.' Over there was one bucket of dirty water. I prayed those army shots were worth something as I stuck my hands into the bucket.

"All I had on me, at the time, was plenty of cigarettes where my pants were bloused at my boot top, and a toothbrush; not one thin dime. While I washed up the attendant's little boy used my toothbrush to brush the filth from between his toes; that took care of my dental hygiene for a while.

"Hopping into an empty boxcar down the road a piece, I waited for another train. Finally one came, but I had to jump off after about six miles as it began backing onto private property.

"Shortly after this, a white family took me in and fed me. They explained that the train was on a spur and would come out that evening heading for St. Louis. They assured me I would be able to catch it because they had a relative working on it. True to their word they placed me in the care of this relative, and I chose my boxcar.

"It seemed like hours had passed when the train slowed down as we neared DeSoto, Missouri. Hearing a lot of voices I took a peek and saw a crowd gathered at what was apparently a station. Something told me to jump and I was gone like a flash. Running down the side of the train, out of sight of the people, I put some distance betwen myself and the train. Later I learned they had gathered there to grab any colored soldier who might be hitching a ride. The flight of a large number of men from the 94th ahd brought out the human bloodhounds in droves; they were at all of the depots. Some of those caught by these animals didn't fare too well before they were handed over to MPs. But then some of those caught by MPs got messed up so it was the devil or his imps.

"When the train pulled out of DeSoto I was ahead of it and waiting. Snagging a gondola, I hoisted myself into it. Night had descended when I was awakened by the loud clanking of the gondola. Pulling myself erect I realized I had slept soundly and was well inside of the St. Louis railway yard. A voice hailed me out of the dark. Not having an alternative I climbed down and found myself facing a middle-aged white man. He looked at me hard and then said, 'You must be new on the road. Don't you know here they shoot first and ask questions afterwards?' Before I could answer he took my arm. To my relief and surprise he took me to his car, drove me outside of that great mass of railroad tracks, and once clear of the yard let me out and waved me on.

"Getting the directions I needed, I headed for East St. Louis, Illinois. I had the address of a buddy's parents, who lived there. We had agreed to meet there if we were separated.

"As I walked along I though I would die of starvation. It's funny; here I almost had it made and such things like hunger and thirst began to bother me. Passing a watermelon stand I just couldn't resist asking the owner if I could have one of the display slices. He glanced at me, then said, 'You don't want that, flies have been at it all day.' With a gesture to follow him, he took me behind the stand into a kind of tent. There he handed me a whole watermelon and a knife and left. I ate every bit of that melon right down to the rind. Thanking the gentleman for his kindness I asked about the bridge to East St. Louis. He gave me some directions that would save time and I was on my way.

"Cars were almost bumper-to-bumper on the bridge, but no one would give me a ride. In the meantime that delicious watermelon had begun to turn my stomach upside down. Somehow I managed to reach the home I was searching for; when my friend's parents opened the door they had a sick, exhausted man on their hands. In a couple of days I was in much better shape, and my hosts saw me safely aboard a train headed due north; this time I was riding up front with a ticket. I was wearing civilian clothes with my uniform in a bundle so I would not be checked by MPs for my pass.

"When I walked through the gates of Fort Custer I was in uniform and the first of the three or four soldiers who succeeded in making it back. I turned myself into Major Theopholus Mann, a colored officer with the 184th Field Artillery Group. He gave me a three-day pass to go visit my parents. I don't know if it made any difference, but it happened that the major knew my Aunt Pearl, in Detroit, very well.

"One day we were called in and told we were to be returned to Arkansas. The very idea made me want to puke. I wanted to shout, fight, do anything, but I was impaled by the United States Army. Four very skittish men headed back to their own little hell. Thank God, on our return, the black MPS on duty at the train station were wearing pistols and had live ammunition.

"When the 94th returned to Fort Custer from Arkansas, Lester D. Simons, soldier who might have cared about the army and the war, was dead; I didn't look for trouble or make any, but I went AWOL every opportunity I got. I didn't care how many days I spent in the stockades or if they docked my pay. As soon as I was out, given the opportunity I was gone again.

"In 1943 the 94th was alerted for overseas and sent to Fort Dix, New Jersey. Fort Dix might be above the Mason-Dixon line, but it is strictly an accident of geography. There we had not only cracker civilians to contend with but cracker soldier boys who were stationed there. Dix had several race riots—I'm referring to the big incidents, not to the almost daily name-calling and fisticuffs between black and white soldiers. One of our men was killed in cold blood there.

"Overseas duty compared to camp life stateside was a lark. The only people overseas who went out of their way to create trouble for us were our good old brethren in uniform, American whites.

"For me the paradox of the Arkansas maneuvers, which should be correctly called the Arkansas manhunt, was whites forced me to run, whites got their kicks chasing me, yet a white family fed me, and a white man probably saved my life!"

On his induction into the armed forces, Sergeant Frank Penick, 46th Quartermaster Company, had a rather unusual experience of army segregation policies. His group arrived at Camp Custer late one day in 1941, and submitted to the complete battery of intelligence and aptitude tests. The weary men were then broken up into two groups according to race.

Frank Penick: "Bone tired as I was, I came out of it when I realized they had placed me with whitey. Man, I wasn't going to have that. I told them they had made a big mistake and they looked at me like I had lost my mind. At my insistence they finally checked back in my record and found they were wrong, and then hastily placed me with my own.

"I did my basic training at Camp Murray, near Tacoma, Washington, in infantry. Six months later I was transferred to Fort McClellan, Alabama, and was introduced to racism and bigotry such as I had never seen. We colored soldiers were greeted by white GIs already there with a lot of name-calling and obscene remarks.

"Here I was assigned to a trucking outfit. All officers at this camp at that time, as had been at Camp Murray, were white. The NCOs were black. With the exception of one real bigoted bastard from the deep south, officers on the whole were fairly decent. Now and than you'd get cracks from some of them that we would make good soldiers for night fighting. This was supposed to be a joke. Civilian treatment of the black GI was just what one expected from white Alabamans, vicious.

"My battalion was shipped out in 1943 and we landed in Oran, Africa. Before allowing us to leave the ship they called us together in a large room and told us the natives were not the kind to take any foolishness off of us. We found out later they were talking about leaving the women alone. We were assured we would be castrated and our genitals stuffed in our mouths, and all kinds of wild things. We were a bit leary about the whole deal. Once ashore we learned this was a lot of bullshit and we got along just fine with the people there. We never knew if the white soldiers on board received the same lecture because we were kept completely isolated from the patty soldiers.

"Going over we had daily fire drills, emergency drills, all kinds of drills to prepare us in the event of an enemy attack. The first day they showed us how to line up, and there was a nice big lifeboat in front of us. The second day we were in a slightly different position. Finally, we Negro soldiers were away from the lifeboats completely. They had shifted us away from the lifeboats the closer we got to dangerous waters. About the third day out, our officers came to our quarters—below the waterline, naturally—and commandeered all of our ammunition. When it finally occurred to us what had happened, we were hot as hell. We determined should anything happen, we might be shot but those white cats were not going to climb happily into those lifeboats while we were held at gunpoint below the decks or stand topside and watch their departure. Now I can't say whether or not whites had to give up their ammo, because as I previously stated there was absolutely no contact between colored and white soldiers. Talk about separatism, the army invented it.

"From Oran we went to Bizerte near the coastline of the Straits of Sicily. They had a huge staging area there as segregated as anything you could possibly find in the deep south. We were placed at the farthest end of this area, which put us the farthest away from the water.

"It was quite hot there so one day, shortly after our arrival, a group of about twenty of us, including Lieutenant Waltz, decided to hike to the beach. As we passed by a white field artillery group on the other side of no man's land and us, they started hollering about the 'niggers,' and dressed this word up with every obscenity their minds could come up with. We turned around to mix it up with them but our lieutenant insisted we forget about them and come on.

"As soon as we got on the beach the guys headed for the water, but before I could join them Lieutenant Waltz called me back and told me to call the men out of the water. I wanted to know why, and he explained that this beach was reserved for others. I had noticed a few white guys sitting on the slopes leading down to the beach sunning themselves and thought nothing about it. There was also a lone man sitting down on the beach itself. The lieutenant said that we would swim further down. I reminded him that the rest of this coastline was very rocky, but he insisted. By then, the fellows in the water, feeling something was wrong, had come out and gathered around us. They asked me what they should do and I told them to swim right there because I could not conceive of this whole stretch of beach being reserved for a handful of men. With that the man who had been sitting on the beach near where the lieutenant had been talking, jumped up, said I was insubordinate to an officer, and directed Waltz to take the proper action against me. With that he called his gang and took off.

"Arriving back at the camp, Captain Fleicher sent for me, and he and Lieutenant Waltz gave me a lecture on disobeying an officer, telling me that I could be court-martialed. I explained that I was a civilian, and a northern one at that, in an army uniform and that was what I would always be and they could court-martial me if they wished. After more talk they let me go, and that was the last I heard of the incident.

"That very same night Jerry came over in waves and, man, they laid down a bombardment that had the earth trembling as much as I was. Between the flares they were dropping and a huge fire in the direction of the beach it was bright enough to pick a dime up off of the ground.

"The next morning the sun was shining brightly and the only thing to remind you of the previous night was the smoke still coming from the direction of the beach area. Curiosity prompted us to investigate. When we reached the field artillery section of the previous day, lo and behold, those peckerwoods had been clobbered! Did we lay it on those in the vicinity of the road! Someone said, 'Goddamn, Jerry bombed the hell out of our big-mouth southern brethren. Well, I do believe, Jerry damn near massacred the bastards, now ain't that just too bad! Those crackers just sat or stood around like they were sick.

"I've often thought of that day and wondered if it was an act of God. Our camp was scarcely a mile away and not one bomb had landed in our area. I felt it then and I feel the same now: they got exactly what they deserved.

"Our outfit was attached to General Patton's command for the

Sicilian campaign. Patton looked just like the picture of him we had seen: two 45s on his hips, spotless uniform, riding crop under his arm, freshly polished riding boots, his battle helmet gleaming in the sun—and his language, every sentence was liberally sprinkled with m.f.

"The Sicilians and Italians really liked the *soldato negro*, and we liked them; they were nice people. A Sicilian who hung around our outfit saved us from being killed by one of those smart-aleck ninety-day wonders. We were moving out across a field when he ran up to this new officer frantically waving his hands and shouting. Mr. Smart Guy assured us that he knew Latin and could understand the man. It happened one of the fellows had picked up enough of the local dialect so that when he heard what the man kept repeating he ran up to the peasant and with a few words and gestures he was positive of what the man was saying: we were in a mine field. You talk about backing trucks up without wavering from our original tracks! If our commanding officer hadn't been busy bitching out Lieutenant Know-It-All we might have kicked his ass ourselves. Mr. Ninety-Day was gone from our outfit in less than thirty days.

"In Italy, one day I was put in charge of twenty men to go pick up some oxygen for the air force. We spent the night in the mountains because the supply depot was some distance away and the terrain was rough. We like to froze to death, and K rations stone cold or worse than ever, so we did without.

"The next day we came out of the mountains into Naples, chilled and hungry. The supply depot was easy to see because it was a mammoth layout. I immediately went to the mess hall and asked the sergeant in charge if he could feed my men. He was real understanding and only too happy to oblige, that is until my men walked into the mess hall. He turned red as a beet and scurried like a scared rat out of the room, returning with an officer. Together they looked at us like we were bacteria under a goddamn microscope. The officer finally found his voice to tell us they didn't have enough food to feed all of us but just five miles down the road we would get all we wanted.

"Talk about a tense situation. I could hear safetys being released on rifles and could feel the anger of my men, not that I wasn't as mad as a hornet. I knew we would be outnumbered and out-gunned in a manner of minutes so I finally prevailed upon the guys to leave, but you believe me when I say they were ready to make their stand then and there. As they put it, they were going to die over there anyway so why not now!

"Just as that cracker sonofabitch had said, there was another supply depot just five miles down the road, all black, excepting of course for the officer in charge. I reported the incident, only to have him inform me in no uncertain terms, war or no war, they believed in keeping the races apart. We could eat at the tables of white Europeans with their families and women, yet not with the white American army!

"One awful problem I had was convincing the Italians I was not *blanco*. The American whites with their arrogance and contempt for these people, which they did not try to conceal, made themselves thoroughly disliked. I always had to have a buddy, who looked negroid in their eyes, explain that I was *soldato negro*. Sometimes they remained skeptical.

"The degree of hositility felt by the Italians toward white GIs was shown in what was not an uncommon occurrence. A white soldier would be knifed, castrated, and his body put in a big barrel and rolled down the hill into the white camp. This came from unwanted advances to Italian girls and women. Some of those guys would get out of line, even when invited as a guest into an Italian home. They never caught the people who were carving up white GIs and delivering them downhill in a barrel. Funny thing, whitey never seemed to learn. I am not trying to say every Negro soldier in Italy was a gentleman. I will say to my knowledge I never heard of one ending up in a barrel.

"Once my unit was mustered out to be looked over by an Italian woman for a rape charge. I give our commanding officer credit for one thing: he made sure she understood she had better know what she was talking about if she selected one of his men. She didn't. I understand being mustered out only once for such a thing was something of a record. The practice was as soon as the word 'rape' was mentioned anywhere the first guys hauled out to be looked over were Negroes, and you know during war rape is a hanging offense.

Frank Penick's description of General George S. Patton's public appearances in impeccable cavalry attire is a reminder that the white cavalry regiments of the United States Army became armored forces in World War II, and that General Patton was himself a former cavalry officer. Black units that became part of the armored forces (see chapter 3) were not built from officers and men of the Regular Army black cavalry outfits. The fate of the 9th Cavalry, a black regiment with a history dating back to 1866, is recounted in the interview with Sergeant Douglas Tibbs.

Douglas Tibbs: "I didn't exactly jump for joy when I was notified to report to my induction center in 1942. I had a number of friends, like Eugene Gaillard, who had been in the service for some time and their letters were something less than enthusiastic. At least I was prepared for the fact that segregation and discrimination were part and parcel of the army for black men.

"When I arrived at Fort Custer the segregation was no surprise since I had been forewarned. It did seem a little strange to be above the Mason-Dixon line and be segregated but I was aware of the fact things could get worse. However, in spite of my wariness of the army I probably am one of the few who can honestly say they had a ball. I can thank Captain Felix McDavid for this.

McDavid was an officer with the black National Guard unit out of

Chicago that was stationed at Fort Custer. We met and one day he mentioned they were forming a special cavalry outfit at Fort Riley, Kansas. He suggested I try for it. Real old-fashion cavalry with horses! The idea appealed to me so I made inquiries. Soon I was on my way to Fort Riley.

"There was a group of us at Riley who were introduced to the art of the old cavalry. We ate, slept, rode, and took care of our gear day-in-and-day-out until we were experts at single file, by twos, fours, gallop, charge, and so forth. Did I say this was an all-black unit with white officers? It was.

"Our uniforms were regular cavalry regalia with the broad-brimmed hat with chin strap, very similar to the Canadian mounties. The shiny boots were kept that way. The spurs (not the western variety) were more for show than anything else. Let's face it, we looked good and we were young enough to enjoy it.

"We had been trained specifically to be a part of a bond drive that would tour all of the big cities in the country. Naturally our act was last, but that worried us not. The young ladies were just thrilled to death with the highly decorative (meaning our uniforms) cavalrymen. We certainly had nothing against being the honey bees swarmed about—we loved it!

"When I returned to Detroit, my home town, on the tour it was like, wow! I don't know how many friends and acquaintances bought tickets to see the show but many a one, females especially, came to our encampment looking for Corporal Tibbs. I guess that's what my rating was then. Oh man, I played it cool with the girls, some I had dated, some I had thought about dating, and others I somehow had overlooked. No doubt a few who knew me real well were tempted to boot me right in the seat of my impeccable uniform.

"The group we were traveling with had a full house wherever it appeared. The show ended with our putting our horses through their paces. Our last thing was a full charge down the field and out the exit with old glory being held straight out by the wind created. This always brought a standing ovation.

"Only one city of all those we toured, north and south, showed its color, Houston, Texas. I shall never forget our grand finale there. As we dashed for the exit with old glory flying the stadium was silent excepting for about a dozen pairs of hands that sounded like shots in all of the quiet. There was no doubt how Houston felt about us.

"I believe there were three white officers with us. One day I had reason to see our commander. He was called away from his tent for a few moments while I was there. He had been writing a letter which I could not help but see. My eyes zeroed in on, 'the niggers are doing all right.' From then on we knew just about where we stood with all three of them. Like the commander, we kept up a good front, did our job, and kept our friendship to ourselves. When the tour was completed we were sent to some small backwoods camp in Texas. We were only there a few weeks when we were shipped to a Port of Embarkation.

"We arrived in North Africa and in short order the 9th Cavalry's regimental flag was furled for the last time, far away from the country its men had so gallantly fought for since 1866.

"My unit became a port battalion and that's what we were doing when the war ended in Europe. You know I really hated to see the 9th Cavalry come to such an ignominious end; it just didn't seem right somehow.

"As I said, with the exception of a few incidents, very small compared to what most black men faced in the armed forces, I had a ball. Who wouldn't? I was in my early twenties, a dashing young cavalryman with the girls chasing me, thinking I was something special. I am one of the few men you will talk to who can honestly say I could happily live that period of my life over again."

Major William Purnell Shelton began his twenty-six years in the service as a draftee in 1941, four months before Pearl Harbor. He was sent for basic training to Camp Wolters, Texas, where he first became aware of "separate and unequal" on the post and in nearby Galveston. He remembers the officers, however, as being "interested in giving us the necessary instructions for handling our weapons properly." From Camp Wolters he was sent to the 369th Coast Artillery (Antiaircraft) Regiment, Camp Edwards, Massachusetts.

Purnell Shelton: "The 369th was one of the few all-Negro units in the army. The commanding officer was Colonel Chauncey Hooper. The 369th was activated from the New York National Guard. I was assigned to Battery A of 1st Battalion. My commanding officer was Captain Edmund Adams, a fine officer and a gentleman.

"There were a large number of Puerto Ricans in the 369th, which with the exception of the replacements, brought in to bring it up to TOE strength, was made up completely by men from New York. All of us were proud of our unit and we were good at our jobs.

"Before going overseas we were assigned to the Four Rivers shipyards in Boston for defense purposes. The unit had no problems in Massachusetts; the people there were most hospitable.

"From Massachusetts we were sent to Hawaii. When we came into Pearl Harbor, we could see the damaged ships, some of which were still smoking; it took the fires a long time to burn themselves out. We were billeted at Schofield Barracks; at night the sky was visible through the many bullet holes put there during the attack on Pearl Harbor.

"Segments of our regiment were assigned to the all-white 1st Marine Division and sent to Camp Malakoli where we were run through various training tests to see if the unit was qualified. In the tests we had no trouble, but here for the first time I ran into problems within the service. There were innumerable fights between the marines and the enlisted personnel of the 369th. There was no overall breakout, but individual and small-group battles were daily occurrences. This disturbed the officers in charge, but marines or otherwise, the 369th wasn't taking any racial guff off of anyone.

"By the way, Hawaii was the first place I saw legalized prostitution. This, done to accommodate the servicemen, was likewise separate and unequal.

"After completion of our training at Camp Malakoli, my unit, the searchlight unit, was assigned to Maui, the garden spot of the islands. Once, while on Maui, a Puerto Rican friend and I were waiting in a store for the GI bus, a truck. Three white GIs entered wearing side arms. They stood silently for a while. Finally one spoke up saying, 'You know I haven't killed a nigger in a long time.' His buddies tried to get this character to shut up but he was quite bellicose. We ignored him since we were unarmed. Upon returning to camp we alerted our CO to the situation and from then on, on or off duty we wore side arms; no more loud mouths.

"In the meantime, I had applied for OCS in artillery. I passed the exams and left Maui for Camp Davis, North Carolina, just outside of Wilmington, newcomers were taken to the camp, where they were given assignments. All of our instructors were white as was our cadre, with the exception of the cooks.

"We Negroes constituted something of a problem. We were housed in the typical barracks, but instead of being in the large area with the whites we were given private dwellings at the end of the building, the quarters of the NCOs. With exception of this we ate at the same mess, attended the same classes, and even used the same latrine.

"There was no social life for black officer candidates since all such facilities were closed to us. Any recreation we got was strictly on pass. Of the 600 men in the class I believe six were black. Three of them passed the course. Three hundred of the total class were punched out. I'll say the officers there were tough on everybody, so I cannot call them unfair.

"On my thirty-day leave after graduating from OCS I went to D.C. to spend half of my leave with a friend. When I got out in front of the train station I hailed a cab. The driver drove right up to me, took a look and said, 'Oh you're a nigger.' He drove right off. That was my first racial experience as an officer in the United States Army, *in our nation's capital*. I was soon to learn I hadn't seen anything yet.

"As an officer I was assigned to the 227th Antiaircraft Artillery Battalion at Camp Stewart, Georgia. I was a specialist in automatic weapons, so was made an officer over a platoon. This first assignment was the beginning of everything wrong for me in the United States Army.

"The 369th had been broken up; it was not going to be used as a regiment, for it would mean a black colonel in command. A number of the 369th were at Camp Stewart. I stayed there in the 227th until the riot. A rumor started that a colored soldier's wife from New York had come to see him and that she was white. They stayed at the guest house on the post. When he took her to the bus station for her return trip the rumor got out that they had considerable trouble. How much was truth I really don't know, but it was enough to turn Stewart upside down.

"I remember one night it looked like a small Battle of the Bulge. Instead of Americans against Germans it was black Americans versus white Americans on an army post that perpetuated segregation and prejudice. There were three soldiers killed, two or three MPs killed, and a large number of troops hospitalized. When the riot was finally quelled, that was the end of the 227th. I was assigned to the 846th, still at Camp Stewart.

"When I reported to Colonel H., the commanding officer of my new unit, his opening statement to the officers gathered was, 'I want all junior officers to sit on the right, senior officers on the left. This automatically split the officers along racial lines since there were no black senior officers. To make sure the junior officers did not misunderstand him he had a few words for us. He said he had been born on the ground this camp occupied. He loved his country and was willing to die for it. He had nothing against 'nigras' but he had never seen, nor had he ever met, a 'nigra' qualified to be an officer in the United States Army. But we had a job to do and he was there to see that we did it. He also assured us that he would see that everyone of us was reclassified before we left his command. Needless to say, the time spent under Colonel H. was unhappy. Also, needless to say, my thoughts about the colonel were and are unprintable. I had visions of one lowly lieutenant torpedoing a high and mighty cracker colonel.

"As an officer you pay officers' dues to maintain the officers' club. The black officers again had separate and very unequal facilities. I never saw the inside of the officers' club during my stay at Camp Stewart.

"One Sunday as I entered the colored section of Savannah, the largest city near our camp, I noticed a crowd of people gathered in the street. Curiosity prompted me to find out what was going on. Once on the periphery of the crowd I could see a black soldier in the custody of the white civilian police. The soldier supposedly had said something about a white male motorcyclist and a white policeman was supposed to have overheard him. For this he was being arrested. There were about ten police cars on the scene but the crowd was growing by the minute. The people living in buildings along the way were hanging out of their windows saying, 'You betta let that soldier alone.'

"I could see that this could turn into one helluva mess so I went up to the police lieutenant. He immediately wanted to know who I was. I produced credentials and than informed him civilian police could not arrest a soldier, only MPs. Since there were none present I would take the soldier in charge and return with him at once to camp and turn him over to the MPs. I suggested that he and his men put their guns away and leave because, having been in one riot, I could smell serious trouble about to break loose. I was pleasantly surprised to find this lieutenant was not the run-of-the-mill stupid southern cop. He saw the situation as it really was; the crowd was still growing in spite of the drawn revolvers, and the smell of hate filled the air. The lieutenant told the officer holding the soldier to release him into my custody. He waved the rest of the men back into their cars and they drove slowly through a sullen mob that was just giving them room to pass.

"I returned to camp with the soldier as I had said I would and turned him in to the MPs. I do not know what the outcome of the incident was, but judging from the friendly demeanor of the MPs I doubt that anything serious came of it.*

"Colonel H. and I had a couple of run-ins about my paying dues for a club I could not attend and a few other such things. The upshot was that I was given his personal attention to see that I was the first to be reclassified. I was as determined in my way to see that it didn't happen as he was to conclude a successful reclassification operation.

"An inspection of our motor pool by the base commander caused him to term it a disgrace and chew the colonel's butt out while giving him one week to bring the pool up to snuff. This set me up for the kill. The colonel sent for me and put me in charge of the motor pool but did not relieve me of my job as platoon leader in weaponry. The white officers in the battalion were supportive of me in that they did nothing to hinder my getting the two jobs done. The motor pool passed inspection the following week. Disappointed in my success and hoping to break my spirit, the colonel assigned me permanently to the motor pool.

"We had a Negro sergeant in the motor pool who was out of Hinesville, Georgia, just a few miles away. He was the true stereotype Uncle Tom. One day when I went down to the motor pool I noticed he was working on a civilian car. It turned out to be the colonel's car. Being a firm believer in rules and regulations, I reminded the sergeant that it was specifically stipulated in the book that no civilian car could be worked on, on government property with government tools or have government-owned parts placed in them. The sergeant thought I had done my duty and that was that. When I gave him a direct order to stop working on the vehicle now, immediately, at once, he obeyed but was stunned. You would have thought I had slapped his face.

---

*Corporal Wadye Gallant, 219th Armored Ground Forces Band, described an ugly situation in Fayetteville, South Carolina, which he observed while stationed at Fort Bragg. Nabbed by white civilian police at night in the town, black soldiers were returned to Fort Bragg the following day, badly beaten. "There was never a let-up on the black soldiers by whites in the area," he said.

Maybe a little-bitty lieutenant isn't supposed to notice rules broken by his superior officer, but as far as our dear colonel was concerned my eyes were strictly on the sparrow. This man had insulted me, been unfair, and was waiting for the opportunity to reclassify me. It was beyond his comprehension that a 'nigra' would dare to strike back. Naturally Uncle Tom went directly to the colonel, hat in hand, to inform him of the incident. Things got hotter for Lieutenant Shelton.

"A few weeks passed, and one day I noticed a civilian car just outside the motor pool fence. It was the colonel's car again. The sergeant had cleverly parked it over a ditch and was working away. When he saw me he smiled slyly saying, 'Well it ain't on government property.' I smiled back as I walked along picking up each tool; they were all government-owned, so I proceeded to jot down each serial number. I walked away at a leisurely pace, leaving a somewhat nervous and bewildered sergeant, went directly to my quarters and wrote up charges against Colonel H. for giving a noncommissioned officer direct orders to disobey government regulations. I submitted those charge sheets close to sixty times. Every time I sent them in they were returned for a comma, a period, any excuse. Finally I got tired of the game of "I've got you blocked." I sent the original copy to battalion headquarters and a carbon copy to the base commander, which is quite legal. I got action.

"The base commander sent for me and asked that I do him a favor in return for a favor. He asked me to drop the charges and I'd have to trust him, but the trouble would stop. I quite frankly told him I accepted, because there was no other alternative.

"He kept his word and the colonel was relieved of his command but not before old H. got in a good solid counter-punch to Lieutenant Shelton. I was transferred to Camp Maxie, Texas. The commander there, as the colonel told me, was an old buddy of his. I was assigned out of my field into an ammunition ordnance. Colonel H. had assured me his buddy would see that I was killed because this group was going overseas.

"I spent some miserable months at Camp Maxie. I put in for a transfer shortly after my arrival there. It finally came through and I went to Fort Sill, Oklahoma, still in ordnance. From there I was sent to the 3755 Quartermasters and ended up in Hollandia, New Guinea. This trucking outfit had black enlisted personnel and mixed officers. We had a little clean-up work to do with the few remaining Japanese on Hollandia. The work in general was hard. Our only recreation was seeing movies. I ended up executive officer of one of the battalions. After three years over there my unit returned to the states with the war's end.

"I joined the reserves in my home state, got out, and rejoined in 1954. The group I was with was the first missile battalion in Michigan. We had the Ajax, then the Hercules missile sites around Detroit. My last job with the reserves was trying to recruit black officers for the Michigan National Guard.

My last report to my superiors was if they wanted black officers they should have started years ago, because out of fifteen hundred officers only seventy-five were black. It is not much better today."

Lieutenant Lacey Wilson, 364th Infantry Regiment, was another early draftee. It was his eventual fate to sit out the war in the Aleutians, after incidents of racial violence involving the 364th at Camp Van Dorn, Mississippi.

Lacey Wilson: "My unit was spread throughout California and Nevada after the bombing of Pearl Harbor. One of our jobs was to guard Boulder Dam. The nearby towns were off-limits to all Negro personnel. We could guard Boulder Dam, an important military installation, against saboteurs, but we could not enter Boulder City. Las Vegas was as segregated as any deep southern city. We were only allowed in the small colored section of the famous gambling city.

"When my unit returned to Fort Huachuca to become a part of the newly formed 93rd Division, I went to OCS. Upon graduating from there I was sent to the 364th Infantry Regiment at Papago Park, Arizona. The enlisted men of this regiment had staged a series of riots against the all-white officers over them and a prompt call went out for black officers. I was the only black officer assigned to headquarters company. Then I was made commander of a newly formed cannon platoon. This was most unusual since this platoon contained 125 men. The platoon was finally made a company and a white captain, white exec. officer, and three white lieutenants were brought in as senior officers, I was low man on the totem pole.

Starting with the captain, each officer in his turn was sent to Fort Benning, Georgia, for special training. When my turn came nothing was said. I inquired into this and was told I was not being sent because I had not finished high school. I reminded the captain that to attend OCS all that was required was a grade school education and an IQ of 110 or higher. I had finished OCS and had handled many weapons in the process. Now I was being told I was incapable of learning to handle one. I still didn't go to Fort Benning. A couple of the white officers in my unit were sympathetic to my situation and gave me all of the printed material that they had brought back with them pertinent to the handling of our weapon. In this manner I managed to stay abreast of the work we did.

"The 364th was sent to Camp Van Dorn, which was most unfortunate. The day after our arrival one of our men was killed by a deputy sheriff right outside the gates of the post and a riot resulted. I can only speak for my immediate area. There was serious fighting between black and white soldiers. We pulled the firing pins from the rifles to prevent real bloodshed. The next day the blacks were confined to their area, which was patrolled by armed whites in armored vehicles. Two months later the 364th was sent to the Aleutian Islands.

"The blacks and whites in the Aleutians got along just fine. There were no women of any race present. In the Aleutians we were all brothers under the skin, but stateside we had better not have put our foot inside of the officers' club on any southern and many northern posts.

"Stateside I encountered every possible racial insult. The one I shall always remember was not in a direct form of a put-down but it was the most disgusting of them all. At a train station in Texas I had to walk down an alley to the back of an eatery to get something to eat. Yet there were white MPs with German prisoners of war inside enjoying each other's company over a steak dinner. It sickened me so I could not eat a bite after ordering. I was a citizen soldier in the uniform of my country and I had to go through an alley to the back door while some of Hitler's storm troopers lapped up the hospitality of my country.

"I think the army, government, or white people, which in the end are the same thing, purposely humiliated blacks in uniform to attempt to make them feel they were less than men.

"Black soldiers of World War II showed more courage just surviving, as well as fighting back by all means possible, in southern and in northern camps, than young people today can possibly imagine. Hell we fought the 'man,' the system, and the Axis powers. The infantry can't go a damned place without quartermasters and engineers, which a lot of people seem to forget."

Lieutenant William Price, whose first assignment as an officer was to the 364th Infantry Regiment while it was still at Papago Park, adds to the picture drawn by Lacey Wilson:

The 364th had had a riot brought on by mistreatment by their southern white officers and hostile surroundings. The men demanded black officers and backed their demand by riotous behavior. I believe fifteen of us were sent there to meet the demand and bring some order to the 364th. Unfortunately a disturbance ensued in Phoenix and the regiment was then sent to Camp Van Dorn, Mississippi. It is not a thing one can prove, but I feel certain Van Dorn was chosen as a punitive measure for the 364th. If these men resented the conditions in Arizona sending them into the deep south would hardly resolve the problem. We hadn't been there anytime when one of our enlisted men was killed, apparently in cold blood. I was not with the 364th when the next punitive action was the Aleutian Islands.

I was with three different infantry regiments and in my opinion the 364th was head and shoulders above all of them. These were men who stood together under good or adverse circumstances. That the government chose to be punitive in their dealings with this group was its loss, for the 364th was a first-class fighting regiment of black enlisted men.

The confrontation at Camp Van Dorn is also described by Technical Sergeant Jeffries Bassett Jones and Private Clyde Blue, both of the 518th

Quartermaster (Truck) Battalion, stationed there at that time. (See chapter 2.)

The name of Fort Huachuca, Arizona, appears from time to time in the interviews, particularly in the following chapter and in chapter 5, which recounts the history of the 92nd Division. Lieutenant Colonel Roger Walden, 555th Paratroop Battalion, who enlisted in 1942, was sent to Huachuca in 1943 after he finished basic training at Camp Atterbury, Indiana. He had become a sergeant in a weapons platoon of the 365th Infantry Regiment, which was to be one of the regiments of the 92nd. "I was quite young when I joined the army," he said, "and my youth coupled with plain naiveness made me quite gullible. These traits got me into more unhappy yet comical situations than I care to recall."

Roger Walden: "At Huachuca it was obvious that very few black officers had command positions in any of the three regiments. White officers who had goofed elsewhere in white outfits were being sent as senior officers to Fort Huachuca and the 92nd. They had no compunction about letting it be known that they were being punished when sent to Huachuca.

"I was gullible but I wasn't stupid. I began to have misgivings about following this kind of officer into battle, and I became determined to get out of the 92nd. One day a team of paratroopers came to Huachuca seeking black volunteers. I honestly didn't know what the paratroops were all about, but they were mighty impressive in their jump suits and shiny boots. It's just a good thing they weren't asking for frogmen that day because I would have volunteered just as readily in happy oblivion.

"We arrived at Fort Benning by bus early one morning. I noticed the high towers in the distance, and someone mentioned those were the parachute towers we would jump from. The towers were actually 250 feet high, but at that moment they looked to me like the Eiffel Tower. I thought, my God, what have I gotten into? I couldn't believe I would go off one of those towers; yet I felt I had a mission that was over and beyond me and I would give it all I had. At the time, bets were made that blacks would never jump. We not only jumped but were darn good. The black civilians in the area were mighty proud of us when we earned our berets. Even the whites in and around the base gave us grudging respect.

"We seventeen NCOs from Huachuca went through regular paratroop training with white trainees. Our instructors were white NCOs and though our black officers trained separately they were also trained by the NCOs. The training we had is quite similar to that given today. There was a gradual body build-up until physically we were in excellent condition. There was a lot of esprit de corps which our instructors can take credit for. Our NCOs were tough on us, but they turned our anger into determination to take whatever they could dish out and do whatever was expected of us.

"Once we learned how to land correctly from a platform, we began jumping at higher levels until the day of the towers arrived. Actually you don't jump from the tower. You are hoisted aloft by a cable and when you reach the top a device automatically releases you and down you come. After the tower came our five plane jumps. Five jumps from aircraft are necessary to qualify for a paratrooper: two straight jumps, one night jump, and two jumps with combat equipment. In those days you packed your own chute. There is a certain comfort in knowing you had packed your own lifeline, so to speak. Two men worked together, each helping the other.

"Only one man of our seventeen didn't make it through. It was after the third or fourth jump he decided jumping was not for him. Instances of this nature are no reflection on the individual; stepping out of an airplane is not a natural thing and not everybody is cut out for it any more than for being a pilot. Some men made it all the way and then asked for reassignment.

"One of the methods of ascertaining whether you have any fear of jumping is you are never assisted, pushed, or asked to go when you jump. Paratroopers jump in sticks; so many men make up a stick depending on the size of the plane and the job to be done. When the time comes to jump you line up to go, after hitching your chute by a line to a cable inside of the plane. This snatches your chute open, once you have fallen the length of the line. However, when you come up to the door and the jump master says, 'Go,' it's up to you. You have to step out on your own.

"By February '44 twenty-six of the twenty-seven men from Huachuca had earned their berets. We formed the nucleus of the 555th or what was called the Triple Nickel. Our job was to train 250 men coming in for a black paratroop unit. From here on the training of black paratroopers would be done by blacks separately. There were over a thousand black volunteers for the 250 places in the 555th, so we could afford to be selective. The volunteers came from all units; there were no restrictions, though we got most of our volunteers from combat units.

"After the 555th went to Camp McCall, North Carolina, I applied for OCS and on acceptance I returned to Fort Benning. Afterwards, I rejoined the 555th since there was only one black paratroop unit and they were not about to send me to a white one! During my absence the 555th had become the 555th battalion, and once battalion training was finished, we expected to be sent to Europe. Instead, we were split into two groups, one going to Pendleton Field, Oregon, and the other to Chico Field, California.

We felt this was a dodge to avoid using us in combat. However, upon arriving at our destination we learned that over a period of time, starting in 1943, there had been a build-up of forest fires in the Northwest caused by incendiary bombs carried by balloons released by the Japanese. It was a magnesium type bomb and was doing considerable damage in the great forests of northwestern Canada and the United States. We had to maintain combat training while learning the art of jumping into forest fires. Forest rangers briefed us on the demonical behavior of forest fires and how to cope with it. Our job was to prevent fires when possible and to fight them when it was necessary.

"Generally, by the time we received information about a bomb the fire had already started. The balloons carrying them were usually so high they went unseen. The contraptions were so devised that the bombs did not drop all together but at intervals to set a number of fires over a wide area. Many of them, carried by the trade winds, were falling into the forests.

"Because of the cold weather, our jump suits were air force pilots' jackets and pants, fleece-lined. We wore something like a football helmet with a mesh front to protect our faces when we fell into the trees. We had gloves we seldom used and always jumped with a long nylon rope. If we landed in a tree we tied it to our auxiliary chute, giving it added length, and we climbed down this chute-rope line. The only man we lost fell to his death when his chute-line in the tall tree where he had landed was fifty feet short of the ground. In this position he couldn't hang on long and he fell, breaking his neck.

"Fire-fighting gear was parachuted with us, even a pump which could be used in the first available stream. Most of our fires were small ones with nine or ten men spot-jumping, so they came in from different directions and could contain the fire for the ground fire fighters to finish the job. Whenever possible, the pilot of the aircraft from which we jumped would find an opening near the designated area and set us down. When no such opening appeared it was jumping and landing in the trees, for which we had been trained. Tree landings are avoided unless necessary.

"The largest fire we had required a hundred men jumping at once. We did find a few of the magnesium bombs that had failed to ignite, or fragments which we carried back to our base for study and further training.

"Later on we were joined in this work by some conscientious objectors from Missoula, Montana. We worked together in several operations. They would jump with us or work on the ground, whichever was necessary.

"When the war ended in Japan we were shipped back to Camp McCall; our type of work was no longer needed. Now there were those who laugh about the black paratroop fire-fighters. As I said, not until we got there did we believe there was a serious job to be done and by skilled men. Combat paratroopers are taught to avoid trees, not land in them. I don't believe any paratrooper would belittle tree-top landings from a plane. Nor would they smirk at jumping when you see the landscape below dotted with small fires rapidly growing into big ones; it's strictly a race against time. No one belittles the parachuting fire-fighters in the west today, a number of whom are ex-paratroopers. We Triple Nickels did a little pioneering in this field."

With the conclusion of World War II, Roger Walden decided to make the army his career. He was married in 1946. He applied for and received a Regular Army commission. Sent to Fort Bragg, he and his wife settled down in the segregated Spring Lake area near the post. In 1949 he was sent to Japan for occupation duty with the all-black 24th Infantry Regiment of the otherwise white 25th Infantry Division. Shortly after the Korean War broke out, he was sent to Korea, where he was in combat until mid-June 1951. He returned from Korea with a Silver Star and malaria. Walden emphasized one fact about his Korean experience: "From the begining, South Korean companies were attached to various outfits. Long before blacks were eating, sleeping, and fighting alongside their fellow Americans, Koreans were living an integrated life in the American armed forces. To deny that this infuriated the black soldier would be ridiculous; it was an affront. This was only one of the 'jokers in the deck' that I witnessed in Korea."

Although the following events occurred long after the close of World War II, they form a significant part of Roger Walden's interview:

"Once back in the states my army career was one of slow, steady advancement. I was stationed at Fort Campbell, Kentucky, when the time was approached for me to make the rank of major. I had been made regimental adjutant after being asked if I would accept the position. All seemed to be going well for about a month, when I was relieved of this job and placed in one below my qualifications at range central. I tried to make inquiries as to why I had been practically demoted and was met at every turn by evasion or silence. I mentioned this to my commanding officer at range central and he quickly slid around the conversation. I noticed when he thought I wasn't looking he would look at me and shake his head. To see my military career, in which I had done a good job, suddenly side-tracked was befuddling and infuriating. I tried to be patient and see what would come of all this. When the promotions for major came up my name was not on the list; twice I was passed over. That did it; I demanded a meeting with the division commander. He received me about a week later and listened to my story. He avoided any answers but said he would look into it. He did!

"Shortly after our meeting I was told to report to a hearing at which I was to be interrogated by officers of the army. At this 'hearing' all of the missing pieces fell into place. Counter-Intelligence had been responsible for the sudden change in my affairs: *I was a security risk.*

"The kind of questions they asked and the methods and manners used in asking them I resented very much. It was as if I was facing the Spanish Inquisition, or more befitting, the Gestapo. I couldn't believe what was happening. I was accused of being a Communist and a traitor. Protest or denial was useless as they bore in like sadistic animals, relishing every minute of their cruelty and power.

"I was angry beyond imagination when they brought my wife into this sorry mess. This was the crux of the whole thing; I saw it as they hammered away at me. My brother-in-law, Captain Charles Hill, Jr., of the Air Force Reserves had, had the attempt made to force his resignation from the service on the grounds his father, Reverend Charles Hill was thought to be, or might be, or could be a Communist.* He refused to resign and fought back. The Secretary of the air force sent him an apology, saying a mistake had been made. However, he was never called to duty in Korea when there was a great need for experienced combat pilots. My wife, Roberta, who was Charles's sister, had been mentioned in the vague non-particulars sent to Charles demanding his resignation.

"My inquisitors noted my car was seen at a certain address on West Grand Boulevard. (My in-laws lived there and my wife visited them a lot whenever I was away.) They said I attended meetings in the basement of Reverend Hill's home, conducted by Paul Robeson, which was a lie. (I met Mr. Robeson exactly once in my life after a concert.)

"I kept thinking, I'll wake up. This couldn't be happening to me in my country—Germany, Russia, China perhaps, but not here. I was stunned that I was considered a Communist because I married the woman I loved very much, who happened to be the daughter of a man I admired very much. He was more than just mouth, he actively fought for blacks, other minorities, the weak, and for justice and democracy in the country he loved. High position and power did not frighten him. I was mentally alert as the interrogation took place but in a state of shock and disbelief as the torrent of lies and insinuations fell upon my head. How long I was in the inquisition chamber with my fellow officers I can't say, but I do know I was forced to stay until they decided I should go.

"I had been *allowed* to go through World War II—I was engaged to Roberta at the time—*allowed* to fight in Korea and to start moving up in the ranks. They could have brought all of their charges out into the open any place along the line, but they didn't. They let me go so far up the ladder, then they pulled the rug from under me. I was flabbergasted and mad as hell.

"My career was short-circuited when I was reaching the level of coming in contact with security material. From here in I was to be kept in inconsequential jobs because I was tied into some kind of conspiracy against the government. I wish I could say I can laugh about it now, but I can't. What was done to me was done against the Bill of Rights, the Constitution, every-

---

*See Chapter 4 for the experience of Captain Charles A. Hill, Jr., also the introduction, above, on the Reverend Charles A. Hill.

thing worthwhile for which this country is supposed to stand. It was the ultimate cruelty.

"If I had listened to my father-in-law I would have brought the whole thing out into the open and fought it then. But I had the naive notion that 'they' would recognize their mistake and all would be well. What an unbelieving fool I was!

"I will never forget Fort Campbell, Kentucky, where my interrogation took place. Nor will I forget my fellow officers whose techniques were straight out of the Gestapo archives. My wife's face, when I came home that evening and told her of the day's events is etched in my memory forever. Roberta is dead now. She died suddenly of heart failure. I will always believe her death can be directly attributed to the fact she was afraid my marrying her had made it impossible for me to climb to the top in the career I had chosen.

"Of course the question of race entering into the whole shabby affair crossed my mind. For a black man it would be abnormal if it had not. I do know there were officers who thought Roberta was white and resented our marriage deeply. We encountered problems along this line often.

"I am sure the tag 'security risk' followed me throughout the rest of my army career. I was promoted in such a manner that I could never become a full colonel, and when you can't move up you move out. We didn't conspire against the government, the army, or anyone or anything else but there *was* a conspiracy, and my wife and I were among the victims."

Determined to join the air force, Major Richard Jennings had first to battle military "efficiency" harder than racism. For overseas service he had to wait until long after World War II, as the 477th Bombardier Group, to which he was eventually assigned, was not completely manned until 1945. His interview describes two tactical victories of black air-force officers against built-in discrimination and concludes on a hopeful note.

Richard Jennings: "During the process of my induction into the armed forces in April 1943, at Fort Wayne, Michigan, I was asked if I wanted to be in the navy, and I declined. I was then sent to a navy recruiter to explain why I wasn't interested in this branch of the service. I told him quite simply that since I was being drafted, the only thing I could do in the navy was wait tables. This I assured him I had not the slightest intention of doing. I was returned to the army side of the induction center and was assigned to the air corps engineers.

"From Fort Custer I was sent to Jefferson City, Missouri, where I underwent a series of tests. I was then given the choice of OCS or topographical drafting school. I explained I wanted to go into the air force, and I learned fast a lot of guys were hard of hearing in the service, particularly when you were talking about something that didn't fit into the picture they had drawn up for you. I did my basic training in Missouri and was then sent to drafting school in Boston. While there I filled out a couple of forms for the air force but received no response. After three or four months in Boston, I was shipped to Eglin Field, Florida.

Disembarking from the train in Florida, I went down in sand up to my knees and quickly decided this was not the place for me. There was no one at the station to meet me and I hadn't the foggiest notion where the field was. I just kept walking around until I ran into a couple of MPs going my way. They drove me to the black area of the field and turned me over to the officer of the day. He gave me a blanket and directed me across the street to the barracks, where I spent the night.

"The next day I checked in for an assignment and they wanted to know when I came in. I explained, and this same OD who was on duty when I arrived insisted I couldn't have come in as I said. I had turned my papers over to him the previous night. I told him just to return my papers and I would be more than willing to leave. They decided to keep me and assigned me to a unit.

"My foremost thought, need I say, was to get out of there as soon as possible. Eglin Field was at that time a proving ground and a testing center. I made it my business to go over to the center and put in an application for air cadet. Without apprising anybody of my activities, I took the written exam and passed it, as well as the physical exam. I had tried to go through channels with no results, so I decided to forget channels.

"The company to which I had been assigned there was alerted for overseas duty. I asked for a furlough. Naturally I was informed by the CO that furloughs were out with an alert notice. I then explained that there really wasn't any point in taking me overseas as I was awaiting a transfer to the air force and they'd just have to pay the expense of sending me back. He was very upset. He said I was a topographical draftsman and very vital to them. I felt that was all well and good, but in the three months I had been there I hadn't drawn a single map. I had done just like the others in this field, gone over to the recreation center and sat around eating ice cream cones; now I was vital!

"Word arrived from Washington that I was assigned to the air force so I was placed in another unit that was remaining until I got my orders. I was soon told to report to Biloxi, Mississippi, for a psychomotor exam.

"When I got to the camp just outside of Biloxi, I was shown to a tent by a sergeant; I was to sleep there. When he got outside I was right behind him. He wanted to know where I was going. I told him, to one of the barracks across the road. I explained I was not just a private coming into the army and he had better believe I had spent my last night sleeping in a tent; I moved into the barracks. My objection to tent living was that after it rained I have seen guys swimming in the tent area; this place proved to be no exception. I can't vouch for the white areas, but I do not believe they spent as much time in inundated sections as blacks did. They got the high ground and we got the swampland with tents. Oh, there were barracks built on stilts but newcomers were generally relegated to the 'swimming pool.'

"I stayed around there a while, but they never called my name so I attached myself to a group and every time they were called to take tests I went right along and took the tests also. After I had taken them, I found five guys were washed out because their names had never been called. The only reason I wasn't one of them was pure brashness on my part; I wasn't going to be left out of anything. I was at Keesler Field two months before they found my records had been there all the time, over on the other side of the base!

"Biloxi was something else, like purgatory, I went into the city one night on pass and was walking down that street in the Negro section where there were no sidewalks. This may sound fantastic but the police tried to run over me! I mean they veered across the street in their police car and if I hadn't leaped across a ditch they would have deliberately run me down. If they were trying to tell me something, I got the message. I got back to Keseler Field fast and I never returned to Biloxi. I made it my business to stay on the base.

"When I had completed all the exams given the group I had imposed myself upon, I was among those who qualified for navigator or bombardier training. At this time they had decided to form a black bomber squadron, so those that qualified went to Tuskegee for pre-flight training, then on to Hondo Field, Texas, for navigation or bombardier training, or both. Thirty-two of us went to Hondo Field from our pre-flight training at Tuskegee. There they set us up in our own little segregated unit, and I do mean segregated.

"Our chief instructor, Lieutenant McPherson, made no bones about the fact he was bucking for a captaincy and if pushing us was going to further his ambitions he'd push. I must admit he really saw to it that we got the material and worked at making as many 'spook' navigators as possible.

"We had a character named Willard Savoy in the group. He had a habit of writing letters to the undersecretary of war. I can't remember the man's name now, but Savoy would leave the letters on his desk. Savoy was from Washington, so the 'wheels' thought. At least they didn't know whether or not he had connections at the capital. Result: Savoy always passed. I have always believed his letter-writing got him through; he plain 'psyched' the 'man.'

"Every Wednesday was open house at the school as far as the cadets were concerned. We had what was called visitation rights at this time, and girls would come in from the surrounding towns. However, this open-house business didn't apply to Negro cadets. Every Wednesday night we were assigned to do something—study the stars, anything. They weren't going to have us ogling the white girls—or colored girls either, for that matter, since they were never invited.

"The post theater had a part set aside for the black cadets. Because of my color and the darkness of the theater they often asked me to please move to the white part of the theater. It was quite humorous, when they recognized their error.

"There was a main PX which was large and well-stocked, and a smaller PX, which was very poorly stocked. One day, rather than go to lunch at noon, I went to the main PX. The base commander saw me and by 1:30 P.M. there was an edict that cadets would not be allowed in the main PX during the lunch hour. This was all well and good excepting we were the only cadets identifiable by color. When we left school at 5:30, the main PX was closed. It was a neat way of keeping us out.

"Three of our men washed out, and the remainder of us went to Midland, Texas, for bombardier training. This course was quite simple. Basically it was a repeat in some areas of what we had already had, DR [dead reckoning], true heading, wind direction and velocity, the ability to come up with a track and to use the Norden bombsight.

"Upon arriving at the base they set aside a barracks, as a white lieutenant-colonel informed us, for all Negro officers. It was arranged that we would eat at the cadets' mess. They told us it would be more beneficial and save us money. We insisted on sharing the burden of any expense so they couldn't very well enforce this. Rather than have us use the officers' club, they built a room in back of our quarters right next to the officers' club. We were told any time we wanted anything just call over and they would see that it was delivered.

"Finally they spelled it out: we were to be treated as cadets, which automatically excluded us from officers' facilities. That did it. Three of us—Savoy, Cyril Burke, and I—sat down and wrote the inspector-general in Washington explaining how we were being treated and what was going on at this USAAF base. We stated if we could not be treated as other officers stationed here, we should be allowed to resign our commissions and go home. We saw to it that one copy was mailed off the base to Washington, another copy was sent to the base commander, and we kept a copy. The letter had been signed by all of the black officers in our group, including Coleman Young.*

"In a couple of days the base commander and his staff were busy little fellows trying to find out with whom the letter had originated. I got the impression that Coleman had clashed with the 'power boys' before, because they did their level best to get each of us to say that he had put us up to this 'foolishness.' Each one answered, when asked if Coleman had written the letter, 'We all wrote it.' That was the only answer they ever got though they tried everything from threats to false promises. About a week later an officer arrived from Washington and turned that base upside down. The base commander was transferred and we were informed that henceforth all facilities on

---

*Present mayor of Detroit.

the base were open to us. So don't ever believe that Negroes can't stick together; admittedly there were only twenty-nine of us. Coleman, who was later transferred to Freeman Field, Indiana, is a member of the 101 Club of the 477th Bomber Squadron; and herein lies a story that must be told, for it clarifies exactly where black air force officers stood with their superiors.

"The 101 Club consists of 101 black air force officers who refused to sign a paper presented to them at Freeman Field, stipulating that should they cause any trouble about facilities closed to them they would be court-martialed and that they understood this. By referring to the original documents I can clarify the situation. A directive was issued at Freeman Field, Indiana, April 9, 1945: Base Regulation, Number 85-2, the title, "Assignment of Housing."

"The first paragraph, which is restated in greater detail over two pages says, 'Army Air Force Standards governing the control and curfew of personnel undergoing training, as differentiated from standards governing permanent party Base, supervisory and instructor personnel, authorize separate housing, messing and recreational facilities assignment to those two classes of personnel.' The last paragraph concludes, 'This order will be distributed to each officer presently assigned or in the future to Freeman Field and will be read by each officer and returned to this headquarters, certifying that he has read the order and fully understands it. By order of Colonel Selway.'

"The members of the 101 Club saw this directive as a very clever way for them to sign away their basic rights and to compound the issue by setting themselves up for a court-martial. Should they infringe on the stipulation in Number 85-2, they would be disobeying a order that they had agreed to in writing. Each of the officers decided against affixing his signature to the individual copy given him. All were placed under arrest April 11, 1945. On April 13 these men were flown to Godman Field, Kentucky, under heavy guard and placed in arrest in their quarters.

"These air force officers realized that there was a good possibility they would be facing a general court-martial. They decided they needed a man with considerable legal knowledge as well as stature in the public eye to act as their counselor. Their choice was Judge William Hastie, who had resigned a prestigous government position in protest against the rampant racism in the armed forces and in particular the racial policies in the United States Air Force.* However, the judge's talents were not needed, for all charges were dropped against the arrested officers. To this day no one knows why, unless fear of what publicity of this incident would do.

"The only comical aspect of this situation was the day the members of the 101 were released from house arrest. The MPs that had been guarding

*See Judge Hastie's article, "On Clipped Wings," published as a separate issue by *Crisis* Magazine, October 1943; also the introduction to chapter 3, below.

them took to their heels with all 101 angry men right behind them. Fortunately for the MPs, the guys were not in their best physical form, having been confined for several weeks. The men felt the MPs had enjoyed their work just a little too much.

"At the war's end I remained in the Air Force Reserves and was recalled to temporary duty for eighteen months after the Pueblo Incident in 1965. My job was with Air Rescue Group 305 as a navigator at Selfridge Field. Those eighteen months with the air force were what it should have been like thirty years ago.

"We went everywhere: from Africa to Iceland to Okinawa. On our last trip out from Okinawa the combined knowledge and training of our crew was used for the worthy purpose of saving lives. We were alerted that a ship was sinking and given coordinates. We located her, a Japanese vessel, marked the area, found help—two other ships were in the area—returned to the disaster area, and stayed overhead until we saw the endangered men being rescued. It was a good feeling to have been a part of the operation and for the first time, twenty-two years after World War II, I felt a sense of accomplishment in the armed forces. Judge Hastie was right, segregation is indefensible. Black and white men, working as a team in the sky, saved yellow men otherwise destined for a watery grave."

Chapter **2**

Servicemen in the Pacific and the Far East

Unwanted, One Black Division

To express his view of the black draftee's or enlisted man's war experience, one of the men interviewed in this chapter (Staff Sergeant Bill Stevens, 48th Quartermaster Regiment), used the comparison of a parade:

The black GIs . . . were on the tail end of everything in World War II. . . . The best example I can think of is a military parade. If you remember back in those days, by the time the white GIs passed the reviewing stand and reached their breaking-up point, black GIs were just begining to march and the affair was drawing to an end. That, baby, is the tail end, and the black GI started there and stayed there throughout World War II.

Although Stevens intended his remark as a general comment, it applies to the specific situation of the all-black 93rd Infantry Division; for when it arrived in the South Pacific toward the end of February 1944 the parade was drawing to an end.

The first of the two all-black infantry divisions of World War II, the 93rd was activated in the spring of 1942 at Fort Huachuca, Arizona. Its nucleus was to be the Regular Army 25th Infantry Regiment (activated 1866), and the new Regular Army 368th, activated 1 March 1941. The third regiment of the division was the 369th, composed of draftees. Black junior officers were assigned to the 25th to keep its composition parallel to that of the other two regiments.

In April 1943 the 93rd went on maneuvers in Louisiana and from there to maneuvers in the Mohave Desert. (One of the men interviewed commented that the 93rd was called the "maneuvers division.") In December 1943 it was alerted for POM.

Towards the end of February 1944 the 93rd was in the Solomon Islands, in the South Pacific. The break-up of the division began. The 368th went to the Russell Islands; the 369th went on to the New Georgia group. The 25th arrived at Guadalcanal the third week of February and spend several weeks thereafter building a bivouac area while about a thousand of the troops worked the docks. Each battalion received about a week's training in jungle warfare, and in March the 25th was ordered to Bougainville as a combat team.

Under the control of the Americal Division on Bougainville, the 25th was broken up into battalions and attached to white regiments. After a period of limited offensive operations beyond the Torokina perimenter in southern Bougainville, the 25th went in June to the Green Islands, between the Solomons and New Ireland, where its duties were security, labor, loading and unloading ships, and cleaning out Japanese stragglers on islands considered secure. The fate of the two other regiments of the division, the 368th and 369th, was essentially the same as that of the 25th, duties that were a necessary part of the war effort but not the duties usually performed by an infantry division. Significantly, Lee notes, "These were the duties contemplated when the 93rd Division was accepted by the theater" (p. 516).

Until the war's end, elements of the 93rd moved from one Pacific island to another, coordinating labor and transportation furnished by the 8th and 6th armies in the Hollandia area, looking after docks and warehouses and going on patrol missions in the Admiralty Islands; furnishing round-the-clock port duty at Morotai (where a 25th Infantry patrol found time to capture a Japanese colonel). In August 1945 the 93rd was made responsible for the surrender of all Japanese troops in the Moluccas, but the formal surrender of the Japanese there was made to the Australians.

At Mindanao in the Philippines during October 1945, the 93rd processed both American and Japanese troops for return to their home countries. (See Lee, chapter 18.)

The interview with Staff Sergeant Stevens, 48th Quartermaster Regiment, appears first since it provides comments by a man who enlisted in 1940 concerning the black Regular Army NCOs of the 25th Infantry Regiment, who were to train the men who became part of the 93rd Division. Stevens's overseas experience began in Australia in 1942, almost two years before the 93rd was shipped to the South Pacific.

Bill Stevens: "I enlisted in the army on my eighteenth birthday and was sent from my home town, Decatur, Illinois, to Fort Sheridan, in my state. At the time of my arrival there, there was a cadre of NCOs from the 25th Infantry Regiment. They were all old in time of service, Regular Army men. There were no new men about, simply because until 1940 there had been a strict quota system on the number of blacks allowed in the armed forces.

"The cadre had come from Fort Benning, Georgia, where the 25th was stationed. They were professionals, well-trained and disciplined. They had no respect for officers, black or white, unless they were professionals, meaning from West Point or a military academy of some repute. Even officers from these academies got little respect if they didn't measure up. Some of the men forming this cadre had been on the best rifle teams in the country, and the officers they worked with treated them with respect.

"Basic training took sixteen weeks. Actually, if you become a career soldier, as I did, you soon learn that every so often you go through another sixteen weeks of training: No one can stay in the service ten to twenty years and not reach a certain degree of proficiency because of this repetitiveness.

"When I entered the service they had not begun conscription, so my first officers were from the Point. They were all pros and there was no tension and no major problems. I made my first maneuvers in Louisiana in 1941, prior to Pearl Harbor. My unit was an unattached service group and everything went smoothly.

"In March 1942 we were shipped to the Pacific. Our first stop was Sydney, Australia, where we blacks were received with some apprehension since the Aussies had never seen such a large number of Afro-Americans before. However, everything turned out all right. From Sydney we went to Brisbane, where we built an airfield. We were attached to an engineer outfit and built a road from Brisbane to Mt. Ira, which is in the center of Australia. Then we worked on a road to Darwin, the northernmost port close to New Guinea. All of this time we had the same officers, white West Pointers who treated us with respect and who we respected.

"In 1943 when the Americans started their campaign to retake those islands held by the Japanese in the Pacific, the officers we had were sent elsewhere. Their replacements were of a different caliber. As soon as white units were committed to battle, the 'brains' were able to weed out those officers unfit for a variety of reasons. These officers were reclassified and sent to black outfits. Did it make a difference with us? It made a helluva difference, for it doesn't take enlisted personnel long to recognize they've got a drunk or yellow-belly in command. Quartermasters carry supplies and do come under fire, and an incompetent can get you killed.

"White officers in general, conceding the exceptions like my original officers, have solidified false ideas about black troops. Their attitude toward black soldiers is entirely different from that shown whites and these attitudes are immediately picked up by white enlisted men. You might not be able to deck an officer for his snide remarks and racial slurs, but you can sure lay on white enlisted personnel. This is why there is so much fighting between black and white enlisted men.

"White commanders in the Pacific theater were notoriously prejudiced. As I have pointed out this kind of thing starts at the top and goes down, so anybody who thinks General MacArthur had any use for black troops had better take a second look at the treatment and use of black soldiers in that area.

"Black troops were just naturally suspected of cowardice, stealing, rape, the whole racial-stereotype lie. White commanders had no respect for black soldiers and it was obvious. Likewise it followed that white soldiers had no respect for their black brothers in arms. In our turn we had utter contempt for them, officers and enlisted men. This whole situation was not helped by the the general knowledge that no commander wanted the 93rd Division, which had all black enlisted men and some black officers. I understand and have no reason to doubt that the 93rd was accepted in the Pacific theater on a direct order from Washington. The word was out that the 93rd was strictly an experimental deal; not much was expected from it. The general opinion of white officers was that black units made excellent labor battalions, and events proved these officers were going to do their damndest to see that black troops were so occupied. Blacks were not going to be given a chance to prove themselves in combat in the Pacific. From where I sat they weren't going to get a chance even if it caused the death of every cracker in the Pacific to keep it that way. The glory boys had to be white!

"The 24th Infantry Regiment, which came to the South Pacific before the 93rd Division, did so much work as labor battalions that I wondered why they did not designate them as the 24th stevedores. I am not trying to be funny. I am attempting to show you how black combat troops in the Pacific were totally misused and humiliated.

"The 93rd came ashore at Guadalcanal; the real fighting had ended when they arrived. This division was split up and scattered all over the goddamn islands. They were put to work unloading ships under the guise of keeping them physically fit. If totin' that barge and liftin' that bale was a physical fitness program, then the 93rd and the 24th should have been in superb physical condition as compared to similar white units. With all of the white casualties our side was sustaining at the time, it seemed a helluva waste of an infantry regiment and an infantry division.

"The 93rd Division, to my knowledge, was never committed to battle as a division. It's too bad, because from all I heard it was a good division with fighting men and black junior officers who were generally respected by their men. They were fairly well demoralized when they realized they would never be allowed to participate in the Pacific theater as infantrymen, the role they had been trained for.

"Prior to the Leyte invasion in 1944, the 5th Ranger Battalion was formed. It was interracial, and the only qualification necessary was that you have a first grade rating. I volunteered for this unit as did all of the other men who became a part of the battalion. Its purpose was to perform special missions before the invasion took place. We were trained in a special area in New Guinea. It so happened we were never committed to battle. We were told things had gone so well leading up to this invasion we were not needed; all of us were returned to our original units.

"It is often said black troops won't fight. I have wondered how this conclusion was arrived at since blacks in the twentieth century have rarely been given the opportunity as combat troops to show their ability, or lack of it. Then too, when you stay in the service as I did, you get a chance to talk to some of the old-timers who are fountains of information on black soldiers. When a greenhorn mumbled about the poor showing of black combat troops they were quickly squelched by remarks like, 'It's funny that General Washington thought blacks did right well in combat. General Sherman, General Grant, and even old turncoat General 'Black Jack' Pershing found no fault with blacks in battle. And old Teddy Roosevelt would never have lived to be president if blacks hadn't saved his hide at Las Guásimas.' You don't see what these men knew in American history books, so the lie goes merrily along, perpetuated by whites, that the black man is a big zero as a fighting man; he is a coward. I find this hard to understand since the average cracker is scared to death to tangle with a black man on a man-to-man, eyeball-to-eyeball deal. It has generally got to be a stacked deck in the cracker's favor.

"Now, about cowardice. In the early days of Korea, during the strategic withdrawal we made—damn near into the Pacific Ocean—those crackers were running so fast to the rear they almost ran over my truck. If they had been forced to make a stand they would have been in one helluva mess. Let's face it, as long as these guys were moving forward and seemingly carrying all before them they were hell, but when the Chinese hit them like a tornado they folded up and ran. You can call it what you want. The army called it a strategic retreat. I was there and it was a rout. Those guys split because they were just plain scared. The black soldier is called a coward before he has even had a chance to stand, or run. This white hang-up about the infinite superiority of the white man to any man of color did not prepare the American white for the Japanese, or for Korea.

"But let us just talk about the Japanese or the little 'monkey men.' You do remember the Japanese were referred to in this and other derogatory terms; they were a colored people so the big bad American marines were going to kick their asses properly and put them back in their place.

"In reality the Japanese were excellent soldiers. They had been fighting in the Pacific for a long time, swallowing up bits and pieces. They had occupied islands, whose names we are all familiar with, and were prepared to be there a long time. Our marines stormed onto the beaches of those islands and they died on them. The Japanese beat the shit out of our legendary marines. That inferior breed happened to be superb contact fighters besides not missing a trick in the book and inventing some new ones. They had all kinds of booby traps. Every trail, every bush, every tree could prove to be disastrous. There were a tremendous number of mental breakdowns among the first marines to hit the Japanese-held islands. We had plenty of physical casualties but the mental breakdowns were not far behind.

"The Japanese took the great white American ego and used it as a weapon against him. They worked on demoralizing our men by doing such things as keeping the marines awake all night by shaking the bushes, sudden noises, and on occasion slithering into a camp and cutting a few throats with a man sleeping beside the victim. The Japanese did everything that kept our men tied in knots.

"American whites are good soldiers, but they met psychological warfare on a scale they had never dreamed possible. And as for cruelty, the Japanese had no corner on this market. I saw souvenirs in the hands of our men, or on their belts, that would have curled the scalplock of Pontiac. There were Japanese women on many of those islands; need I say more?

"It does not surprise me that no black won the Congressional of Honor from 1898 until 1950. Hell, if Dorie Miller didn't receive it in World War II what other black could earn one?* The reason for this 'oversight' is quite easy to understand if you know the military. Most of your military officers come from the south and this is particularly true of the army. In black divisions few blacks reached the level of captain, and it is officers who put a name in for a medal. The recommendation to receive any medal can be stopped all the way up the line of command. The Medal of Honor was beyond us as soon as the recommendation reached the level of major. I think you know there were no helluva lot of Distinguished Service Crosses awarded to our men; less than eight received it. The cracker officers thought they were doing you a damned favor when they 'gave' you the Bronze Star. Notice I said 'gave.' We Negroes never earn anything; they 'give' us medals out of the 'kindness' of their hearts.

"In World War II one of the best artillery units in the Pacific, if not *the* best, was the 49th Coastal Artillery Group. It received a commendation from General Kreber. The 49th may have been designated as coastal artillery but it was used as field artillery and everything else where artillery was needed. The 135th Field Artillery, also black, supported the 37th and Americal Divisions, both white. Strangely enough there are few if any complaints about black artillery men.

"Black-and-white relationship in the South Pacific during World War II can best be summed up by this fact. As a service unit, if you were hauling supplies for a white unit you had better take your own food. You could have been hauling for a couple of days but if you asked for something to eat the reply was, 'The kitchen—mess hall, in army lingo—just shut down.' "

As Sergeant Stevens said, "Quartermasters carry supplies and do come under fire." On 8 March 1943, near Porlock Harbor, New Guinea, Private

---

*The heroism of Dorie Miller is mentioned in part 2 of this chapter with the interviews of men in the United States Navy.

George Watson, of an unidentified quartermaster unit, was on board a ship that was attacked and hit by enemy bombers.

When the ship was abandoned, Private Watson instead of seeking to save himself, remained in the water assisting several soldiers who could not swim to reach the safety of a raft. This heroic action, which subsequently cost him his life, resulted in the saving of several of his comrades. Weakened by his exertions, he was dragged down by the suction of the sinking ship and was drowned.

His Distinguished Service Cross sent to his next of kin, a sister in St. Louis (General Order 52, Headquarters, United States Army Forces in the Far East, 15 June 1943).

Interviews with men of the 93rd Division begin with 1st Lieutenant George Looney, a member of the cadre of the reactivated 368th Regiment. As a commissioned officer he served with the 25th Infantry Regiment, and was transferred to the 368th in the last months of the war. Except for Colonel Queen, Looney is the only one of the men interviewed who was actually born into the United States Army. His nostalgic childhood recollections of Fort Huachuca contrast sharply with what some of the draftees remember about it.

George Looney: "My ideas and attitudes will probably vary to some extent from the majority of the men you have interviewed because I am what is often referred to as an army brat. The rude awakening for most black draftees upon induction into the armed services had always been a part of my life. Perhaps my background can give you a fair idea of what the black GI was going to encounter, particularly at Fort Huachuca.

"My father was a regular army man serving with the old 9th and 10th cavalries and the 25th Infantry. I was born in Douglas, Arizona, October 28, 1923. When I was two years old the family moved to Fort Huachuca and there is where I grew up. My mother was a school teacher at the fort and my brother was born there, so you see Fort Huachuca was home. Was it isolated? Was it beautiful, ugly? Questions like this I can't really answer. It was home and I had a relatively pleasant childhood there.

"It should be pointed out that the United States Army, pre-World War II, was one big family; this was particularly true on permanent army posts. Huachuca had about 800 men stationed there when I was a kid. There was no such thing as juvenile delinquency because all of the children belonged to all of the soldiers, so to speak, and if you were caught wrong your backsides were warmed by the person who discovered you up to no good. In the summer the teenagers earned $25.00 a month doing KP for the soldiers who would rather pay than do the job themselves. The soldiers' salaries were $19.00 month. At the end of the summer the kids had $75.00 and they had been kept occupied.

"I attended the all-black elementary school on the post. There was a white elementary school there also for the children of the officers and white civilian workers' young ones. Separation at the elementary level was Arizona law, which somehow took precedent over federal law in that it could be imposed on federal land. Those of us young blacks who were continuing our education at the high school level were bussed 28 miles to and 28 miles from Tombstone High School in Tombstone, Arizona. It was an integrated high school, again Arizona law. Our bus was purchased by the soldiers chipping in. They bought the parts and assembled the bus at the Motor Pool. The only license plate the bus ever had was a tin plate that said Fort Huachuca. The state never bothered about demanding a proper plate.

"White kids attending the same high school in Tombstone, and coming from Huachuca, were picked up by a bus starting somewhere in Cochise County that wound its way to Huachuca and on to Tombstone. Our bus driver was a soldier who drove us to school, waited throughout the day, and drove us back to the fort.

"Tombstone High School was my first integrated experience. There were no breast beating and dire threats when the black kids from Huachuca went to Tombstone High. I played in the band and was a member of the football team, so the school was obviously well integrated. I am sorry to say that my graduation class was the last to have blacks from Fort Huachuca; a high school had been built for black kids on the post.

"Fort Huachuca's only entertainment that brought out all of the various groups living there was the movie. The picture was shown in a large, old building. There was no separation of those in attendance. In 1931 a new movie house was built and to the surprise of the black soldiers an area had been roped off for them and their families. They boycotted the show, and to make sure no soldier showed the 'white feather' the largest and toughest men in the regiment were stationed along the pathways leading to the show. Blacks, being by far the majority in numbers, really hurt the new theater by their non-attendance. In less than a week the ropes came down and only four rows were reserved for the officers and their wives. There was a black chaplain on the post, so even that section was not entirely white.

"I should say now that the white officers of those days were an entirely different breed than those that were to come with World War II. There were exceptions, but as a rule most of them were West Pointers. All knew of the excellent fighting records of the regular black cavalry and infantry and were glad to be a part of these units.

"When I finished high school I had hoped to go to college and study music but circumstances necessitated my getting a job to help support the family. Not prepared for anything in particular but well acquainted with the army, I chose to enlist. The only hitch was no black could join the army unless one was leaving; there was a strict quota system in operation. Luckily one of the buglers went permanently AWOL and I was allowed to join the infantry at Fort Huachuca. I wanted to join the band but the older fellows advised against this if I hoped to move up in the ranks. They pointed out that the band was a one-way street; promotions and advancements did not exist. Since my instrument was a trumpet, they suggested I become a bugler. I would still be able to play my horn but would be a regular infantryman. I took their advice. Being able to carry a forty-five instead of a rifle impressed me. Besides, buglers did not have work details in the afternoon; they withdrew to the drill field and practiced. There were 27 buglers on the post at the time, so we only stood duty every 27 days. Anyone living on the post could tell who was on duty because each bugler had his own sound.

"There were two calls we knew but never practiced because they were only used during the real thing, the call for a fire and the call to arms. One day on my way to the drill field I was stunned by the sounding of the call to arms. Reacting automatically, I headed to the supply room on the double. There I grabbed my forty-five and was given a helmet full of old bullets. (In those days the white soldiers got all of the new equipment and the blacks got the cast-offs. This was true of everything, including bullets.)

"It turned out Mexico was going to have an election, and these usually ended in rioting. Our job was to see that the Mexicans rioted on their own side of the border. We were to go to Naco and Nogales. For transportation the regiment had a handful of old Indiana trucks. Those going to Nogales were loaded on the trucks. The group going to Naco started marching. Once the Nogales group was deposited, the trucks doubled back and picked up those marching to their destination. Nothing happened at the border, and in about a week we were recalled. This time the men at Naco were loaded onto the trucks and those at Nogales started marching back to be picked up by the trucks later.

Huachuca's first draftees arrived in November 1940. They were quartered in pyramidal tents used by the Arizona National Guard when they came to Huachuca for their yearly training. Cadres from the 25th Infantry Regiment were sent to the cantonment and I went as the bugler. In the meantime the 25th was sending cadres all over the country for the formation of service units. The famous Red Ball Express came from a cadre of the 25th.*

"To give you an idea how the men were being sent out in cadre: by December 1940 there were only four buglers left at Fort Huachuca. These men were regulars, they were soldiers, they knew their jobs, and they were good.

"In 1941 the government decided to reactivate the old 368th at Fort Huachuca; the original 368th had been a regiment in the 92nd Division in World War I. I was chosen as a member of the cadre which consisted of a 1st sergeant, Edward Branch, four platoon sergeants, a supply sergeant, and a company clerk, Bobby Walden. This was the beginning of the 368th in World

---

*More on the Red Ball Express is found in the following chapter, interview with Chester Jones.

War II, or if you prefer, the 93rd Division at Huachuca down below the railroad tracks.

"The young men who came to us at that time were predominately from the coal fields of Ohio and West Virginia. These were some rough troops. I was kind of young for a platoon sergeant, and one big fellow from the mines of West Virginia let it be known that no young punk was going to tell him what to do. One day his blouse was not completely buttoned. I told him to button it up. He told me to button it. I was just about to oblige him when the top kick intervened. Later, this miner and his buddy became two of my best friends. Once the men realized I knew what I was talking about and wanted a good platoon, they relaxed and became just that.

"On Sunday, December 7, 1941, I was home with my mother, who lived on the post. When I heard the news of Pearl Harbor, I couldn't believe it. Incidentally, draftees until then were only called up for one year. A number of the men had their separation papers on the desk in the office to be picked up the following morning. Many of the men had purchased their tickets home; the declaration of war froze these would-be departees into the armed forces for the duration.

"Late in December we got our first orders, moving us out to guard various installations considered vital in the west. My particular unit, 2nd Battalion, E Company, was sent to guard Boulder Dam, a popular tourist spot. Boulder Dam furnished electrical power for several of the western states, and it was essential that it not be sabotaged. We replaced the 125th Infantry Regiment, white, which was immediately sent to the South Pacific. It has to be said, they did have a little more experience than we did. White soldiers trained with trucks marked 'tanks'; we trained with horses and wagons marked 'trucks.' There was sort of a trickle-down policy, but by the time it trickled down to us it had trickled out.

"Boulder Dam could not be closed to the public because a main highway crosses it. What we did was stop all cars at a given spot. When there were about twenty of them a truck with a mounted guard led the convoy across the dam, bumper to bumper, with no stops allowed, flat tires included, and another truck with a guard brought up the rear. The people were instructed in advance that anyone opening a car door would be shot down without question. Manned machine guns were strategically placed along the sidewalks on both sides of the highway for this purpose. All guns and cameras were confiscated by Rangers on one side and put on the lead truck. Rangers on the other side returned them to the owners. Some people were thoroughly outraged by such actions; others must have gotten a bang out of it—they would cross over and get in the returning line for another go at it. We also had small units guarding water tanks used by trains in the desert. Remember most things were transported by rail in those days, so keeping those water tanks intact was important.

"In May 1942 the government activated the 93rd Division. The 368th was pulled off of guard duty and returned to Fort Huachuca. The 369th Infantry Regiment was then activated, making the three infantry regiments necessary for an infantry division: the 25th, the 368th, and the 369th. Training then began at Fort Huachuca. The cadre for the yet-to-be-reactivated 92nd Division would come mainly from the 93rd.

"During this time we still had all white officers. Some of our regular white officers were being sent out individually to new white groups or National Guard units. With the rapidly increasing military population at the fort, new white officers were coming in. Soon the good breed would be gone and a new breed would be in charge. A sprinkling of black officers came in, fresh from OCS, with the formation of the 93rd Division.

"The army was losing officers so fast in the fighting, each division was given a quota to produce men for OCS. The 93rd could not meet this quota because of a large number of 4 and 5 AGCTs. Desperate, they decided they had better test their regulars. I made class 1 and was asked what group I would like to join; my preferences were cavalry and then ordnance. I ended up in the infantry OCS at Fort Benning, Georgia. Later events were to show the army had no use for black cavalry, still using horses while the white cavalry used tanks.

"At Benning I was assigned to 10th Company, 2nd Student Training Regiment. All 22 blacks were put in squads I and II of the 2nd Platoon. As we attended school in units, we were quite effectively segregated. Most all of our training was separated from the whites. The day before graduation all white officers-to-be had been assigned, mostly to overseas outfits. No black received any orders. Upon graduation we were kept in a holding center for a month; then we were all sent to Camp Swift, Texas. The air force was in need of airfield guards.

"At Camp Swift everything was separate: living area, recreational facilities, etc. The camp bus went through our area last, so by the time it got to us it was usually full. I was three hours late getting to my wedding, waiting for a place on the bus.

"In the middle of '43 the army decided it no longer needed extra air force base security guards so our unit was disbanded. Instead of taking all of these well-trained enlisted men and putting them into combat units, which meant infantry, the army wasted all of their skill by converting them to general engineers. The black officers could remain as engineer officers or go to the 93rd Division. I was given no choice because of my infantry background. I asked for my old regiment, the 368th, but was refused because once you have become an officer you cannot return to the unit from whence you came. I was assigned to the 25th Infantry Regiment. All of the others opted for the infantry so we went to the Mohave Desert where the 93rd was on maneuvers.

"The change in officers at the senior level of this Fort Huachuca division was glaringly apparent to me. The animosity between the white and black officers permeated the air and our arrival certainly didn't help to improve the situation; it just meant the senior officers had more black lieutenants to keep in their place, second lieutenants. Ninety-five to ninety-eight percent of the white officers were southerners. I think I was in a position to say that the majority of the white officers with the 93rd were people who could not have made it with the 37th or 87th divisions, or any white division of any caliber. They might have been all right in the quartermasters, or some laundry units. Instead of being sent to jobs they were fit for, they were sloughed off on the 93rd. I understand what we didn't get of these misfits ended up with the 92nd Division. The black officers as a whole were superior to their senior officers in the 93rd and the black officers knew it; dissension was bound to arise. Then too, those white officers, though Lord knows they would never admit it, knew they were outclassed by their junior officers and this heightened *their* resentment. They took advantage of their rank to strike out at black officers.

"This hostility between junior and senior officers did not abate once we were in the South Pacific. We landed at Guadalcanal early in 1944 and were immediately put to work unloading ships. Now I do not know what MacArthur's racial policies were for the South Pacific. I do know that *all* men landing in the area were put to work for the first month there stevedoring. There were two reasons: no place in the United States has the climate of the South Pacific; it is extremely hot and humid day and night, and acclimatization is necessary. There was a shortage of men to unload the ships. However, I will say black combat troops did a lot more stevedoring than whites, and I'm sure we became acclimated just as quickly as they did.

"At Bougainville we held a perimeter at Augusta Bay. This perimeter permitted an airstrip to be built from which our planes could take off for an attack of other islands. Again I do not know what had happened previously. I understand the divisions holding this perimeter had been there for some time. They may have relaxed their vigilance because things had been quiet. They may have become tired, for the climate can be debilitating. Whatever the cause, the Japanese broke through the perimeter on Bougainville.

"A call came through for the 25th Infantry, reenforced as a combat team, to be sent to Bougainville. We were joined by the 24th Infantry Regiment, black, which had been working the docks when we arrived. Together we were called the Brown Brigade; *black* was not an 'in' word then.

"We arrived at night, and the next morning we went on the front line. I was the heavy-weapons platoon leader, so I had to place our weapons and then go on the line as forward observer. It was all very interesting but uneventful. I finally volunteered for a patrol. I got a chance to see the jungle but nothing spectacular happened.

"One of the companies was sent out beyond the perimeter and the first person back was the white company commander, the captain. As a few more men straggled in later we learned they had been ambushed and the captain had run off at the first shot. His black lieutenant died along with the main body of men trying to make possible the escape of a few. The captain was not court-martialed for deserting in the face of the enemy. However, as long as he was on Bougainville, which was only a short time, a bodyguard with an automatic weapon was assigned to guard him at all times. He was transferred to the battalion staff.

"Another white captain was assigned to replace him. If his predecessor was inadequate as a commander, this character was inadequate in all respects. He detested blacks and did not try to conceal it; we reciprocated in kind, we despised him. I was assigned to a patrol under him that was to probe beyond the perimeter and spend the night in foxholes. We had been told not to fire our rifles but to use grenades if we thought we heard something since a grenade cannot give away your position. After some hours in our holes some of the guys got restless or frightened and shot off their guns. Captain Petty climbed out of his foxhole and went up and down the line saying, "This is Captain Petty, cease firing." With all of the animosity that man engendered in each of us, no one took a shot at him or tossed a grenade, though he was a perfect target. Now today's generation might think of us as "Toms" for not killing him but I think two things prevented this. How could you be sure the guy with you wouldn't tell? Second—I believe of greater importance—even though we thoroughly disliked the man, we couldn't shoot a man down in cold blood. In the heat of anger, in a fight, yes, but to cut him down out of the dark was assassination, and that was just not our bag, I am happy to say.

"I was involved in another reenforced patrol sent to locate a missing recon patrol. I was in charge of the heavy-weapons men. When we found the patrol the bodies were a sickening sight. We were told to bring them back. The men resented this bitterly, for they feared being ambushed. Somehow or other amidst the confusion I ended up with men not known to me carrying the last body. We were the last to leave the scene of the ambush and were a distance behind the others. This distance kept increasing because of the terrain. There were exactly four of us carrying the body in a make-shift stretcher. This did not help since each of us had one hand occupied with the stretcher. Finally the men said, "To hell with it," and insisted on leaving the body. As previously stated, I did not know the men and they did not know me. More important, in the Pacific no officer wore anything identifying him as an officer; snipers singled them out. The result was I could not command them to do anything. We hadn't gotten fifty yards from the body when a white colonel appeared with his black bodyguard, a sub-Thompson machine gun artist. He recognized me and chewed my butt out. Explanations were useless, so I got thoroughly blistered.

"I was put on the colonel's shit list for this incident. To my knowledge it was the first mark against me although I will admit I probably stepped on some toes now and then. I was army all the way and I knew when some bullshit was being put down and I would let it be known. This wasn't necessarily going to endear me to my senior officers.

"Assigned to lead another patrol, I got all of the necessary data from the G-2, a young white 1st lieutenant. I was to take my patrol 4000 yards beyond the perimeter and relieve a patrol that was in a forward observation post. When the lieutenant gave me my directions he assured me there was no other American patrol out so if I ran into one it wasn't ours. May I say that intelligence officer was wrong on every detail he gave me. We came upon a wide stretch of winding road, just as the lieutenant had said. We had moved about twenty-five yards down this road when we spied another patrol coming in our direction just as they saw us. Everyone hit the dirt. God alone knows why none of us fired. It turned out to be a white patrol from another unit and in talking to the officer in charge I found out that he too had been told by his G-2 officer to look out for enemy patrols since there were none of ours out there. When I finally reached the point I was directed to, there was no small hill with an observation post on it. By radio, smoke, and anything else we could think of I finally got the right directions. Changing our line of march we were within 150 yards of the forward post when suddenly the jungle opened up and the hill was directly in front of us. Climbing up to the position we found the other patrol gone and to make matters worse our radio had conked out. I positioned the men, but the information I was to receive from the officer I was to relieve as to procedure was back at the perimeter with the departed patrol.

"My radio man was totally illiterate. Everyone considered him a hopeless case but he loved the radio so I let him be the radio man even though I had had to teach him how to turn it on. One thing—if communication could be made with the instrument at all, he could bring it in or send it out. We carried no spare parts for the radio so it was impossible for him to get it working. He volunteered to go back and get another radio. I explained that I could not spare the men to escort him. He was hurt that I had not understood he had meant to go alone. I decided to send him back with my platoon sergeant. They were back in no time with a new radio and extra supplies.

"Here this man who had been shucked off as some kind of a joke was a natural soldier; all he had needed was a chance to show it. In going for the radio he had demonstrated courage and the sergeant said he had an uncanny sense of direction. He unhesitatingly and unerringly had led the sergeant back to the perimeter. Our illiterate became one of the most dependable soldiers on the line.

"When we returned to the perimeter four days later, upon being relieved, I was again royally chewed out for incompetency in not having located the observation post immediately; I was to be court-martialed. A buddy of mine, who knew something about law, got together with me and we reconstructed the whole thing. We rechecked the directions, which showed the G-2 officer had given me wrong information. When my commander learned I had every intention of fighting the charge, it was withdrawn, or so I thought. Nobody ever called in the white G-2 who had damn near got us killed and evidently could not read a map.

"I said the charges were dropped against me but one day I found I was booked for General Johnson's school for bad boys. Those black lieutenants they considered not up to snuff, one way or another, were to be the students. The program instituted at this "school" was not too bad, if you didn't mind doing your OCS training again. All of us had to read a paper called 'Johnson's Plan for Success in Battle.' Nobody but we black junior officers had to read this, and I was of the opinion, what good was it going to do if our white senior officers were ignorant of all of this accumulated wisdom?

"Lieutenant Scruggs and I were called in by the colonel one day. He frankly stated he was to get facts to reclassify us but had been unable to do so. He then had the temerity to ask us if we would help him so he could get on with it. I told him with equal candor that if he was going to try and reclassify me, he most certainly was going to do it without my help. Scruggs took the same position. The colonel was terribly disappointed in our lack of cooperation.

"Failing to reclassify us, he transferred us to the 368th with an admonition to not mention the reclassification attempt. The first words that greeted us upon our arrival at the 368th headquarters were, "So they couldn't reclassify you!"

"The 368th was involved in mopping-up operations when the war ended, September 17, 1945. We were then sent to Mindanao, where I became an officer with the MPs. This was shortlived for I dared to ticket a white colonel for speeding.

"Once rotation back to the states on the point system began, I was shifted from one spot to another in the Philippines. I wanted to stay in the army with my rank so though I had more than enough points to get out I stayed on. One day I was called up before the board as to my remaining in service as an officer. I got by the board all right but on my physical it seems I had picked up a tropical bug and that ended that. After thirty-seven months in the South Pacific I finally shipped home.

"One group of black soldiers had to have an armed escort to get them on board a ship sailing for the states. I'm not so sure this reluctance was love of these islands or the fact that they had some kind of lucrative enterprise going. I had run into them previously, and they were wheeling and dealing then.

"Upon reaching the states I went to Georgia, where my wife was living. I was bored quickly with having nothing to do as I tried to use up all of my accumulated leave. When I took a job and the man called me 'boy' a couple of times I went straight down and reenlisted so there would be no break in my service record.

"I was made a master sergeant and sent to Fort Knox, Kentucky, as NCO in charge of the motor pool. From there I was sent to Fort Bragg. My papers were all in order excepting someone had goofed and put down white for my race. I said nothing, looking forward to the reaction at Bragg. Fort Bragg had Detachments I (white) and II (black). Naturally they were separated on the post. With my papers I had to report to Detachment I. The reaction was swift. There had been a mistake and I should report immediately to Detachment II. Since I was unexpected at II, I spent a week counting the fire extinguishers on the post. I had a ball goofing off seven days. While at Bragg I volunteered for the Triple Nickels, the 555th, the black paratroopers. Before I could start jumping I was switched again. When the Korean conflict came I was with a combat engineers unit at Camp Hood, Texas. We were ordered overseas at once.

"We went all the way up to the Yalu River and all of us, black and white, strategically withdrew as fast as any army in retreat ever did. I will never forget the day we got back to the beach from where we had started; it was 35 degrees below zero. It was no weather for swimming, but for a while it damned sure looked like that's what we were going to have to do.

"I did two tours of duty in Korea, only the second time around I was infantry. I was still supposed to be a paratrooper even though I had yet to make my first jump. I managed to get switched to the 187th Airborne in Korea, but don't you know I still never got to jump. I was still fighting on the ground.

"The most glorious day of my life was the morning we could stand up in our foxholes in Korea and stretch our arms and not have to worry about being shot at; the war was finally over. I stayed with the airborne and when I retired I had made sixty-two jumps and had returned to the officers' ranks. It was a long road back, but I finally made it.

"I think it is readily apparent that I was a soldier by profession and choice. I can easily understand the problems of a draftee adjusting to life in the armed forces since as a young man I had trouble trying to adjust to civilian life. I knew there was prejudice in the army but I was reared within this framework, so I not only could work with it but I could fight it—the racial situation. I had to mature to realize I could function outside of the army and still fight for my rights as a man and an American in a civilian society."

The interview with 2nd Lieutenant Walter Green, 25th Infantry, like the preceding one, touches on the problems of morale and leadership accompanying racial policies of the army at the officer level.

Walter Green: "My route was no different from the rest of the fellows:

induction, reception center, camp for basic training, and then, for me—which I thought was lucky at the time—OCS.

"The policy of separating officers according to race and then assigning them to units that had black enlisted men caused an unusual situation at Fort Benning, Georgia, in 1943. Over a period of a year, each graduating class of black officers in infantry went home on leave and then reported back to Fort Benning awaiting assignment. White lieutenants went home on leave and then were immediately assigned, usually to some unit going overseas because it was thought that there was no more training necessary other than experience in combat. The black officers reporting back to Fort Benning began to accumulate even though only a few graduated each week in each class. I was one of those who graduated in May 1943, and like my predecessors I landed in the officers' pool. I found men there who had been waiting for months for assignment. An inspector-general came through the officers' pool and observed that there were 92 officers lounging around the area with absolutely nothing to do. I understand he was appalled when he found out the prevailing conditions and had an order cut, shipping all 92 of us to the 93rd Division.

"At this time the 93rd was in the Mohave Desert undergoing hardship training. When we arrived there we found companies so short of officers they were being commanded by one lieutenant: They were delighted to see us because it meant all of the white 1st lieutenants were suddenly going to become company commanders with some 2nd lieutenants to command. There were a few black 1st lieutenants. A system had been worked out where white lieutenants were assigned to regimental and staff positions, while black lieutenants were assigned to platoon leadership, which meant the latter did all the hard work.

"However, if the black 1st lieutenant had brought his company up to a high level of performance and his supplies and company record were in good order, he would be assigned to the battalion staff as an assistant to a white staff officer. Then a white 1st lieutenant who had been on the staff would take over his platoon and within a few months would be elevated to the rank of captain; this bit of chicanery gave a white officer a basis for promotion. Since he had no experience in the job, ofttimes his company would flounder under his leadership. Then he would be transferred out from the company and a black 1st lieutenant would go back into the slot to build it back up again.

"Lemuel Penn, the black officer who was shot to death on the highway while returning from reserve training in the south years ago, was so highly competent in working with platoons and bringing them up to top shape that he was transferred in and out so many times it was comical, but he was still a 1st lieutenant when I left the outfit two years later.

"The black 1st lieutenants often had this rank because they had been ROTC graduates. The rest of us were ninety-day wonders who came into the army and went to OCS. I never rose above the rank of 2nd lieutenant until

1950, when I was given a direct appointment by Governor G. Mennen Williams to the Michigan National Guard. I did learn that I was up for promotion while overseas after Bougainville, but my commander learned I was one of the 'bad boys' and he withdrew it. The 'bad boys' were the rebellious 2nd lieutenants of the 25th Infantry, and we were rebellious, no doubt about it, because we had everything to be rebellious about.

"But getting back to the Mohave Desert. At Camp Clippert, the few little towns scattered around the desert were off limits to black personnel. Those of us who disobeyed the law and sneaked around watching for white MPs saw white officers and enlisted men walking with no such worries. The real sickening thing was the MPs were black, so it was black arresting black. In western towns, in particular, you had the problem of getting served in a restaurant. Some would serve you, and others would not; but they had the upper hand. They knew that by military orders you were not supposed to be there, and they could cause you serious trouble. This was a bitter pill to swallow.

"We went through desert training from August '43 to January '44. In the latter part of December we were alerted for movement overseas. We knew we were going to the South Pacific but not where.

"We arrived in Guadalcanal in February 1944. The marines had lost a lot of men at Bougainville, but they had stabilized the situation. They had established a perimeter about ten miles long and five miles deep. Our purpose was to island-hop, as you recall, going back to the Philippines and on to Tokyo. Instead of trying to command the whole island we just took strips of the island, continuing in the direction of the Philippines.

"One of the disappointing things to us was as soon as we arrived in Guadalcanal we were put to work loading and unloading ships. As a matter of fact, we helped load the supplies for the last marine group to go to Bougainville. We actually got over there in time to receive awards for participating in the Battle of the Coral Sea but in all honesty we were not involved in it at all. It was just a matter of time. We happened to cross the Coral Sea while it was still considered a naval battlefield.

"In one way we could feel we had never left home, for our racial problems still plagued us. The white officers kept to themselves, completely out of touch with the black officers, unless it was in the line of duty. There was no socializing or rapport between us when not on the job. The thing that aggravated us was that there were military laws that were enforced against us but not against the whites. There is no defense for that kind of corruption. For example, a general order was issued that no officer was to drive a vehicle. This was only enforced against black officers. You could see white officers driving all the time. If a black officer did this he was pulled over by MPs, hauled before the commanding general, given a summary court-martial and fined $150. This was true of many other laws that were only laws when black officers were involved. A large number of the white officers were southerners, and they seemed to feel they had some kind of mission endowed by God to make sure you were subjected to every possible indignity that they could conceive. They even tried to segregate us at mess in the South Pacific. This was one thing I exploded about. Being very young I would have my say and that ultimately got me into a lot of trouble. Enough hell was raised that no black officer would enter the officers' mess tent, so the Arkansas mess officer had to drop the procedure. Of course, rank segregated us to a great extent anyway excepting for the doctor and the chaplain.

But going back to Guadalcanal for a moment. The division was split up and the different regiments sent to various places. Then came the call for the 25th to go to Bougainville as a combat team. The reason we were going was that the Japanese had decided to carry on one of their wild banzai attacks to break through the American perimeter and had succeeded only too well. The 37th Infantry and the Americal divisions were holding the perimeter to make it possible for the air force to operate from Bougainville, striking at other islands. In desperation they reached back to Guadalcanal for the 25th, reinforcing us with other parts of the 93rd and with additional service units needed to make up a combat team.

"At Bougainville we filled in the gaps where the Japanese had broken through at the cost of something like 2,000 of their men. I understand they were never able to mount another offensive like this. We had paid a heavy price also in men in the 37th and the Americal divisions.

"The Japanese were now dispersed throughout the jungle in this rather hilly and mountainous terrain. Our job was to keep this perimeter intact and to go out on what were called jungle patrols to see if they were bringing up any equipment or trying to build any installations for mounting another attack. The result was numerous encounters between small bands of Japanese and our patrols. Men were getting killed and wounded in these fire fights. I believe, and I can only say, someone was looking out for my patrol; we never had a serious fire fight. I was combat patrol leader. We went on patrol every day, at least the lieutenants went out every day with different men. We did not engage in the main battle of Bougainville. The marines were moving out as we were coming in. We were in the combat situation of these patrols for about two months, every day, seven days a week.

"The last patrol I recall, a big one that included my platoon, involved the Divisional Reconnaissance Team. They had been called in because they were supposed to be experts. They were to penetrate deeper than had been done, beyond the perimeter and into enemy-held territory. The purpose was to find out if there was a Japanese force of any size out there. These men were armed with automatic weapons only. They were to gather information and were not prepared to fight. The young black lieutenant in charge, who seemed quite sharp and was a fine fellow, stayed with me the night before the operation began. The next day probing far beyond any previous probe his group ran into an ambush and was wiped out. Many were killed, and some wounded dispersed.

"We were preparing to leave for New Guinea when we were ordered to find what was left of that recon patrol and bring them back. At the time we did not know what had happened since all communication was cut off. This time half of our company was going, the captain and the exec., white, and two black 2nd lieutenants, of which I was one. We went well prepared for trouble, heavy weapons, grenades, the works. Our orders were to find out what had happened to them. If they were under fire or whatever, get them back. It was a real rugged trip through the jungle, always on guard against an ambush. You more or less had to stick to the trail because it was practically impossible to cut your way through the surrounding jungle. We had to go through several bamboo forests. It was a day-and-a-half before we reached them. We found their bodies, stripped of everything the Japanese could use. After three days of jungle heat, the bodies were bloated and covered with flies. I was ordered to contact the base back at the perimeter and tell them what we had found.

"When we contacted the base, the commanding general got on the radio and personally ordered that we were to bring those bodies back. We had no equipment for doing this, and I knew this when I gave the captain the general's order. The men rebelled on this and sat down. They did not want to touch those putrefied bodies. Fortunately, one of the enlisted men had been a mortician in the states. He had us take our shelter halves and succeeded in making litters to carry them and cover them. I believe there were eight or nine bodies. We sprayed the remains liberally with sulphur powder to help keep the flies away and to keep down the odor. We managed to get them back but we were afraid every step of the way. The insistence for bringing the bodies in was because we would be leaving in a week and they wanted to have made proper disposition of American dead before this.

"On leaving Bougainville the 25th was split up, going to various islands. I went to Hollandia, New Guinea. By this time we had a new commander, General Johnson. Our other commander had injured himself falling off a cliff.

"The racial antipathy in our outfit had worsened and it was said the White House had gotten wind of it. Johnson, a Texan, was the result. He is said to have been with the 9th and 10th cavalries. Before the war I understand he was with an oil company. Johnson took over the command when we moved to Green Island for what was some kind of rest period. Here the racial pot began to boil; the whole thing was repeating itself—laws that were for black officers only. We were not allowed to visit other outfits where we were welcome. Our senior officers would not permit this; our only recreation was a movie.

"Now the black enlisted man did not get this kind of pressure from white officers. As a matter of fact they could be almost decent to the dogfoot soldier, but their hostility to the black officer bordered on paranoia. A black man as their peer they could not stand, and they did their damndest to break you through humiliation and frustration. Some of our black officers were able to sublimate and take this better than others like myself. We 'bad boys' were continually in hot water and being punished for our protest that showed itself in one form or another. And they were quick to punish us at the slightest infaction.

"General Johnson had been apprised of the situation as soon as he arrived; there were 'bad boys' spread throughout the islands in various units; they were the ones who rebelled against the racist practices.

"General Johnson formed what he called the 'bad boys school.' He brought all us so-called obstreperous black 2nd lieutenants from all of the units together on Treasure Island. He said our problem was that we had not been properly trained so they actually set up training 'school' and we did practically the same things we had done in basic training: pushups, setups, and so on, a whole lot of foolishness at this late stage of the game. They treated us like enlisted men. The whole idea was, of course, to break us. But he had made a foolish mistake; General Johnson had gathered all of his vocal rebels in one spot, so we had each other for moral support. Separately we had been dubbed trouble, now we could become double trouble.

"When I was with Headquarters Company on Green Island I had gotten friendly with the warrant officer, who was the general's secretary. He deplored the situation and informed me that to use officers in this manner was illegal. To keep it hidden from Washington the general did not maintain a morning report. We were being carried on the morning reports of the outfits to which we belonged, like all was well. It suddenly penetrated: I could not be court-martialed for refusing to obey an order in the 'bad boys school' since I wasn't there. The first thing they would ask for at a trial would be the morning report of my regular unit and since I was listed there, how could I be disobeying orders on Treasure Island? They might even ask the general how this could be. So one day, without mentioning it to anyone, when reveille sounded I failed to fall out. (I should add the white officers in charge were afraid of us because they had heard all kinds of things we were reputed to have said or threatened, some true, some not. Word had gotten around that we were quite capable of doing them in. Even though they ranked us you could see the fear in them; when you wrong men your own guilt stimulates this fear.)

"When the officer came into my tent to find out why I was not outside, I told him I wasn't going and he said, 'You are supposed to do your duty.' I answered I was aware of this, but hadn't the slightest intention of going any place. My two roommates found out when they returned that I wasn't ill, so the next day they didn't report. In about a week nobody was going to 'school.' Then they started to reclassify us, a wrist-slapping thing to disgrace you by sending you to an entirely different outfit. It takes a lot of paper work so they couldn't get to more than one or two a week. In the meantime, we were sitting around doing nothing.

"One day the captain in charge confronted me in my tent and said, 'You don't intend to do anything around here do you?' I replied that the school was illegal and therefore I had no business being in it. He countered, 'You really mean that I can't tell you anything because I have never had any battle experience.' He left himself wide open and I told him, 'You are absolutely right captain. You can't tell me a damned thing because you haven't been in combat and I have.'

"He went back to division headquarters and told them he just couldn't get along with me. Another officer came down to talk to me, a Texan. Well by that time, every time I heard that cracker's accent I just about went into orbit. He started giving me a lecture, the con line about what a good job I had done in combat, and so forth, ending on, 'I just can't understand.' To which I replied, 'Its simple, I just can't stand all of this goddamn racial prejudice.' He gave me a brilliant answer, 'Of course you know *we* don't have any control over what happens in the armed forces.' I looked at him and said, 'I don't even know who my enemies are. I think the white officers are more my enemy than the Japs.' That rattled his teeth, as he said a man with my attitude had no business being in service. For once we were in accord and I told him so. He assured me he was going to speak to the general about me.

"The general was red-faced mad, shaking his finger at me, when I reported to him two days later. He said he heard I had been stirring up trouble down there, 'Now you get back down there or I am going to court-martial you Green, do you hear me, I am going to court-martial you!' His message was coming through and now 98 percent of the white officers had their eyes upon me waiting for me to breathe hard.

"They decided to send me up to Division Headquarters where I could be watched. I learned from a white captain from the east, who did not countenance the racial intolerance, that when I arrived up there the white officers had been told to watch my every move and for the slightest twinge I was to be court-martialed. I had suspected something like this when told to report there. Need I say 2nd Lieutenant Walter Green was letter correct in deportment, appearance, and kept spotless living quarters. I had made up my mind that those peckerwoods were not going to break me nor catch me in a trap.

"They decided to put me in charge of training the division's defense platoon. It was a minor kind of training with 30 mm weapons with which I was familiar. But I knew I had to get out of there because nobody can be under constant surveillance without spitting out of the wrong side of his mouth accidentally.

"The opportunity for me to make a move didn't come until we were in the Molucca Islands near Morotai. My commanding officer would not allow the black doctors to touch him so whenever he was ailing he flew to one of the islands where the doctors were white. My warrant officer friend told me when he was leaving for a few days for medical reasons. As soon as he was gone I went to the doctors and asked them for help. They knew what was happening and they did what they could. That was to send me away to an aid station. As Dr. Bob Bennett put it, 'Its the best we can do, now it's up to you whether you get out or sent back.' My gratitude was limitless.

"I was flown to Biak as suffering from combat fatigue. I found I had been placed in the mental section of the hospital when they sent a psychiatrist to talk to me. He wanted to know what was wrong and I told him, 'I am sick and tired of this goddamn United States Army and all of its goddamn prejudice and discrimination. I am fed up and I am not about to participate in getting myself killed for a bunch of blankety, blank, and blanks.' I said I didn't care what happened to me; they could do anything they wanted to with me. I told him what had been happening from beginning to end. He asked me, 'Lieutenant, do you have the urge to kill anybody?' I asked him if he meant anybody besides the Japanese and when he nodded in the affirmative I said quite casually, 'I wouldn't mind killing that goddamn commanding general of ours!' He closed his book and had no further questions.

"He wrote me up for evacuation back to the states. I had to go through medical channels. I was classified as everything from 'combat fatigue' to 'psychotic.' I was placed in a ward with patients where we were locked in. I returned on a hospital ship, finally arriving at Letterman General Hospital in San Francisco. My wife came to see me and it was then I learned they had censored my letters so they looked like paper cut-outs and she had no idea as to what was happening to me. I had tried to write the NAACP but I know those letters never got through.

"I was being considered for being medically relieved. Then I learned my medical consideration had been dropped and they planned to return me to the South Pacific. The War Department had changed their medical findings, I should say ordered them changed. The bomb was dropped on Hiroshima, the war was over, and they decided to let me go through regular channels. I was given an honorable discharge.

"Remember when I mentioned the reclassification of the fellows at the 'bad boys' school.' Well, a few never really stopped attending voluntarily, but had to stop because there was just a handful and it was a farce to try and keep the 'school' going. These men were reclassified because the higher-ups had had enough time to give an evaluation on them which naturally would be very poor. Those like myself, who stopped, couldn't be evaluated for this reason. Those men who had tried to comply were all given dishonorable discharges.

"When I got home I was bitter as gall and it was a while before I realized that hate destroys the hater. Then too, I was out from underneath the fascist southerners. Since I did nothing about my military career I was carried on the reserve roster. Felix McDavid talked me into thinking over becoming an active reservist in the Michigan National Guard. I told him honestly about my army career and that I didn't think he could get me a commission. He asked me to let him try and I agreed. As I said, Governor Williams made me a 1st lieutenant in the Michigan National Guard by direct appointment and the necessary papers deactivated my regular army reserve commission."

The second black lieutenant on the patrol to find the reconnaissance platoon was George Looney. The similarity of parts of Green's interview to Looney's made possible, a few hours after the interview, a reunion between two "bad boys" who had not seen each other since their days in the South Pacific.

Acceding to the request for an account of his war experiences, 2nd Lieutenant Albert Evans, 369th Infantry Regiment remembered "nothing pleasant, with the exception of the few close friends I made and the loyalty of my platoon, that would cause me to particularly want to recall those days. But maybe people should know what World War II and the Negro soldier was all about."

Bound for Camp Wolters in late September 1941, he was one of a large group of black soldiers from the north who had a surprise welcome on their arrival by train at Mineral Wells, Texas.

Albert Evans: "Our unofficial welcoming committee was quite a gathering of young white children, who yelled racial epithets at us as we disembarked. This was a new experience for most of us since we were from Detroit, Cincinnati, Chicago, Philadelphia. Our official greeters were white officers and Negro NCOs; they took us over to the camp.

"Camp Wolters was rigidly segregated. There were whites and Negroes stationed there but the whites had their area, their theaters, their post exchanges, and we had ours, our theater, our post exchange, which we were told were ours. We were also told not to patronize those in other areas. Need I say, separate is never equal.

"After thirteen weeks of basic training at Wolters I was selected to remain there in the cadre. I trained two or three groups of young soldiers before being sent to OCS at Columbus, Georgia.

"In January 1943, after I received my commission, I was ordered to Camp Swift, Texas, where they were training men for air base patrol duty. A number of black officers from a variety of outfits: tanks, artillery, infantry, and so forth, had been sent there. It was a very interesting course with a lot of innovations. However, it was here that I began to notice that all of our command positions with rare exception, had gone or were going to white officers. We had black lieutenants as platoon leaders but the executive officers and the captains were always white as was our battalion commander and the battalion staff.

"We had an incident on a night march at Camp Swift, where a white captain had kicked a black soldier. This happened after the soldier had fainted from exhaustion. The next day I was acting company commander, when a sergeant brought this man to me and told me what had taken place. I wrote a letter to the commanding general, Special Troops, 3rd Army. This letter never got to him. Some two or three months later a white officer came out on the firing range where I was and asked me to withdraw the letter, which I refused to do. He made it quite clear that he had a feeling I was going to have a very limited career in the army. This was laughable; I hadn't the slightest desire for an extended stay in the armed forces. I just wanted the war to end so I could depart as rapidly as possible. I waited another month and nothing happened so I now knew the letter had never left the immediate area. I gave a copy of the letter to the chaplain, who could take it directly to the commanding general without going through channels.

"Upon receiving the letter, the general of the 3rd Army Special Troops removed the captain from command and placed him in position where he had no troops under him. He also had it put in his file that he was never to be placed in charge of any troops as long as he was in the army. I knew this would ruin any chance I would have for promotion in the army, but you have to live with yourself and sometimes things are required of you, no matter what the cost. An officer's job is to lead, he has to be respected, and his job is also to look out for his men. If he fails to do these things he might wear the officer garb but he is not an officer.

"By September some of the black 2nd lieutenants in the battalion were beginning to be promoted to 1st lieutenants. I remained a 2nd lieutenant and had a black lieutenant over me, but I remained the executive lieutenant in charge of tactics on the field and the training of the troops. This happened because the white captain of our company was a fairminded man.

"That October all of this training for airfield guard duty for blacks was dropped and all of the black officers in the outfit were sent to join the 93rd Division in the Mohave Desert. Our arrival there I remember well because the regimental commander had us meet with him. He said, 'What you have previously been in was no more than a station complement, and now you are with a fighting outfit.' This did not set easily on our shoulders for we thought we had come from a well trained unit. In a not too subtle manner the commander was letting us know we weren't much.

"We went through maneuvers on the desert with the 93rd from October '43 until January '44. This division again epitomized the white master and the black subject. They had one all-black battalion, and the pressure was always on it. While the other guys were sacking out they would be picking up paper or policing the area. They never had a let-up and whatever they did always had to be a little better than anybody else, which I did not think was fair, but this was the situation, the way the 'man' felt.

"In the other battalions, mine included, there were all white officers down to the platoon level, or the lieutenant level. From my previous experience and now this one with the 93rd I became convinced that generally black army units were given the inferior white army personnel. I've seen white officers who hardly knew how to give a marching command to a platoon. They were inept; it was pathetic. They didn't even have the ordinary horse sense to open an army manual and read up on tactics, weapons, or the use of a particular type of terrain. I really felt sorry for the fellows who would eventually go overseas with these white officers because I knew they were going to have inadequate leadership.

"The men of the 93rd were proud soldiers. They felt they knew their jobs and if sent into combat they would do well. The morale was high even though they had just come off of six months of maneuvers in Louisiana. I don't know of any other outfit that was subject to this kind of thing. On maneuvers you are subject to forced marches; sometimes you don't eat for thirty-six hours. Maneuvers can often be more rugged than combat, the only difference being you are not getting shot at.

"In January 1944 we went to our POE in San Francisco. Twelve days later we anchored off of Guadalcanal. Up until that time every new outfit going to the South Pacific staged at either Australia or New Zealand. This gave you a chance to check your gear, which took about three months. I presume it was also a chance to offer the men some last recreation. Yet the 93rd came directly from one year of maneuvers to Guadalcanal. I think it is commendable as well as remarkable that we had no trouble with the men because of this. In spite of what the 'man' thought, these soldiers weren't stupid.

"To my knowledge there was no fighting on Guadalcanal when we landed there. We stayed there about six weeks checking our equipment. When we left, the division was split up. The battalion I was with of the 369th went to Munda in the New Georgia Islands. On Munda there was primarily an airstrip. After a month there we were sent to the north end of Munda to Enogi Inlet. We set up an outpost there to keep the Japanese from reenforcing their decimated remnants still in the area. I never saw any Japanese though we put our patrols on three- and four-day stretches. Upon leaving Munda our battalion was sent to the Admiralties. This is where we were used as stevedores completely.

"We went from the Los Negros to Biak in the Netherlands East Indies. There I was taken out of the 3rd Battalion to join the 2nd Battalion going to New Guinea at Sansapore. This spot was properly called the hell-hole of New Guinea because of the ashy terrain. Scrub typhus was prevalent. The food was bad. It was the rear end of the world in all ways. Our forces were trying to evacuate this island, but the Japanese were quite active and aggressive. We ran patrols and suffered our first casualties there. The Japanese kept us awake with mortar fire at night, and one of our patrols was ambushed. One of the major problems was that they had evacuated the hospital so there was none on the island. Although we had a doctor with us, lack of a hospital still was a very strong morale factor. All of us knew if you were wounded right after the plane for the wounded departed in the afternoon there would be no possibility of hospital care until its scheduled return the following afternoon. We stayed on Sansapore about three months then returned to Biak.

"At one time the 368th was at Hollandia. I can't say what their job was." [The 368th was doing the work of stevedores at Hollandia.] "I will say that quite often they used the 93rd Division as stevedores and this was a true morale destroyer. The men felt they were first-class fighting troops and believed they were not being used for what they had been trained. During these labor details you could see the demoralization setting in; carelessness in dress was one sign. However, the officers had no problem with the soldiers as to following orders, no matter how distasteful.

"At no time did I have any problem with my men. I always had the greatest respect for them and they appeared to have the same for me. We had been on some rough patrols together. One I remember, we had to cross a river and two of the fellows lost their shoes. Those men didn't complain, and they kept up. We found an old abandoned army dump and there were some shoes there, damp and fungus-covered but those fellows put on those shoes without a word. This was the wonderful thing about them: they gave one hundred per cent, to my way of thinking.

"I have a great deal of admiration for the black soldier. There is no doubt in my mind that he is a good soldier anywhere. But the southern so-called 'aristocracy' runs the army and their thinking prohibits the proper use of blacks in the army or anywhere else over which the army has jurisdiction. This has been traditional and in World War II any black officer will tell you it is true. It seemed the white upper echelon in the military would sit up nights trying to think of ways to keep the Negro soldier, particularly the officers, in 'their place.'

"One of the most ridiculous situations possible occurred to keep white over black. We received a number of new replacement officers, all white captains or first lieutenants. They were all made either company commanders or executive lieutenants under white captains. To effect this it was necessary to transfer two black captains into one company; that is the army! Furthermore we had separate and unequal officers' clubs, not overseas but right here at home. At times it actually seemed that the white man would rather lose the war than give the black man the recognition he so clearly deserved.

"I have a very bitter taste when I think of the army. I wanted to be a soldier like everyone else, but this was impossible for a black man to do in World War II. I don't think the situation has really changed too much."

Technical Sergeant Willie Lawton, 369th Infantry Regiment, Bronze Star, underwent basic training at Fort McClellan, Alabama, in 1941 and was held over as part of the cadre there for some months before being sent to Fort Benning, Georgia, where he first earned his sergeant's stripes.

Willie Lawton: "My views on the south just aren't very good. The Negro enlisted man was never allowed to forget he was a Negro and the Negro had a place to stay in both in and out of camp. All of my officers at these two southern camps were white and they had a great capacity for not remembering names so substituted things like, 'Hey you with the black face over there, boy.' If you showed any signs of intelligence, belligerency, or acted like a man, you were immediately put on their 'smart nigger' list. These officers found some pretty nasty ways of trying to break the spirit of those who did not fit into their way of thinking on what kind of behavior and attitude a Negro should exhibit. I finally just couldn't take it anymore and asked for a transfer. Besides I figured I was in the army to do a job and I might as well go somewhere, where they supposedly were going to do this job. I have already said my transfer was granted, but not before I was busted back to a private. I was sent to Louisiana where I joined the 93rd on maneuvers. I should say the 93rd became known as the maneuvers division. I doubt if any division in this country spent as much time on maneuvers as this outfit.

"When I reported to the 93rd, they looked at my record and noticed I had been a training sergeant. I was assured that I would not remain a private long. When the Louisiana maneuvers were over we were sent to the Mohave Desert in California for further maneuvers. The 92nd Division had moved into Fort Huachuca so I guess they had to send us somewhere.

"The 93rd had some Negro officers, particularly at the junior level. In all honesty my first encounter with a few of them made me almost wish I was still at Fort McClellan. They were aloof and arrogant and often tried to exhibit more intelligence than they had. Fortunately, there were others who were really down to earth, and they were the ones who had a lot on the ball. They knew how to communicate with the guys. Those bars on their shoulders hadn't made them think they were little tin gods.

"After the ups and downs of the California desert, which was hardly the ideal place since we were miles from civilization and the heat was terrific, and I might add it didn't look like we were going any place either. The *Chicago Defender* began to lambaste the government as to why Negro combat units were not being sent overseas. They didn't let up the pressure until we were at last shipped out. We went in the direction we figured on, the South Pacific.

"Our first landing was in the Solomon Islands, and we went from there all of the way up to the Philippines. Our division was put in the category of mop-up, meaning we came in after the fighting. We were given patrol duty for the purpose of keeping contact with the enemy forces, which were usually small, to see that they were not reenforced and to keep them in check. We were also given holding positions. This was a little boring, but it had interesting moments.

"When the war was over we were in the Philippines, and by then I had had the army right up to my neck. Promotions were given on the basis of whether or not you were a 'good nigger.' I found throughout my military career that the Negro of some intelligence and freedom of thought definitely was not wanted and wasn't going very far. These things you expected in the states and particularly in the South but not after you are some thousand and more miles away from the United States.

"We had an incident in the Philippines that just missed being a bloody war; the 93rd vs. the Dixie Division. This white outfit was there when we arrived. I do not remember the name of the place but it was in the vicinity of the Dole Pineapple Company. Our men had been overseas nineteen months without seeing any women to speak of so when the guys hit the Philippines they went hog wild. The Dixie Division couldn't stand the Filipino girls going for the Negro soldiers. After several days there were small battles. The ultimate finally arrived; the Dixie Division was lined upon one side of the road for about two miles or more and the 93rd was lined up opposite them. Both sides had fixed bayonets, their guns were on load and unlock. It took the colonels of every battalion from both divisions to get their men and bring the situation under control. They were real busy riding or running up and down that road to keep down outright war.

"The next morning the colonel of my battalion called a meeting of all of the officers and NCOs. He marched us to a field and instead of talking some kind of sense we were severely reprimanded, so we knew where we stood. The thing we kept thinking about was those Dixie boys wouldn't have been caught dead with the Filipino girls back home. Anyway, we were told that anyone would be busted in rank should he become involved with the girls of the country. Neither the officers nor the NCOs liked this directive, and instead of telling the enlisted what we were supposed to we told them exactly what had been said.

"The colonel, being the colonel, was the only person who had a generator to furnish light in his tent at night. That night several men cut loose with their .30 caliber rifles on that light and the upper part of his tent. Man, he came crawling out of that tent screaming bloody murder. The whole thing was settled without another word; he had gotten the message and there was no problem about our mixing with the women who came into our area.

"Shortly after this incident I had enough points to come home and I arrived in Frisco, December 24, 1946. I thought about the past few years and there were some pleasant memories. In Alabama the Negro homes were open to us, all of the homes, rich and poor alike, and the people were most hospitable. When you left the post there you had something enjoyable to look forward to. However, I just couldn't stomach the 'pigeon roost' to see a movie so I only saw one movie off of the post the whole time I was stationed in this state. Now California was something different, and I do mean different. We often went to Los Angeles on leave from the Mohave since it was the closest large city to our outpost. Of course all of California, from San Francisco down, is a naval area, so servicemen were old hat. I found L.A. to be a big city on the take, and everybody was out to take the soldier. If you didn't have a dollar bill in your hand you were out of luck for just about anything. Los Angeles was the only town I saw where servicemen were hustled by men, women, and children. I found this rather appalling. Now I came from around Beaubien and St. Antoine in Detroit and there was no silver spoon in my mouth and I had seen life in the raw but I had never seen anything like L.A. during the war. The people who invited you to their homes were from all appearances nice respectable people, and they were gracious hosts, but when you got ready to leave there was a bowl at the door where you dropped a little gratuity. Now, nobody had told you this was a 'rent party.' If you were caught a little short then they were willing to settle for sending them back a carton of cigarettes or whiskey, any little old item that was hard for civilians to get. I guess this is human nature, but I found it hard to take.

"The only civilian jim-crowism we saw in the South Pacific was among the Spanish people in the Philippines, who had big plantations and were the business people that our forces had saved from the Japanese. The daughters of these people were too good for our soldiers, black or white. A few ranking white officers might have received a less than hostile greeting but on the whole they were off limits. We called them 'the untouchables.'

"The relationship of the Negro and white soldier in the South Pacific was farcical. The very guy who would make your life miserable in the states was your best buddy over there. I have never quite figured this out. Oh, we accepted the friendship offered but we never forgot that one day we would be going home and not to take this buddy-buddy bit for real.

"As far as my experiences go, the army is the poorest-fed branch of the services, and the Negro soldier is on the rear end of this. We ate goat from New Zealand, horse meat from Australia, and dried eggs; that was our regular fare. In the Philippines on Sundays, for a decent meal, we went to the nearby naval station. It was quite large and the guys, who were white, welcomed us aboard and stuffed us with good food; that was the only decent food we had.

"Right now we are talking in terms of 'he or she is black.' I am a Negro or an Afro-American and reject the term *black*. The first time I heard the word used as it is today was overseas when we were working alongside some Aussies defending an island. They would come down and have tea with us. They used the word *black* and I was offended until I learned they do not think of the words *colored* or *Negro* and always use the word *black*, but the intent was not to malign. None of the white Americans picked this up because they would have gotten a fat lip if they had, just the word 'nigger' provoked a whole mess of trouble.

"All and all I look upon my experiences in the army as a racial thing that should not have happened to anyone. Al Evans and I used to discuss these things, and he was as outspoken as I was and he didn't bar rank or color. There were numerous times they tried to set him down to reclassify him. In one instance I got hold of the deal and alerted him. The ironic part was the trap was being baited by a few black officers bucking for a promotion at any price. This is one of the things that hurts us as a group.

"Today the Negro soldier does not have to undergo much of what we did because white officers are really afraid of him. Today's Negro soldier will 'frag' an officer in a minute; toss him a live grenade or booby-trap his bed with one. In World War II a white officer might get a warning shot fired at him, or he might get shot, but nothing like the fraging incidents that have taken place in Viet Nam. Negro officers are not subject to this kind of thing. It has nothing to do with their race; they know when they have over stepped their bounds and they back off. 'Patty' is like the child who doesn't believe fire will burn until he sticks his hand into it.

"I most certainly think the Negro GI of World War II did play a great part in the changed overt thinking and behavior of the white military because we'd take so much and that was all. But if I had it to do over again I would take off for Canada like many of the fellows have recently done. We were supposedly sent over there to do a job, fighting for our country, when it really added up to traveling half way around the world to endure the same insults from the same people.

"I have very few good things, if any, to say about white officers. I read the manual for officers at Fort Benning on how to handle Negro soldiers; it was asinine, and this is how they tried to run the Negro in the army.* They didn't know the Negro then and they don't know him now. One of the big factors is so many army officers are from the south and this is as far as they will ever go in life.

"The men were brave; they did whatever job was assigned to them and they did it well. We had no instance of cowardice or mutiny. But the officers could have made life more bearable and left us with a little dignity. The 93rd was a discriminatory, bigoted organization from the lowliest white lieutenant right up to the commanding general, H. H. Johnson.

---

*This manual is described by Lieutenant Earl Kennedy, 332nd Fighter Group, chapter 4, below.

"The war was a thing I wanted to forget. I've never put on my uniform since I took it off. I've never marched in any parade. I have never applied for my citation. It is something I'd rather forget because it was a bad dream, a real nightmare."

Pigeonholed in the Navy

The black soldier was invisible in the U.S. Army during World War II because he was not mentioned; he was invisible in the Navy because, until President Roosevelt's Executive Order 9279 in December 1942, the black American was hardly there.

In the peacetime years preceding the war, the U.S. Navy employed blacks only as mess attendants; the traditional steward's mate in the white jacket was even being replaced by Filipinos, Chamorros, and Japanese. During the early years of World War II, neither the navy nor the U.S. Marines used the draft as a source of manpower. Neither accepted black enlistees, except that the navy continued to employ a few mess attendants.

Following the executive order, the navy began to accept an increasing share of black enlistees and draftees. Interestingly enough, Lee records the army's irritation with the navy for "siphoning off" the cream of the nation's engineer and building trade manpower for its construction battalions (Seabees), contending that their functions were not "always properly those of the Navy" (p. 406).

The rigid policy of the navy, ostensibly adopted to prevent "mixing of the races" aboard ship (Lee, p. 22), did not prevent the performance of acts of heroism by some of the very men forbidden by category to handle weapons. Neither Dorie Miller nor Leonard Harmon, both mess attendants 1st class, would have won the Navy Cross had they merely filled the slots they were supposed to occupy. Dorie Miller was cited for "distinguished devotion to duty, extraordinary courage and disregard for his own personal safety" during the Japanese attack on Pearl Harbor 7 December 1941:

> While at the side of his captain on the bridge, Miller, despite enemy strafing and bombing and in the face of a serious fire, assisted in moving his Captain who had been mortally wounded, to a place of greater safety, and later manned and operated a machine gun directed at enemy Japanese attacking aircraft until ordered to leave the bridge. [For the President, signed, Frank Knox, Secretary of the Navy]

Almost a year later, Leonard Harmon was serving aboard the USS San Francisco during action against the Japanese in the Solomon Islands, 12 and 13 November 1942. His citation for "extraordinary heroism" was posthumously awarded:

> With persistent disregard for his own personal safety, Harmon rendered invaluable assistance in caring for the wounded and evacuating them to a

dressing station. *In addition to displaying unusual loyalty in behalf of the injured Executive Officer, he deliberately exposed himself to hostile gunfire in order to protect a shipmate and, as a result of this courageous deed, was killed in action. His heroic spirit of self-sacrifice, maintained above and beyond the call of duty, was in keeping with the highest traditions of the United States Naval Service. He gallantly gave up his life in the defense of his country. [For the President, signed, Frank Knox, Secretary of the Navy]*

Three of the navy men interviewed here saw service in the South Pacific. Steward Ray Carter, nineteen-year-old-Detroiter, enlisted the day after the Japanese attack on Pearl Harbor. After the routine examinations, he was slated to go to Great Lakes Naval Training Station in Illinois, but his assignment was speedily changed.

Ray Carter: "As they were getting my papers in order I was asked my nationality. I answered, 'I'm colored.' The redneck s.o.b. doing my paper work quickly changed my orders. The letters behind my name AS3, apprentice seaman third class, became MATT3, mess attendant third class.*

"At this point I could not have cared less. Besides at that moment I hadn't the slightest idea what MATT3 meant. What's that saying about ignorance is bliss? I was so proud that I had volunteered to fight for my country, this great democracy of ours, changing a few letters besides my name didn't dim my burning patriotism.

"At the post office, after our induction, we were given little pins to put in our lapels saying, 'I volunteered for the Navy.' Then we marched down to Union Station where my parents were waiting. I felt very gung-ho and very proud of myself for getting into the fray immediately. The train finally pulled

---

*Of the men interviewed for this book, one served with the U.S. Coast Guard, which offered opportunities for advancement to the black recruit, but limited the use which could be made of his technical background and training. Coast Guardsman Bernard Coker, stationed at Curtis Bay, Maryland, found himself "segregated both by race and rating." At first assigned to a ship, he became a landlubber after the first shakedown cruise and a promotion. "All blacks who had a rating above messman were excluded from sea duty; that meant me."

Coker advanced from fireman 3rd class to machinist mate 1st class while at Curtis Bay. "The higher my rating got the less chance I had of going to sea. They weren't about to have a black over whites. A white machinist mate with the same rating as mine came to the base. He had done sea duty and had been told he would be permanently stationed here. He sent for his family, and soon as they settled down he received orders to report for sea duty. I tried to get them to take me instead because he was married and had a couple of kids. We both literally begged them to let me go but I was the wrong color so he had to go back to sea. Those in charge would rather make a white widow than have a black machinist mate on board ship: that was the service–period."

The irony of this situation is that Coker had to request that "Negro" be specified on his enlistment papers. Had he gone to sea, those serving under him would never have known the difference.

out, and we were off to Norfolk, Virginia. Until then the farthest south I had been was Windsor, Ontario, Canada.

"Upon arriving at Roanoke, Virginia, the conductor shifted us to another coach, a Jim Crow coach. I said to myself, this won't happen again once I get into my uniform. Man, was I a real fruit cake! Anyway, smug and secure in the magic of the navy blue I could not care less at such behavior.

"When we got to Norfolk the white boys went into the waiting room and we were escorted to the colored waiting room. The navy bus soon appeared and we were ushered right to the back of the bus. The whites got on last, occupying the seats up front. This was a state law, as they explained it to me. We went out to the naval base and it was beautiful, really beautiful. However it was at this point I got sick. They drove us Negroes to a fenced-in unit of several acres, called Unit B. I often wondered if the B stood for 'black.' This is where I joined the black navy, the segregated navy.

"In Detroit they had told us to have our teeth fixed, socks mended, everything just so. In Unit B there were guys in overalls who could not read or write their names. I thought, well, I'll just make the best of this and try to get into another unit. It was purely illusionary on my part because Unit B was all there was for blacks. After my basic training was over I was given a ten-day pass. I returned home and went straight down to the post office to see if I could get out of the navy. This was impossible so I asked for a transfer into the army; that too was impossible. I didn't want to go back, period.

"During our boot training we were given little white coats. I wondered what they were for, oh man, I was a real dum-dum! I soon found out that mess attendants wore these little white coats to wait on the officers. Here I had enlisted to fight for my country and my great contribution to the war effort was to wait on whites. When I left on furlough I hadn't the slightest intention of returning to Norfolk, but the wisdom of my parents prevailed and I unhappily went back to waiting table.

"After boot leave we were assigned to ships and stations. I was sent to San Diego, California, to go aboard the USS *Gregory*, an ATD, attack transport, an old four-stacker from World War I.

"My quarters was an exclusive little section just for us 'house niggers' who were assigned to the ward room. Cooking, waiting on table, shining shoes, the whole bit; this was the job for Negroes in the navy in World War II. It made me angrier than hell. Here I am spoiling for a fight with the enemy and the question begins to arise, just who the hell is the enemy?

"My battle station was on a four-inch gun on the foc's'le. I was a hot-shell man. I wore asbestos gloves and caught the shells ejected as the gun fired. I didn't mind this because I was topside, right up front. Most of the cooks and mess attendants, black and white, were below deck passing ammunition.

"After running all over the damned Pacific Ocean with hit-and-run attacks we joined the invasion forces for Guadalcanal. Our job was to transport men and supplies from the New Hebrides and New Caledonia to Guadalcanal and Tulagi. We were attached to the 1st Marine Division. They were one of the first American units to clash with the Japanese and they learned the hard way. It's one thing to think a race inferior and another thing for that race to be inferior.

"On September 5, 1942, we had been shuttling between Guadalcanal and the Solomons; no problem. On this particular evening we had gotten word that a Japanese cruiser was in the area. I believe this was about the time the USS *Vincennes* had been hit and all ships in the area were maintaining semi-battle stations. General quarters was sounded about 1:00 A.M. Our sister ship the USS *Little* was under attack by the Japanese cruiser. We were in a position between the *Little* and the cruiser but somewhat forward and silhouetted as the firing began. Our ship had gotten off about thirty rounds when we were hit. They didn't have the intercom system on our ship like you see in today's navy. The captain had been killed, and the exec. told the boatswain to tell the men to abandon ship.

"I donned a life jacket and took a running jump, landing as far out as possible away from the ship. I can still remember the 'glug-glug' sound of a ship passing close by me. There was screaming, crying, hollering all over the place. The Japanese shot off a few flares, I believe to finish her off, because right after the flares went off the *Gregory* went down like a ton of bricks. Oh, I had put some distance between me and the *Gregory* before I looked back to see what was happening. When I say she went down I mean she went down in what seemed like seconds.

"While the ship was sinking, before the kill, our ash cans, depth charges, on the back of the *Gregory* which evidently were not set properly began to explode at 50- or 75-foot depths. I could hear them going off and I thought, God help anybody swimming in the vicinity because of the tremendous concussion they would cause.

"With the *Gregory* gone I just turned and started swimming. How far I swam I haven't the slightest idea and where the life raft came from I don't know, but when I saw it I swam to it and pulled myself aboard. On board was a chief Sheehan who was badly hurt, and towards morning passed on. There were 115 men aboard the *Gregory* when she was hit. There were 70 survivors of the *Gregory* and the *Little*. They all ended up on or around this raft. After what seemed like the longest night ever, day broke and soon a plane came flying out about 150 feet above the water. When they tell you, you can tell the difference between planes under any circumstances they're full of crap because all of us were scared to death, sure it was Japanese. Fortunately it was one of ours and he tipped his wings to let us know he had seen us. In about three hours a ship had been sent to pick us up. It was at this time I learned there were 70 of us out of approximately 230 men, the total complement of both ships.

"I really must inject the no-segregation bit while we were floating and swimming around in the warm waters of the Pacific. Talk about togetherness; we were straight out of *The Three Musketeers*, all for one and one for all. Brotherly love just oozed all over the place.

"Our rescuing vessel put us ashore on some island where fighting was going on. Now my land battle training was a big zero. The Japanese were knocking our ships out right and left and turning our marines everyway but loose and we navy survivors are landed on an island that in exactly twenty minutes after we disembark hoists a red flag with the words run to a fox hole. Hell, I didn't know what a foxhole was; we sailors had to be told. When I dug the meaning and its purpose I dove into a foxhole fast with my navy knife to protect me, ain't that a bitch. An hour later I was wearing marine boots and a forty-five.

"In three days we boarded the USS *William Ward Burroughs* and headed for Hawaii. Two more of our comrades died en route. One was buried at sea and the other at Esperito, New Hebrides. When the *Burroughs* arrived in Honolulu I learned a good friend of mine and a real hero had been killed aboard the *Pensacola.*

"Coming home we were put aboard the *Lurline*, and we Negroes began to feel the old racial prejudice once more. We were back again in our separate but unequal slot; brotherhood died fast. We landed at San Diego in the great land of democracy and milk and honey. Bullshit! San Diego was overrun with survivors. The *Wasp* had been hit and two other carriers.

"For entertainment we had to go down to 5th and Market to the Imperial while the white boys were welcome everywhere and given every consideration. This is one reason I won't give the damned Red Cross a lousy penny, today, tomorrow, or 3000 A.D. Our pay was held up because naturally our papers went down with the USS *Gregory*. The white boys received health and comfort money from the Red Cross, and we had a helluva time getting fifteen lousy cents. We were given survivors' leaves, thirty days, and we couldn't get a seat on a train or plane but the 'patty' boys did; we ended up on the Trailway bus; our families had wired us money.

"Three of us traveled together, James Curry, James Forman, both of Chicago, and myself. Everything was swinging until we got to New Mexico and Arizona and then we started having trouble. The race problem popped up again. In Texas up through the Panhandle we were refused food. We couldn't eat in their restaurants yet we could see German prisoners of war just gulping down succulent steaks and having a ball. Here we had just taken a long swim in the goddamn Pacific Ocean and a lot of men had died horribly and these 'mothers' were sucking up to the enemy and refused us food. That did it. I said fuck the navy, I'm not going back to sea again. I returned home and stayed thirty days, which stretched into sixty days; I just wasn't going back.

"I was picked up by the SPs and taken to the Great Lakes brig, *c'est la vie*! I was then sent back to San Diego and from there to the navy shipyards at Seattle, Washington. They were putting a new destroyer into commission and I was to be part of the crew. She was one of the latest models and a beauty.

"I had become a hardened old salt by then. I knew my way around the navy and I knew how to 'shook' and 'jive.' I made a couple of rates and I wasn't waiting on table any more. I had some boys under me, I had arrived. My new ship was the USS *Endicott*, and I was the senior 'nigger.' I use these words because that's what 'the man' thought. I'd have been drawn and quartered if they could have read my mind. They wanted to be boys and play games; I played right along with them, laughing at their gullibility.

"A new ensign, fresh out of Annapolis, was assigning battle stations. As usual the 7th division, or the lackey detail (meaning us), was being assigned to battle stations below deck. When I saw my name on the list I told him, 'I got news for you, you can send me to Portsmouth Naval Prison, give me a dishonorable discharge, or do anything you choose but you damned sure are not putting me at a battle station below deck. After a hassle I was put on the number one antiaircraft gun. This wasn't too cool because I wasn't a gunner, I just passed ammunition but at least I was topside.

"We had our shakedown cruise and ended up in New York. I was just too close to home so I went over the hill.

"The SPs finally caught up with me again and it was the routine procedure, back to the brig and this time I was busted in rank. After my brig time was up I was sent to Baltimore, Maryland, and put aboard a tanker carrying oil and gasoline. Scuttlebutt had it that the invasion was coming so I thought we were going that-a-way but not me, back through the canal and out into the Pacific where we stayed at sea from sixty to seventy days refueling carriers, destroyers, cruisers, etc. We even refueled Admiral Halsey's flagship.

"Japanese aircraft attacked us when we were down in the China Sea. I am here to tell you that you don't know what fear is until you are aboard a tanker under attack. Tankers will blow to kingdom come if hit in the right place. If they don't blow they can be turned into blazing infernos. Burning oil covers the water; in short it's a bitch either way. Luck was with us, for we sustained no serious blows but I'll bet you all of us on board aged twenty years while the action was going on.

"We then began spending time in and around the Bay of Okinawa. At night we would enter the bay and nets would be put out to protect us. One night a two-man Japanese sub had gotten inside of this protection. About 5:00 A.M. the sub cut loose with two torpedoes and our sister ship was blown clear out of the water. We put out to sea as fast as possible and our next port was Hawaii. It took us four months to get there and we refueled at sea.

"I wish I could remember more but I can't; it was a long time ago. To prove it I have two sons, one twenty-five and the other twenty-two. Then, too, one tends to forget the ugly incidents and remember the good. And of course there were good times: the girls, seeing the world, making new friends. Believe it or not, I once tried to get my sons to go into the navy because I had been in it and thought only of the good things. Your asking me to recall the whole deal for you caused me to sit down and look behind the scene and remember how it really was. I am glad my sons decided one navy man in the family was enough.

"If I had it to do all over again, or if I had to do it today, for what 'they' call 'our democracy' I would not go in, I would go to jail first. Remember the saying, 'I'd drink muddy water'? Well, baby, believe me I'd drink muddy water before I would enter the armed forces of my homeland; I've been that route once and you made me recall what a lousy deal it was for blacks. I have yet to see, after careful consideration, where I or my people, benefited from the time I spent in service and the insults and humiliation I endured as a man. I can find no reason to make me want to take up arms to save 'democracy.' What democracy?

"The officers I served under as a whole weren't too bad. There is always the exception; a sonofabitch named McCormack called me a 'nigger.' I threatened to beat the shit out of him and we got things straight. One thing, I was Portsmouth-bound* if I had to take that crap. A steward's mate named Smitty broke an officer's jaw for referring to him with this word. Were 'they' embarrassed when Smitty was brought up for charges! Smitty was wearing all of his ribbons earned: six major campaigns, two medals, the Purple Heart, two ships shot from under him. He also had spent six days in the Pacific floating around on a life raft. The charges were dropped but Smitty was put on the first ship going back to the war zone. Justice? I am glad to say Smitty survived the war, unlike Dorie Miller, a real hero of Pearl Harbor and the USS *Arizona,* who went down with the USS *Lipscomb Bay*.

"We black servicemen of World War II can set down and talk and laugh about the war but we know deep down inside the war struck at our manhood by trying to make menials out of us at every opportunity. Some of our men were broken by racism in the United States armed forces. There are always a small number of real Uncle Toms. However, the majority of the black men who served in World War II fought back in innumerable ways. The most obvious were the riots in the camps all over the country. To this day the public is unaware of the number of open rebellions that took place, just as they are ignorant of the number of blacks who died at the hands of white MPs, SPs, white civilians, and civilian police, particularly in the south. Had black servicemen been good 'boys' these slayings wouldn't have occurred. If the 'man' thought he knew how to handle blacks when they went into the various services he learned he was wrong; not that this changed his methods. To this

---

*The naval disciplinary facility at Portsmouth, New Hampshire.

day whites who were in World War II cannot tell you what the blacks really thought because blacks are masters at only showing one side of their faces. They are 'one-eyed jacks.' I daresay those who did see the other side are not around to tell about it.

"Maybe, just maybe, some of the things we went through paid off. We now have several ranking officers who are black. Speaking for myself, all I know is I went through hell. I lost a ship, I was kicked in the ass everyway possible excepting physically, but I think I came out a better man than those who were wielding the power. I survived everything the 'man' threw at me and I fought back in every way I could think of. Today I respect the young blacks who are hostile and don't give a damn who likes or dislikes it. After all, they were sired by the men of World War II!"

Steward's Mate Eddie Will Robinson of Cleveland, Ohio, enlisted in the U.S. Navy in August 1942. For reasons explained in his interview, he requested service on a submarine. Following World War II, he enlisted in the army, served in the Korean War, and attained the rank of captain.

Eddie Robinson: "Being a seventeen-year-old patriot burning with a desire to smite the little bastards who had dared to fire on the flag of my country, I had delivered an ultimatum to my mother. Either she sign so I could enlist to fight for my country or I was going to run away from home. She really should have kicked me in the pants, but being a wise parent she decided to let me experience my growing pains under the guidance of the armed forces. Later there were times I wished she had locked me in the closet and thrown the key away, but who is more worldly wise than a teenager approaching maturity?

"The Secretary of the Navy, Frank Knox, made no bones about the fact that as long as he was secretary there would never be a mixed navy. This somehow or other had not penetrated my thick skull, full of chauvinistic fervor. I was quite disappointed when I ended up with all the other blacks as a steward's mate.

"I was sent to Bainbridge, Maryland, where I did my basic training. I decided since I was going to be in a position of subservience I might as well be in the elite servitude class so I volunteered for submarine duty. My training for this was done in Hawaii. I was a natural for subs since I was five feet four inches and 100 pounds dripping wet.

"My first ship, which I picked up in Honolulu, was the USS *Thresher*. (The old *Thresher* was retired at New London, Connecticut, after many successful encounters. Her namesake the new USS *Thresher* was the new snorkel-type sub that dived some years back and never came up.) How well I remember my first day as I strutted down to the *Thresher* prepared to board. Just as I was nearing the deck a great big white seaman looked down on me and said, 'And who's your mother, little boy?' The battle flag was hoisted and all

100 pounds of fighting, flaying fury, charged into him headfirst. He sidestepped, and like I was a toy he grabbed me by my collar and the seat of my britches and dropped me unceremoniously in the drink. I swam to the dock and climbed out. Back I marched to board the *Thresher*. Just as I reached the same spot my white friend was there to greet me again. Again like an enraged minature bull I charged. Once more I hit the drink. As I swam ashore I began thinking, 'You know, Eddie, this doesn't make any sense, you'll be swimming all day.' When I climbed out and went back to board again I still strutted, if one can looking like a wet shaggy terrier. There he was. He made his speech and I stuck my nose up in the air and jumped aboard. My big friend grabbed me, tossed me up in the air, shook my hand and we were buddies from then on.

"One night in Honolulu he put out a 'Hey Mac' call because the madam at a house of iniquity said they did not service blacks. It so happened most of the *Thresher* crew was thereabouts. They made a shambles of the joint. I'll bet that was the most expensive ungotten piece that madam ever ran into.

"Our patrol duty was in the Pacific and we had many an encounter. Don't think we escaped unscathed. Once all of our communications were knocked out, including the radar. We headed back to Pearl for repairs. The USS Destroyer *Litchfield* whipped our ass for two days in the meantime. We had no way of letting them know who we were and they did their damnedest to finish us off. The man that was our captain was one of the greatest guys who ever lived. He finally managed to get us on the surface. He had refused to shoot at the destroyer even if it sank us. I can't say the crew was necessarily in accord. What the hell did they think we were doing continuing to dodge and evade instead of getting off a torpedo or two! As I said, after two days of being clobbered by the *Litchfield* we finally managed to surface and let those bastards know by semaphore that, 'Hey motherfucker, we're on your side.' You talk about the desire to walk the water and kick a few butts on that destroyer. Our sub was steamy inside from the sweat we had exuded while those depth charges were exploding all over hell. I will give our skipper and the captain of the destroyer credit for knowing their business. Ours had us ducking and dodging. He did everything but hide the damned sub in his pocket, but that destroyer captain hung on like a damned bull dog.

"While the *Thresher* was in drydock for repairs I was transferred to USS *Flying Fish*. It was on the *Flying Fish* that we went into the Sea of Japan and tore up the ships we caught there. Our Captain, 'Killer' Kane, was a total man of war. He believed in it, loved it, and thrived on it. I said we had blasted the hell out of Japanese ships in the bay; the whole place was aflame. Everybody, officers down, suggested discreetly that we get the hell out of there. But Killer wasn't satisfied, he was hungry for more kills. He wanted to lay on the bottom and wait for more game. Well the *Flying Fish* made the bottom all right but not under her own power.

"The last thing I remember was our ship being blasted clear out of the water. That's all I recall. Alonzo Harrington, just a kid, a friend here in Detroit, grabbed hold of me and hung on paddling until a Japanese ship picked us up.

"We spent the rest of the war working in the salt mines of northern Japan. I can't say our treatment was unduly cruel. I remember on one occasion they got us up in the middle of the night, handed us shovels, and pointed to the ground. We could hear the bolts of their guns sliding into position. I had thrown up something like twelve shovels of dirt when it dawned on me I was crazy as hell. I threw my shovel down and the nearest guard practically stuck his gun up my nose. Now I don't know if he spoke English but he got my point which was I'd be goddamned if I was going to dig my own grave, so he could shoot me and I'd conveniently fall into a grave I had gotten blisters digging.

"It must have been wild, as I look back on it. As I stood there arguing nose to a gun I told him to pull the fucking trigger then get busy and dig a hole to stick me in.

"The others continued digging with their eyes rooted on me. The guard finally withdrew to talk it over with others. And there I stood in righteous indignation. Isn't it wonderful to be young, waiting to get shot? Nothing happened excepting every now and than one of them would come to look me over. I decided later that like black man in the south the crackers leave alone because they have concluded he's crazy, my keepers thought I was a bit of a nut. They weren't alone, so did the other prisoners. Perhaps my color played some part in it also but I think perhaps my size was the important thing. They didn't have to look up to me, and I was all of nineteen years old, looking like fifteen.

"Now don't misunderstand and think henceforth I was a privileged character because I wasn't. But being the irrepressible type, perhaps the word should be idiotic, I was a one-man big mouth. I didn't push them but when I felt they were going overboard I'd be running my big yap protesting. I just got that odd look and they ignored me. Don't ask me what prompted me in my being the unelected spokesman. Probably the fact the young believe they are indestructible played a part of it.

"Finally our troops came, and strangely enough my big mouth was in it again. Some of the soldiers and ex-prisoners wanted to torture the guards and kill them. I raised hell. I reminded them that these guards had only acted on orders and if they would think about it that they had done things that would make these guys look good. I could remember watching and taking my turn machine-gunning the survivors of a Japanese ship. It was like shooting fish in a barrel. We even bet on whether or not we could hit a certain one right between the eyes. Now I know we Americans don't do these things, but the cruelty in the Pacific was a Mexican stand-off. If anything we led by a nose. Some of the souvenirs our marines and soldiers collected off of Japanese women—oh yes, some were on those islands—caused battle toughened veterans to puke when they realized what the object was. Scalping in the days of the Indian was kind in comparison. No, the war was over in my book and I wasn't about to buy a more holier-than-thou attitude. It was over and done, and I let everybody know just how I felt.

"Whenever our sub put in at Pearl I ran the biggest floating crap game in Honolulu. Oh, I was an enterprising young man. I know you have learned that black-marketing is a big thing during a war. Gambling is, war or no war. The problem in both instances is sending the money home so you'll have a stake when you return. A serviceman is only allowed to send the equivalent to his pay home. Of course one can get around this by the well known pay-off. For every hundred dollars I raked in as house man I paid seventy-five to the right people to get my twenty-five home. Ah, man, wartime produces some sweet rackets. The one time I got suckered I bought a jeep from a guy on an atoll in the middle of the Pacific. When I was back at sea I learned this cat had sold that same jeep to about twenty other men at fifty bucks a throw. He was doing all right because he knew few of us would return to that spot.

"My last interesting submarine trip was at Eniwetok when they dropped the atomic bomb there. My sub was one of those manned entirely by volunteers, standing off from the island to see what kind of effect the explosion would have on all the various naval ships there for this purpose. After the explosion I was supposed to be sterile and I wanted papers to prove it so I could have a ball. You can believe they were wrong because I have the kids to prove it!

"What did I see? The same thing you saw in the movies, a great big mushroon billowing skyward. I don't know what I expected but I was not impressed.

"When I was released from the Navy I went to visit my mother, who was living in Alabama. A few days down there convinced me I preferred the service, only this time I went to the army. I eventually was sent to OCS and was one of the black lieutenants with the 24th Infantry Regiment in the 25th Division. I was in that mad backward rush from the Yalu River. I must admit I was one of those fools who kept taking and retaking Pork Chop Hill.

"I came out of the services after twenty years of what was a rather interesting life.

"Would I do it again? Hell no, I'm old enough now to know better."

Steward's Mate Thomas Pruitt describes in a few paragraphs the background of northern black draftees entering the U.S. Navy in 1943 and after, the kinds of work to which they were assigned, and the stress imposed by their predetermined role.

Thomas Pruitt: "Four of us blacks were sent from Detroit to the naval station at Quonset Point, Rhode Island. I was an apprentice tool-and-die maker at Ford's. Tim Kennedy, the second member of our foursome, was a musician and had just received an offer to join Duke Ellington's band. J. E. Williams, Jr., was a mortician. Bob Davis, though he worked at the post office, held a master's degree. He was just one of the many 'degreed' blacks who could not get jobs in their field because of color.

"Upon reaching our destination we were told we were going to be steward's mates. At that time that is all a black could be in the navy.* The job entailed serving the officers' meals, making their beds, and if the officer was high enough in rank you did his laundry and polished his shoes, in short, you were a male maid. To say we were upset is putting it mildly, but they were hardly going to change the navy and its customs just for us, so we settled down to the routine.

"After basic training they let us do a little bit of marching occasionally to make us feel we belonged to the military. We were also assigned to the bachelor officers' quarters so we could do our housework. I must say we looked quite cute in our little white jackets buttoned up to the neck and our spotless blue trousers. Williams was assigned to the pantry making salads. Tim Kennedy did get the opportunity to play with the navy band at certain times.

"I soon received a promotion and was removed from the dining room and assigned to the captain as his 'boy.' This word 'boy' I found in the Navy's Blue Jacket Manual. I became the captain's valet. I had moved up in the world; I was the head 'niggah.' Nobody messes with the captain's boy. The captain was an officer and a gentleman. He never called me 'boy' nor did he treat me as a flunky, which I appreciated.

"Many of my buddies saw a lot of action in the war. Though all of us were taught to fire small arms, we could not put our little pinkies on the big guns. Their job under fire was to 'praise the Lord and pass the ammunition.' They weren't permitted to throw rocks at the enemy.

"A black's ability to progress up the ladder in the navy then was nil. Rear-Admiral Samuel Gravely was a steward's mate 1st class when I was at Quonset Point. Over the years it was heartening to me to watch him, via the newspapers, go from steward's mate to captain of his own ship, and finally to rear-admiral."

Asked about the kind of work done by the Seabees, Machinist Mate

---

*Seaman 1st class Norman McRae received his basic training at the Great Lakes Naval Training Station in 1944. By that time the U.S. Navy had begun a program of officer training for the black enlistees, and he met several black ensigns at the station. Selected for training in the Navy's V-12 program, he was sent to Hampton Institute in Virginia. When the program was closed down, he was sent to Hawaii where he found that "no matter what your training all blacks ended up stevedores." McRae worked in the rigging loft splicing cable which, he said, "any idiot could have done."

Edward Oldham, 19th Navy Construction Battalion, said, "We often had to go in before the marines to build landing bases. When we encountered the Japanese, well, the army had tanks—we had half-tracks and other heavy machinery and rifles. Remember we were called the 'fighting Seabees.' "

Edward Oldham: "I was thirty-one when I was drafted and could have been exempt because of my age and family. I felt my age was against me in the army, so I went into the Seabees where you had to be twenty-six or over. I was sent to Camp Peary, Virginia. I followed orders and never volunteered. I stayed out of trouble. There was a black and a white side to the camp with signs designating which was which. One day the black guys tore down all of the signs. The authorities split our battalion and sent the northern fellows north and the southern fellows farther south.

"I was asked if I wanted to work with a water-purifying team. The job necessitated some learning. I believe my white officers thought they had a fool, and this was a little game they were playing. Much to their surprise I learned the water purifying process with ease so I became part of a white team.

"The officers' subtle put-down of me was they always referred to me as 'Eddie, the model Seabee.' I was not given a rating. When we finally arrived in New Guinea I asked my immediate superior why no rating since I was a model Seabee. He said it was because I was so perfect they didn't even know I was there. It dawned on me model Seabees didn't get ratings so I did an about-face. I started gambling, drinking, buying and selling—the black market thrived in the Pacific. In no time I moved from seaman second to first, to machinist mate. I found this quite funny. However I did not let my new way of life interfere with doing my job and doing it well.

"Oftimes there was shortage of drinking water on the various islands on which we were stationed. It was for me to determine how much water a man could have for the day. For a short period we were down to a canteen a day and some of the men didn't like it. Our commanding officer specifically charged me to shoot anyone who tried to get more than his share of the water. He made it quite clear there were to be no exceptions to this order. This same officer, several hours later, appeared at the water storage tank, emptied his canteen on the ground and reached for the tank spigot. I said, 'Sir, you ordered one canteen a day for all personnel, with no exceptions, because it is necessary so you don't get any more.' He looked at me, snorted, and reached for the spigot again. I warned him, 'Sir, if you turn that spigot I will be forced to kill you.' He looked at me for a minute then turned and walked away.

"Would I have killed him? Without a qualm. He expected me to shoot anyone else under the same circumstances and when he issued the order he made no exceptions because he knew officers would take advantage otherwise.

"No, I wasn't court-martialed; I wasn't even called in for a friendly conversation. It was never mentioned. From that day until the day I was discharged my superiors treated me with a new respect, not their usual brand of b.s.

"I have no hard feeling about the service. I went to do a job and I did it. I remember in danger the white man was like my brother but I wasn't concerned with that one way or another. I was concerned with doing my time and getting back alive, so I learned everything they taught for survival and fighting. I took it seriously. Some of the guys did not and when the chips were down they died or were maimed for life. I never lost track of the fact, this is the white man's world. I had every intention of living in it, not dying for it.

"My best friend while I was in the Pacific was white. We went through hell together, gambled together, chased girls together, and came back together until we passed under the Golden Gate Bridge, and my buddy disappeared. I never saw him again. Disillusioned? Hurt? Not really. The bridge said it, we were home again, back to reality."

"All Seabees have a lot of battle stars. I have sixteen."

Driving the Ledo Road

During World War II, a 271-mile section of road was constructed from Ledo, Assam, to connect with the old Burma Road to Kunming, China. It functioned both as combat support road and supply route. The 518th Quartermaster (Truck) Battalion, sent overseas in 1943, began driving the precipitous mountain roads still under construction when that unit arrived in Assam in early 1944. Their main job was supplying allied troops and airfields with ammunition and gasoline. When the last link was completed, they drove "over the Hump" to China.

In one sense, the men of the 518th were already veterans by the time they arrived in the CIB theater. Sergeant Jeffries Bassett Jones, drafted in 1942, had undergone basic training at "the backside of hell," Camp Van Dorn, Mississippi, where, he says, "I saw and participated in more fighting than I experienced in all my days overseas."

Jeff Jones: "While at Camp Van Dorn we were once sent on a detail to Arkansas because of a flood. It was all right with us; we thought we'd be rescuing people; driving them to high ground and the like. It turned out we were to be used as a labor battalion to clear up some farm acreage that belonged to an Arkansas politician. Our unit was predominately from Detroit and Chicago and cleaning up some Arkansas cracker's backyard after the flood certainly did not appeal to our humane instincts, so we refused. We were informed we could be court-martialed for refusing to obey an order. We told our lieutenant that we'd just have to take our chances; we were truckers, not a damn labor battalion. When Lieutenant Dozier, white, found all three platoons were adamant in their refusal he said he didn't blame them and that ended that. Unfortunately Dozier was injured in a jeep accident so was lost to the outfit; he was a pretty decent guy.

"We hadn't been at Van Dorn long before we got a new commanding officer, Major Downs. This 'little' bastard, I mean little in all respects, had us gather around him on a platform so he could look down on us. He told us, 'As far as I am concerned I have never seen a 'nigra' I felt qualified for OCS or Warrant Officers School and I don't expect to.' Well the high scorers on the AGCT now knew their chances of going to OCS were nil. Not one member of our unit was ever sent to OCS and we had some really high IQs in the group.

"Major Downs took ill just before our departure for POE. I have often wondered if the major got wind of the troops' wish that they could catch him alone on deck one night when we crossed over. The guys weren't kidding about seeing the major swim.

"The night I returned to Van Dorn from my furlough home a riot was in the making. In a few hours after my arrival it was in full swing. The cause I learned was the senseless slaying of one of the soldiers of the 364th Infantry Regiment, black, that had recently been sent to Camp Van Dorn. The 518th had no access to arms, but the 364th did so this night the two groups joined forces. It was wild. The word got out that the whites were going to attack the black areas with tanks. One of the officers from the 364th went into the white area and warned them if this were true not to do it because the men of the 364th antitank company had sworn they would blow to hell any tank they saw coming near their area. All kinds of rumors were flying, along with fists, feet, cudgels, everything. It was a small war.

"After the riot the 518th was split up and shipped out. It was in August 1943. My unit was told we were going to Sicily. We actually landed in North Africa on the first leg of a trip that eventually took us to the CIB area. My first view of Oran was quite a surprise. I was expecting half-naked natives, mud huts, and wild animals. Instead I was looking at a beautiful modern city, Oran. Their dress in many instances was quite similar to ours. I thought about us dumb Americans, so sure everybody else is backwards. For something like four months we wasted time doing not one constructive thing towards the war effort.

"Finally we were put aboard a British ship bound for Bombay, India, by way of the Suez Canal. Two-thirds of those on board were white Britishers, but there was no segregation. From Bombay we went to Calcutta and eventually ended up in Assam. Our first bivouac area was the Bamboo Motor Pool, a natural camouflaged area under palm trees.

"I thought I was quite capable of driving a truck, so at the first call for volunteers, I was ready. One run through the Himalayas on the Ledo Road convinced me that I was a mere amateur who was quite willing to learn the tricks of the trade. I planned to stay alive. Principles used on flat terrain just don't work in the mountains and I was a real nuisance to the convoy my first night out. It wasn't long before I caught on and was driving the Hump as natural as breathing.

"All of our first convoys were carrying gasoline or heavy ammo to be used at an American airbase in Kunming. The trucks were always over-loaded. In the states we would have been court-martialed for the loads we were carrying as we drove the Ledo Road at night. This was at the time when the road was being rebuilt and added to. The work was done principally by black combat engineers. I take my hat off to those guys, talk about cliff-hangers, and in bulldozers, no less. They took the turns out of the road and made curves. They also widened it into a two-lane highway for about 75 percent of it's length. Those guys were there when we arrived and they were still there when the 518th left. To my knowledge none of them got furloughs, but their officers were rotated every eighteen months.

"During the monsoon the mud on the Ledo was worse than driving on ice. The road often was washed away in places or there would be a landslide. Those engineers would go to work in the torrential downpour and get the road back in use as quickly as possible. They had to work on the road in the day time, so kept their rifles at hand because of snipers. These men were not Boy Scouts; they built and fought at the same time and they got the job done.

"We drove twelve months a year, monsoon season and all. It was a real bitter pill when the Ledo and Burma roads were finally connected and the official opening took place. The black units had 'ass bad': there was one black driver in a convoy of fifty trucks that passed across this new juncture. Usually the ratio was just the opposite on the road.

"After eighteen months we were assigned a new commanding officer, Captain Sullivan. He was an old, and I mean *old*, army man. Our commander had been Lieutenant Fred Weedham. He drove the Road with us many times when he knew we were pooped. If he could do it, we could, and we did.

"Captain Sullivan's first words to us were that henceforth all dents, bumps, and other damage to our trucks would be deducted from our pay and we would be court-martialed if it were serious damage.

"Chosen by the men as spokesman for them I suggested to Sergeant Sterling, his 'boy,' and I mean 'boy,' that the captain ride the Road first before making this an irreversible order. The captain hedged but finally agreed. We gave that cracker a ride he'll never forget. When we reached the spot you start down-grading—now remember this is the highest mountain range in the world—we threw caution to the winds and hit into those curves just about five to ten miles faster than usual. Captain Sullivan, who was riding with me, turned as white as a sheet in spite of his beautiful suntan. Finally we reached our rest area. The good captain, try as he might, couldn't hold his hands still long enough to light a cigarette. He never said a word the whole time, but when we returned he canceled his order. I should add the captain never rode the Ledo Road again.

"We never had any trouble with the whites stationed around us. We had all purchased some kind of weapon since our carbines were kept under lock and key and the whites knew this so we sort of kept each other straight. That old-buddy stuff, which we knew was overseas b.s., just came naturally and we went along with the program for the duration. Actually we needed the weapons more stateside when we were at Camp Van Dorn where we walked guard duty with broom sticks and the crackers up the road had loaded carbines. You knew that Walter Winchell called Camp Van Dorn hell's half acre?

"The CBI area was famous for no furloughs, rest camps, or anything else along this line. The Red Cross notified me my father was critically ill and wished to see me. After days wasted on red tape I finally boarded a plane home. My father had been dead and buried a month when I got back."

Corporal Charles Pitman, of the 518th, was inducted in Decatur, Illinois, in 1944, and sent in a few weeks to Camp Lee, Virginia, for basic training, which was followed by a course in driving skills and technical training as a mechanic. Sent with a group of men to a camp near Philadelphia, he was pulled out of his unit after two months and was on his way to a POE in California.

Charles Pitman: "We boarded a train heading west. Between Pittsburgh and California we ran out of food. For two days we lived on fruit provided by the army, and then this ran out. At stops along the way we bought what we could and cooked it in the galley. Arriving at our destination at three in the morning, the hungry men headed for the mess hall—again nothing to eat. The next morning the commanding officer of the post explained that food had not been ready because we were not expected until two months later!

"We soon shipped out. Once aboard ship we learned our destination was the South Pacific. There were whites on board also; we had segregated sleeping facilities but could move freely about the ship. After thirty days on the water, we refueled at Melbourne, Australia. No shore leave was granted to anyone the twenty-four hours we were there. We proceeded to Bombay, India, where we disembarked.

"The East Indian troops we encountered under British command would have nothing to do with Negro soldiers. They looked upon us as outcasts. We learned later about their caste system and untouchables. The Indian people were cool to us at first but once they found we were not like the lies told about us they became friendly. You know we as a people are naturally gregarious and the Indian people were just naturally curious so it ended well.

"In a short time we were transported to Assam, which is near the foothills of the Himalayas. I was a replacement for the 518th Trucking Battalion. I arrived at my new home on Christmas Eve. There were five of us who were sent to one company as replacements and since we were new we were asked if we would like to make a run that night. Being new, and if you like stupid, we all accepted. I might add this particular run gave me my first battle star. I was hauling airplane bombs on my truck and thought it all very exciting. It was. I was trained for night driving so that didn't worry me.

"There were about fifty trucks in the convoy as we took off. Now there was not much I could see because we were using blackout light and my concentration was on the truck in front of me. I realized we were elevating by the shifting of gears I was doing in keeping with the guy ahead. What was really happening was we were climbing almost straight up for six miles. After our short run from the foothills and then this six mile climb we stopped to gas up; the pipeline running through India into Burma and China was finally connected and working. We than drove 125 miles through the mountains to the other side. Once on the other side there was a seven-mile downgrade. Now the idea is, don't wear out your brakes while descending because of the heavy load in your truck and if your brakes went you were in trouble. Once the trip came to an end the trucks were unloaded and we started our return trip. Without a load and having become somewhat accustomed to the driving I began to glance around me. When I reached the stretch of six miles of downgrading instead of climbing this time. The convoy stopped to gas up again as before for the final stretch and it was beginning to get light. Than I saw where I was. Like looking down there was nothing. I started thinking about the night before and all that time I didn't know there was nothing on my right side but space for a helluva a long distance down. I broke out in a cold sweat. I was a wee bit provoked at the older guys for sucking me into this run, but at the same time I have to admit that maybe ignorance was bliss. The deed was done when I was really aware of the kind of runs we had to make. After I got down on the ground again, cussed, cleaned my truck, got some sleep, it was time to go again; I went.

"If a truck were stalled and broke down on the road we never saw it again. There was a group that was supposed to pick up these trucks, but unless they were literally on the scene when the breakdown occurred the Chinese would come down from the hillsides, strip the truck, then push it over.

"In spite of the snipers that made it necessary to drive at night only, we carried no government-issued arms. All arms were taken from us and locked in the arms depot. The weapons we had were those we purchased from the Burmese and Chinese. These were small arms and knives.

"When the Chinese began to lose too many trucks during the monsoon season and we were covering over three hundred miles each night without losing any, they put in a new phase of operation—driving the trucks for the Chinese into China. We would leave the trucks there and fly back. I will tell you quite frankly I didn't like flying around the Himalayas. Once it looked like we were going to have to jump, I think my heart stopped beating for a minute. When the light came on that all was well, I started breathing again.

"Ah man, we had some real 'thrills' in the Himalayas. On my first trip into China, crossing from Burma into China, we had to drive on a rope bridge over the Salween River. My hair stood up on my neck when I learned that bridge was constructed of rope. Only one truck was allowed on it at once. Swaying back and forth between the mountains over a river that looked like a nightcrawler it was so far down, put a lot of doubts in your mind that this contraption was going to hold but it did. How the Chinese ever got that kind of bridge across that river in the first place was an engineering feat I haven't figured out yet. We had to drive very slowly and be ready for its bobbing and weaving. Need I say we were damn good truck drivers? We weren't called 'F and F' for nothing. It meant fighting and freighting; we delivered the goods wherever we were directed.

"Another outfit with us was the 45th Trucking Unit. They were a rugged outfit and we were often sidetracked to let them go through; they moved. Some of them might have been called reckless drivers and their trucks showed the wear and tear but they got the job done and perhaps a wee bit faster than anyone else.

"I was awarded five battle stars for the night-driving in sniper-infiltrated areas. Finally the Dare Devils, planes with flame throwers, wiped the sniper out. Because of my battle stars I was able to come home early once the war ended. I was stationed there one year, eight months, and twenty-one days.

"Everyone was anxious to get home and felt things would not be the same after the particular hell we had been through. It turned out that we were wrong. I will say the unbelievable poverty and the total lack of value put on a human being's life in the Far East would make anyone glad to return to this country. I don't believe Americans, particularly white ones, know how fortunate they are."

Private Clyde Blue was drafted in 1941 and, like Jeffries Bassett Jones, was assigned to the 518th Quartermasters (Truck) Battalion at Camp Van Dorn. His extended interview can serve as a conclusion to the chapter for its references to—or expression of—situations and attitudes encountered thus far, with a significant addition. Clyde Blue knew the Ledo stockade from the inside.

"I went into the army strictly as an interested observer," he said, as he began to talk. "My father had served with the Buffaloes, 92nd Division, World War I. I expected nothing and the army didn't disappoint me."

After being sent to Fort Custer with other draftees for the usual round of tests, Blue soon found himself on a train heading south.

Clyde Blue: "Everyone aboard was in good spirits, and we played guessing games as to where we were going. Our first stop was somewhere in Indiana, a small town. It was evident dining arrangements had been made in advance but it was apparent that we had the wrong paint jobs; the frost darn near gave us chilblains. Our revenge was to buy out the one liquor store in the town. At least his steady customers would have to wait until he restocked, we hoped.

"The next stop was Memphis, Tennessee, where we encountered our first open racial discrimination. We were shunted onto a siding in the Memphis train yard to prevent our going through the Memphis station. A white MP told us this little fact of life and said we were not allowed in the station. Memphis had a large colored section so we felt no further pangs of racial discrimination during our short stay.

"Upon reboarding the train we soon knew in what direction we were headed. Anybody with a smattering of geography knows if you stay on a straight line in the same direction, as we were, we were going dead south.

"On the train when we went to the dining car we ran into the color line again. A screen was placed around us shutting us off from the other people. One white army officer got up and protested; he attempted to remove the screen. While the steward explained the rules to him we told him to forget it. We didn't want him to get into trouble for a good deed, so he finally took our advice. As we ate I thought to myself we had run into a lot of firsts since had left Custer. It occurred to me there would be a lot more before it was all over.

"After dinner we got gloriously drunk. The train was backing down a single track when we came out of the alcoholic fog. There was nothing around us but mud and woods. When we climbed down at the end of the track there were white officers waiting to take us to Camp Van Dorn, which none of us had ever heard of. This was natural enough since it was near Centerville, Mississippi. Well, at least we knew where we were and if I tell you it made us feel any better I'd be telling a damn lie. All of us were northerners and Mississippi was synonymous with brutality to and the lynching of Negroes. But we were in the army so we followed our leaders.

"The camp was under construction and the grounds would qualify for a massive mud puddle. There were no streets that is, paved just uneven stretches of mud. I seriously doubt if a nature lover could have found much to redeem Camp Van Dorn. I'll bet that's one place they couldn't even give to the Indians.

"Our cadre of NCOs, I hate to say, were southern blacks who at best were semiliterate with the emphasis on *semi*; I'm assuming they could write their names but the English language was completely alien to them. The topkick was the only exception. All of our white officers were new boys; 90-day wonders, I suspected, with little experience, overburdened with their self-importance, and a fair share of stupidity.

"In my case they called me in to ask how I had such a high AGCT. They were convinced I cheated on the exam. As I said they were a bunch of boys; that a Negro could have a high IQ was inconceivable to them. Their insinuations about my cheating on the test did not disturb me one bit. I let them discuss the possibilities. Why should I bother, it's a waste of time talking to ignorant crackers. I did ask about OCS. They informed me 'perhaps later, but first they would have to train me there.' If I still wanted to go after this I could. I soon learned none of us were going anywhere, not even if we were Einstein.

"We did thirteen weeks of basic training. Passes were granted afterwards but I flopped on this because of improper shaving. It was just as well since the fortunate guys left at 5:00 P.M. and were back shortly after 6:00 P.M. Some were bruised and bandaged. It seems the town of Centerville had no appreciation of Negro GIs and the white MPs agreed.

"On my first furlough my buddies and I went to New Orleans. We did what soldiers do, get drunk and chase girls. We stayed over our time, naturally. After a few days we decided it was time to return to the devil's domicile. We entered the bus station and got in line to buy our tickets. A Negro janitor brushed the floor around us at least a dozen times mumbling something under his breath. When we got to the window we understood what he had been trying to tell us. 'Niggers' bought their tickets at another window, in the alley. Well, we got the tickets but when the bus came whites boarded first and when they finished there was no room for us. The driver, feeling kindly toward us, offered to let us ride in the baggage compartment. Can you just imagine any man in his right mind riding in that compartment locked in! We declined his generous offer without telling him where he could put the compartment and the whole state of Louisiana. Another bus arrived and we sat in the middle since it was practically empty; we were ordered to the rear. When the bus stopped for food and nature's call we could not enter the lunch room and were directed to the woods beyond to relieve ourselves. That did it, we were glad to get back to Van Dorn before we did something stupid under the circumstances. Oh, we were punished for being AWOL but after the bus station and the ensuing trip, walking up and down with a full field pack didn't seem so bad.

"The 'bad guys' or 'boys' if you prefer, meaning the white officers, tried to be clever, or else they thought everybody else a low-grade moron. Take guard duty as an example. Instead of laying it right on the line as part of the job they'd be cute. They'd make it sound like something special, something you couldn't do unless your shoes were shined just so, face shaved just so, uniform immaculate, weapon cleaned—that's a lie: our weapon for guard duty was a broom stick. The white soldiers down the road a piece had the real thing with live ammo. Anyhow they'd give you all of this bilge for the privilege of walking around outside in the dark, rain, and everything else. The clincher was anyone failing to measure up to the required standards would be denied this marvelous opportunity. I knew they were playing games. 'Patty' loves to play games with us to show what a brain he is and what jerks we are. I decided to play with them and I took them at their word. I muddied up my shoes a little more and didn't bother to shave. The inspecting team came in and denied me the chance to walk guard duty. After three or four nights of my sacking out while the others walked duty the 'boys' became suspicious; I was stuck on KP. Well by the time I had served less than a fourth of the men there was no more food. The mess sergeant blew a gasket. He took me to the colonel and told him he didn't care what he did with me but keep me out of his kitchen.

"The game gets more interesting. I obviously had not capitulated to their 'Negrology' meaning, knowing how to handle Negroes. They weren't about to do the sensible thing, like give a direct order; they had to demonstrate that they were smarter than me. You know my IQ actually worried them and it was passed on to new officers coming into the unit. They'd look at me like I was a freak and I'd look as innocent and stupid as possible wondering what their next move would be. I could tell when they planned something new that they were sure would tree the 'coon.' What they didn't realize was the 'man' had been trying to tree me from the day I was born and I wasn't about to be had by a bunch of 'boys' in army uniforms. I did not respect them and this in turn built no respect in me for the uniform.

"One bright day I was invited to the office to have a man-to-boy talk; who the boy was was strictly a matter of opinion. They came on with the concerned paternalistic approach. I was too smart to be wasting my time. I should earn some stripes; I quickly agreed. Well they had a job for me to help me achieve this goal. I thanked them from the bottom of my, well, I thanked them, and went forth wondering what the brainless wonders had contrived this time.

"I was sent to the captain's headquarters where I was told to shine his boots, make his bed, clean the room; in short I was to be his personal boy. I saw a pornographic book lying on a table and spied a half-empty bottle of bourbon. Between the book and the bourbon I had a ball. I fell asleep and was discovered; so ended a promising flunky's career. But so much for the 'bad guys' because they were always with me as you will see.

"We had hardly passed through the gates of Van Dorn when we learned there was a black PX and a white PX, the latter being out of bounds to us. This was also true of the shows. Entertainers came and entertainers went; I guess they didn't know we were there since we never saw them.

"We objected but on the whole our guys were regular fellows, they weren't 'causophiles.' They ran their mouths and let off a lot of steam but that was about as far as it went; causes just weren't their bag. Then too our white officers weren't receptive to our ideas, nor were our dum-dum NCOs. As I said the men talked a lot, which is usually par for the course in the army.

"The inspector-general was sent to Camp Van Dorn. He is supposed to learn what is wrong and correct it. Our hopes soared with his visit and when we had our chance to have our say we told all. He was most understanding and sympathetic to our problems, agreeing such things should not be happening. We were naive, that sucker had hardly cleared the gates when reprisals began to fall on those who had told it just like it was.

"I took this in stride, chiding myself for daring to hope. The inspector-general visited Van Dorn quite regularly and every time he was there a friend of mine, who was as outspoken as yours truly, got a truck detail with me which took us far enough away from camp that the gentleman was gone by the time we got back. One thing was sure, in spite of the inspector-general's regular visits, nothing changed.

"An alert came that we were going overseas. Many of us found we were not going to be given furloughs. When my New Orleans buddies and I were sure we were on the 'it' list we did, what I must confess was, a masterful job of writing out our own papers. Stamping them properly we were off for the 'Big D.' After a while the MPs were covering our hangouts in the old home town so we decided it was time to return.

"In Chicago we were stopped by white MPs, who suspected our papers. They looked us over and one of them asked, 'You are going back to Camp Van Dorn in Mississippi?' We told him we were. They let us go saying there was nothing they could do to us there that just being in Mississippi wouldn't do to us in spades.

"When we returned to camp our commanding officer was getting his kicks ticking off the charges he had ready to press against us. I most humbly reminded him that on page such-and-such of the Army Manual it states that no man shall be taken overseas without having had a furlough home. Now this curve ball threw him; he wanted desperately to check out a manual lying on his desk but he opted for looking contemplative. I had made it my business to learn the Army Manual by heart: page, chapter, and verse. As an uneasy silence descended upon the room the word came in the 364th Infantry Regiment was arriving. Our commander hastily dismissed us under the pretext of having to make preparations to meet the new unit about to enter his domain. I could not help but smile to myself as I wondered if our commander knew the 364th had all black enlisted men and NCOs and a fair share of black officers. If he didn't, *that* should finish ruining his day. Anyway we were off the hook.

"The 518th was very impressed when the 364th marched and rode through the gates of Van Dorn. They had mounted guns, artillery, the works. Their men carried their carbines. The only time we had ours in our hands was on the firing range. Afterwards we had to turn them in with all ammunition. The real thrill for us was when we saw our first black officers; they were mostly lieutenants, but they were officers. With the coming of the 364th a whole new ballgame began.

"When the 364th learned about the separate and unequal accommodations at Camp Van Dorn they acted at once. They confronted one of the white shows joined by men of the 518th. I guess the whites were thunderstruck, for they let us in. Half-way through the show the lights came on and we were ordered to leave.

"The next day the 364th invaded the off-limits PX. They were served because most of the guys working there were black and they were more frightened of their own than they were of the whites.

"Some of the white soldiers were in agreement with the black soldiers but the majority followed the lead of the white superstructure in their non-mixing of the races. (The way they acted you would have thought it was a division of white WACs.) The post commander sent the white commander of the 364th a letter saying he expected him to see that his boys obeyed the ground rules. The commander of the 364th presented himself to the post commander and told him his *men* were American soldiers with all of the rights implied by the word; he was with his men.

"The 364th hadn't really gotten settled at Van Dorn when one of their men was killed by a deputy sheriff near the gate of the camp. The result was small fights that grew into big fights that mushroomed into a full-scale riot.

"I had seen white hatred many times; the black wears many masks which conceal his true feelings, but that night at Van Dorn the black mask was dropped and I saw stark black hatred. Guys of the 518th got into the fighting. I saw two or three black soldiers jump one white and give him a brutal beating. I am neither condemning or condoning, since many thousands of blacks have been in the same situation as that white soldier with white antagonists, I am only stating how I felt. I guess when something like a riot gets started all reason departs and the worst comes out in men. Then too, I believe some of the southern blacks who had never had the chance to swing on a white were making up for lost time; they were getting rid of generations of hostility.

"The next day the provost-marshal ordered the white infantry at Van Dorn to place the 364th under arrest. Both units, white and black, met in the drill field in skirmish lines facing each other. Both units were armed. Both white colonels told their men to load and lock. (If you want to know where the 518th was, we were on the sidelines watching. There had been no order to arrest us. The 364th had already had trouble in Arizona. Don't misunderstand me, what I am trying to say is the men of the 518th were playboys, comparatively speaking. The men of the 364th had become soldiers under black officers they respected and they didn't play games. We were on the sidelines where game-players belong.)

"At the command 'Arrest these men,' the white unit did not unlock. Their colonel relayed the message to the provost-marshal that his men refused to fire on the 364th. To sum it up, white enlisted personnel showed more understanding than all of the 'big brains' on that huge post; it could have been a bloody mess. Moreover the first stray bullet that had hit the 518th would have given them no out but to join in what would have been outright warfare; even game-players fight when the alternative is death.

"For their understanding, the white unit was shipped overseas,

half-trained, to a battle area. I am happy to report they distinguished themselves in action. The 364th was shipped to the Aleutian Islands to literally sit
out the war; a real gung-ho group with esprit de corps to spare were junked.
Now many deny this was punitive action on the part of the 'boys upstairs.'
What would you call it?

"The 518th was not forgotten as 'rewards' were being passed out.
We were alerted for overseas duty again. To show you the efficiency of the
army, we were sent to an eastern POE and our equipment was sent west; it
never caught up with us. We ended up in Africa with winter coats, no less.

"At Camp Patrick Henry, our POE, they put us through a combat
course. If you refused to take the training you could not go overseas; I refused.
They put it on my record, but guess who was on that Liberty ship when it
pulled out to sea! Speaking of Patrick Henry, don't ask me how, but a goodly
portion of our NCOs and officers copped out. They had it rigged somehow and
we went overseas with practically all new men in their places.

"Our transport was in a large convoy; the naval escort was most
impressive. I immediately secured three life preservers. No one bothered to tell
me they would all become water-logged at the same time, nor that at the
present water temperature a man's survival limit was eight hours.

"One morning a freighter made an incorrect turn and ran into us.
Our ship's captain had the cargo shifted so we tilted quite a bit to keep the
gash in our side out of the water. After this we were more or less on our own,
since we could not keep up with the convoy. The kitchen section of our ship
had been destroyed in the collision so our meals were cooked by steam in the
boiler room; diarrhea was the direct result. To add to our little comedy the
toilets were on the side tilted out of the water so you can imagine what was
happening.

"We limped into Gibraltar. While they were repairing the ship, the
518th was given shore leave. We hit the liquor stores, and that night they
rounded us up and put us aboard our ship. The captain was given sailing orders
than and there, and we left during an air raid. Somehow I think the British
didn't appreciate us. The next day we arrived at Oran, North Africa. We were
taken to some isolated place and told to pitch tents. K rations were dumped,
and those spit-and-polish officers of ours departed quickly. It's not talked
about generally, but in every unit there is a whiskey man and a woman man,
meaning wherever they land they can locate these little incidentals in a short
period of time, even on a desert island.

"Our 'where-the-action-is men' had located a little town called
Fleurus. The tents were pitched, our officers had cut out, so what else was
there to do but go to Fleurus? We were balling back when our captain returned
the following morning to find the tents empty. To reach Fleurus by vehicle
necessitated winding around a hill to its bottom. The captain drove a truck
down to the town and started gathering up the men. It was sometime before he

realized as he deposited the guys back at the camp they simply walked up over the hill and down to Fleurus. I guess he had delivered about twenty or thirty of the same guys back at the camp before all blacks stopped looking alike to him; he was furious. His revenge was to take four of the fellows who had been court-martialed aboard ship for being AWOL in the states and try to get them incarcerated in the African Disciplinary Barracks. Much to his chagrin the commandant there would not take them on such a frivolous charge. He said his stockade contained only murderers and rapists.

"We finally found our way to Oran from our little outpost. Having no assigment, Oran was just for us, a military city—soldiers and sailors everywhere. The port battalions and quartermaster units stationed there turned thumbs down on us after we discovered the thriving black market going on and cut ourselves in on some of the goodies. More than half of everything going into those North African ports never got any farther, as far as the war was concerned. It's a fact of life in the army.* In three months the 518th had succeeded in wearing out its welcome in this port city.

"Just before we took our requested embarkation from Oran my captain, ever hopeful of getting rid of me, had filled a request for infantry replacements at a nearby Repple Depple with a quota of one, me. I was there but a few days when I had to have surgery for hemorrhoids. In five days I was up and around again; however the infantry had no use for me now so I was returned to my old group. When my ever-lovin' captain saw me, the look of frustration, dismay, and rage was interesting. I think he was tempted to either cry or shoot me. You see we had never stopped playing games, even with the change in officers at the POE. The captain alas, thought he had won the game but fate had intervened and there I stood, a real eager beaver.

"On board ship, headed for a new destination, my surgery caught up with me. The ship was British and I made haste to see the ship's doctor. He gave me a gallon of mineral oil to take regularly. This confined me to the latrine area. I was ordered to report on deck and I didn't, rather I couldn't due to unavoidable circumstances. For this I was court-martialed, charged with refusing to obey an order in a combat zone. Being up on the Army Manual I knew this was a capital offense they were hanging on me. I went to the doctor and asked him if he would appear at my hearing and he said yes.

"My trial board was what is called a stacked deck: two colonels, two lieutenant colonels, and a captain. There were no junior officers who might be

---

*Corporal Warren Harris of a quartermaster unit stationed in France, had this to say when interviewed: "Any guy in the quartermasters knows when there is wholesale stealing some of the officers in the unit are in on the take, too. A white railhead unit just got carried away with profiteering. They weren't satisfied stealing the merchandise in the boxcars, they started stealing the whole boxcar. Finally, they took a whole damn train, engine and all. It's kind of hard to explain the disappearance of a whole train. The whole damn unit was court-martialed, from top to bottom."

a little sympathetic. Were they surprised and angry when the doctor testified in my behalf. The case was dismissed. I was isolated in that I could not participate in any activities and was to be ignored. This went on until a torpedo bomber gave us a rough time just before we entered the Suez Canal. 'All God's children' got the hell scared out of them, officers included, and as they say, families that pray together stay together so all was forgiven, for the moment anyway.

"During my period of isolation I had done a lot of thinking. My officers had tried to make this 'smart nigger' conform, in other words to break me. I knew the game and I played it instinctively, but I had forgotten that this was not the game as played in my hometown of Detroit. This was the army and my opponents were white southerners protected by a uniform. Aboard ship they had tried to hang a capital offense on me. It hit me all at once that if they couldn't break me they would settle for my life. So I viewed my acceptance back into the family—under the threat of being sent to the bottom of the Mediterranean—with a jaundiced eye.

"When we were passing through the Suez Canal we first ran into drugs. Viet Nam isn't the first place American soldiers encountered pot.

"In the canal there are places dug out so one ship can pull aside to allow another to pass. Little native boats are out in the canal all the time and when a ship pulls over they come right along side your ship and peddle their wares. They must have been selling drugs because we were all potted pretty soon. I am referring to the smoking kind only, the thing we use to call a reefer. The whites over there stayed loaded, scotch, gin, and rum; half of that red color is not suntan. The poor natives can't afford liquid intoxicants so they get high on their native grass, which grows wild. They use it and they sell it. I should say it is not the cut junk you buy in the states; it is pure. When we left the ship no problems, no hangovers, no addicts.

"We finally came to Bombay, India, where we spent three days. It was necessary to round us up and put us on the train as usual. However in those three days old Asia had caught up with us. All of that luscious fruit we had enjoyed biting through the shiny skin to get to the meat had turned on us in all forms of dysentry. No one had told us to peel the fruit before enjoying the succulent inside. Our 'brilliant' officers were as ignorant of this fact as we were so every man jack of us ended us sick as one can get without dying. There was a German doctor with us who thought asprin cured everything from the measles to snakebite; he was one big mistake. You would have thought the train was hauling cadavers excepting for an occasional moan. The lucky few who hadn't bit the dust soon joined the rest of us as they happily bought fruit at the various stops still unaware of the cause of our ailment.

"You have asked several times what we were doing in the war effort. I am telling you, absolutely nothing! The 518th, at least the five or six companies of the 518th that were on this bummer were, well I honestly don't know what you would actually call us. We had been sent out from Camp Van

Dorn to get rid of us; the fruits of Asia almost did the trick! In a very short time we realized no plans had been made for us anywhere. The guys then went their way until they caused enough trouble and were moved on.

"There was no reason why the 518th shouldn't have been as good a quartermasters group as any other, but it was doomed from the start. It was a conglomeration of misfits; demoralized officers as well as demoralized men. Our officers were rejects. When an officer can't cut it any place else they send him to the quartermasters. It takes little or no talent to be an officer in the quartermasters. My personal opinion is every officer we had was totally lacking in those qualifications necessary for leadership, which is what an officer is all about.

"From the train our remains managed to climb aboard barges that were towed by boat; we reached Ledo, Assam, in this manner. We knew we were in a combat area because we could hear guns in the distance. Here they had to accept us because there was no beyond.

"We were attached to the 25th Quartermasters and given four-man tents as temporary quarters. All of the men, except me, were given trucks and assigned to the inner supply route. On the first haul they found the black market in full swing with one difference—the middleman was Chinese.

"I was given no driving to do until the group was to take its first trip to Hell's Gate, up in the Himalayas. I saw them mounting weapons on our trucks. Knowing they anticipated trouble and not having driven a truck in months, I absented myself from the scene. I was threatened with a court-martial. This time the Japanese came to the rescue. Somewhere they had broken through, and technically we were surrounded. My court-martial was forgotten like yesterday.

"We went on emergency and evacuated the hospital to the airstrip. Than we were told we were to be the rear guard. When we asked how we were to get out the reply was, 'Fight your way out.' Fortunately the situation improved I am glad to say, since the 518th had fired .50 caliber machine guns twice at Camp Van Dorn. Our familiarity with carbines left a lot to be desired; we were more familiar with broom sticks than rifles.

"Things got back to normal and we, including me, on occasion, were put to driving the Hump. Even on this road the supplies never reached their destination 100 percent intact. Not allowing me to drive was considered punishment. Have you ever seen the Himalayas? A whole lot of guys would have liked to have been on punishment.

"In the CBI area they played on the fellows' chauvinist instincts like Van Cliburn plays the piano; duty, the Almighty, country, they didn't miss a note and always fortissimo. To me it was nauseating hypocrisy when all I had to do was look around and see the comparative luxury we lived in compared to the men up front. The most lucrative black market in the world was operating right under our noses. Everybody was involved. Thirty-thousand and home was the slogan of a large number of the nurses and Red Cross workers. It was not, I later learned from other GIs, confined to the CBI area alone. These ladies sold their wares, regardless of color, at certain rates and when they had socked away the desired amount they got pregnant and were returned to the states. Everybody had an angle.

"Nothing I ever saw in the CBI area made me feel patriotic. Oh I *saw* patriotism there; I also saw the price it exacted. Merrill's Marauders* came through Assam. This unit had been declared medically unfit for further action but somehow the military 'wheels' got them committed to one more mission; to take an enemy airfield 250 miles inside Burma.

"The men of this unit I will never forget. Their camouflage clothing was torn and dirty; their boots worn. With all of the loot stashed around our area these men were not even offered new clothing or boots. Yet many, many members of the quartermasters alone could change clothes, skin out, top to bottom, five or six times a day if they chose and still have plenty of extras.

"Around the eyes, all of Merrill's men looked alike no matter what their coloring; they had the eyes of dead men. A smart MP grabbed one of them when they first arrived. The marauder just looked at him and the MP loosened his grip like he had grabbed the heated end of a soldering iron. I suspect he realized he had come about as close to death as possible without dying. These men had become professionals in the art of killing, working behind enemy lines. They had been at it too long, killing and being killed. They had seen too much violent death, and in turn had become messengers of death. An overzealous, immaculate officer snapped one of them up for not saluting. For his trouble he got a contemptuous visual sweep from toe to head and was brushed aside like so much dirt! Talk about a red-faced major!

"These guerilla fighters took up with blacks in the area. I guess there was a natural empathy; we were at the bottom of the barrel and they had finally reached it. They couldn't stand the griping of the white soldiers about trivials such as the food, pay and their duties. The brief time they were in Assam they spent with us. They seemed to want to talk, to have someone listen to what had happened to them before they choked on it.

"The take-off point for the Marauders to their objective was something like forty miles up the Road. Trucks were up and down this road regularly, but do you know no trucks were designated for them. They walked the distance. I have never figured out why. These men, medically unfit, going

---

*A contingent of American troops commanded by Brigadier General Frank D. Merrill. They left Ledo in February 1944 and marched into the Burmese jungle to outflank occupying Japanese troops. In May 1944 they captured the airfield at the north Burmese city of Mitkyina and, assisted by Chinese partisans, continued fighting until they captured the town of Mitkyina itself in August 1944. The taking of that town permitted the extension of the Ledo Road (later called the Stilwell Road) to a junction with the old Burma Road. (See above, interview with Jeffries Bassett Jones, on the link-up.)

to do a tough job that only they could possibly do successfully had to walk to their take-off point. That is the army.

"When the remnants of Merrill's Marauders returned to the states there was no ticker tape parade for them down Fifth Avenue. There were no headlines. They had to have been fired with patriotism to do the kind of work they did; they had become killers for 'God and Country.' Who cared when they left Assam with the exception of the blacks they buddied with? The others were afraid of them and were relieved to see them go to whatever fate awaited them. I also think their presence pricked whatever little conscience the fearful ones had left.

"I should add that discrimination was just beginning to sneak into our area when Merrill and his men came to Assam. They broke up this foolishness fast, for wherever they went they took their black comrades and nobody bothered or questioned them. To have tried to force for-white-only on us after the Marauders left, was just too ridiculous to contemplate, so that ended that.

"Allow me to give credit where it is due—the CBI war in *my* area was one big, lousy joke. At night when the sun went down the fighting stopped. The funniest thing was at night on occasion a Japanese soldier would sneak down to our outdoor movie and watch the show. The only way we knew was if Chinese happened to see him. The biggest *fist* fight you ever saw would be the result until the Japanese broke for the bush; nobody ever went after him. If what I've read about war in books or seen in the movies is war, then either they are lying or they certainly weren't having a real war in my area.

"My captain was displeased with my behavior one day and to make sure that I did not escape the prescribed punishment he saw to it himself. He drove me in his jeep about forty or fifty miles up the Road, and smiling happily as I stepped down, he told me to get back the best I could. This actually meant I was to walk back. He hadn't been gone five minutes when a truck came along and I stuck up my thumb. Hopping aboard, I passed my gloating captain in about twenty minutes. I am sure he could visualize the blisters I would have on my feet when I finally hobbled into the camp. I was seated on a make-shift chair in front of his headquarters set-up when he pulled up. When the captain saw me, it was the first time I had ever known him to be speechless, that is for about thirty seconds, and then he blew like a surfacing whale. He talked about me in every way possible within the confines of the Army Manual; I don't think he quite trusted me so kept that little book of rules in mind.

"Eventually he ran out of words and ordered me to accompany him to the colonel's quarters, which I did. Once there he explained in detail my behavior and the punishment he had determined upon. The colonel finally got around to asking me about the situation and I agreed with the captain up to the point of my stepping out of the captain's jeep. I said, 'Sir, he specifically told me to get back the best way I could, and I did just as he directed.' The colonel asked the captain if this is what he had said. Sputtering, red-faced, dog-mad he admitted those were his exact words. The colonel tried hard not to laugh as he said, 'Under the circumstances I think he showed excellent judgment, for I certainly would have done the same thing.' I was home free once more, thanks to the stupidity of a petty captain. If he had sent me up the road with MPs, the usual procedure, they would have put me out and said, 'Walk back, buddy.' I would have had no alternative but to obey.

"I finally was court-martialed for disobeying an order. I was sent to the Ledo Stockade for six months hard labor and docked half my pay for the same period of time. The stockade was a barbed wire enclosure with watch-towers at each corner. The men lived in tents which appeared to be a block long. They slept on cots practically touching each other and were allowed one blanket though it got quite cold there at night. The captain in charge had been a big cheese in a Georgia chain-gang penal system. He had a ball practicing his trade, sadistic brutality.

"The day I entered the gates of Ledo stockade I was greeted by a white guard who started a tirade of obscenities each of which was modified by the adjective 'black.' I watched his performance and said nothing. Angered by my silence he said, 'Oh one of those smart niggers!' I thought of my IQ problem which had pursued me half way across the world and I answered softly, 'Everybody's gotta die some day, sometime, somewhere; this place is as good as any.' Play day was over as I saw it. If they thought they were going to play physical games with me they were dead wrong; I'd be hanged first. The guard was ignorant, illiterate, stupid, and sadistic but he understood exactly what I meant, any rough stuff from anybody and I'd make it my personal business to kill him come hell, heaven, or a tidal wave. There were no more words exchanged and I didn't have any trouble and I wasn't the exception. I found the captain and his crummy crew were selective; they knew the weak men instinctively and preyed upon them. Oddly enough a goodly number of these were the rough and tough football-player types. The quiet puny types were more likely to be omitted from severe punishment, or any punishment for that matter.

"Everybody was supposed to do some kind of work and if none was assigned to you, you had better find some. They had various kinds of punish-ment. One of the milder ones was having a group of men walk around in a circle until their feet had made an ankle deep rut; then they would start a new circle. This would go on from dawn until dark. One of the tougher deals was the sweat box. It was two feet wide, four feet long, with cement sides and a metal corrugated roof. There were no windows; the door had a slot through which they pushed your slop to eat and water when they felt like it. Your toilet a tin can was also passed through the slot in the door. They had a habit of leaving it inside with the occupant for long periods of time; you can imagine how sickening this could be. Blacks who spent time in there came out ashy white and whites came out a peculiar blue-white. The real punishment of the sweat box was a man could not lie down, stand up, or sit down, he had to stay in a bent position of some kind depending on his height. Few men were able to walk out of this contraption. The guards dragged them out. The punishment system always stayed within, just within, the limits of killing a man but they damn sure broke many of the men in their charge.

"All of the guards were white but one black, tomming sonofabitch. Punishment usually was the result of their getting one man to inform on another; I never got on the punishment list.

"I only served a little more than two months of my time. Why I don't know and I didn't bother to ask. The war ended soon after I returned to my company. I had enough points to get out but decided I'd stay on and return with the whole group. However one of our trucks, including the driver, went over a cliff; then a plane crashed, loaded with drivers returning to base. I concluded the groups' luck and had run out so quit observing and headed for the states.

"Ledo Stockade back in the woods? No indeed, it ran along the main highway. They wanted the soldiers on the outside to see what went on; it was a veiled threat. To my knowledge nobody every protested against what went on there though the guys' screams most certainly could be heard at times.

"I arrived home after having spent four years observing the 'man' at work, or play, as I saw it. He still plays games with the whole damn world crashing down around his head. One day he will be incredulous. How did it happen, or what did I do to offend God? Oh yes, I haven't the slightest doubt that he'll turn to the very God he mocks every day of his life when his turn comes. Nobody lives forever; no civilized barbarian's society has lasted forever.

"Young blacks today do not play games with the 'man.' They are not subtle but demand a confrontation. His only answer to them has been brute force, which exposes his limited mentality."

14. Cadet Graduation Class of '44, left to right. Back row: ——
Calhoon†, Gordon Rapier, James Hall, Rixie McCarroll,
—— Merton, Sam Rayner, R. C. Brown, Walter H. Brown, ——
Ayles; Middle row: Peter Whittaker, Chas. L. White, —— Mar-
shall, John Porter, H. H. Haywood, Chas. Williams, Roosevelt
Stiegert†, —— Young†, Wm. Brewer. Front row: —— Nightin-
gale, unidentified, Chas. Wilson, Vincent Dean, —— Rohlsan,
Wm. Wheeler, Al. Hutchins, W. S. Price. *Official Army Signal
Corps photo.*
† died in action or in crash overseas.

15. Pilots in the Class of '43F. Of the twenty-four men in the photograph, only six can be identified. Back row: 6th from left, Robert M. Alexander; Middle row: 2nd from left, T. D. Moore; 3rd from left, Jimmie _____, 4th from left, Bill Williams; Front row: 3rd from left, Wilson Lacey; fifth from left, Chas. McGee. *Official Army Signal Corps photo.*

16. Fighter pilots of the 332nd. Standing, left to right: Hicks, Clifton, Moody. Seated at the controls of the P-40: Williams. *Official USAAF photo, AAF Training Command.*

17. Captain Wendell Pruitt, DFC, fighter pilot who downed three German planes (note swastikas on fuselage) and helped to sink a destroyer.

18. General Strothers pins the DFC on Captain
Campbell, 99th; Lt. Gray, 99th; and Captain
Heywood, 302nd Fighter Squadron.

19. Captain Joseph Elsberry, DFC, fighter pilot
of the 332nd, credited with three kills in one
day. He led the group that scored a direct hit on
a destroyer and sank it in the Adriatic Sea.

20. Major George S. ("Spanky") Roberts (center), with Captain Baugh (left) and Captain Lawrence of the 332nd Fighter Group.

21. Major "Spanky" Roberts, photographed overseas with Col. B. O. Davis, Jr. (center) and Major Edward Gleed, DFC (right), and two unidentified visitors. Gleed led a 332nd escort mission in the bombing of Berlin, with the 15th Air Force. On leave from the 332nd, Gleed was a test pilot in North Africa.

22. Captain Joe Christmas, the "black-white" classmate of Major Robert Pitts at OCS in Miami. (See chapter 4.)

23. Lieutenant Robert W. Diez, of the 99th Fighter Squadron, saw action over Anzio in 1943 and was one of a group credited with 5 kills, 27 January 1944.

24. Captain Mac Ross of Dayton, Ohio, killed in an overseas crash, was one of the first pilots to graduate from Tuskegee.

25. Colonel Howard Donovan Queen, commanding officer of the 366th Infantry Regiment in World War II. *U.S. Army Signal Corps photo, 1944.*

26. Members of the World War II officer corps of the 366th Infantry
Regiment, photographed on Capitol Hill with one of their members
who became a senator. From left to right: Colonel Hillard, Colonel J. J.
Martin (ret.), Senator Edward Brooke of Massachusetts, Colonel Queen
(ret.), and Major General F. Davison. *Photo courtesy Republican Policy
Committee, U.S. Senate.*

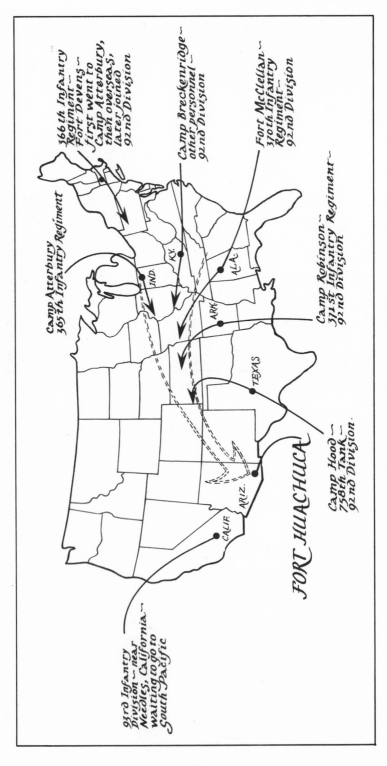

366th Infantry
Regiment~
Fort Devens~
First went to
Camp Atterbury,
then overseas,
later joined
92nd Division

Camp Breckenridge~
other personnel
92nd Division

Fort McClellan~
370th Infantry
Regiment~
92nd Division

Camp Atterbury
365th Infantry Regiment

Camp Robinson~
311st Infantry Regiment~
92nd Division

Camp Hood~
758th Tank~
92nd Division.

FORT HUACHUCA

93rd Infantry
Division ~ near
Needles, California~
waiting to go to
South Pacific

IND.

KY.

ALA.

ARK.

TEXAS

ARIZ.

CALIF.

1. Scattered training camps for elements of the 92nd Infantry Division
   preceding 1943 transfer to Fort Huachuca, Arizona.

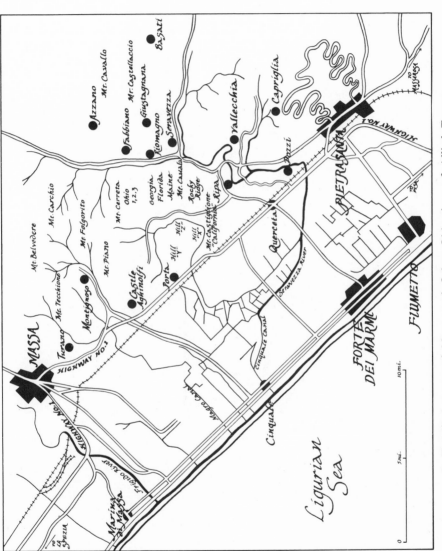

2. Fortified town of Massa and Other Objectives of Allied Troops before and after Cinquale Canal Crossing, February 5–8, 1945.

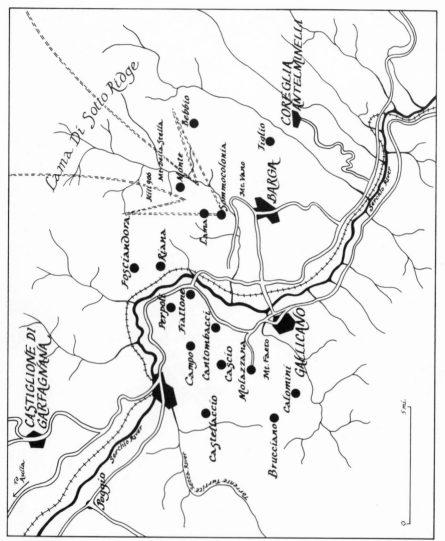

3. Serchio Valley Sector, Italy, Fall–Winter, 1944–45.

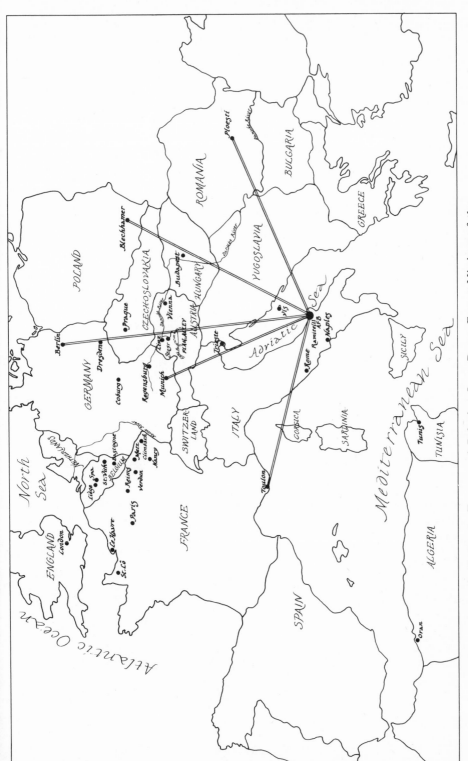

4. Towns in France and Belguim; Long-Range Escort Missions of the 332nd Fighter Group.

Chapter **3**

"Seek, Strike and Destroy":
Men in the Armored Forces

Most of the men whom the reader will meet in this chapter were members of two highly successful combat units, the 761st Tank Battalion and the 614th Tank Destroyer Battalion. Both served at various times with General Patton's 3rd Army, and references to the general appear frequently in the interviews. These two battalions have a similar history in their seldom being committed to combat as whole units, but rather as companies, platoons or even smaller groups in support of infantry divisions. In reading an interview with a member of either of these armored units, the reader should keep in mind the size of the group he was involved with. (See Appendix, Table of Organization of an Infantry Division.)

Included in this chapter also are interviews with members of the 578th and 969th Field Artillery battalions, fighting in the same areas at the same time as the tankers and tank destroyers in the late fall of 1944 when Patton was advancing toward the Siegfried Line and in December when an all-out effort was made to push back the German offensive in the Ardennes and to relieve the besieged city of Bastogne (the Battle of the Bulge).

Also included is an interview with a driver of the Red Ball Express, which kept Patton's army supplied in its drive to the east.

The 761st Tank Battalion

The 761st Tank Battalion was activated in 1942 at Camp Claiborne, Louisiana, and received intensive training at Camp Hood, Texas. Landing at Omaha Beach, Normandy, 10 October 1944, and committed to battle by the end of the first week of November, it was the first Negro armored unit to see action. In the first engagement, units of the 761st were attached to the 26th Division for an attack on a group of small towns south of Liège, where there were pockets of German resistance still to be cleared as Patton made his way to the Siegfried Line.

The performance of the 761st Tank Battalion at Morville-les-Vic, Dieuze, and Guebling in November 1944 won them special commendation from the commander of the 26th Division, General Willard C. Paul, who cited their "great bravery under the most adverse weather and terrain conditions."

Staff Sergeant Ruben Rivers of Company A won the Silver Star for gallantry in action, 7 November 1944, near Vic-sur-Seille:

> During the daylight attack on *** Staff Sergeant Rivers, a tank platoon sergeant, was in the leading tank when a road block was encountered which held up the advance. With utter disregard for his personal safety, Staff Sergeant Rivers courageously dismounted from his tank in the face of directed enemy small arms fire, attached a cable to the road block and had it moved off the road thus permitting the combat team to proceed. His prompt action prevented a serious delay in this offensive operation and was instrumental in the successful assault and capture of the town. . . . *[General Order 47, 26th Infantry Division, 2 December 1944]*

Less than two weeks after the event, Rivers was killed in action, and the award sent to his family in Oklahoma.

Sergeant Warren Crecy of the 761st also won the Silver Star for gallantry in action, 10 and 11 November:

> During offensive operations near *** and *** Sergeant Crecy, a tank commander, lost his tank when it was knocked out by enemy antitank fire. He immediately dismounted, took command of another vehicle which carried only a .30 caliber machine gun and wiped out the enemy antitank gun and crew. On the next day of the offensive when his tank was bogged down in the mud, he fearlessly faced enemy antitank, artillery and machine gun fire by dismounting and attempting to extricate the vehicle from the mud. In the course of his work, he saw the advancing infantry units crossing open terrain under enemy machine gun fire and unhesitatingly manned the tank's antiaircraft gun from an exposed position, neutralized the enemy machine guns by direct fire, thereby aiding the infantry in its advance. Later in the day he again exposed himself by mounting his tank turret and destroying enemy machine gun nests by direct fire and aided in silencing one enemy antitank gun. . . . *[General Order 47, 26th Infantry Division, 2 December 1944]*

For 183 days, the history of the 761st was one of continuous commitment. When the 26th was relieved for a rest in December, the 761st was attached to the 87th Division, crossing the German border on 14 December, only to lose most of their tanks from enemy action and mechanical failure. Throughout January they engaged in successful actions in Belgium and Luxembourg.

Early in February, they were attached to the 95th Division, XVI Corps, awaiting the 9th Army drive to the Rhine. Switched to the 79th Division in the Rhine offensive, they crossed into Germany 3 March after cutting the Roermond-Julich Railway at Malich. At Schwannenberg their *assignment was to mop up pockets of resistance bypassed by the 2nd Armored Division.*

> *Not much more than a week later the 761st was attached to the 103rd Division, and 20 March a platoon of C Company, supporting the 411th Infantry Regiment attacked Nieder Schlettenbach, neturalizing 13 pill boxes, 12 machine gun positions, capturing one antitank gun intact, and killing 30 of the enemy. Another platoon of C Company in support of the 409th Infantry Regiment before Riesdorf, a key to the Siegfried Line, reduced 6 pill boxes, killed eight of the enemy, and took 40 prisoners.*

> *Light tanks of the 761st, with the Reconnaissance Platoon of the 614th Tank Destroyer Battalion, spearheaded the advance of Task Force Rhine, 22 March, into enemy territory beyond Riesdorf. When the task force had advanced 14 kilometers through enemy territory it had destroyed 150 vehicles, 31 pill boxes, 49 machine gun nests, 29 antitank and 44 self-propelled guns, killed 170 of the enemy, and taken 1200 prisoners.*

> *On 28 March 1945, the 761st was attached to the 71st Division, 3rd Army. During the following weeks they frequently spearheaded the advance of the 71st to the Danube. Tanks of the 761st entered Steyr, Austria, on 5 May; the following day they met the forces of the USSR at the Enns River.**

> *The first interview is with Captain John D. Long, Commander, B Company, 761st Tank Battalion. Long exemplifies the soldier who rose from the ranks to become a professionally expert officer. A gourmet and excellent cook, he was a cook at Fort Knox, Kentucky, when he was accepted for OCS. He and Ivan Harrison (interview below) became the first two black 1st lieutenants in the United States Tank Corps. During the interview, Long asked to see Lee's account of the 761st; his comments on recorded events in which he actually participated make part of the interview.*

> *In the first battle described, Company B was attached to the 26th Infantry Division. Their assignment was to take the town of Morville-les-Vic. (See Lee, pp. 662—63, for his version of the events.)*

John Long: "Not for God and country but for me and my people. This was my motivation pure and simple when I entered the army. I swore to myself there would never be a headline saying my men and I chickened. A soldier, in time of war, is supposed to accept the idea of dying. That's what he's there for; live with it and forget it. I expected to get killed, but whatever happened I was determined to die an officer and a gentleman.

"I was and am proud of my tankers. They were as good or better than most of the tankers in the whole European Theater. There wasn't a white

---

*This capsule battle history of the 761st Tank Battalion depends upon Lee, pp. 660–67, and Trezzvant W. Anderson, *Come Out Fighting: The Epic Tale of the 761st Tank Battalion, 1942–1945*, for statistics, names of units, routes, locations, and dates.

outfit that wasn't damned glad to have us after our first engagement at Morville-les-Vic; we were fighting sons-of-bitches and our reputation came before us. We were supposed to spearhead and give cover to the infantry and we did our job well.

"Upon our arrival in France we were addressed by General Patton, commander of the 3rd Army to which we were attached. He told us, 'Men, you are the first Negro tankers ever to fight in the American army. I would never have asked for you if you were not good. I have nothing but the best in my army. I don't care what color you are as long as you go up there and kill those Kraut sons-of-bitches. Everyone has their eyes on you and are expecting great things from you. Most of all your race is looking forward to your success. Don't let them down, and, damn you, don't let me down!

'If you want me you can always find me in the lead tank.

'They say it is patriotic to die for your country, well let's see how many patriots we can make out of those German motherfuckers.'

"The 761st, consisting of headquarters company, a service company, companies A, B, C, and D, was a detached and self-sustained unit up for grabs by anyone who needed it in the 3rd Army. As a result of our fighting ability we spearheaded a number of Patton's many-pronged thrusts deep into enemy territory. It was the 761st who forced a hole in the Siegfried Line through which Patton's 4th Armored Division poured into Germany.

"Our motto was 'Come out fighting.' We fought in France, Belgium, Holland, Luxembourg, Germany, and were the first Americans to meet the oncoming Russian troops at the River Stey in Austria.

"Ulysses Lee's version of the 761st at Morville-les-Vic, in his book on Negro troops in World War II, is part truth and the rest of it is a goddamn lie. I don't know where his butt was during the war or what archives he got his information out of, but I was there. The victory of Morville-les-Vic belongs to the enlisted men and the junior officers of the 761st; they just happen to be black. The two white senior officers of our unit he credits with Morville-les-Vic didn't have a goddamn thing to do with our victory.

"Lieutenant Colonel Bates, our commanding officer, credited by Lee with the taking of Morville-les-Vic, which was our initiation into combat, was shot in the ass the night before and had to be evacuated. They never found out whether or not he was accidentally shot by an American soldier or hit by sniper fire. The next man in command, Major Wingo, the morning of the attack, turned his tank around and went hell-bent in the opposite direction. He just plain chickened and that s.o.b. was evacuated for combat fatigue. Hell, we hadn't even been in battle yet.

"There were six white officers in our outfit. Only two were worth a good damn, Captain David Williams and Colonel George, who was sent to replace Bates *after* Morville-les-Vic. These two were real professionals; the rest weren't worth shit!

"The town of Morville-les-Vic was supposed to be a snap but it was an inferno; my men were tigers, they fought like seasoned veterans. We got our lumps but we took that fucking town.

"A German officer we captured in the town said the heroism of one of our tank crews in the battle was only equalled by that of a Russian tank crew under similar circumstances. He was referring to a tank of B Company, the first into the town of Morville-les-Vic which had been knocked out by a bazooka. Two wounded men of the tank crew were pulled to safety under their useless vehicle by their comrades who then seized automatic weapons, knocked out the bazooka that had disabled them, and put at least six German antitank gunners out of action.

"Sergeant Roy King, leader of the crew, left his safe fighting position to go to the aid of a white infantryman who was hit several yards away. As King was assisting the man he was wounded but refused to be evacuated. Twelve days later King was killed in action.

"I didn't believe in asking my men to do anything that I wouldn't do myself; I always took the point. I did put my finest sergeant on the point for a while for a specific reason, but I was in the next tank. I am sure my men thought I was a bastard and hated my guts but they followed me. They were a well greased fighting machine.

"I was captured while on reconaissance with my jeep driver, Tech. Sergeant Fred Fields. The sergeant was a big, awkward kid from Denison, Texas. He gave away my liquor, my cigarettes, wore my underwear; he was real generous with my things, but he was loyal. When I sent him on an errand, only death would have kept him from following orders; I could trust him completely. Sometimes when I was going out in the jeep to look things over I'd tell him he didn't have to come along but he always slid into the driver seat and said, 'I'm with you, sir.'

"There was only one time that my sergeant ever hesitated about an order, but you couldn't really blame him. The unit was settling down for the night. There were wounded men with us and the medics were busy tending them. A shot rang out and one medic keeled over. Some sonofabitch had shot him right through that cross on his helmet. A second medic was killed before our guns located the sniper. When they brought the sniper in, he was bleeding to death from a bullet wound in his upper thigh; this was quite obvious from his color. I looked around for the other medics and they were very busy elsewhere, carefully avoiding looking in my direction. In one second I knew I wasn't about to ask those men to tend this bastard who had chosen the conspicuous crosses on the medics' helmets as a target. I told my sergeant to shoot the sniper. The kid turned ashen then fumbled for his gun. It was an unfair order so I pulled my revolver and did it myself. Don't think it ended there. He was the first man I had killed whom I could see close up, his face, his features; for years I dreamed of him. But back to my capture.

"Sergeant Fields and I were cut off from the main body and taken prisoners near a town whose name I can't remember. I should, because as they led us through the town the women there got their kicks spitting on what they called the *schwarz* captain of the 'elite *schwarz* panzer division.' I do know we ended up in a citadel called Walhalla, which I believe is near the city of Regensburg.

"I expected to be killed, for our tank battalion had mopped up Jerry when and wherever we encountered him and these things don't remain a secret. We took thousands of prisoners, but those who wanted a fight to the finish got just that. The fight-it-out boys were usually SS troops.

"I refused to talk to non-commissioned personnel so finally they told Fields to stand up. They were going to take him outside and shoot him. I died inside, but all I said to him was 'Remember you are a soldier.' I'll never forget his reply, 'I'm with you sir.'

"It turned out they were bluffing, and soon a general appeared. He asked me, 'What are you doing in Germany, you rich Americans?' I answered, 'Sir, we found you in France!' He slapped his thigh and started laughing.

"To my surprise they abandoned the citadel the next morning and left Fields and me there, unharmed. My men found us soon afterwards.

"It was on crossing the Enns River that the men thought I had lost my mind. I got out of my tank and walked in front of the tanks. I had my reasons. We would be entering into Hitler's well-touted Austrian stronghold once we were on the other side. Here was this bridge standing intact at the entrance. I knew the danger of possible snipers, but I damned sure could spot mines, dynamite charges, weak spots in the structure better on foot than in my tank, which wouldn't protect any of us a bit if that bridge was a trap. I felt better when we were on the other side, I will admit. There we faced the famous 6th SS Alpine Division, which we found to be much less formidable than rumored.

"Replacements for our outfit came from volunteers of the engineers, port battalions, quartermasters, etc. They were completley untrained in tank work but they wanted to be with us because they were proud of our unit. Many of the men took a reduction in rank to be a replacement with us. We trained them right on the line, and though not battle-tested they were damned good. White tank outfits had trained replacements waiting at a Repple Depple for them.

"In my opinion the Battle of the Rhine was the toughest. We were suppose to act as a diversionary force in crossing the Siegfried Line. Only one thing was wrong, Jerry wasn't fooled and everybody got into the act with all of the firepower they could muster.

"War is a strange thing. You are trained to do a job, even to the killing of men, but you do your job. It is an impersonal thing, at least it had better be or you are in for a lot of trouble. This was the way I looked at the Germans until the day we liberated our first concentration camp.

"Have you ever seen a stack of bones with the skin stretched over it? At the camp you could not tell the young from the old. When we busted the gate the inmates just staggered out with no purpose or direction until they saw a dead horse recently struck by a shell. Have you ever seen ants on a few grains of sugar? They tottered over to that dead carcass and threw themselves upon it, eating raw flesh. We cut ourselves back to one-third rations and left all of the food we could at the camp. There was just one thing wrong, we later learned our food killed many of them.

"Why didn't someone tell us not to give them food? But then, what do you say to a person hardly able to stand or talk but is begging you for food. Somebody should have told us!

"From this incident on Jerry was no longer an impersonal foe. The Germans were monsters! I have never found any way to find an excuse for them or any man who would do to people what I saw when we opened the gate to that camp and two others. We had just mopped them up before but we stomped the shit out of them after the camps."

Captain Long's plan to remain in the army following the war was cruelly and abruptly cancelled by a jeep accident in 1946 which resulted in the amputation of one of his legs.

Two of the men in the following four-way taped conversation, Sergeant Edward ("Eddie") Donald and Corporal Horace Evans, B Company, 761st Tank Battalion, comment on Captain (then 1st Lieutenant) Long as a CO. The two other participants were Colonel Ivan Harrison, at the time a 1st lieutenant in Headquarters Company, and Sergeant Horace Jones, Service Company. The conversation is presented in the order in which it occurred, the first references being to the German mid-December 1944 breakthrough in the Ardennes Forest. Later, the conversation takes up the November action near Morville-les-Vic. Throughout, battle experiences are interwoven with recollections of the training camps in the states.

Eddie Donald: "To your question is there any objection to the use of our names in print, the answer is absolutely no! If I can't afford to say what I think, then I wasted a helluva lot of time fighting in World War II. As you see the others are in accord.

"Its funny but your question for some strange reason brings the Battle of the Bulge to my mind. It was one of our roughest fights. I guess the connection is we earned the right to speak our minds. The 761st had just punched a hole through the Siegfried Line. It had taken us three days of steady fighting, and then Patton's 4th Armored Division started pouring through that hole into Germany. As the 4th entered Germany the news of the German breakthrough in the Ardennes Forest reached the general and the 761st was diverted north along with other Patton tankers."

Horace Evans: "I would like to point out that the 4th Armored received all the credit for the breakthrough on the Siegfried Line, and we did the work. The 761st did not even receive an honorable mention. But let's get back to what Eddie was saying."

Eddie Donald: "We headed north as fast as tanks can go and the closer we got to the Ardennes the colder it got and I do mean cold. It was so cold that where my eyes were watering from the wind and my nose running, this was freezing on my face. Horace Evans had the nerve to look up at me and asked, 'Didn't your mother teach you to wipe your nose?' I would have laughed but my face was a frozen mask.

"We reached the Ardennes and became a part of what is known as the Battle of the Bulge. The 761st was given as its objective a town called Tillet. I shall never forget that place. It took us one week to drive the Germans out of this town. They were really dug in. After an hour of fighting we knew we were fighting SS troops we had tangled with before. It might sound odd, but if you have a return engagement with a unit you know it. You recognize their style of fighting. We finally moved Jerry out, and we were right we had fought them before. It was the same group that had held Patton up at Normandy.

"I mention Tillet because every group that had been assigned to take it had taken a severe beating. There were tanks, artillery, and infantry inside the Ardennes. All had tried Tillet; all had failed. Of all the tankers with Patton it was the 761st that was given Tillet. We took the town and drove the Germans some miles in full retreat. You can find Tillet in many books on World War II but you won't find one word about us."

Horace Evans: "Just like our reunion group met in Kentucky in 1969. We visited the Patton Museum and to our astonishment and anger nowhere in that building was there a black tanker, much less the 761st."*

Eddie Donald: "You want to know about the black soldier as well as his combat roles? Being in an all-black outfit in which we lived together, fought together, bled together, I found my own experience with the, quote, black soldier was that he performed no differently than white soldiers in the terms of heroic deeds, in the terms of his feelings towards typical war situations;

---

*This omission is remedied in the new Patton Museum, Fort Knox, Kentucky, which opened in November 1972.

moments of despair, moments of happiness. The Negro soldier felt the same emotions as did any other soldier.

"I feel that past history, if that is what it can be called, has tended to distort these things and use a stereotype Negro who would run the moment a gun was fired, or could not be trusted, or would steal. My experience was that the Negro soldier was no different from the white soldier in any respect."

Ivan Harrison: "In regards to the Negro soldier preferring to serve under white officers rather than black ones; they prefer serving under officers they have confidence in, black or white, and they will serve such an officer faithfully regardless of his race."

Horace Evans: "Digressing for a moment I wish to get something straight. The movie *Patton* infuriated me for several reasons; but correct me if I am wrong, gentlemen. The very beginning of the picture was a bit twisted. If my memory serves me correctly that speech was made to us, Negro tankers, the day before we went into our first battle.* We were called up on a hill, and Patton stood upon one of our tanks and spoke to us. It was the same speech, excepting they left off part of it. He also said, 'There is one thing you men will be able to say when you go home. You may all thank God that thirty years from now when you are sitting with your grandson upon your knee and he asks, 'Grandfather what did you do in World War II?' You won't have to say, 'I shoveled shit in Mississippi.'

"Patton let us know that he had asked for us. He said he sent a m.f-ing message asking for more tankers. The answer was the best tank unit they had was black; the general only took the best. He replied, 'Who the fuck asked for color, I asked for tankers!'

"That Patton was something else. When he got a message asking him if he had crossed the Rhine, he sent the reply, 'Have crossed the Rhine and I pissed in it.' "

Horace Jones: "That speech they used in the movie was most certainly made to us. But getting back to the black soldiers working under black or white officers. Having been an enlisted man and an officer, I feel black soldiers respond to the kind of leadership given them. Give them an incompetent officer, color notwithstanding, you are going to get slipshod soldiers. There were two white officers in our outfit who I would rate almost as superior because they had the knack, ability, mental attitude, to convey to the troops what they wanted done, and they got it done well. Black officers did the same thing."

---

*For the rest of the speech see Captain Long, above.

Ivan Harrison: "Going back to General Patton, he believed in rewarding outstanding work on the spot. He carried medals along with him and he pinned them on when earned, regardless of race.

"To cite an instance, a Sergeant Johnson in the 761st, who was later killed, fired one round into a German bunker on orders from General Miley. Everyone was sure he had missed it. Johnson assured the general that the round (one shot) had gone into the bunker. He was proven to be correct and the general, following the lead set by Patton, pinned the Bronze Star on his dirty uniform right there. But unfortunately there were many unheralded instances of skill, dedication, and heroism.

"One well-known black correspondent, Roi Otley, found most white correspondents lived in Paris, while we were in Germany. They would visit the various hospitals in Paris and write front-line dispatches for the states. They didn't see it, so chose what appealed to them. It wasn't first-hand knowledge in any sense. Many books on the war are written from the material secured in this manner; that is one reason why there are so many errors in them.

"In 1957 I was in Bamberg, Germany, and an officer who had been with an all-white division in World War II had a copy of his division's history. I was glancing through it, and it showed them taking Coburg, Germany. I violently disputed this, because we took Coburg, and I was later able to prove it to him. It was at Coburg that we found a slew of refrigerator cars full of fresh meat; the first we had had in a long time. But there this was written up as victory for an all-white unit; yet I was there and so were these three gentlemen sitting here.

"Concerning segregation in the army, there were definite instances of segregation before combat and immediately afterwards but during combat it did not exist."

Eddie Donald: "I would agree with Ivan, there were incidents of segregation and discrimination, but very little if any on the front line and this is where we spent 183 days. We definitely broke the segregation barrier by being the only black combat troops on that front at that particular time.

"We fought side by side with the 101st Airborne, 26th Infantry Division, the 87th Infantry Division and we slept together and ate together. Yes, there were a few racial flare-ups but all in all we were there for a job and I think we got the job done."

Ivan Harrison: "A slight variation but an illustration of the difficulty sometimes in pinpointing white feelings. Paul Robeson appeared at Berchtesgarten. Ours was the only black unit in the vast audience of GIs. They had a concert pianist who called himself Franz Liszt. The white soldiers booed every time he swept up and down the keyboard then yelled, 'Are those 88's?' A very attractive girl came out and tried to sing, and they gave her the same treatment.

They were just plain rude and unruly. For some reason Paul Robeson had the stage lights lowered excepting for the one on the mike. He walked quickly on stage, over to the microphone and started singing and then he talked. You could have heard a pin drop in the audience. He received a tremendous ovation. Why the audience reacted in this manner, I can't say. Afterwards he joined our outfit and had a bottle of wine with us."

Horace Evans: "Speaking of the Negro soldier being cowardly in battle. I recall and I am sure Eddie can bear me out, an incident where white soldiers of the 87th Infantry that were fighting with our tanks for cover could have been called cowards. We had to plead with them, coax them, put their packs on their backs, beg them to go on with their outfit. They could be shot for desertion, we pointed out, because they were determined they were through fighting. They just weren't going to fight any more and they were in tears. I don't ever recall a black soldier in my outfit crying. I've witnessed a lot of cussin,' but not crying."

Horace Jones: "I was in a jeep, tank, or some kind of vehicle, I don't remember which but I'll never forget what happened. A white officer ran down the road to where his troops sat or sprawled in various positions. He told them to get on their feet, we were all moving up. As the captain passed on, this white soldier, obviously a hillbilly, said, 'By God if I'm going,' raised his foot, took his M1 rifle and put a bullet through it.' "

Ivan Harrison: "An M1, he must have damned near shot his foot off at that range."

Horace Jones: "Right, and that was a whitey and I witnessed that with my own eyes."

Horace Evans: "While we are speaking of Negro soldiers being cowards in World War II; that wasn't so. It was we had fought so much at home in those southern camps to survive that by the time we got overseas we were just plain exhausted. [A roar of approving laughter convulsed the guys for a moment. Evans continued in a more serious vein.] Somehow I got a Purple Heart and was away from my outfit for at least a month. You won't believe this, but I was glad to get back to my group, I was treated so badly in the hospital, which was American by the way, and during the time I spent returning to the group.

"One incident that always will remain with me happened in the hospital. Being a walking patient, having been wounded in one arm, they asked me to attend a white patient who had had an amputation. They didn't have enough help. I stuck with that soldier for a solid week and tried to do what I could for him. Near the end of the ordeal he called me a 'nigger,' and that is the one time I cried. I couldn't believe it, but that is what he did. From then on I had nothing to do with him.

"After I left the hospital and started working my way up to my outfit, passing from one group to the next heading in its direction. I was called out of my tent at least a dozen times with other black soldiers to stand in line to let some German girl look us over to see if we had raped her the previous night. I was real glad to get back to the front line because there was much more freedom up there!"

Horace Jones: "In the closing days of the war orders came down that gasoline was to be issued henceforth to certain outfits only. We had been in combat something like 178 days then right on the front line. The word was that the war was ending shortly; this was in May. No gasoline was to be given to the 761st. We were to drive our vehicles as far as we could and that was that.

"I took our supply trucks back to Kohlgrube, which had an ammunition and gasoline depot. Ammunition we could get, all we wanted, but no gas and with armored groups you have to have gasoline to move on. The only way I got any gasoline was by going out and talking to the men in a black quartermaster unit. I told them how long we had been fighting on the front line and were now on our way to meet the Russians at the Stey River in Austria.

"In actual fact I stole 30,000 gallons of gasoline. Those guys were out on the airstrip stealing drums of gasoline like crazy.

"Gasoline was rationed to the 13th or 14th Armored Division, white naturally. They were to make the great spurt to meet the Russians.

"By going out and begging those enlisted men, telling them who we were, and what we wanted, and what had happened; we had come this far and we wanted to go all the way. They agreed, helped, and sent me on my way saying just get there first!

"When I got back to the outfit and told the commander we had 30,000 gallons of gasoline he was overwhelmed. He wanted to know how I had managed it and I told him, 'Colonel, if I tell you, you will be an accessory after the fact.' He grinned and dismissed me. That is how we managed to get down to the Steye River and meet the Russians; on stolen gasoline."

Eddie Donald: "One of the things I very clearly recall was our being thrown into battle for the first time. We were told by our company commander that they had a little town over the hill they wanted us to take and we were going to spearhead, quote, spearhead the division. This was the first time I had heard the word *spearhead* and I really did not know what it meant until the following morning when I found out.

"We were to go in and soften up the enemy; we really weren't expected to come out of it. We were supposed to soften up things so the troops behind us than could capture the town without too much difficulty."

Horace Jones: "What Eddie is talking about is we had been told that because we were green troops they were going to give us a little combat mission.

"Seems there was a little pocket of Germans in that town and we were suppose to ride through it, shoot up the town, throw some hand grenades around, and wipe out the town. You know get a little blood on us so we would be eligible for the real thing.

"When the truth came out it was some 'pockets' that General Patton's 4th Armored Division had bypassed because they were a little tough to fool with, which would slow the 4th Armored down. Our mission was to go into that little cluster of towns and let the Germans spend their ammunition on us green black tankers so the white infantry could come in and mop up. As Eddie said, it was to be our first mission, also our last one. No more black tankers to worry about. How we got through that I don't know. We hit that place and it blew up in our faces like TNT.

"The guys in B Company were given Morville-les-Vic with orders to go right on into the center of the town, blast away and drive right on out."

Eddie Donald: "There was only one problem, Jerry was waiting for us with the proverbial kitchen sink. I swear they had bazookas mounted on some roof tops. Our first tank was hit as soon as it entered the square and this tied up those behind. We might have been green but we fought like crazy while they got the equipment to move Sergeant King's tank.

"I believe it took us a couple of days to cruise on through that town as we had been directed. We lost something like 32 men killed, plus those injuries we sustained. Somehow we survived it and emerged victorious veterans.

"Our first mission was supposed to be the last one. It was a suicide mission, we later learned."

Horace Evans: "One time we had been in so many battles and lost so many vehicles they had to give us patched-together junk to fight with."

Eddie Donald: "Comparatively speaking, our tanks were inferior to most of the German panzers. Their tanks were far superior in terms of fire power and that, generally speaking, is the name of the game. We dared not get within range of their 88 mm artillery piece mounted on their heavier tanks which gave them greater range and fire power. Our gun was 76 mm mounted on a 16-ton medium tank. Our tank in contrast had greater speed and maneuverability. We were trained to take advantage of this, but we all definitely feared the German fire power."

Horace Jones: "The Germans had a hand-operated turret, while we had an electric system we called 'Little Joe.' It made it possible for us to swing our gun and turret into position faster than Jerry could. It was like in the days of the old west, it was often a matter of the fastest draw."

Eddie Donald: "I was inducted into the service in March '42, shortly after Horace Jones. After two weeks at Custer, I received orders that I would be moved to a place unknown. I was placed on a train with other soldiers in a veil of secrecy. The shades were pulled and we were not allowed to raise them until we reached our destination; it was Louisville, Kentucky.

"After we arrived at Fort Knox, we were told we were an experimental outfit; we were going to be prepared as the first group of black tankers in the United States Army.

"Our officers for the most part were white. However, there was a cadre of black NCOs who gave us our basic training; Horace Jones was one of these men. Our six-weeks basic training period was very comprehensive and gave each soldier a chance to select the special training he preferred in the armored division. A tank crew consisted of five men and each man had to be able to do another man's job; we were interchangeable in case a crew member was wounded or killed.

"After completing our training we were sent to Camp Claiborne, Louisiana, a totally segregated camp. Black soldiers were quartered on the back side of the grounds in what I would call swampland, the most undesirable area of the whole camp. White soldiers were at the other end of the camp, on good ground with the highway nearby and bus facilities to take them to town. We were soon to learn we had our own PX. We were strictly and completley segregated. We were not allowed in the white area and they were not allowed in ours.

"When we went into town we had to go to the ghetto. We learned, with some difficulty, to accept this. White northern soldiers had their problems but they were a different kind. They were called 'Yankee' and adjectives of the uncomplimentary kind were generally attached.

"While there, I noticed that a number of German prisoners were in the camp in a special area, not swampland. They were given freedom of movement and had access to facilities denied black American soldiers. They were given passes to town when black soldiers were confined to the area and did not have their privileges. This was one of the most repugnant things I can recall of the many things that happened to Negro servicemen."

Horace Jones: "Once we had an exhibition of infantry and armor working together. We were all put in tanks and set on the side of a mountain to show how these tanks would fire over the area. The infantry was under fire in their fox holes. They had straddle trenches dug for the infantry, and what got me was these were segregated."

Ivan Harrison: "At Camp Hood Jackie Robinson was in our battalion. Of course, we had our black officers' club. One day Jackie was on his way to town when he realized he didn't have enough money. He stopped at the white officers' club to get a check cashed and they barred him at the door; he wasn't allowed across the threshold. Jackie became very bitter about this. Some days later he boarded a bus and another Negro officer's wife, who happened to be quite fair, was sitting down near the front. He knew her so sat down beside her. The bus driver was going to throw him off until Jackie stood up and he saw his size. The driver went for the MPs. Jackie refused to be arrested by noncommissioned men. They in their turn went and returned with a major who ordered Jackie off of the bus. Jackie bowed low from the waist and with a flourish swept off his hat and swept it across the floor in front of the major saying 'yassuh.' He was charged with being disrespectful to a superior officer and was to be court-martialed.

"The NAACP, his fraternity, and the Negro press soon learned about Jackie, and the messages began to pour in demanding to know what happened. They moved Jackie to another camp, then answered he was no longer a member of the 761st. Of course the black underground soon notified them where he could be found and messages began to hit his new place of residence. He was moved again only to have the procedure repeat itself. It was beginning to be such a hot potato that they held what I am sure was the shortest court-martial in the history of the armed services. One officer read the charges as fast as was humanly possible, and on his last word another gaveled the desk and said 'not guilty.' Then messages went out in answer to the inquiries, saying, 'Jackie Robinson not in trouble!' "

Horace Evans: "You know black soldiers were on the 'shorts' in everything and in every way. In the blistering heat of a Texas summer the patty boys had ice for their water, drinks, everything; we didn't have any. It was these little, petty things that really burned you and made you know just what a vicious, scheming character patty was.

"By the way, overseas we were known as a bastard outfit. It meant we didn't belong to any group permanently; we fought with any outfit that needed us. Sometimes we didn't see each other for a week or more. One company might be sent to the 87th, three or four tanks to some other outfit, and so on, so we'd be all over the place. It was definitely a ploy to keep from committing us together as a battalion as much as possible; whole units get credit while a few isolated tanks, no matter whether they saved the day or not, are overlooked.

"Units that fight together continuously become your better outfits because they know each other's, you could say, techniques. Fortunately for us, splitting us up so often did not disturb our effectiveness as a battalion when we were committed in total.

"The army simply was not interested in a black combat outfit that functioned with precision and know-how. We just fooled them because we were damn good; our esprit de corps was a solid tie."

Eddie Donald: "As Horace said, we were good. No one ever objected to getting the 761st in part or whole. We gave the infantry regiments or divisions we worked with the best protection possible; it meant their lives. That they were white never crossed our minds. As I said before, the closer you are to the front the less prejudice, and the front was where we lived. Those infantrymen wanted to live just as badly as anybody else, so color is no object when you take the heat off of them and keep that dream of getting back home alive! Oh yes, Ivan Harrison was promoted to major before the war ended, and in a black combat unit that was not an easy accomplishment; it was rare. We were all very proud of him."

Horace Evans: "Even in moments of extreme danger there are those times when humor injects itself into the picture. Whitey may call us clowns, but thank God for our sense of humor.

"Whenever I was going into battle I would have a nervous stomach. I shall never forget, nor will the crew I was a member of; Eddie was our sergeant. This time instead of a nervous stomach I had a mild attack of dysentery.

"If you have never smelled the smoke from the firing of a 76 mm, count your blessings. It alone is bad enough. Then throw in the body odor of five men in a confined area and one member, meaning me, with diarrhea as we are racing into battle. Now I was the cannoneer and radio man, an important part of the team, particularly at this time. Picture if you can a tank cannoneer sitting on an upturned helmet lined with a letter, firing away at his targets, and his best friend who is head of the crew, managing between giving orders and cursing the foulness of the air to tell the others they ought to put me in the gun and fire me at Jerry with my secret weapon."

Eddie Donald: "Digressing a bit, speaking of colored officers, Horace and I were in B Company of the 761st. Our company commander Captain John Long, was a leader extraordinary, a fine officer. Our white infantrymen called him 'the black Patton.' "

Horace Evans: "Johnny was every inch a soldier. He asked nothing of his men that he would not do himself. He was courageous, shrewd, able, and an evil s.o.b. There were times we hated his guts, but we had to respect him.

"When we would batten down our tanks with shells falling all around us we could see through our slit opening and he'd be out there walking around in that hell, calmly surveying the situation.

"That man had the luck of the Irish! One night on our way to an objective we came smack up against a mine field. To go around would have taken valuable time. John Long got out of his lead tank and walked ahead and guided us safely through that field.

"Another time his tank was knocked off a high embankment. By the time we got down to him he was climbing out unhurt and blistering the air about the time we had lost.

"When we got to the bridge over the Enns River, leading into Austria, you can bet we were sceptical about the bridge and the fact that we had experienced no opposition so far. This was known as the entrance into Hitler's redoubt, and it was heralded as impregnable. Captain Long got out of his tank and walked across that bridge ahead of us looking for weakness in the structure and booby traps. He was wide open to snipers and if that bridge had been mined he wouldn't have had a chance, but his phenomenal luck held."

Eddie Donald: "You know he almost court-martialed the whole lot of us."

Horace Evans: "He sure did, and I think it cost Eddie a battlefield commission."

Eddie Donald: "We were to take another one of those innocent-looking little towns; only this time we knew the details. There was only one way for us to get into this town and that stretch of road had been thoroughly mined and machine guns had been set for a deadly crossfire. Johnny explained this, and I said I didn't like it. He agreed, but said his orders were to take the town and that's exactly what he was going to do.

"I talked it over with the other fellows and they didn't like it either. I told Johnny. He just looked at us and asked if we were going with him; nobody responded. He walked quickly past us and grabbed the field telephone, called headquarters and told them he was proceeding as ordered. He then told them what we had said and that when he returned he was going to court-martial every damned one of us. He wasn't kidding."

Horace Evans: "Sergeant Mike Word's tank happened to be sitting in the forward position and the sergeant and his crew were still aboard for some reason. The captain ordered Mike down from there. He jumped on that tank and sent it down the road toward that booby trap like a bat out of hell. Sergeant Words, stunned, jumped into Johnny's tank and took out after him."

Eddie Donald: "I said, if he's fool enough to go alone, then I am big enough fool to follow him. We all hopped into our vehicles and took off. We could see him, and when his tank hit that trap he cleared it safely, guns blazing away and full throttled. Mike's tank hit a mine and was out of action; so did mine. The others, following his example, tore through that space, guns spitting; they made it and in the process rendered the trap harmless. Just a few mines remained that sappers could remove, but the machine guns were silenced permanently.

"When we walked into town, all was quiet, and we found John Long comfortably ensconced in someone's kitchen, cool as you please, smoking a cigarette. He received three or four Purple Hearts but never was out of action for any length of time. That guy was something else, but he was a professional soldier all the way."

Horace Evans: "After this incident the captain told us, 'I lead you across France. Now I'm going to kick your asses all the way across Germany. As I said he was an evil son-of-a-bitch, but no one can deny his leadership ability. His strategy when going into battle was uncanny in its effectiveness."

Eddie Donald: "One thing is obvious—whatever happened overseas, good or bad, welded us all together because to this day we are all friends and meet yearly somewhere in the country. We get an honest-to-goodness pleasure out of being together again and going over the times we had together.

"David Williams, the only white officer who stayed commander of a company throughout, always meets with us. He is the blackest white man you would ever want to know. He is one of us. His men, all black, would follow him to hell and a few steps beyond, so you see its not the color that Negro soldiers respond to but the leadership exerted and the trust, respect, and confidence the officer can engender."

The 614th Tank Destroyer Battalion

The 614th Tank Destroyer Battalion was activated 25 July 1942, at Camp Carson, Colorado. Its original cadre of five officers and 156 enlisted men came from the 366th Infantry Regiment, Fort Devens, Massachusetts. Sixteen other men came from Camp Wolters, Texas. Advanced training for the 614th began in May 1943 at Camp Hood, Texas, where it was reorganized from a selfpropelled to a towed battalion—one using an older model of antitank gun, towed by a truck. In the interviews, "splitting trail" refers to the work of separating the weapon from the truck before firing. Expert crews, like those of the 614th, could split trail and be on target ten to fifteen seconds after reaching their firing position.

Lieutenant-Colonel Frank Pritchard, whose name appears frequently in the interviews, became battalion commander 16 October 1943. The follow-

ing summary of the 614th's service record is taken from the battalion history, "Seek, Strike and Destroy", which he compiled at the war's end:

> *No one knew [at the time of its formation] that before its standard would be furled for the last time this new battalion would see service that would take it from Colorado to Texas; across the Atlantic to England and after a month across the English Channel to Normandy, France, then north to the battle ground that is Metz; into Germany for a few days in November of '44; then back into Alsace, across the Siegfried Line into Germany and Austria; then, as the war ended back into France to be broken up at Marseilles; then the end of the war in the Pacific and a change in orders that sent it back to Germany with the Army of Occupation.*

He mentioned particularly combat at Climbach (to be described in the interviews), the work of the gun companies in support of the infantry, and the work of the reconnaissance platoons "that led the way across Germany and Austria into the Tyrolean Alps, the city of Innsbruck and the valley of the Inn River." Colonel Pritchard records that the personnel of the 614th won three bronze stars for taking part in Northern France campaign No. 1, the Rhineland campaign, and the Central Europe campaign; that one enlisted man won a battlefield commission and the Distinguished Service Cross; that eight members won the Silver Star, 28 the Bronze Star medal, and that awards of the Purple Heart medal went to 79. On leaving the 614th, 16 October 1945, Colonel Pritchard said: "I am proud to have served with you, proud of you and the record you have made. I consider it an honor to have had some part in your achievements" (Lee, p. 666).

Lieutenant Christopher Sturkey is the enlisted man who won the Silver Star and a battlefield commission. A Detroiter and a draftee, he was one of the men who completed basic training at Camp Wolters, Texas, and was part of the cadre sent to Camp Carson to become officers for the 614th. Acute appendicitis and surgery delayed his entrance to OCS. By the time Sturkey was ready for something other than light duty, his classmates were well into their training at OCS, and he remained an enlisted man.

Christopher Sturkey: "I was sent to Camp Hood, home of the 614th. When our black officers-to-be finally graduated from OCS and came to Hood we were all mighty proud of them. My best friend, Charles Thomas, who I was to attend OCS with, was now my superior, but he was a helluva nice guy and a top officer so all I could feel was pride in spite of my disappointment.

"I had not been idle after arriving at Camp Hood. I attended the enlisted men's school and the weapons school. I made sergeant and was assigned to teaching the use of heavy weapons. Eight hours every day I taught weaponry half of the time, the remaining hours were spent teaching men who were totally illiterate to read and write. These men, to a great extent, had come from the backwoods of the south: Louisiana, Mississippi, and Alabama. They had earned from seven to thirty dollars a month in civilian life. There were many sharecroppers among them. They became very good at their jobs, showing a tremendous adaptability at things demonstrated to them. Their coordination and ability in team work was outstanding. They became some of the best TDU gun crews in the army. We had the champion TDU gun crew that could split trail and have their guns firing in ten seconds and I mean firing accurately. This talent would save C Company of the 614th at Climbach when seconds meant life or total annihilation. It also made Climbach our victory.

"There were seven hundred men in my outfit and when retreat was sounded those with passes would line up at the bus stop, as would the white soldiers from their camp some distance from us. The Negroes had to wait until the whites filled up the bus with the exception of the back seat. When this was done those number of Negroes the one back seat would accommodate were allowed to board. Waiting to get a seat to town could be a pretty hopeless task. A lot of guys like myself gave up trying. Besides when you got there, entertainment for black soldiers was two hole-in-the-wall dives.

"In the meantime we were continuing to train and daily becoming more proficient, thinking we would have to fight for our country and of course, to defend democracy!

"Time kept passing, and according to the papers we weren't exactly winning the war and could use all of the help we could get, but for want of anything else to do with this battle-ready outfit they made us school troops. We did the problems for the OCS near by; they would set up tactical problems and we would then perform like trained seals. We did this so long I figured the war was over for us. I had been in the army three years and hadn't moved from Texas and yet they were fighting and fighting over somewhere.

"Our battalion commander, Colonel Frank S. Pritchard, was doing everything possible to get us overseas. We were sent on maneuvers in Louisiana and then back to Camp Hood. Again we played school troops to the OCS. The *Pittsburgh Courier* was screaming its head off about no black combat troops in action but by now I was kind of indifferent about it all; I figured I would grow into an old man right there in Texas playing war.

"In August 1944 we were sent to Camp Shanks, New Jersey, our POE. The 758th, a black tank outfit, part of the 92nd Division, was on the same ship with us. Thirteen days after our departure we arrived in Southampton. After camping temporarily in England, we entered France by way of Omaha Beach where we began moving up hedge row by hedge row to join General Patton at Metz.

"Patton talked to us, saying he didn't care whether we were black or white, all he wanted was fighting men. You have my word his language was just as pithy as reported. The general had just streaked from St. Lô to Metz and was impatiently awaiting supplies.

"We started moving up again and soon I could hear the sound of guns. I recall my platoon leader coming back to me and saying, 'This is it, Sturkey.' I remember it was early in the morning and a kid was shooting dice. He stood up and threw them away saying, 'Well I won't be needing these any more.'

"We left going into battle with Lieutenant Walter Smith, a Negro, in command of our company. He took us into action to relieve a white tank outfit that had been holding the flank of the German 6th Corps.

"As they pulled out—you know tanks make noise and they did! All hell broke loose! Jerry threw everything he had in our direction. The men were scared and felt like running. Some did, but not away; they were seeking better protection. You really can't blame their reaction. This was their first time under fire and they were getting a real baptism.

"As we hit the dirt, the platoon leader called for me to form up the men and come up front. I couldn't even find them at first. Some were still crouched in the half-track, others had dispersed in the area, and shells were falling like a heavy downpour. The kid who had thrown his dice away that same morning was the first to die.

"When it finally quieted down, we had forty seriously wounded men. Those still fit for duty numbered twelve enlisted men, one officer, and me. We were to do the job that at minimum required fifty-four men, and we did it. We stayed three days on that flank until relieved. Sleep was out of the question since the fox holes were half filled with water. Besides we could not take the chance of infiltration. Had they mounted an assault they could have run over the top of us. Oh, we could have killed a number of them before they broke through, because as I said we were tough on rapid firing and accuracy and our weapons were placed for maximum damage, but in the long run we would have bought it for sure due to superiority of numbers.

"It was at this time I earned my Silver Star and a battlefield commission for the deploying of my men under the circumstances, keeping them together in an emergency, and continually covering that six-hundred foot line we were holding to make sure all was well. Machine guns take only one man but a two-incher takes two men, one to load and the other to fire, so you can see we were spread mighty thin. Naturally when we were withdrawn we had to refill our vacancies to bring our group back to full strength. To do this we had to go to the Repple Depple for replacements. The black men we were given at the depot had not even had basic training. How the hell they ever got to Europe I will never know! These men were untrained and illiterate, and they were replacing veteran soldiers of a long period of training in the states. Many had never fired a rifle, but they were proud to be joining a combat unit. We had to train them on the line. They tried hard and did a good job. They might not have been highly intelligent but they had spunk and the stamina to fight, and fight they did. All of the originals of the 614th were wonderful soldiers. They wanted to be good and they were. Those who took their places did a darn good job of living up to the standards set by the first group of men.

"I've already said we had some of the top gun crews in the country for TDUs and we had the older model antitank gun where we had to split trail. All of the white outfits I saw had the new self-propelled jobs which you just had to swing into action. Ours was towed by a truck, but that's all right, we could still split trail, beat them to the draw, and hit the target.

"Whether or not we were given the old-style gun had to do with our being colored, I honestly don't know. I do know the white military opinion was Negro troops were only good for service units to white combat troops. We wasted in Texas, though combat ready, and the brass said we were too dumb to fight, we'd kill each other. I always will believe the only reason we finally got into the action was because of all the hell the Negro press was raising.

"As we came into Germany the people would draw their shades and peep out at us. They later said they had never seen black soldiers before, but I doubt that since the British and French had African troops with them. I heard they had been told we had tails, and a lot of other such garbage, but once they got to know us they were quite nice.

"When 1st Lieutenant Charles Thomas was critically wounded in the battle for Climbach, the officer in charge of my platoon was switched to lead the company in Charles's place and I was put in charge of the platoon. I was the rare sergeant who sat in briefing sessions with nothing but commissioned officers.

"I fought from Climbach, which Charles will tell you about, until February 15 as leader of my platoon with the rank of sergeant; on the 15th I was awarded a battlefield commission by General Patch, commander of the 7th Army. Charles, still critical, had won a Distinguished Service Cross. All of us thought he would surely win the Congressional.

"We had been detached from Patton's 3rd Army, leaving us open to call by any group needing us. We were getting a good reputation and Climbach clinched it, we were in demand!

"The white infantry unit we were joined to after leaving the 3rd Army seriously doubted our competency until the battle at Climbach. After that we became 'jug' buddies. Our units were so close it was not unusual to see a couple of our guys going along on one of their patrols. Now these eager beavers might have just returned from a skirmish with their own TDU outfit but there they were going back into battle. Some had a good friend in the infantry group going on patrol, others I guess just couldn't relax so this was a way to keep occupied. We never lost any of our men who went along on these infantry patrols, and it was not a fun-and-games thing. It seems our guys were just as proficient with a machine gun as they were with our big guns.

"The friendships established were not one-sided affairs. We were continually running some of the patty boys back to their camp so they wouldn't miss roll call. I'll never forget one white kid from the deep south, he must have been all of nineteen, who couldn't understand why he couldn't stay with us since the two outfits were traveling together. We patiently explained that he could get shot for desertion; that he understood but he was back with us every chance he got.

"I said our guys knew how to fight, they did and they also knew how to die. You'll have to forgive me but I get real pissed off when some jackass declares a degree is necessary to get a first-class fighting man. Audie Murphy was illiterate, at that time, and so was Sergeant York of World War I. Is white illiteracy somehow different than black illiteracy?

"We had no problem with the regular German soldiers we defeated in battle. However, their officers wanted to surrender to officers of equal rank. Since this was impossible such formalities had to be dispensed with; we didn't have time to be scooting all around the country looking for a general as a matter of protocol. We had to kill SS men because they wouldn't surrender and wanted to fight to the death; they wanted it the hard way and that's just the way they got it.

"My group was moving south toward Italy when the Bulge happened. We were reattached to Patton's army, which was far advanced, when the orders came to fall back and straighten out our line. All infantry in advance was also ordered back and we were to cover their retreat in our sector. Our orders to effect this were to hold a certain crossroad until midnight. It was cold and snowing. The platoon's guns were mounted to straddle that road and to stop anything, with an emphasis on *anything* coming down it behind our troops. A platoon against an army wasn't a comforting thought. I just hoped the Jerries were having as much trouble with the weather as we were.

"Midnight finally arrived and we started to withdraw. The roads were frozen and slick as glass. I was forced to destroy two of our guns because they slipped into a ditch. We got back to the line with a jeep, a truck cab that towed one gun, and all of the men.

"When I received my commission, my superior officer insisted I have a drink with him. I asked for a rain check because I had some men in a forward position in the little town ahead. He made the drink an order, that order kept me from being captured by the Germans, who overran the position. Another time I was on my way out of the door of the briefing room when I remembered something I had left behind. I turned back and the fellow who went out in my place was killed by shrapnel from a bomb exploding in the courtyard.

"When I returned to the states I went down to the defense plant where my wife worked, to surprise her. I had on all of my paraphernalia: battle stars, campaign ribbons, the works. I was early so thought I'd have a hamburger at the White Tower around the corner. I ordered it and the counter girl told me, 'We don't serve niggers in here.' Now this is where I thought the battle should have begun, in all of the little places where little people get their pleasure in telling us we are not good enough to eat in, drink in, shop in, the whole bit, their little places of business. Here I was supposed to be some kind of a hero returned from the war and the first thing I hear from some poor white hash-slinging bitch I've been fighting for, is 'We don't serve niggers in here.' "

Lieutenant Claude Ramsey's interview adds a postscript to the previous one, and underlines Christopher Sturkey's assertions about the relationship—or lack of it—between illiteracy and ability in combat.

Claude Ramsey: "Frankly the whole time I spent in the army was an unpleasant experience that I have never had the slightest desire to recall. I am sure other men you have interviewed have told you of the rampant racism in the armed forces. Civilian life is one thing, but to be drafted to fight to save the world for democracy only to find that you have entered the most undemocratic and racist organization in the whole country is quite another thing. This as the young people today would say, 'turned me off' completely as far as the army was concerned. I did a job I had no choice about to the best of my ability but as far as wishing to remember those days I don't.

"I will say the 614th was fortunate in having a fine leader, Colonel Pritchard. He respected and liked his men and they reciprocated this feeling. Our officers were black and white. As soon as a white officer transferred or was lost to our battalion Colonel Pritchard always replaced him with a black officer.

"Of course I have many friends from my army days. I can say in all honesty that our recon platoon was probably the best in the business. It spearheaded the whole division we were attached to when we were taken from under Patton and headed south. Our gun crews were superior. The 614th as a combat unit was outstanding, and my feeling about the army in no way reflects on the superb combat record of this group.

"The victory at Climbach in December '44 belongs to Captain Charles Thomas and the company he led into that valley where they would be like clay pigeons in a shooting gallery. Charles had several things going for him. His men believed in him and they were proud of their unit and their ability. They were good, damned good. At Climbach speed and accuracy made the difference, plus guts, and these things they had to spare. Climbach was an important victory and it was made possible by a black captain and a company of black soldiers. More than fifty per cent were casualties, but they held that valley. In the process the company so engaged picked up fourteen medals: one DSC, four Silver Stars, nine Bronze Stars, and a unit citation.

"When Sergeant Sturkey won his Silver Star, in November '44, it was the first time his platoon was under fire. It demonstrated the fighting ability, tenacity, and leadership of black soldiers, their NCOs, and their officers.

"The enlisted personnel in the 614th completely destroyed the fallacy that illiteracy is a definite handicap to a fighting man. Many of the enlisted men in the 614th were barely literate, if not illiterate, but they were completely at home with weapons and under fire. Leadership makes the difference."

Captain Charles L. Thomas, a Detroiter, started his army career as did many other Detroiters, at Fort Custer, where he first encountered segregation in the army. His one recorded memory of Camp Wolters, Texas, was of the little town nearby where there was a big, fenced-in hotel, where "we could peek through the fence and see the whites having a ball." After OCS, he reported to Camp Hood, Texas, where the 614th was in the making.

The battle described by Captain Thomas took place 14 December 1944. Climbach is a town in Lorraine, just south of the Rhineland border.

Charles Thomas: "Our intelligence said that three Mark VI had been seen in the vicinity of Climbach, one of the northernmost entrances to the Siegfried Line. They did not want enemy reenforcements in this area. Moreover, Climbach had to be taken to break up communications between it and Lembach. Climbach was a town high in the hills, looking down on a valley which was surrounded by woods. It was down the only road through these woods we came on our way to take Climbach.

"A small task force had been formed under Colonel Blackshear. It was composed of a battalion of infantrymen. I don't remember their number but they were out of Arkansas and were not particularly pleased when they saw the artillery was a company of black men from the 614th Tank Destroyers. Colonel Blackshear with his tankers made up the rest of the task force. I believe there were about 250 men in the company I commanded.

"As we neared the valley entrance, for some reason Colonel Blackshear stopped. I pulled up beside him and told him I would take it, meaning I would take my men on into the valley first.

"Why did I volunteer? I can't honestly answer that any more than why the colonel stopped.* I know I was as aware as the colonel that the valley was undoubtedly mined and certainly would be covered by something like the 88 mm German field piece. Perhaps somewhere in the back of my mind was the fact that we had the only guns that could match the firepower of the Mark VI tanks. But to get on with it, we entered the valley. The Germans held their

---

*The citation for then 1st Lieutenant Thomas, General Order 58, 7th Army, 20 February 1945, omits to mention that he *volunteered* to take the lead; likewise, Lee.

fire until we were well into it when they cut loose. My half track was hit and so was I. I was hit again, hard, as I got out of my vehicle.

"As to your question did I deploy my men? Yes I did. Yes I refused to be evacuated until an officer who had commanded a company before was brought up to replace me. This was hardly the place to learn.

"Yes, I was conscious the whole time and in command until the officer arrived to relieve me. My men were getting their guns into position with the whole world erupting around them. They were doing it swiftly and in good fashion in spite of the casualties we were beginning to sustain. In just a few minutes they were returning the fire. They were functioning to a lesser degree, as I was, automatically. I knew what had to be done. That is why I would not leave or should I say allow myself to be evacuated until the officer to replace me was on hand and all of our guns were firing.

"They say men under stress can do unusual things. I imagine this was true in my case. I wonder how many men who earned medals can give you a detailed account of what happened? I know I hung onto one thought, deploy the guns and start firing or we're dead.

"Thinking back on it I knew if the job could be done these men could do it because they could and would fight; they were proud and they were good. Training and discipline were the key and they had had plenty of both. No doubt my men seeing me hurt and still doing my job pushed them to even greater effort.

"I was badly hurt but I didn't have time to think about it. Thinking is your worst enemy in war. It can scare you to death as well as immobilize you. My training had been to *do*, particularly in an emergency. I, and many others like me, are proof of the proper automatic behavior that continual training and discipline brings about. Remember an officer's deportment carries tremendous weight with his men. He is also responsible for them. I suppose all of these things were in the corner of my mind.

"I learned afterwards that my men thought I had bought it. I'm pretty sure I was no longer on my feet but I was not stretched out on the ground either. I just kept giving orders and made sure my line of vision was not blocked. No doubt a medic or someone was supporting me.

"They told me later I was a mess to behold, a bloody mess that kept giving orders and urging them to do their best. I cannot tell you about the actions that won the men in my company their medals. Its strange but my vision was limited to the gun crews and the enemy guns.

"You really know a lot about me and Climbach. Yes, I guess you could say I was just about cross-stitched by a machine gun. I didn't know this until I got to the hospital. I was also carrying a fair share of shrapnel.

"I would like to repeat, my men were a fine disciplined bunch and their deployment on my orders was as normal as breathing even under the heated circumstances. Normally, the one who gets off the first shot is the victor. We didn't have this advantage but their speed and accuracy made up the difference.

"You have to adjust to living with death in war, but don't let anyone tell you, you are not afraid. The officers and noncoms are less afraid, not because they are better men, but because they are continually moving to encourage the men and to see that all is well. The enlisted man, however, sitting and waiting for whatever is to come has plenty of time for thinking so he has more time to build up fear, with good reason. When you don't have time to think you are not afraid but when you can sit down for even a minute fear creeps in.

"Stateside, there was much more formality between the officers and men. Once we got into action it became quite informal. The formality was no longer needed, for the discipline was already there.

"As to the high number of illiterates. The army was inducting men who could see lightning and hear thunder.* How they came into the 614th I don't know. All of a sudden they were there. One thing, they learned to fight and to fight well. For many the 614th was their first outside attachment from the rural south and they were proud of their unit. These were not ignorant men by any means; they were unschooled. Need I say I was proud to serve with them."

Captain Thomas's faith in his men was not misplaced. Less than an hour after he was evacuated single soldiers were doing the work of ten-man gun crews: loading, aiming, and firing. With the 614th's numbers cut in half the Germans launched an infantry attack. A worse time could not have been chosen, for the men of the 614th were running out of ammunition for their remaining big guns.

Corporal Robert Harris, a trucker carrying ammunition, sitting it out back on the road with the remainder of the task force, sensed what was happening by the small-arms fire. He climbed into his truck and started to move out. Colonel Blackshear forbade his action as sheer madness and an impossibility. According to his comrades' version of events, the corporal almost ran the colonel down as he tossed a few pungent words in the colonel's direction and headed, full throttle, into the holocaust. He succeeded in driving his truck right up to the two guns left and began to help unload. The timely arrival of this ammunition helped to save the day. The Germans had become so involved in trying to kill off an outfit that just wouldn't die, the 411th (the white infantry regiment of the task force) was able to slip in behind the Germans and seize the town of Climbach. Corporal Harris received the Bronze

---

*Dr. Rudolph Porter, an examining physician at Fort Huachuca, Arizona, for the 92nd Division, found one infantry man who was blind in one eye and had only partial vision in the other.

Star for his gallantry in action,* and the men of the 614th and 411th became friends.

Colonel Blackshear, the commander of the task force, described the action of the 614th as being "the most magnificent display of mass heroism I have every witnessed" ("Seek, Strike and Destroy," p. 13). Individual deeds of heroism described in the following citations need no comment.

Lieutenant George W. Mitchell, Silver Star:

For gallantry in action. During the daylight hours of 14 December 1944, Lieutenant Mitchell as second in command of a tank destroyer platoon, with a task force attacking * * *, took command of the platoon, when his platoon leader was wounded. Constantly exposed to intense enemy artillery, mortars and small arms fire, he magnificently and efficiently directed the fire of his guns against enemy positions. Numerous times, with utter disregard for his life, he moved from gun to gun supplementing the gun crews as the complement of gun positions were reduced by enemy action. In one instance Lieutenant Mitchell gallantly manned a gun, loading, sighting and firing it single-handedly. He courageously exposed himself, to aid in the evacuation of the wounded from the front line to places of safety and many lives were saved by this action. Lieutenant Mitchell's display of coolness under fire and magnificent courage was an inspiration to all and contributed to a large degree in the successful capture and occupation of ***, with a minimum of casualties to the task force. [General Order 89, 103rd Infantry Division, 28 December 1944]

Private William H. Phipps, Silver Star:

For gallantry in action. On 14 December 1944, in the vicinity of * * *, Private Phipps was seriously wounded while driving his quarter ton truck through an artillery barrage. Private Phipps, with utter disregard for his life, on his own initiative drove his platoon leader to a gun position without revealing his bitter wounds. He courageously drove forward in face of intense enemy artillery and bazooka fire, firing his weapon until he collapsed from his mortal wound. His valiant action assisted materially in the success of the infantry's mission. . . . [General Order 89, 103rd Infantry Division, 28 December 1944]

Corporal Peter Simmons, Silver Star (posthumous):

For gallantry in action, during the daylight hours of Dec. 14, 1944, in the vicinity of Climbach, France. Corporal Simmons, a member of a task force in the attack, went into position in open terrain under severe enemy artillery and small arms fire to man a three-inch gun. Although his position was in direct line of enemy fire and in full observation, he brilliantly and skillfully directed fire into enemy strong points. The intensity of the fire became so severe that the area was blasted by hostile fire wounding and killing his comrades on all sides. In face of certain self-destruction he

---

*General Order 88, 103rd Infantry Division, 27 December 1944.

gallantly stood at his post manning the gun with the assistance of one other comrade. He continued to pour fire into the enemy with such relentless furor and utter disregard for his life that they became confused. An enemy bullet found its mark and Corporal Simmons fell mortally wounded. As a result of his display of outstanding gallantry and superior calmness in the face of devastating fire he materially assisted the attacking infantry in reaching their objective. . . .*

Field Artillery Men: The 578th and 969th Battalions

Master Sergeant Floyd Jones, of the 578th Field Artillery Battalion, saw action in Europe from September 1944 until the war's end. His outfit had advanced beyond Bastogne to the southeast, he recalls, when the German counteroffensive in the Ardennes began, 16 December 1944.

Floyd Jones: "From the very beginning, when I realized there was going to be a conflict in which I would participate, I determined I was not going to allow myself to be warped by war. Therefore the time I spent in service was something I set outside of the mainstream of my life. I did my time with but one thought; in spite of hell I was going to return just as I left physically and mentally. While I was in the army I was a soldier, not an interested spectator, asking no quarter and giving none. When I stepped out of my uniform for the last time I stripped off the last vestige of army life and took up my life, to a great extent, where I had dropped it.

"This may sound strange but I had no illusions about World War II. World War I had been fought to end all wars and yet scarcely twenty-four years had passed and we were out to save it all over again. The result, on my part was, I was not carried away with chauvinism nor consumed with hatred of the enemy as so many people were.

"I had no qualms as to whether I would serve. My roots are here in this soil. In no way is this a denial of my African ancestry, rather an affirmation of the fact that I am an American. I hated the atrocities I read about, of course, but not the Japanese or the Germans. Can you pin the acts of a few sick, depraved people upon whole nations? I did not expect to save the world again or right any great wrong. I served because it was my job and I don't dodge jobs I feel I must do whether I like them or not. My concept then and now is life is much too short to let man's foolishness warp it, at least for me.

"The time I spent in service was one of the greatest experiences I ever had. I saw much of the world I would most certainly would not have seen otherwise. I did not see the victims of the war that an infantryman, or a front line man, would encounter. I saw devastation but not the victims. I am sure this

---

*Corporal Simmons's citation is quoted from *Seek, Strike, and Destroy*, p. 13. His posthumous award was sent to his family in Silver Street, South Carolina.

helped me remain an actor who would eventually remove his makeup and become himself once more.

"About race prejudice, the Europeans in our line of march, had no racial hang-ups. Those my group met were the French, Belgians, and Germans. Now I ran into prejudice and discrimination in Europe, don't misunderstand me, but it was marked, 'made in the United States.' Ole 'Mister Charlie' was there to make sure you never left home, so to speak.*

"I got the hell beat out of me soon after my arrival in France because I was alone and unarmed. I never soloed again. I was always accompanied by a 45, a knife, comparable to the Bowie knife, and a couple of live grenades. I wasn't attacked again; I wasn't wearing that arsenal for fun. No bunch of white GIs was ever going to beat the shit out of me again for fun and games; they were going to get a full-scaled war. I planned to enjoy my passes and furloughs whenever, wherever, and with whomever I chose. When I went on furlough I looked like an infantry man heading for the front line. Whenever I saw a bunch of white GIs heading my way I just unbuttoned my coat, and as the saying goes, 'let it all hang out.' Believe me they walked on by. But so much for how I managed to have a wonderful time when I was not on duty in the battle zone.

"When the draft came into existence I expected to be 1A so I enlisted. The navy, coast guards, and the marines had excuses for turning me down. I joined the air force and was grateful for a deferment in order to finish college. In April '43 this went out the window and I was called into the army, not the air force.

"I reported to Fort Sill, Oklahoma, for training in heavy artillery. There I was offered OCS but I turned it down since I aspired to ASTP. From Sill I went to some camp near Paris, Texas. I don't recall the name because I was soon sent to ASTP at Ohio State University. As luck would have it this program died a sudden death, and I was back at the same old stand. This time I went to Fort Bragg to help form the 578th. My rating was corporal.

"I must confess I made a career out of going to NCO service schools for two reasons. First, to delay combat duty as long as possible. Second, to be well prepared for all eventualities. Besides my training in heavy artillery I attended Intelligence School at Camp Lee, Virginia; Chemical Warfare School in New Jersey; and Ordnance School at Aberdeen Proving Grounds.

---

*The coastal artillery unit to which Sergeant Warren Carter belonged moved up the west coast of France the summer of 1944 and was never fired upon. The only hostility he personally encountered overseas was from American whites, "just natural-born haters." He found the French people, like the English whom he had previously met, kind and hospitable, but "the race problem followed us overseas. After all, the same characters here were transported with their venom abroad." He reported "one strange thing. Though our outfit had a comparatively easy time we had five suicides."

"Racially the south, USA, was the south and my situation was no different than any other Negro stationed a hundred miles south of hell. I stayed out of the south's way. I do recall a bit of racial madness that occurred at the camp in Texas.

"Twenty-five of us had been confined to the area for three days, awaiting orders to move. We were out in a field playing baseball when a tank came rolling down the nearby road. White civilians were riding on top of this metal monster. Instinctively I knew this tank didn't mean us any good. I noticed its .50 caliber machine guns were aimed in our direction. Having been well trained in all kinds of weaponry as it moved towards us I slowly, but casually, kept out of the range of those guns. I was too far away to hear what was said but I could see the action. Suddenly the white officer who had us in charge came running like crazy down the road. He reached the tank, and there was more talk. Finally the tank turned around and went shopping for victims elsewhere. It seems there had been trouble in town the night before, and they were looking for the 'niggers' who did not know their place. They were looking all right with an army tank; one of the men on top was the sheriff. Our officer had vouched for the fact that we had not been off the post in three days.

"As I said, I stayed out of the south's way. In the north, stateside, or in Europe, it was different; you didn't have to worry about a damned posse hunting you down. Their damned posses only went on the prod when a Negro was victorious in whatever fracas occurred. Whenever a Negro GI was killed down there it was never investigated, by anyone, and was chalked up as an accident, suicide, or provoked. One of their suicides was hanging from a tree with his hands tied behind his back!

"My final assignment was with the 578th Heavy Field Artillery. I can say with pride we had a creditable record of 98 percent hits. We could hit a man's handkerchief 22 miles away. Perhaps this clarifies why I can say I didn't see the victims that happened to be in or around our targets. Our work was almost as impersonal as a pilot's. Sometimes we saw our target; often we didn't. If we did, it was usually several days later and by then it would have been hit by a variety of other weapons so we certainly didn't bother to try and pinpoint our work.

"There were a number of excellent black field artillery units. Most of these used the 155 mm howitzer whose range was, I believe, something like 8 to 10 miles. Other groups used the 90 mm guns. They were smaller field pieces. As far as I know the 578th Battalion was the only black outfit firing the 155 mm Long Toms. Our maximum range was 22 miles. The German gun that might be called comparable to the Long Tom was the 88. It lacked our range but it made up for this in versatility. The 88 had a muzzle blast cover that muffled the sound and made its flame invisible on firing. Our gun had no such cover. In order to pinpoint our guns at night they used what is called sight and sound. They would see the fire coming out of the guns, pinpoint the time it took the shell to hit, then compute the distance and knock out our guns. To avoid this we had to do our firing during the daylight hours.

"The 88 was a very sophisticated weapon. It could be mounted on the Germans' heavy tanks, used as a very effective antiaircraft gun, and then as a straight field piece. The Long Tom was strictly a field piece. We were called on to mow the man down from a distance, giving those who had weapons with less range a chance to move in for the final kill.

"We arrived in Wales shortly after the Normandy invasion. A month later we were somewhere near Lille, France. Our first engagement was in September 1944, and from then on we were on the move. We were on call to General Hodge's 1st Army, Patton's 3rd Army, the 7th and 15th Armies, all of which composed the 12th Army Group. In short we were a Group Artillery Unit and could be placed anywhere in that Group.

"We enjoyed being with Patton because of his well-known vocabulary and remarks that were passed right down the line. Patton kept his superiors uptight; they never knew for sure where he was, excepting beyond where he should be.

"The battle I remember best that we participated in was the Battle of the Bulge, or if you prefer, the Battle of the Ardennes Forest. One would hardly forget 40-degrees-below-zero weather. Man, when the wind blew it made you think you had forgotten your drawers. You mentioned that some fellows said it was so cold they couldn't dig in their pieces, yet others did not have this trouble. Remember, the weather varied around an area as large as the Ardennes, so both groups are telling the truth.

"I am a little hazy on our exact position when the Bulge happened. This I am sure of, when we began firing we were firing to the west which means we were beyond Bastogne. We had dug in southeast of Bastogne, expecting to pull up and move further east, when all hell broke out in the Ardennes some days before Christmas. We were firing over Bastogne, trying to keep the Germans from sealing off the town.

"You notice I said we were awaiting orders to pull up and move on. Unless we were specifically en route and stopped for a rest, whenever we stopped we dug our guns in. It takes about a half-hour of hard work to dig those damned Long Toms in and a special truck to pull them out. There are 15 men to each gun and four of them are necessary just to carry the projectile to the gun. Each man has his job to do, and nobody stands around holding his hands when we were in action. We could fire about every 10 to 15 seconds when ordered to fire at will. In good weather a good gun crew could dig in and be ready to fire in 18 to 20 minutes.

"After we dug our guns in, we would wait for instructions, which came some 12 to 72 hours later. Our targets came from forward observers in Piper Cubs or fire direction centers. I generally worked in the fire direction center. There we could observe through powerful binoculars and radio instructions to the gun crews. When given directions, number one gun would fire and then the other guns would zero in on that particular target; each gun was a complement to the others.

"We had just been sitting around awaiting orders when news came of the German breakthrough, so—get ready for action! This is the way it was with Long Toms, for days nothing, and then we would be busy for hours. When we went into action at the Bulge, we were firing for several days and nights without let-up. German 88s were concentrated at the breakthrough point, so we didn't have them to think about at night. Actually in this instance I don't think it would have mattered. They would have had to think of something to keep us firing because at that time the Long Toms were just about all the allies had.

"At the Bulge we had something like 64 Long Toms over a ten-mile spread but every gun could fire on the same point. In our battalion my gun was the number one gun most of the time. Every battalion had a number one gun; every gun to the left or right of number one counted off from that gun. If we were firing, say ten miles at a target, every gun to our left or right would have to adjust a number of degrees to come in on the same target. The guns behind would have to make the same adjustment, plus adjust for elevation. Now, you understand we could spread fire; so many guns on several different targets. In short, we could batter the hell our of a number of targets at once or we could zero in on one. With all that fire power on one objective, obliteration was the result. All artillery pieces are at their best somewhat short of their maximum range. At the Bulge I believe we were firing 12 to 14 miles.

"The 578th was not supporting the 101st and 82nd Airborne. If my memory serves me right, those two divisions were trapped within the Bulge. We were trying to smash the German supply line, prevent the encirclement of Bastogne, and break up the crack panzer units the Germans had brought up for this breakthrough. Any support we were giving was to our troops that were trying to get into Bastogne who were to help those inside of the Bulge breakout, or if possible to hold Bastogne. We didn't see the targets, but we knew this was a crucial. Later we learned artillery made the difference in the early days. Fog and snow had grounded allied planes, so though we dominated the air to a great extent at this time they had to sit on their hands and pray for clear skies. Patton was on his way back to the rescue, but he had to have time; the artillery was fighting like hell until help could arrive. There were tanks inside of the Bulge, but our tanks were never a match for the heavy panzers and certainly not when outnumbered. I understand a division of infantrymen, not too long off of the boat, were on the perimeter or just inside of the Ardennes; they damned near got wiped out.

"Very few people know that two black artillery battalions were trapped inside of the Bulge, the 333s and 969th. Both fought like hell on the inside. The 333s sustained the heaviest losses of any artillery unit of the VIII Corps Artillery Unit—a handful of officers and over 200 men. Some of those guys fought as infantrymen when they lost their field pieces.

"I guess I remember the battle of the Ardennes Forest best because we were getting information regularly via our communications as to what was transpiring. They wanted us to know it was one hell of a mess and a lot of our men were dying. We fired around the clock, for how many days I can't say, but we never worked like that before or after.

"The skies began to clear, and old 'blood and guts' arrived. And in his division, I say with pride, was the crack black tank battalion, the 761st. We could let up then, but they had their work cut out for them because a good many of the Germans facing them were SS men. I learned afterwards they had been absolutely merciless on the Belgians and many of their allied captives.

"Eisenhower broadcast during the breakthrough asking for volunteers because the Germans were really cutting a swath through our guys. They wanted volunteers for the infantry from service units—quartermasters, engineers, cooks, everyone. This meant they welcomed blacks to pick up a rifle, get a little training, and jump into that cauldron. Something like 2,500 Negroes volunteered. They never show it in the movies, but a lot of 'us' fought and died at the Bulge. To my knowledge these volunteers, and they did right well, were not returned to their previous condition of servitude when it was over. They remained infantrymen attached to a white unit.

"A couple of buddies and I got drunk and under the influence got carried away and volunteered for the infantry. We went to the officer in charge and expressed our desire. He told us to go to hell. He wanted to know if we were out of our minds; three of his best men. Afterwards when sobriety returned I knew I must have been out of my tree for such a brilliant idea. I am forever grateful that they weren't about to let what they considered skilled technicians go running off to the infantry.

"After the Bulge we didn't see too much action. We crossed the Rhine at Dusseldorf and took part in the Battle of the Rhine.

"The biggest enemy to artillery is counter-artillery and air raids. Fortunately for us when we arrived, the skies were just about controlled by the allies. We had what was called anti-aircraft machine gun battalions that were to protect us during an air raid. I don't know the number of the unit but there was one such unit, black, that had a 100 percent average, having never lost any artillery, etc., guarded by them."

After VE Day, Jones found himself headed across the Atlantic Ocean not for home, but for the South Pacific. He was on board ship for 47 days and spent three weeks that "seemed forever" in Hollandia, New Guinea, before returning to the states.

Master Sergeant Jesse Cummings was in the 969th Field Artillery

Battalion, trapped inside the Bulge in December 1944. The 969th was awarded a Distinguished Unit Citation for its work there, on recommendation of the commander of the 101st Ariborne, General Maxwell Taylor.

A midwesterner, Cummings was sent for basic training to Fort Sill, Oklahoma, and from there to Camp Gruber, also in Oklahoma. There he encountered an aspect of racial discrimination unlike any reported in the previous interviews.

Jesse Cummings: "On my first pass to the nearby town I asked a girl for directions to the colored USO. Before I had finished the sentence a police car pulled up. The cops wanted to know what I was doing talking to the girl. I told them and they said, 'Move on and don't let us catch you talking to our white women again.' I was flabbergasted. White? She was darker than I am and I certainly am not fair. I later learned she was an Indian girl and in Oklahoma, at least during the war, Indians are considered white. I found this to be about the most ridiculous thing I had ever heard. Indians who are treated like dogs, no, worse than dogs and have been for years by the whites were white in Oklahoma and a black serviceman could not speak to one of their women. The real pitiful part was that dumb chick was pleased that the police had dipped in, because that made her white for a moment. I suppose she would have frothed at the mouth had she known I only spoke to her because I thought she was a colored girl which in my book was paying her a compliment. Hell, the American Indian is so far down on the totem pole whites have forgotten they exist.

"At all of the camps where I was stationed my officers were always white and the NCOs black. My training was in artillery so I ended up with the 969th Field Artillery, which turned out to be one of the best damned field artillery units this country produced. I'll say now my unit was never given the credit it should have received, simply because it was black.

"The 969th consisted of two firing batteries, howitzers, and two service batteries. It was a part of the 333rd Field Artillery Group. Our sister unit was the 333rd Field Artillery Battalion, whose complement was similar to ours.

"When we left New York for overseas our first stop was Wales. We did more maneuvers there and then went to England. General Patton visited our unit. He told us some of us could get killed, but that was war. He added that we would be under him, and we were most of the time. This in itself was a compliment to our ability, because it was generally known that Patton would not accept anything but the best in his command. General Patton was admired by the average dog-face simply because he was always where the fighting was, right in the middle of the fracas. He wasn't a behind-the-lines general with some maps on a wall. I must say he kept us busy shifting us wherever we were needed. We were so occupied that it was a year before I got a pass and the war was coming to an end. The Germans dubbed the 969th the *'schwarz* with automatic weapons.' It meant we could fire our piece rapidly and effectively.

"From England we went to St. Lô, France, where we dug our pieces in amidst a lot of dead soldiers and cattle. Anybody caught smoking could be shot, we were that close to the enemy. We had been brought in to replace a white outfit that not only were missing the objective but were firing so low they had killed some of our infantry. Our job was done in St. Lô in short order, and we were off and running to the next one. I don't remember the town but we were brought in to take out a church that was being used by the enemy for observation. It was a shame we had to dig our pieces in. It took us exactly three rounds to bring the building down; all three were on target.

"From France we went to Belgium, and for a bit of rest we were stationed in the Ardennes Forest. The whole country of Belgium to choose from and we get the Ardennes! It was beginning to get cold, so with all of that timber around we built some makeshift cabins. We made one mistake, which was natural since this was a rest period: we did not dig in our pieces. Suddenly the German breakthrough came and there we were with field pieces we could not fire effectively. Fortunately for us the Germans didn't know this. It was in December '44 when all hell broke loose in the Ardennes. I suspect our orders were to hold where we were. We were then shifted several times before we were ordered to the 101st Airborne's perimeter near Bastogne. I should add that we were able to dig in at our other sites and get out some mail.

"Our sister unit, the Triple 3s, had been moved out of our bivouac, and when the breakthrough came they were face-to-face with some SS troops. They lost a lot of men. The Triple 3s also had the bad luck to have one of their top officers, white, chicken on them and just walk away. The men finally started to drift away as a result. Another officer appeared on the scene and had no trouble getting them back into action. They were eventually joined to our unit on the perimeter. Because of their heavy loss of men they could not function as a separate unit.

"I think you will find it interesting that the 333rd Field Artillery Group, besides including the 969th and the Triple 3s, had a white unit, the 771st. The 771st had been shifted around until it ended up at Chenogne. The Triple 3s were near Chenogne, and the 969th was near a place called Villeroux. The 771st position was between the 333s and us. If I recall this correctly, a white infantry unit out in front of the 771st broke and started to withdraw through the 771st. The 771st got the fever and they took off also. The Triple 3s and the 969th stayed put. We heard when the army caught up with those men they were half-way across Belgium.

"I believe it was at this time the 333s officer showed the white feather. I think I can say that the 333s and the 969th were left with an open flank with the unexpected departure of the 771st. We were pulled out before the Germans knew about the gap in our lines. Of course, they were pretty busy raising hell elsewhere, or should I say everywhere, and that might explain why they did not exploit this hole at once.

"We had had some pretty scary moments to have nothing to fight with but field pieces, so the 969th armed itself with automatic weapons from the bodies of the dead of the 101st and 102nd Airborne. Some of them were in the Ardennes when the trouble started. Others had apparently tried to relieve them because some of the bodies we took weapons from still had parachutes on.

"The 969th dug in, in and around Bastogne, and we were real busy getting out the mail. Patton's arrival and clear skies could not have come at a better time because we were getting a little low on shells.

"I should say our commanding officer was an Arkansas cracker, but he was a good officer and a fair-minded man. Several members of our unit won the Silver Star and these weren't just being given away to blacks.

"My unit fought all the way to Berlin. I most certainly did not like the ways of the army, but I was and am mighty proud to have been a part of the 969th.

"I guess I must have suffered a minor case of shell shock, because when I got back to the states and my home town I applied for various jobs for which I was qualified. It ended up that I went to work in a factory doing the same dirty work allotted to blacks. Nothing had changed stateside, and that shoulder-to-shoulder crap and brothers-under-the-skin at Bastogne were just the exigency of the moment. It simply was we had better fight together or we damned sure were going to die together."

Driving the Red Ball Express

The 1942 oversupply of qualified applicants for the air force program meant that Staff Sergeant Chester Jones (3418th Trucking Company) would be a tank ordnance man and a driver in the Red Ball Express rather than a flyer. He and a childhood friend, white, were inducted at the same time in Wyoming, and stayed together for basic training at Fort Carson, Colorado, although Jones, being black, narrowly escaped assignment to the table-waiting detail at the officers' club. On reaching Aberdeen, Maryland, they were separated and assigned to segregated groups for training: "We might as well have been on different sides of the world, for Aberdeen was two separate worlds, one black and the other white. Clark and I saw each other again four years later when we were both out of the army and back home in Wyoming in 1946." For this young westerner segregation and discrimination were completely new experiences.

Chester Jones: "At the proving grounds I was assigned to Tank Ordnance

School. There one learned the mechanics of tanks of all weights; how to replace their treads, and repair their engines. We drove tanks up and down hills, through mud holes, and into trees to see if they were ready for action. We would often go from Aberdeen to Camp Pickett, Virginia, and that was something else. Pickett was more segregated and rigid in its discrimination than Aberdeen. If you got caught on the white side of Pickett during meal time you were out of luck. You couldn't enter any of the white PX's to buy food and they darned sure weren't going to suggest you eat with them. If you knew you were going to Pickett the better part of valor was to carry along a sandwich, just in case.

"We had a minor skirmish one time at Pickett. A whole company of our ordnance was there and we were stationed out in the woods. Entering the first PX we came to, it turned out to be white. The men in charge turned their noses up like they were smelling something bad while they informed us they couldn't sell to us and we'd have to go to the colored PX. We promptly turned out the joint and then headed back to the woods. Nothing came of it because they didn't know who the culprits were other than we were black, and you know we all look alike.

"We stayed at Camp Pickett two weeks doing advanced ordnance work; learning how to handle 18-ton wreckers to pull tanks back to ordnance depots for repairs, how to handle the winchs and all things that were used in handling disabled tanks. In my basic ordnance training all of the NCOs were black and the officers were both black and white. There were even a few black captains.

"When our training was finished we were given two weeks furlough. Upon my return several of us were told to report to Camp Reynolds, Pennsylvania, which meant our next stop would be POE. I was at Reynolds about a month and where the Pennsylvanians weren't the most hospitable people in the country we were fortunate in being near the Ohio border. Camp Reynolds could just as well have been in the deep south since it too had its black army area and white army area and never the twain shall mix or meet.

"Our orders finally came to us to report to Boston, our POE. When our train got to Boston it pulled right out onto the dock, and when we stepped down the ship was just about 25 yards away. I think that was the saddest day of my young life. I was eighteen, and along with thousands of other fresh-faced boys I marched up the gang plank with my 125-pound pack on my back. We were given pamphlets forbidding gambling and drinking. However as soon as I stepped aboard there were crap games and card games everywhere; there was no place to buy anything to drink. There were six or seven thousand of us aboard and we composed what was called a pool. We didn't belong to any unit yet so there was no separation along racial lines. Once we reached England this was quickly corrected.

"In England we went to the 10th Replacement Depot. If you had not known the army was segregated before you found it out there. Colonel

Killian was in charge. White soldiers were stationed at an old English army base in sturdy brick buildings. The Negroes were in a valley in pyramidal tents, four to a tent. After two weeks there it was a real pleasure to leave. We had work details in or around the nearby hamlets out from Birmingham. The work consisted of unloading officers' luggage and supplies for the 10th Replacement Depot. Birmingham and the surrounding hamlets were off-limits to Negroes.

"At night the colonel would have retreat and than there was a roll call for both black and white. Any infraction of the rules, at least in the eyes of the colonel was then dealt with, with sentences ranging from three to six months in the stockade. This particular stockade, along with the 10th Depot, had an infamous reputation. As a matter of fact in '47 or '48 Drew Pearson ran a long series of articles on the mistreatment of the soldiers meted out by the colonel at both the depot and the stockade. Colonel Killian was court-martialed as the result. He was found guilty, but I don't remember his exact punishment.

"Upon leaving the depot I was sent to the 3418th Trucking Company, which was soon to be called the Red Ball Express. I was assigned to this trucking outfit because of my mechanical background in tank ordnance; never did figure out what trucks had to do with tanks or vice versa but nevertheless I joined the 3418th as a mechanic.

"After the proper introduction to the ways and means of trucks my group left for France June 15, 1943. Celebrating our departure, I got stoned. The fellows poured me onto a truck as we took off for Liverpool.

"When we reached the big city we proceeded right on down to within a block of the docks. There we saw all kinds of supplies waiting to be taken across the channel. Our group camped right there in the street and we slept under the trucks.

"Three days later we boarded our ship, one of those deals with a rather flat but rounded bottoms. I noticed they had chained the trucks and tanks down and wondered why they bothered; why not just put them in gear. By the time we reached the middle of the channel I knew why; talk about the rock-and-roll waltz. That old tub waddled like an inebriated duck, did several dipsy doodles, and a few bumps and grinds. The English Channel is rough and I am here to tell you that puking became the order of the day; guys were sick all over the place.

"When we drove our trucks off our landing ship the following morning the water was five feet deep or more in some places. That's one time truck drivers needed life preservers. I was lucky in that my vehicle made the beach and climbed up with no trouble. The allied forces were something like ten to twelve miles inland and the evidence of their landing June 6, was still there; dead bodies floating on the water, laying along the shoreline, on the beach, dead soldiers strewn everywhere. If you were not conditioned to seeing the dead you received an unforgettable initiation on the beach.

"Our group set up camp about four miles inland. Immediately the truckers took their vehicles to the nearby ammunition and gasoline depots, loaded up and headed for the front. These men came under fire as soon as they were within range of the enemy's artillery.

"After Cherbourg was captured and the combat troops had moved further on, a big Red Cross center was set up in this city. That Red Cross center was off-limits to Negro soldiers until a Negro chaplain with the rank of major heard about the situation in England. He came over and got it straightened out so black, English, etc., troops could use the Red Cross facilities. From that day to this I have never contributed a dime to anything concerning the Red Cross nor do I ever plan to. This was the second time I had encountered discrimination within the Red Cross. The first time was in England. We had been delivering some big tank wreckers to a designated area and stopped in Manchester at the Red Cross to get a hot meal. They refused to serve us. There were white soldiers all over the place eating. One white soldier spoke up saying he didn't see why we could not be served like the rest of them. His courage changed nothing, and we dined on K rations. We did not expect them to give us the food and were prepared to pay, but they did not cater to our kind. Cherbourg washed me up with the Red Cross forever. To serve humanity, the Red Cross, bullshit!

"It was after we left Cherbourg that the Red Ball Express was formed. There were a few white companies in this group but it was overwhelmingly black, except for officers. It was composed of six trucking companies. My company was one of those assigned to pick up supplies at the beach and haul it to the front. As the combat troops moved further, of necessity we had to split the trip at a half-way point. One driver would drive from the beach to the half-way point, where another driver would take over. The second driver would take it to the front, return to the half-way point and the first driver would be on his way again back to the beach. All of this driving was done at night with black-out lights. I believe that the Red Ball Express set a record for moving supplies both in speed and amount. When General Patton was breaking through and running all over the place, it was the Red Ball that kept him supplied. Our truckers did a fantastic job driving with those slits, cat-eyes as we called them, at night loaded with high octane gas and all kinds of ammunition and explosives. Our speed was thirty to forty miles an hour no matter what the weather, and we drove every night.

"The road over which the truckers passed as they went from the beach to the major cities in northern France and Paris was renamed in their honor. It became known as the Red Ball Express. There was a joke about a soldier missing for two days with his captain's jeep. When he finally appeared the captain wanted to know where the hell he had been. Tired and a little angry himself the soldier replied, 'On that goddamn Red Ball Express. I accidentally got into one of their convoys and it was 100 miles later before I could get a chance to turn off.' This actually happened many times. If a vehicle got in between us, it was just there until we stopped.

"We had some accidents; after all the men were human and vehicles do have mechanical failure over which man has no control. The one I particularly remember involved Boswell, a soldier from Louisiana. My group was than at the half-way point that went to the front. While waiting for our loads we had managed to buy some chickens from nearby farmers. Our cook had really cooked them. Boswell loved the gizzards, and a lot of the guys gave him theirs; he had a mess kit full of them. We were late taking off that evening because our trucks from the beach were late getting in. When they arrived we gassed up and were on our way. It must have been two or three hours later that we were winding through some little town—the road was one *S* curve after another. Boswell apparently decided to pass the truck ahead of him on a curve as we entered the town. He couldn't quite make the turn and hit one of those cement telephone poles, shearing it off. In some manner the wires held the upper part of the pole and swung it right into the cab where Boswell was sitting. We stopped right in the middle of the town, yet strangely enough no one in trucks immediately in front or behind me knew why, nor did I. It was pitch black, so what, we decided to stretch our legs since we had stopped. A sergeant came running up to ask if any of us had any first-aid equipment; that was the first time we knew something was wrong. All of us ran back to Boswell's truck, which was about midway in the convoy; he didn't need first-aid. Half of his head had been caved in by the pole. Pushing his truck to the side of the road, we had to leave him. He was our first casualty. This was sometime in July, when we were supplying Patton's 3rd Army. I should say most of the officers we encountered in Patton's army were fairly decent guys but there are dogs in all outfits, and there were a few in his.

"While supplying Patton's army with guns, ammunition, and food, we happened to be carrying gasoline, which they were running short of, up to a place called Spa, and we ended up in the Battle of the Bulge. Gasoline, food, and ammunition dumps were on secondary roads around a place called Bergilers, about fifteen miles from Liège, Belguim, a big city. When supplies were needed up front, we would load up at the proper dump and take off. If the Germans could have captured Liège they would have been back in business with all the supplies they needed.

"At the time the Battle of the Bulge started, our trucks got trapped between Liège and Spa, near the border. A hole was finally located that our trucks could get through and we left the Bulge carrying soldiers who had been forced out by the Germans or who had run out.

"Were there infantrymen on our trucks? I think they were all infantrymen. No, I don't remember their number—whatever troops were along our route were the ones we picked up. It struck me as strange they were leaving the scene where their kind of action was. We picked up a batch of them at Saint Vith. You have to remember one thing. Before they found the hole we escaped through, everything we were hearing was bad. They didn't want our trucks to fall into German hands. We drivers didn't want to fall into German hands, either. So you see I was less interested in who got into my truck than in getting the hell out of there.

"When we finally got our trucks back to Bergilers, combat officers were coming around asking the truckers to volunteer for infantry duty at the Bulge. My opinion was: they said I didn't have sense enough to be a combat soldier stateside—well if I didn't have it then I damned sure didn't have it in their emergency. They did get quite a few volunteers from black service groups: cooks, bakers, truckers, engineers, etc. Those who volunteered were in mixed groups because they didn't have enough blacks to make entire black companies, or maybe they weren't too particular at the time. Those blacks who did volunteer did a creditable job, which shows all they ever needed was an honest-to-goodness chance.

Patton was called back to relieve Bastogne and all those little villages trapped in the German encirclement. Hundreds of soldiers were being killed, more white than black, because until the volunteers, the primary black combat units in the Bulge were artillery.

After Patton returned and the siege was lifted, we had to take our trucks across the Remagen Bridge, over the Ruhr River. This was the bridge the Americans were able to capture before the Germans blew it up. However, it had been weakened by the Germans' attempt to destroy it. After 25,000 allied troops and tanks had crossed, its structural safety was questioned. They held us back, to test it first and then decide—fortunately for us, for late that afternoon one of the spans gave way. We spent the night where we were, and come morning black and white engineers, side by side, were building a pontoon bridge across the river. Around 3:00 P.M. it was completed. We proceeded to cross. It was a hairy experience staying a truck's length behind each other in low gear on the metal-covered pontoons. The bridge would stand the pressure all right but you had to keep your wits about you as it would bob and weave every now and than. Sniper and artillery fire aimed in our direction added to the discomfort of the situation. The engineers had constructed the bridge under the same enemy fire.

"Once we crossed the river we saw integrated combat groups; they were the volunteers from the Bulge. There were black riflemen, BAR men, etc., mixed right in with the whites. It seems the blacks had done such a good job at the Bulge no one thought of sending them back to the kitchen because they were still needed.

"After the Remagen Bridge crossover, I was assigned to the 961st Tank Ordnance. This unit was stationed at Liège and I was going to get my first opportunity to utilize the training I had received at Aberdeen Proving Grounds. We had to go out in 18-ton wreckers and pull in damaged tanks for repairs. The Germans had an armor-piercing shell that cut through the exterior of a tank and then exploded. Aberdeen had not prepared us for this. When you opened the hatches of the wrecked tanks that could be repaired, some of the most ghastly sights you could ever imagine were exposed; what were once human beings were scrambled all over the interior of these tanks. You didn't stop to figure out which leg or arm went with which remains, if there were a whole torso. You just put it all in a plastic container and cleaned the spattered brains and blood from the inside of the vehicle. I was a tank mechanic, but cleaning out those wrecks went with the job. You got used to it; you had better or you would never keep any food down and you'd blow your stack besides.

"There were always those instances when some unexpected horror would be revealed and you'd discover you were not as used to the blood and gore as you thought. We were grateful for one thing, the cold weather. We got a slight idea what it really could be like when we would pull in a tank whose interior for some reason was still slightly warm. The sickening odor began to hit you as you started loosening the hatch. Thank goodness these were few and far between.

"My remaining soldiering days were uneventful. When the war ended we were sent to Bremerhaven in preparation for our eventual return to the United States. Here the old racial bug-a-boo came back in full force. At night we would go to Bremen, a large city, for entertainment. I ran into a lot of my trucking buddies there. One night they rented a cafe for a party and several of us at Bremerhaven were invited. Two of the truckers went to pick up their girls. They stopped at a bar en route to have a drink. At the bar they encountered a group of whites from the 29th Division. Any Negro in Europe during World War II knows the 29th. It was an all-cracker division that had a real 'thing' about blacks. In Bremen Negro soldiers did not go out on the streets alone at night because they not only got stomped but members of the 29th enjoyed killing them.

"My two friends who had stopped in the bar were forced to do a jig while these crackers shot at their feet, the ceiling, everywhere. The truckers were finally sent on their way with shots to encourage their haste. They returned to the party and told what had happened. About twenty-five men at the party returned to the scene of the jig and shot it up. Five or six of the 29th bit the dust. The fellows from the party quickly returned to the party and gave their guns to the German cafe owner, who hid them. In about six minutes the places was swarming with MPs and their officers. They took all of us to a school building and lined us up. They picked up all the Negroes they ran into within a half-dozen square blocks of our cafe. Two MPs came in with two Negro soldiers saying they just entered the area. The captain in charge said, 'Bring them in anyway and line them up with the rest of the niggers.' After making us stand a while they brought in the men of the 29th who had been at OK Corral and had not been shot. They were to identify the assailants, but as you know and as I have said, we all look alike so they were unable to single out one man. I have an idea making Negro soldiers do the jig did not long remain a favorite form of entertainment among the men of the 29th.

"One evening, shortly before leaving Bremerhaven, an older soldier in our group, who liked to take walks alone around the base, with a bottle, left for his nightly constitutional. As far as could be ascertained he never left the base perimeter, but in about an hour he staggered into the guard house with a gaping chest wound. He had been shot by an unidentifiable white assailant. Captain DuPree, the fairest officer in our outfit, had me assist him in taking the man to the hospital. I do not know what happened to him because we were soon homeward bound.

"In case you think this kind of thing was just common in Germany, I almost got killed in Paris by a white American soldier. This incident occurred while I was still a trucker. We were trucking supplies to Paris at the time and stopped at a given spot since we had no further orders. Two of us decided to sneak a quick peek at Paris. We left our carbines in the trucks and walked about four blocks when we saw a bar empty of patrons except women. I was too green to understand at first, but my buddy was inside and upstairs before I could blink an eye. Upon my return to the bar, my buddy was still occupied so I had a drink with my companion. Just than two white soldiers entered. Both had been drinking and one was stoned. The drunk soldier staggered over to me and said, 'You black-sons-of-bitches don't sit with white women at home, and I'll be damned if you'll do it here when I'm around.' The next second I was looking at his forty-five leveled at my chest. There was nothing to be said on my part, all things being unequal. He ordered me out of the bar and I left with him following me with his gun practically between my shoulder blades. I expected a bullet any minute but I still worried about my buddy in the bar upstairs unaware of the turn of events. As soon as the white guy turned back to the bar I ducked into a doorway, only to have that pistol-packing ass turn back, find me, and start marching me again. This time I knew I was dead but after we covered a block he turned back after making it quite clear to me I had better not come back. I was standing there wondering what to do when I heard the sound of feet; it was the rest of the group. I told them what had happened and when they hit that bar they were like a juggernaut. One fellow teed off on the pistol packer with the butt of his carbine. He knocked him halfway across the room and was on him with both feet before he stopped reeling. I kind of hated to see the other guy get stomped, but I reasoned silence gives consent and he hadn't opened his mouth when I was on the receiving end. The truckers tossed them out into the street after mopping them up. They didn't return with reinforcements. I'm not so sure they were able to talk for several days. If there is a humorous side to this incident, my friend joined us downstairs eventually totally unaware that anything out of the ordinary had transpired.

"I have one last thing to say. The day I received my discharge papers from the United States Army I was the happiest man in the whole world."

Jones mentions the call for black volunteers at the Bulge and notes having seen black BAR men in what looked like integrated combat groups at a later date. Because of the acute need for infantry replacements in December 1944, Lieutenant General John C. H. Lee, after consulting with General Eisenhower, sent out to his base and section commanders a call for volunteers December 26. It included the statement "It is planned to assign you without regard to color or race to the units where assistance is most needed" (Lee, pp. 688–89). An upset over this statement followed at Supreme Allied Headquarters; frantic efforts were made to suppress it, and a revised version was hastily issued.

General Lee had made his suggestion with the purpose of ending hostilities "without delay"; those upset by it cited departure from official policy, embarrassment to the War Department, and provocation of "every negro organization, pressure group and newspaper" by a willingness to integrate in a life-or-death situation only. The upshot was that small groups of black volunteers, of company size or less, were used as replacements for similar white units. (See Lee, pp. 688–92 for details of the episode and for an account of the superior performance of the black units in combat.)

Edward A. Carter, Jr., a volunteer, was assigned to the Seventh Army Provisional Infantry Company No. 1, attached to the 56th Armored Infantry Battalion. He won the Distinguished Service Cross for "extraordinary heroism" in action near Speyer, Germany, 23 March 1945:

> When the tank on which he was riding received heavy bazooka and small arms fire, Sergeant Carter voluntarily attempted to lead a three-man group across an open field. Within a short time, two of his men were killed and the third seriously wounded. Continuing on alone, he was wounded five times and finally was forced to take cover. As eight enemy riflemen attempted to capture him, Sergeant Carter killed six of them and captured the remaining two. He then crossed the field using as a shield his two prisoners from whom he obtained valuable information concerning the disposition of enemy troops. [General Order 580, 7th Army HQ, 4 October 1945]

Some of the men whose citations for valor are included in this chapter could not pass a literacy test. Were they thereby less qualified to be soldiers and leaders of men than their white counterparts?

Chapter 4

The "Spookwaffe":

Airmen of the 332nd Fighter Group

The United States Army Air Corps began to accept Negro applicants for aviation cadet training in March 1941, although some months elapsed before such training began. Eventually there would be four squadrons, with 200 pilots, a token representation of the Negro in the air force.

The government invested millions of dollars in constructing the Tuskegee Army Air Field, which would maintain racial segregation. Officials at Tuskegee Institute had urged the building of the base there, their reason being that Tuskegee already had a civilian pilot-training center. With the new government installation, Tuskegee was given a government contract for the primary training of all Negro aviation cadets.

Strong opposition to the Tuskegee plan was expressed by Judge William Hastie, civilian aide to the secretary of war, who observed that the school "promoted and tied itself advantageously into a Jim Crow army program."* Hastie fought hard to get black men into the air force, but frustrated by the "reactionary and discriminatory practices of the Army Air Force affecting Negroes," he resigned his post with the Roosevelt administration. After his resignation, he wrote an article, "On Clipped Wings," published in October 1943 by "Crisis" magazine, in which he charged that black men were allowed to enter the air force only as fighter pilots, qualified for the most difficult type of combat flying. Hastie accused the air force of dragging its feet in the training of black air force mechanics. He further noted that Negroes who were already specialists in flying or ground work were overlooked as material for Tuskegee. Fred H. Hutcherson was flying bombers to England from Canada but could find no position available with the USAAF. James L. Peck, a veteran combat pilot from the Spanish Civil War and a writer on aviation, was only in

---

*See Judge William Hastie, "On Clipped Wings," *Crisis*, published as a separate issue, October 1943. Quotations from Judge Hastie in this paragraph are drawn from the article.

his early thirties when he vainly offered his services to his own country. He represented the one black man who could have given black air cadets the benefit of his knowledge and experience of having flown successfully against Luftwaffe. James Redden, Negro infantry officer, held a civilian pilot's license but was too tall for pursuit flying. He was assigned to the glider pilots' school, but on arrival was ordered to return to the infantry.

The first Negro airmen to go overseas were the men of the 99th Pursuit Squadron. Although activated in 1941, it was not until April 1943 that the 99th sailed for North Africa and was slowly introduced to combat. In August 1943 its squadron leader, then Lieutenant Colonel B. O. Davis, Jr., was returned to the states to command and to complete the training of the 332nd Fighter Group, made up of the 100th, 301st, and 302nd fighter squadrons. Davis's place in the 99th was taken by Major George S. ("Spanky") Roberts.

At this time the fate of black pilots was actually in question. Most reports received from ranking air officers in Africa were uncomplimentary, and on 16 October 1943, Lieutenant Colonel Davis was questioned by the Advisory Committee on Negro Troop Policies (McCloy Committee) concerning the unfavorable reports received. The committee had under consideration a proposal to reduce Negro air units and reassign those in existence.

In the interval, the fortunes of the 99th had changed. Under the leadership of Major Roberts, the 99th was fast becoming a veteran combat team. In January 1944 its men saw action at Anzio. The October proposal of the advisory committee was not acted upon.*

The 332nd Fighter Group, under the command of Lieutenant Colonel Davis, arrived at Taranto, Italy, between 29 January and 3 February 1944, and was attached to the 12th Air Force. On 7 June the 332nd flew its first mission with the 15th Air Force. On 29 June the 99th Pursuit Squadron became the fourth fighter squadron of the 332nd, as was intended, and the 332nd was on the way to becoming one of the most respected fighter groups in all of Europe. Records kept by Lieutenant Colonel Walter Downs, summarizing the exploits of the 332nd, support this evaluation:

> The 332nd destroyed 111 enemy planes in the air and damaged 25. It destroyed 150 enemy aircraft on the ground; damaged 123. The group also destroyed 57 locomotives, damaged 67; destroyed 58 boxcars, damaged 506; sank one destroyer; sank 16 barges and boats, damaged 24 others; destroyed 2 oil and ammunition dumps, one radar installation, 6 motor transports, 15 gun implacements, 15 horse drawn vehicles, damaged 7 tanks on flat cars; destroyed 3 power transformers, damaged 2; and damaged 23 buildings and factories.
>
> The 332nd flew 1,267 mission in the 12th Airforce and 6,381 sorties. In the Strategic Air Command they flew 311 missions and 9,852 sorties. Their total missions flown were 1,578; sorties flown 15,553.

---

*See Lee, chapter 6, for details summarized here.

Captain Lee Archer, Captain Joseph Elsberry, and Captain Edward Toppins all had four kills. Captain Elsberry, Lieutenant Clarence Lester, and Lieutenant Harry Stewart all had three kills in one day. Captain Wendell Pruitt had three kills and a destroyer.

The pilots of the 332nd received: 865 Legion of Merit, 95 Distinguished Flying Crosses, 1 Silver Star, 14 Bronze Stars, 744 Air Medals and clusters, 8 Purple Hearts, and a Presidential Citation for the group.

Lieutenant Green received the Partisan Star M Class from the government of Yugoslavia. He bailed out over friendly territory, the Island of Vis, and helped a British mission fly supplies to Tito's men.

Major Lee Rayford flew two tours of duty and won the DFC with cluster.

With few exceptions, the men whose interviews appear in this chapter were part of the 332nd Fighter Group. There is a recognizable esprit de corps within this group, even after a lapse of almost thirty years since the end of World War II. The interviewer had constantly to be aware that the pronouns "I" and "we" are almost interchangeable with men of the 332nd, so close-knit were they. Their sense of group loyalty and of empathy is particularly noticeable in the interviews with communications officer Captain Samuel Fuller and with Captain Charles A. Hill, Jr., a pilot who owes his life to men in the control tower.

Two members of the 332nd interviewed, Lieutenant Colonel Henry Peoples and Captain Hill, remained in the Reserves at the conclusion of World War II. What they have to say of their later experiences is given added significance when related to the following facts: Executive Order #9981, signed by President Harry Truman in 1948, was intended to begin the desegregation of the armed forces. In 1950 the President's Committee on Equality of Treatment and Opportunity in the Armed Forces published Freedom to Serve, outlining a procedure for integrating the armed forces that has been credited with accelerating service desegregation during and after the Korean War.*

Gilbert Cargill was first a civilian instructor at Moton Field, Tuskegee Institute, beginning in 1941, before Pearl Harbor. In 1944 he became an advanced flight instructor at Tuskegee Army Air Field, with the rank of 2nd lieutenant, returning to civilian life in August 1945. He still flies when he can. Gargill has clocked around 11,000 hours as a pilot.

Gilbert Cargill: "One day in 1941 at my home in Cleveland, Ohio, I read that the government was offering pilot training gratis for those interested. I was definitely interested but fully expected to be rejected because I was colored—'black' was not the 'in' word then. To my surprise I was accepted.

---

*See Robert Twombly, ed., Blacks in America since 1865, pp. 333–34. See also above, publisher's intro., note 12.

"There were what they called three phases to be passed before you started in the government-sponsored program. First, the IQ exam. I had finished college so this was no problem. Second, a physical examination which I passed, though I had been highly sceptical and with good reason. In August 1940 I had had the same physical to qualify as an air force cadet. I was rejected because I had a 'malocclusion': it simply means my teeth didn't fit properly together in front. So I was going to fly with my teeth? My malocclusion was not mentioned the second time, but of course I was not aspiring to be a cadet in the USAAF, just a trainee in a government program. The third phase was a board review, which was an interrogation, I suppose it was to see how you would react under stress. I fully expected to get the axe here. However I was told the results would be mailed to me in about a week. This had taken place sometime in April.

"To say that I anticipated good news would be a lie. When you have had the door slammed in your face all of your life because of skin coloring you look for the worst if as nothing other than a defense mechanism. In a week the letter arrived to inform me that I had passed all three phases and in a month I would be assigned to a training school.

"In June I was assigned to Horn's Flying Service in Willoughby, Ohio. There the program consisted of four phases: primary, secondary, cross-country, and flight instructor. Only the top ten percent of each level would go on to the next. Still pessimistic, I figured I would make it through primary and then be rejected, but I decided to go as far as allowed in spite of my scepticism. I passed the primary exam with a good score and was asked if I was interested in phase two; I was. This consisted of bi-winged aircraft with about 225- to 250-horsepower engines. These were usually used for acrobatic flights. One particular maneuver I had difficulty with, but the day before the exam it came to me how to do this maneuver and I did so easily. Again I sailed through the written test and checked out quite well in my flight grades. It turned out I was always second or first throughout the entire program. Having completed this phase I was asked if I wished to proceed further; I did. They said they did not have an immediate opening for me but would have one in three or four months. This was in February. Come June I received a letter asking me to report to Akron, Ohio. There I learned if you finished the cross-country phase you automatically went into the instructor refresher course. I ended up with a commercial license and a flight instructor rating.

"On leaving Akron, those who had finished the course satisfactorily were told they would be contacted by the air force. A letter arrived at my home a couple of months later directing me to report with my credentials to Maxwell Field, Montgomery, Alabama, to become an instructor for the air force.

"Throughout my training I had been the only black in the program at least in the Ohio area. My name gives no indication of racial origin, so I was asked to come to Maxwell Field to instruct their cadets.

"When I walked in, the military person seated at the desk assumed I had made a mistake. I assured him I had been asked to come there and produced the letter. He was stunned and hastily disappeared into the back office. When he reappeared he was at least honest; they had not anticipated a Negro instructor. He informed me there was an airfield about 90 miles away, Moton Field at Tuskegee Institute, and that if I went right over they would take me. I figured I had come this far so 90 miles more wouldn't matter. I took a bus to Tuskegee.

"Upon my arrival I met those in charge and was pleased to see so many black pilot instructors of whom I was totally unaware until that very moment. Since all of the programs I had participated in were all white with the exception of me, my ignorance was understandable. These men, including me, gave the air force cadets of the original 99th Pursuit Squadron and later the 332nd Fighter Group their primary and secondary flying lessons. Black civilian instructors taught black cadets their basics at Moton Field; from there they went to Tuskegee airbase, which was like next door, and did their advance work under white air force officers.

"The black instructors were: Jack Johnson, Cecil Ryan, Wendell Lipscomb, James Wood, W. Foreman, Adolph Moet, Sherman Rhodes, Charles A. Anderson, Lewis Jackson, Abe Jackson, 'Chief' Allen, Jimmy Hill, Nathan Sams, Charlie Francis, Robert Terry, O. R. Harris, Hector Strong, John Pinkett, Robert Gordon, Robert Gray, Matthew Plummer (the only instructor I recall being lost during flight training), Joseph Ramus, Archie Smith, Jim Taylor, Jim Plimpton, and 'Muscles' Wright. Most of these men had received their training at Tuskegee. We instructors lived at the institute, usually at Fletcher Hall.

"Black cadets were already there when I came to Moton Field. The first group, including B. O. Davis and 'Spanky' Roberts, had finished their training.

"Five cadets were assigned to an instructor. We generally flew half of the day and each cadet was allowed to handle the plane 45 minutes per day when he first started. After he soloed his accumulation of airtime would increase. The Tuskegee cadets were of the highest caliber. All were college graduates; they were mentally and physically tops and they really wanted to be pilots.

"I cannot document this, but we instructors felt that in many cases men were washed out or eliminated because of some quota system set up determining the number of black pilots. My reason for my own feeling, in support of this, is I lost some cadets, washed out, who were natural pilots; they were good. These washouts were picked at random by the air force people without consulting the instructors. The white officers who did the picking were not working with the cadets so they had no way of judging their ability.

"Whenever a cadet went for an unannounced check ride he was through. If he happened to be a student of mine who I might think was the greatest and he was tagged for a check ride I could write him off. They had a hearing afterwards but it was just a matter of form. It was unfortunate, for some of those fellows were very disappointed: They knew they had a natural talent for flying; you know when something's right for you. Cadets could be eliminated in this manner right through the three phases of training. I would be willing to bet that 70 to 80 percent of those eliminated by this means should have passed.

"Now if the instructor felt the guy couldn't cut it, he would ask for a check ride. Of course there were some who weren't cut out to be pilots; it doesn't take a good instructor long to recognize this. One of the biggest things is the fear of coming down. I had one cadet who was pretty good on take-off but, when it came to setting her down he just wasn't the same; even he recognized he could not overcome this obstacle.

"There was a Captain McGoon, when we saw him coming we had a saying, 'Here comes McGoon and he's going to get himself a coon.'* It never failed; when McGoon said, 'I'll take him,' that was it. The set-up was army and we were civilians and there was not one thing we could do or say about it. Naturally it hurt when you saw a real hot pilot going down the drain without even a by-your-leave. I have often wondered what it did to those men who had it and knew they had it. They had picked up the challenge that black men can't fly, endured a lot of nonsense, and then were washed out evidently because of a quota system.

"We instructors had numerous check tests ourselves by the air force to see that we were still on the ball. The funny thing was in many instances we had more flying time than our checkers and were better pilots. We could see the flaws in their maneuvers which we were then asked to perform. The intelligent ones told us what maneuvers to do and left the flying to us. You have to realize these men were only flying two or three times a week and we were flying every day.

"There was one checker who was so sure of himself and his greatness that his ego actually blocked him from realizing the instructors had gotten so they never took over the controls. They just let him fly the plane. The result was we always got excellent marks when he was the checker and he never caught on to what was happening. He was a good pilot on surface, but a man who doesn't know when he is or is not in control of his plane would give me second and third thoughts as to his reliability—and ability.

"In my opinion the selection of cadets was poorly organized. There were more ways than the check ride to eliminate a cadet. Some of the

---

*Alexander Jeffersen, who interview appears below, passed his McGoon check ride, however.

instructors took the exams given the cadets out of curiosity and flunked them; yet we were as good as any flyers in the air force and better than most. We took those exams after we had passed flight check after flight check. We wanted to know why some of the fellows we knew to be good were washed out. Interestingly enough, not one of us was ever called in for flunking the exams; the subject never came up.

"That I am not exaggerating when I say the civilian instructors at Moton Field were top flyers is proven by the fact that in November 1944 those of us who wanted to go down to the base [Tuskegee, USAAF] as advance flight instructors were invited to apply. To do this you had to join the air force, which stopped most of the guys, but a few of us decided to make the move since our civilian instructor hours would be counted in our records for date of release. All we had to do was take a written exam, and all of us who decided to change over passed it.

"The last six months of my stay at Tuskegee I was a 2nd lieutenant. The planes there were faster than the trainer planes we had at Moton Field, but this presented no problem. Once you learn to fly well, it is not hard to transfer from one plane to another. Eventually we got the P-40 and I checked out on the B-25 bomber also.

"The P-39 was used a lot at the base but it had its motor behind the pilot's seat. It was known to go into a flat spin and was hard to pull out. If you had to crash-land you had the weight of that motor behind you. There was also the P-63 or the King Cobra. It was very much like the P-39, only slightly larger.

"I certainly must say that all of us black instructors took great pride in our students and in the 99th and 332nd. They were a fine collection of pilots and men, and we were proud of their accomplishments."

Sergeant-Major Ralph Jones, 318th Air Base Squadron, was part of the original enlisted personnel at Tuskegee Air Field, which was still under construction at the time of his arrival in early November 1941. He elected to stay at Tuskegee rather than go overseas with the 99th Fighter Squadron in 1943. As a result, his eventual request for overseas duty meant attachment to a POM unit, with the "overseas" destination of Adak, in the Aleutians. "I should have stayed put," he commented, "only a geologist could find anything stimulating in the Aleutians."

Ralph Jones: "I do believe my name was one of the first to come up for induction into the armed forces: I was drafted October 16, 1941. My AGCT was taken at Fort Custer, Michigan, and I was among the enlisted personnel selected to go to Tuskegee Air Base.

"We arrived via train at a little station called Cheehaw, in Alabama, which describes the place quite adequately. From Cheehaw we were trucked to the base—really what *was to become* the base—for on our arrival we immediately dubbed it 'tent city.' There were no permanent buildings for the army personnel and the airstrip was still under construction. It was about November 10 when a cadre from Chanute Field came to tent city, and we paraded through the town and onto Tuskegee's campus.

"The 318th Air Base Squadron consisted of my group and the personnel from Chanute Field, who took care of the airplanes. They were considered part of the 318th until such time as they were made a separate unit and so designated. The only white people at Tuskegee at this time were a quartermaster group and some instructors. There was no race problem because all whites lived in town; they didn't even take their meals at the base.

"Shortly after Pearl Harbor, we received five air cadets, including Captain B. O. Davis, Jr. This initial group which would become the 99th Fighter Squadron started from scratch—an understatement. I believe I can say with certainty that white air bases were already set up and did not have the same problems to confront: white cadets did not have to endure a tent city or try to hear instructors in one subject while another was being taught behind a thin partition in a temporary building.

"I began assisting Captain Davis with the office work and soon became affiliated with the cadet corps. My rating at this time was corporal.

"Each succeeding class had no more than eight cadets in it while I was at Tuskegee—sometimes less than eight, never more. You can see how anxious they were to build a black air-force as rapidly as possible by the tremendous number of cadets in each class. They did not have enough pilots to form even a skeletal squadron until late '42. Men were washed out even in these small classes but this was not indicative of lack of ability; rather it was evidence of much higher standards set for black pilots. I am sure you will learn this from some of the pilots themselves. If you can talk to a primary flight instructor—these were all black men—he will undoubtedly tell you cadets with superior talent were washed out right along with those who actually could not do the job. Comparatively few men came to, or should I say *got* to, Tuskegee who could not cut it.

"The first five cadets to graduate from Tuskegee Airbase were: Lieutenants Custis, Ross, DeBow, Roberts, and Captain Davis. I know Mac Ross crashed overseas.* I believe the other four are still living; actually the only one I'm not sure of is DeBow.

"If my memory serves me correctly, we had some trouble in the city of Tuskegee in 1943. The Negro officer of the day had been snatched from his car and his driver had had a tooth knocked out. They were then sent back to the base. When the news spread over the base the men were all for storming the city, weapons or no weapons. Cooler heads managed to control the situation.

---

*See the interview with Major Robert Pitts, below.

The whites were getting the idea across that blacks from Tuskegee Air Base, officers included, were not welcome in their town.

"I think probably one of the most revealing incidents as to the white mentality on the base revealed itself in this manner. A small group of psychologists were needed to determine whether a pilot would make a better fighter pilot or twin-engine man. The committee had four members: Dr. Moton, Ph.D., psychology, black; Sylvester Q. Doty, Ph.D., psychology, black: an enlisted man with an M.A. from the University of Chicago, black; and a white lieutenant, fresh out of college with a B.S. The white lieutenant was appointed as head of this committee. Is there any more to be said?"

Major Robert Pitts, intelligence officer of the 332nd, started his military service in 1941 as a member of the group to which Ralph Jones was assigned. Like Jones, Pitts was one of the 300 black enlisted men who, after a battery of tests, were selected to form the first all-Negro fighter squadron. Pitts's examinations placed him in the supply administration category.

Robert Pitts: "The air force, being a segregated institution, saw to it that all of our classes were taught at Chanute Field; normally a person who was going to have my job was sent to Denver, Colorado, for such training. Chanute Field was the air force's mechanics' school, so it was ideal for them. Nevertheless, all of the black members were changed into one large group at Chanute, which also included the meteorologists. Oh yes, we were called cadets.

"After about four-and-a-half months of training we were told we were going to Montgomery, Alabama, and then to Tuskegee. I recall one of our officers was a Captain Maddox, a West Pointer and a nice gentleman. The rest of the officers, white also, were quite biased. At this assembly we were given the behavior pattern that was expected of us since many of us had never been south before.

"We were en route to Alabama when word came through that they could not receive us at Tuskegee yet. Instead we went to Maxwell Field, white, at Montgomery. Instead of a short stop there we had to remain for a while in a most hostile atmosphere.

"One night a number of us were on the bus returning from Montgomery to Maxwell Field. The driver directed us, in the typical southern fashion, to move to the back. Those of us who were more docile crammed into the back while Milton Henry and a few others said they weren't going back any further because it was as far as they could go. The bus driver than stated, 'I ain't movin' this bus 'til you 'niggers' move to the back.' Milton called him a few choice words and the driver grabbed his pistol. At that point some British cadets sitting up front—they were doing flight training at Maxwell—jumped up, crowded around Milton, and pushed him off of the bus. Two of their group contained the driver and succeeded in keeping him on the bus and talked him into driving on. All of us black cadets had gotten off the vehicle by the rear door. Later we were picked up by a half-ton truck and taken to the field. If it had not been for those British cadets Milton Henry would have been killed and it was apparent Milton was ready to die because the British cadets had to restrain him from trying to get at that cracker, gun and all. If those had been white American cadets he would have been a dead man. I feel sure Milton's time spent in the armed services of his country had a tremendous influence on his future actions.*

"A few members of the administrative personnel journeyed to Tuskegee to get our offices ready. I was one of those in this group, and my first time at Tuskegee was quite a shock. There was nothing but tents available to us. B. O. Davis and the other flying cadets were occupying tents in a nearby area. I can remember staring in awe as Captain Davis put the other cadets through their military routine.

"Our day was taken up because the offices upon the hill were beginning to take shape and we had to set them up as fast as one room was completed. The leader of our group at that time was Sergeant Thomas J. Money, who had come from Camp Walters, Texas. Like myself he was regular army, having enlisted. As we proceeded to develop the administration, the base began to grow.

"By living adjacent to the cadets we were able to watch their development. We saw the air base grow into the home of the 99th Fighter Squadron and then the 332nd Fighter Group.

"I must not leave out our real indoctrination at Tuskegee. We were to participate in the Army Day parade. We did, at the end of the line, and with wooden rifles to boot. Shortly after this shall-we-call-it 'patriotic' farce, Pearl Harbor day came. Then there was mass expansion and more cadets began to flow in. They had now gotten around to accepting the huge number of twelve cadets a month. When you wash out seven of these you have 5 left; now that's wanting to really create a fighter squadron in a hurry!"

Major Pitts recalled an incident that "came close to" a riot and resulted in another kind of "indoctrination":

Pitts: "It would have occurred in Montgomery, carried out by the men of Tuskegee. One of the colored nurses returning to the base from Montgomery had been severely beaten and thrown off of a bus by a driver for refusing to move to the rear. The men had broken into the MPs' station, secured a few weapons, and commandeered a truck, when some cooler heads prevailed and

---

*Milton Henry is a Detroit attorney and civil rights activist. His courtroom technique combines brilliance and pugnacity; the latter has more than once earned him a penalty for "contempt of court."

they did not descend upon Montgomery. However, the pot continued to boil and B. O. Davis, Sr., came to visit us. All of the black troops never really knew what happened.

"The senior Davis was closely guarded by the base commander, Colonel Kimble. Finally the word trickled down to us: 'You are in the South, there are certain laws and customs you must abide by. The army is not to take part in any incidents. Those who get involved do so at their own risk and must suffer the consequences.' Needless to say there was still much unrest.

"My assignment finally became S-2 sergeant at headquarters. I stayed in this position until October 1942. My job was to prepare papers against those considered to be dangerous to the United States government. In those days anybody reading the *Pittsburgh Courier* was considered suspect. Particularly was this true if they read George Schuyler and, believe it or not, Westbrook Pegler. We started a processing dossier on such individuals, and they were transferred elsewhere. I would not have such a job again.

"I asked my boss one day about the chances of my going to OCS. I was in his good graces, having done a good job, and I was sent to the administrative OCS at Miami, Florida. I graduated in 1943 with 19 black candidates and one white-black candidate. And this of course is the beginning of an amusing story.

"Upon arriving at Miami Beach, in our particular group were twenty prospective candidates from Tuskegee. Joe Christmas was strictly the Nordic type; so when they paired us off for rooms they put him alone, where he was later joined by a white lad. After about two or three weeks they were still looking for the twentieth black candidate from Tuskegee. They must have turned it over in their minds enough times to finally realize that Joe had arrived at the same time we did. They called him to the VIP's office building and asked, very apologetically for having to subject him to such a question, if he were from Tuskegee. He replied in the affirmative. They said, 'You are not a Negro—or are you?' Joe said he could hardly keep a straight face when he said, 'But of course.' They closed that whole base down for the day. They could not understand how a man as fair as Joe with features that made many of them look right 'negroid' could be a Negro. When they recovered we were then evenly paired off. Joe Christmas had many interesting little experiences like this, and we always referred to him as the white-black candidate. Oh yes, we all graduated.

"On returning to Tuskegee, I met my old boss again, Edward C. Amber, from Roanoke, Virginia. He said he had an assignment for me; I became intelligence officer for the 332nd Fighter Group. In March 1943 we moved to Selfridge Field, Michigan. Shortly after our arrival nine of us were sent for ninety days to Harrisburg, Pennsylvania, to Intelligence School. In August B. O. Davis, Jr., joined the 332nd Fighter Group as its commander, to train it for combat and lead it overseas. He was taken from the 99th Fighter Squadron, which was overseas at the time.

"During our stay at Selfridge the Detroit race riot occurred. Those who were on the base were restricted for five or six days at which time the establishment confiscated all of our weapons and we were more or less surrounded by white troops from Fort Custer.

"I don't know if anyone mentioned it, but the pilots in our group were definitely of the opinion we were given the worst planes and they were not being properly maintained. The result was we lost a number of pilots in Lake Huron and Lake St. Clair. There were many flaps about this.

"One ironic thing was we were provided with all of our facilities, including our officers' club in one building yet we had to pay to support the main officers club which we were forbidden to attend. We went on a sit-down strike about this and their answer was to enlarge our facilities. I believe Milton Henry was one of the ring-leaders in this. In spite of our efforts we never crossed the threshold of their lily-white officers' club.

"The 332nd Fighter Group arrived in Italy in February 1944. We started out at Naples as a harbor patrol unit. After a few months the 'wheels' decided there wasn't enough work in this area for a fighter group so we were shifted east of the Alps to Ramitelli. While this was going on, the 99th, with the 12th Air Force, was doing close ground support work: strafing, dive bombing, this kind of thing.

" 'Spanky' Roberts had become the new leader of the 99th. Under him the dudes of the 99th decided they could and would do as well or better than any white squadron. One of the members of the 99th, Bill Campbell, a superb flyer as well as a man of exceptional leadership ability, can take credit, along with 'Spanky,' for the relatively smooth injection of the veteran 99th Fighter Squadron into the new 332nd Fighter Group. 'Spanky' had developed a strong, aggressive fighter squadron, He, Campbell, Hall—the first member of the 99th to shoot down a German plane—and a few others gave the whole group tremendous esprit de corps.

"The S-3 officer—who is really the key to making things go—was Mac Ross, an original member of the 99th. Unfortunately, because of his administrative responsibilities he had less flying experience than others. Under the pressure of transitional training from the P-47 to the P-51 Ross was killed in a crash. The big question was who would replace him since he had been so well liked by the men. B. O. Davis selected another Davis, no relation, and to everyone's surprise he took hold as it had never been done before. I remember his first briefing well. He said, 'This morning we are going to attack the southern part of France to destroy radar installations. I do not want a single plane landing at Rome. I want all planes back at this base.

"Now prior to this five to ten planes would land at Rome or Naples returning from a mission with the excuse of running low on fuel; hence they could not make Ramitelli. The consequences of this were the effectiveness of the 332nd would be reduced for the next day's mission. With the new S-3 officer the shortage of gasoline stopped abruptly and those guys came home unless there was severe damage to their aircraft. This was the last bolt that needed to be tightened to make the 332nd a strong, well-knit, first-class fighter group.

"It was just about this time we lost our other West Pointer, Lieutenant Robert Tresville, commander of the 100th Squadron. He was a fine young man and well liked by all. There is no doubt he had a great future ahead of him. On a low-flying mission over water, to avoid detection, I am told he mushed into the sea when switching tanks, and that was the last anyone ever saw of him.

"Captain Wendell Pruitt, perhaps we could say, was the maverick of the 332nd. He was the only pilot that B. O. Davis, Jr., never seem to be able to severely reprimand. Pruitt was the ground crew's and technicians' pilot in that after each mission when all of the other pilots had landed he would put on a show for the ground crew. He would circle the base, tip his wings, go into a chandelle and a couple of rolls. After about 10 or 15 minutes of beautiful flying he would come in for a perfect three-point landing. Any other pilot would have been chewed out by the boss. To my knowledge B. O. Davis, Jr., never said one word to Wendell Pruitt for doing this. Maybe it was because all of the men on the ground and particularly his crew chief really loved the guy; he was that type of man. Everybody respected him, and he knew the guys that kept them flying would like to see a little show now and then. He never failed to demonstrate for them after a mission.

"Wendell Pruitt was probably—no, positively—the most popular pilot in the 332nd. The second such man would be Lee Archer. Both of these men had something very important in common. They were both top flyers, they were superb in the air, and they were veteran flyers, but both had time to talk to and give advice to a novice. They flew like birds but they kept their feet on the ground.

"Pruitt crashed after returning stateside, doing a victory roll at Tuskegee. When tthe news was heard in Italy, no one wanted to believe that he was gone. There are many opinions as to what happened, but I think most of the pilots believe that for a second Pruitt forgot he was flying one of those beat-up old trainers and not a P-51 when he did that roll.

"Pruitt was highly honored by the city of St. Louis, his home town, when he returned to the states. He had an excellent record. AMVET Post No. 8 in the city of Detroit is named after him. Wendell Pruitt was a one in a million, he was a gem, he was a champ.

"The highlight for the 332nd was when it was called upon to fly top cover for the Berlin mission with the 15th Air Force. They made three trips there: one escort mission, one top cover mission, and one withdrawal mission. The first—a penetration mission—was an all-out effort. B. O. was to lead the group, but he aborted because of engine trouble, and either 'Spanky' Roberts or Gleed led the group. Both men were excellent pilots.

"The 332nd Fighter Group was also te first to down the ME-263, German jet."

Captain Wendell Pruitt, mentioned in the preceding interview, shot down three enemy aircraft (two ME-109s and an HE-111). He won seven air medals and the Distinguished Flying Cross:

> *Throughout many long and hazardous combat missions against vital strategic targets deep in enemy occupied territory, though confronted by heavy enemy opposition from highly aggressive enemy fighters and intense and accurate anti-aircraft fire ... [he] consistently displayed outstanding courage, aggressiveness and intense devotion to duty. ... Heedless of severe and adverse weather conditions encountered over rugged mountainous terrain and surmounting many other major obstacles ... during these hazardous missions, ... [he] gallantly engaged, fought and defeated the enemy with complete disregard for ... personal safety and against overwhelming odds. [By command of Maj. Gen. Twining, 15th Air Force, 15 Oct. 1944] ***

Lieutenant Colonel Walter ("Mo") Downs, DFC, leader of the 301st Fighter Squadron, had signed up, during his senior year at college in 1941, to become an aviation cadet, and had been informed thereafter that the air force would be in touch. In the interval, he settled down to the quiet routine of teaching high school in Tahoma, Mississippi, and was married in 1942.

Walter Downs: "The words 'I do' had hardly passed my lips when I was called to Jackson, Mississippi, and told to report to Tuskegee, Alabama. At the air base, I went through the usual routine for cadets anywhere; training by the instructors and harassment by the senior cadets. I rather enjoyed it since one could look forward to the next bunch of cadets as low man on the totem pole.

"Things progressed at a normal pace, for Tuskegee, until one of my instructors tried to show me how to do a crash landing. Instead of showing me, he actually crashed. He struck some trees and down to the ground we went. The engine stuck into the earth and we were hanging by our safety belts in one of the many swamps in Alabama. Because of this the people in the immediate vicinity could not find us. However we succeeded in freeing ourselves and made

---

*The citation is so phrased that it would apply to all personnel receiving the award at that time. No mention of the sinking of the destroyer appears in either the air medal awards or the above.

our way to the highway. By listening we could hear the planes at the base, so hitched a ride in that direction.

"Back at the base I was requested to have a physical and an interview before they would put me back on flying status. The same was required of my instructor. I was returned to flying once the interview ascertained that the crash had had no adverse effects on my attitude towards flying.

"My training was completed in February 1943. I was sent to Selfridge Field, Michigan, for combat training. At Selfridge I was made operations officer and helped to train other pilots for combat duty. Our job was to train replacements for the 99th Fighter Squadron which had been sent to the Mediterranean Theater in April 1943, and attached to the 12th Air Force Command.

"Oscoda, Michigan's air base, became home to a large part of the 332nd Fighter Group. Here combat training was taught with emphasis on gunnery. We did a lot of acrobatics and succeeded in thinking up tricks not in the book, that brought the wrath of you-know-who down on us.

"One morning I was out with a flight, and it struck us to play peek-a-boo with a train. We'd fly straight at the engine and then pull up. To enliven things we did all kinds of loops just in front of the engine. We enjoyed ourselves immensely, though I suspect the engineer was not nearly as delighted with our antics as we were. You might say he lacked a sense of humor. There were those, including our commanding officer, who had news of our performance before we got out of our planes, who thought we lacked sense, period. The colonel chewed us out in the proper military manner; he didn't miss a syllable, comma, *or* period. Our punishment was to walk around the entire base with parachutes on our backs until he gave the order for us to stop. He halted the march about our second time around. We didn't mind the walking because we had really enjoyed playing dippsy-doodle with the train, but we didn't repeat it.

"In another instance the farmers were complaining about us buzzing their farms and the result was their chickens weren't laying; they had gone on strike. Besides the farmers said we were shattering or cracking their china, or causing it to fall off the wall. These charges were hard to prove, but it would be foolish now to deny the escapades. Our problem was we were overtrained and chafing at the bit to get overseas.

"The 332nd Fighter Group actually left Selfridge for POE at Christmas of '43. We arrived in Newport News, Virginia, and our ground personnel found they had run into a very active form of segregation. The base theaters were segregated and our men weren't buying it. They returned to their barracks and got their rifles. Going back to the show they let it be known that they sat anywhere they chose to or nobody was going to sit anywhere in the theater. This was immediately brought to the attention of the commanding officer of the base. As long as we were there our fellows sat where they wished in the theaters.

"It should be noted that the 332nd Fighter Group, and I am including the 99th Pursuit Squadron, undoubtedly had the most highly educated men of any flying group in the country. Up through most of 1943 all 332nd pilots were college graduates; a goodly number held more than one degree. In 1943 you could be accepted if you had two or more years of college training. White cadets only had to have a high school diploma. As cadets I daresay we had more educational background than our advanced instructors unless they were West Pointers. I make a point of this because of the excuses made by the white military to try and keep black men out of the sky. The air force said blacks were afraid to fly; so they volunteered. Then it was said physically blacks were unable to fly because above certain altitudes they couldn't function. How they arrived at this conclusion has never been clarified. This idea was proven to be fallacious anyhow. Their last gimmick was a black man had to have education far beyond whites to comprehend the rudiments of flying. Strangely enough, today, a black instructor has been teaching ghetto dropouts how to fly quite successfully. Nevertheless the standards black pilots had to meet in the 40's far exceeded those of white pilots.

"The 'washing machine' as we called it, took care of a large number of would-be pilots. Those of us who went overseas will always remember this washout system because we always lacked the necessary replacements. Members of the 332nd often flew an excessive number of missions straight in a row because of this. White squadrons did not have a replacement problem so they did not lose any men who went down simply because they were exhausted. The USAAF never got the black replacement situation corrected.*

"The 332nd flew a variety of missions. One that we all claim a part of was actually carried out by six of our men: they sank an enemy destroyer. You see destroyers aren't sunk by fighter planes; fighter planes don't generally try to sink them either. A destroyer can put down too much fire power for a fighter plane to go up against. But the only destroyer ever sunk by fighter planes was sunk by six members of the 332nd.

"It was in June 1944 that a group of twelve planes under the leadership of Captain Joseph Elsberry was to try and intercept enemy troops coming from Yugoslavia to reinforce their units in Italy. The fighters were to fly to Ancona on the Adriatic and up the coast to the Pola area of Yugoslavia. Due to strong winds they were blown off course and split into two groups heading back looking for targets on the way. Captain Elsberry, who had three kills in one day, Captain Wendell Pruitt, Lieutenants Henry Scott, Joe Lewis, Charles Dunne, and Gwynne Pierson spotted a ship in the Trieste harbor. It was

---

*See chapter 5 on the replacement problem in the 92nd Division.

moving out, and they soon recognized it as an enemy destroyer. Forgetting the saying 'fighters cannot sink a destroyer' they moved in for the kill. The destroyer, knowing that they had been spotted, began to lay down a barrage that seemed inpenetrable. Elsberry led the attack, followed by Scott, Lewis, and Dunne. Wendell Pruitt went in next, making a direct hit that set her afire. Pierson, following Pruitt, also made a direct hit causing the ship to blow up. Because of the heavy smoke now covering the ship, they gave the destroyer several more passes until they could see a goodly portion of it sliding under the water. Pruitt and Pierson were credited with the kill since they were directly responsible for sending the ship to the bottom.

"When the men returned and reported what they had done, no credit was given them in spite of the number of witnesses, as was usually done. Not until the film in the cameras of their planes had been scrutinized with a magnifying glass was it conceded that black fighter pilots had done the impossible, sunk a destroyer. The pilots had been wise enough to know that there was going to be considerable scepticism because of who they were, meaning black, so they hung around until she was going under. Everyone of us were so proud of this feat that it is not unusual to hear any member of the 332nd say 'we sank a destroyer.'

"If white fighters had sunk that ship it would have been on the news wires all over the world. As it is, outside of the 332nd, few people know that black fighter pilots accomplished what was thought to be impossible.

"The same scepticism arose when my squadron shot down the first German jets to be downed by fighters. It was March 1945, on a return trip from Berlin, that Captain Roscoe Browne, Lieutenant Earle Lane, and Flight Officer Charles Brantley each bagged one of Germany's new threats in the sky. The rest took off after those three were taken out of play just like any other ordinary fighter.

"A strange thing happened as I was walking to the debriefing room. BBC announced my name and said my squadron had shot down three of the enemies' new jets. How they found out I'll never know. This had no influence as to credit for the job, nor did the corroboration by the other pilots. Only the film in the cameras got the men the credit due them. This was not always a fair method because sometimes your camera went on the bum, and if they didn't want to accept the word of witnesses that was that.

"How did we succeed in this undertaking? When first apprised of the new German ME-263 we sat down and discussed what we would do should we encounter one. Gathering all the available data we went over and over it until we concluded there was only one way they were vulnerable. They were faster climbing and diving and just as maneuverable as the P-51. However, they could not make as short a turn as we could. Therefore we had to become the target; let yourself get in his range, then turn sharply. Jerry would follow, but as you completed your turn he would be crossing in front of your guns. It worked!

"One week after our Berlin run we scored thirteen enemy planes on a single day. It was our highest number bagged for one day. We came close with an even dozen shortly afterwards. When our missions allowed dog fighting, you can see the Red Tails knew this end of the business as well as anyone.

"At Ploesti I almost bought it. We were shooting up an airfield which was covered by small guns, not the regular anti-aircraft weapons. As I was firing my guns on one side stopped. Looking over to see what happened I almost dug into the ground. Pulling up fast I flipped onto my side to see what was going on with this wing. As I looked down the wing I looked right into a German gun. I went down fast and knocked it out. I don't know if it had anything to do with my gun fouling up but I felt better after I clobbered it.

"One of our squadrons escorted three empty bombers to the vicinity of Ploesti to pick up American airmen who had parachuted and crash landed successfully. Ploesti was a real bad scene, as they say today, for bombers. Those empty bombers loaded up under the watchful eye of the 332nd and we took them home. We did quite well on the Ploesti raids considering the Luftwaffe was dodging us like the plague and jumping all over the groups in front of or behind us. In one run to Ploesti we bagged eleven Jerries and we did not run off and leave our bombers. It was after this particular shoot-out that they really left us and our birds alone. The price was just too high since they could not divert us away from our bombers.

"Anzio was the roughest ground battle in which the 99th Fighter Squadron took part. The ground fire was heavily concentrated and it was difficult getting in and out without getting shot up.

"It takes Charles Hill, talking about his friend Heber Houston who was with the 99th, to give you an idea just how hot Anzio was. Charles swears the fellows of the 99th were always ribbing Heber about Anzio. They said that every time they saw Heber he was crash landing at Anzio, shot down, or he was arriving back at the base via a vehicle on which he had hitched a ride, then he climbed into another plane and was off again to repeat the process. Houston actually was shot down two or three times at Anzio. I think one might safely say he was shot down more than any other guy at Anzio and lived to tell about it. As far as I know he was never seriously hurt.

"We made several escort missions into the Brenner Pass, which is the northern entrance into Italy. The obstacles there for both bombers and fighters were high mountains and the overcast. The latter would obscure the pass and the bombers would fail to knock it out, which meant we'd have to do it all over again. The mountains were very close together and the pass quite narrow, which certainly didn't help matters. We would have rather taken on the whole Luftwaffe than be flying around in those mountains. The tops of the mountains often jutted out of the overcast to add to our problems. Mountains or overcast alone are bad enough but combined they are a pilot's nightmare.

"I cannot pinpoint the exact time, but it was on one of these missions in the mountains that we lost Dixon. Next to Pruitt he was the idol of the ground crew. He developed engine trouble and the last anyone saw of him was his pushing back his overhead shield. Several months later Italian peasants found his body in his plane perfectly preserved by the extremely cold weather.

"Just as I was due to return to the states the squadron leader of the 301st Squadron was shot down and 'Spanky' Roberts, then commander of the 332nd asked me to stay on. As usual we were short of replacements. I agreed to stay as the operations officer of the 301st, but I couldn't stay on the ground so I went with the squadron most of the time. I chalked up quite a number of missions because of this, somewhere around a hundred."

Captain Samuel Fuller, communications officer of the 332nd, graduated from Howard University. He received his commission as an officer from the ROTC in 1939. Trained as an infantry officer, he was surprised when he was transferred to the air force.

Samuel Fuller: "When I was ordered to report to Tuskegee in July 1942 to become part of the newly formed Negro air group, I was intrigued. I had visions of what it would be like, you know, like any other air base. When the group with which I was traveling stepped off the train at some godforsaken place, we stood in dust up to our ankles. I had never seen so much dust in my life. We were finally picked up and driven to the base. My bubble of what an army air base looked like burst as I noticed the tents everywhere and the temporary buildings. Construction was going on, and the noise was awful, with planes taking off and landing to add to the din. I saw that at least the headquarters building was complete and I felt there was some hope for what at first sight appeared to be utter confusion.

"There are no *ifs*, *and*s, and *but*s, Tuskegee was a Negro air force base, separate and apart, entirely on its own. We had no misconception as to this eventually becoming an integrated situation. I am sure this was felt by both the enlisted men as well as the officers. We knew it was a segregated set-up and believed those whites there would eventually be replaced by blacks. In short we saw Tuskegee as black and expected no change in this; we were right, from Tuskegee to North Africa to Italy we remained a black air group.

"While I was at Tuskegee I was sent to Yale's communications school, where I spent two months or more, with others like me, being crammed with every minute detail about communications in the air force. The enlisted men who later served under me overseas received their special training at a school somewhere in Florida. They were crackerjacks at their trade and ofttimes enlarged upon my lessons at Yale.

"It was a big disappointment for the 332nd when we left the deep south for what we thought would be God's country, the state of Michigan and Selfridge Field. We were about to leave behind the oppression and racism under which we had lived, or should I say survived. Up north there would be no white enlisted men who ran across the street to avoid saluting a black officer; up north things would be different.

"Well they were—the city of Detroit had one of the biggest race riots in the country, and housing for blacks was almost impossible to find. Many of us had wives, so this lack of housing directly affected us. But the blacks of Detroit were the most hospitable people we could have hoped to encounter anywhere at any time. They opened their doors and hearts to us.

"Now Selfridge Field, that was a horse of several different colors. Upon arriving there, we found we were entering a base that was essentially white and soon learned it had every intention of retaining its whiteness. We had envisioned an integrated Officers' Club, officers' quarters, etc. How wrong can one be? We were isolated completely with quarters of our own. Our sleeping facilities were those of a dormitory and we had little or no affiliation or association with the rest of the base. Our air force ceremonies were strictly ours. In no way at any time were we an integrated part of Selfridge Field. During the Detroit race riot members of the 332nd found themselves not only confined to their isolated area but surrounded by armed white infantrymen.

"As for Oscoda, our gunnery practice base, when I was there it was cold as the devil and I stayed put. I presume the natives were white. I never heard the men who did venture off of the base speak of them so again I presume, like the weather, they were frigid.

"In January 1944 we went overseas, landing at Taronto, and moving up from the bottom of the Italian boot to Capodicino. Our airstrip was close enough to the Naples city airport to be an occasional target for the Luftwaffe. Later we settled down permanently at a new base, Ramitelli.

"My position as communications officer is self-explanatory. The communications group erected and controlled the entire communication system on the base wherever the 332nd was stationed. We had radio or telephone connections from squadron to squadron in Italy. We had a control system which took care of the monitoring of our planes when they took off on a mission and returning them to base when they were lost. Many times the guys would get into a fight 'upstairs,' and some of them would lose contact with the squadron. We had a beam which they could tune into and be returned safely to base. Anything pertaining to communications was our baby; sending and receiving messages up and down the peninsula, erecting and maintaining telephone lines from one squadron to another. All of this was our job; to erect, to operate, and maintain everything that existed in the line of communication.

"Monitoring the pilots was always interesting. It was a matter of simply listening in but some of the things that were said under pressure by the pilots were priceless gems in the use of the king's English and a Venetian gondolier's obscenities. Of course, overseas many times the pilots were on radio silence. Such times were determined by intelligence. Occasionally this silence would be broken in the heat of battle. We could hear the enthusiasm of success and a definite down tempo when someone had been lost. Actually by the time the guys landed, those of us in communications knew just about all that had taken place.

"Atmospheric conditions made it possible for us to pick them up at greater distances sometimes. There were those days we could monitor them all the way to their target and back. We were armchair fighter pilots because emotionally we were right up there with them fighting. There were times that we would actually be exhausted by the time they returned, to give you an idea just how real it was to us. When one of the pilots would holler, 'Look out,' we didn't have to hear names because we recognized their voices, and until the right voice responded we were suspended in space. If there was no answer I believe each man in the communications tower died a little bit. Eventually, we would hear the confirmation of our private hell. Someone would ask where is so and so? A quiet reply could be heard, 'He got it.' 'You're sure?' 'He was on fire.' 'Do you think he got out?' Silence and then the final answer, 'I didn't see a chute. I saw smoke and flames behind the hill where his plane went in.' Silence. Eventually someone would pick up the conversation but they would talk only of the fight. Soon others would join in, but we could tell the difference in their tone of voice as we thought about the guy who had bought it; all the little things you ever knew about him. By the time the pilots had landed our moment of mourning had passed. It had to, because they could not mourn and go up the very next morning.

"The squadrons in the group had an inter-squadron rivalry. They were highly competitive, but this never spilled over into their support of each other. When assistance was needed they never failed to be there; it was really wonderful to see. I am very proud to say, it was a Negro air force indeed, first class all the way.

"Could we monitor the men at Ploesti? Most of the time, when there was no atmospheric interference. They had so many missions over that oil depot I daresay we missed no more than three of these long-range missions via monitoring. Now, there was a place you got some interesing comments from the pilots as they saw their bombers coming out of that ring of hell. I never actually saw Ploesti, but through their eyes it was as real to me, with its monstrous doughnut of ack-ack fire overhead, as if I were there. Our guys were really spoiling for a fight when they gathered up their wounded birds and headed back. They got their wish a couple of times but after those encounters where David, us, smote Goliath Jerry, so hard, the Luftwaffe let the Red Tails and their birds go their way unmolested and zeroed in on some other group.

When our pilots could see Jerry sitting off in the distance letting them pass, their remarks were worthy of posterity, if they were printable.

"One incident I shall always remember occurred in Italy while we were at Ramitelli. A white bomber squadron landed at our field because of weather conditions. They remained with us either two or three days. Of necessity they had to eat with us, sleep with us, and a lot of guys gave up their beds and slept on pallets on the floor; they were our guests. We talked together, played cards together, had bull sessions together, did all of those things normally done by pilots and crews when they are socked in. Their enlisted personnel stayed with ours and received the same hospitality extended by the officers. This was, to my knowledge, the only time a white squadron had a chance to live with Negroes and find out what we were all about. They found we lived the same, spoke the same language, didn't smell up the place, and were doing the same job they were doing and doing it well.

"There were some good friendships developed in those few days. Some of the guys actually had tears in their eyes as they bid us goodbye. It was a good social experience. It stands out in my mind even today because it took an act of God, bad weather, to integrate the black and white air force for a few days. I have found over the years this to be true, only an emergency or something most unusual can bring about a healthy integrated situation.

"Everything on our base was maintained by us and every officer in every job was black: meteorology, communications, intelligence, aircraft maintenance, ground crews, the works, and our base ran like clockwork.

"Even though the 332nd was not integrated, the air force command in Italy considered us tops, and each one of us officers, and enlisted men as well, felt this. We did our job and we did it well. The enlisted men under me had a lot of initiative and were quite innovative. At Rametelli something happened to our generator which supplied the base's electricity. My guys got together and built one from the other and it worked just as effectively; we had no further problem along this line. (Electricity was an absolute necessity for it was used in tuning up the planes.) There is no doubt about it, the men were superior in their work.

"If I sound proud I am. I am just as proud today as I was then of these men and their expertise. I am proud as hell of the whole 332nd Fighter Group. If there is ever an example of the fact that black men do not have to have white leadership, the 332nd is the proof."

First Lieutenant Alexander Jefferson volunteered for the air force in June 1942, following his graduation from Clark College. He found the written examination no problem and passed it easily; the physical examination offered a different kind of hurdle: "I was a big 117 and you had to be 118 to be accepted. The guys at the recruiting center told me to go downstairs, buy some bananas, eat all I could, drink some water and come back. I did. I weighed in a little over 118. I think I was the skinniest thing that had come along for the air force—that must be qualified, for the black air force—until Whitehead. He was so emaciated looking the guys dubbed him Mr. Death."

After taking the examinations, Jefferson was told to "go home and forget it." He was called up just as he was "all set for graduate work at Howard University."

Alexander Jefferson: "I started my cadet training at Tuskegee in April '43 and I think there were ninety fellows originally in the class. When we finished in January '44 there were about twenty-five of us. To tell the truth I don't remember much about primary training except getting up, running, and, oh, those push-ups. There was preflight, primary, and basic training for a cadet. I remember soloing, bouncing about five or six times as I landed, scared to death. I believe anybody who says he is not scared on that first soloing bit is a damn liar.

"Oh yes, I managed to ground-loop in every phase of my training. Anybody who ground-looped in primary was out; by some miracle or other I stayed in. Man, they check-rode me regularly yet I came through in spite of my, shall we say, idiosyncracy. I even had the infamous McGoon check-ride me. It was well known that a check-ride by McGoon was the end of your flying career. It was one helluva check-ride but I miraculously survived McGoon.

"I can say, not necessarily with pride but with the knowledge of doing something different, that I successfully ground-looped everything I flew up to the P-40; then I stopped. Maybe the P-40, probably a hand-me-down from the Flying Tigers, was such a son-of-a-gun I was too occupied with other things to add it to the list. That old girl, the P-40, had a bad habit of pulling to the left as you were going down the runway for a take-off. I would have to stand on the rudder pedal, with all of my 112 pounds, the excercises had reduced me a mite, applying all the pressure I could to keep her from running off into the woods. The nerves in my leg would be quivering like crazy as we fought it out. I was one mess and scared to death but I was determined to be a pilot, and this old clumsy plane seemed to be determined I wasn't as it taxed every ounce of my strength. I graduated and was kind of pleased with my accomplishment. After all, I had come up in the Buck Rogers period and flying was the thing.

"My memories really start at Selfridge Field, Michigan, where we flew the P-39. Now I had another reason to be scared with that big Allyson engine sitting behind me. Besides, when out for gunnery practice the recoil from the planes weapon would come back within two inches of the stick.

"Once we were firing at stationary targets in the lake; we were in a string, one behind the other. Clarence "Red" Driver, a nerveless, crazy sonofabitch, who is still flying, fired his 37 mm at the target from approximately 2000 yards away.* He was too low. The darn shell hit the water and a big plume of water gushed up 20 or 30 feet. Red flew into this with his left wing and it looked like he was going to mush in. He managed to pull up and we could see his prop spitting water, and it scared the hell out of all of us; we just knew he had bought it. But the gods were on his side. When he got back we looked at his wing and it had been beaten back about six inches. The rest of us were still scared, but not Red, that stupid, maroony s.o.b. laughed at us and the incident.

"The group I was with was never sent to Oscoda, we did all of our gunnery practice from Selfridge Field. When on pass we zeroed in on the girls in Detroit. The 'Big D' was a real hospitable town to the flyboys and I've never heard a member of the 332nd knock it.

"Routine flying at Selfridge got boring at times. One night we had a 'luftberry,' flying in a circle around the top of the Maccabees Building. We thought we were showing off our flying ability for the 'gals,' forgetting that black girls did not live in this area at that time. Our motors were roaring like mad as we circled, moving in and out. I heard the switchboard lighted up like mad at Selfridge Field. When we got back we were innocent as lambs. They didn't restrict us, but somebody caught hell for it at the higher level; it was a gas.

"We went under the Blue Water Bridge between Port Huron and Sarnia. The Ambassador was old hat; besides it was too high. However, I'm not going to lie, I think all of us were scared when we did it, but you just don't show the white feather on such occasions.

"As far as being battle ready, I can only speak for myself. We were trained for the job, but 'psychologically ready,' I'm not sure. Look, we were just plain black civilians turned fighter pilots. One thing, none of us wanted to walk or be menials. Let's face it, it was an honor in that our people were so proud of us for having picked up the challenge when it was offered. We were looked up to by them, we were heroes. The fact is we were vainglorious. I'm old enough now to know this is quite human for a bunch of young men. Psychologically ready? No! As a matter of fact, I believe you have to get into action before your mind picks up the reality of 'destroy or be destroyed.' Self-preservation is a very strong instinct and one doesn't have to learn it; it is a built in mechanism that turns itself on when needed.

"The 301st, 302nd, and the 100th squadrons were formed at Selfridge Field. The whole time the 332nd was stationed there no black officer on the base was permitted to attend the permanent officers' club there, a huge red brick edifice with all kinds of facilities.

"The black pilots at Selfridge when I was there were replacement

*"Red" Driver was killed flying in Viet Nam a few months after this interview.

pilots. We kept clamoring about the discrimination against us, our focal point being the officers' club. Our black officers' club was a small wooden building with a bar that literally shouted, 'Okay "niggers" this is good enough for you.'

"One day an order came over the radio for all officers to report to the post theater immediately. This meant all of us, black and white. Remember there were ranking white officers who were a part of the permanent base personnel. There were also white instructors. Some of us were out flying when the message was received and we headed in quickly. We went directly to the theater in our flying suits since the order was to 'come as you are.'

"All of the black officers with few exceptions were 2nd lieutenants. The 1st lieutenants were ground officers, and I think Milton Henry was one of these.

"Five or ten minutes after all were present someone hollered, 'Attention!' Down the aisle strolls a two-star general with all of his entourage. I remember he had a great black mustache. He said, 'At ease, gentlemen.' We sat back wondering what the hell was going on. The general made a few introductory remarks which I have forgotten but his message I can still quote by heart. 'Gentlemen this is my airfield, as long as I am in command there will be no socializing between white and colored officers! Are there any questions?' As we sat thunderstruck he continued, 'If there are any questions I will deal with the man personally.' Unquote!

"He stood there and looked at us and we looked at each other. He hadn't mentioned the officers' club but you can bet your buttons he had gone straight to the heart of the problem. The good general then looked at his flunky, who again hollered, 'Attention!' We all stood up and the general walked out as he entered, trailing lower-echelon rank in the rear. That was it!

"To the best of my knowledge this was on a Thursday. We black officers were immediately restricted to the base. They locked the gates, cut off the radios, telephones, and all means of communication and they kept us locked up. Now during World War II officers were not restricted in this manner, but we were. That Saturday we were loaded on a train and never told where we were going. We went to Port Huron, crossed to Sarnia, Ontario, recrossed to the states at Buffalo, New York, and then headed straight south. When we stopped we hadn't the foggiest notion as to where we were. We had been told to prepare to detrain so when we stepped down we were sharp in our dress uniforms. Greeting us were white soldiers in full battle dress every twenty feet. There we stood, dumbfounded, asking, 'Where are we? What's going on man?' In something like fifteen minutes the armed guard disappeared.

"Later, in talking to some of them, we found out they were a part of a permanent crew of housekeepers. They had put on their battle dress and had live ammunition to meet us because they had been told some bad 'niggers' were coming in on that particular train. They were equipped to contain us!

"My stay in what turned out to be Walterboro, South Carolina, was very short. I was in the first flight over the town and we buzzed the hell out of dear old Walterboro. Dryden, our leader, caught hell and MacIvers, a graduate of my class, for some devious reason and by some devious method was given a dishonorable discharge. Along with the rest of the culprits, I was among the first replacements sent out from Walterboro. To this day I have never figured out why these men were singled out for such heavy-handed treatment and the rest of us actually went unpunished. There were fifteen of us single-engine replacement pilots that were sent to Hampton Roads POE. The other members of my class were sent to Louisville for twin-engine training. They would become bomber pilots in the newly forming 477th Bomber Squadron, all black.*

"Seven days after our departure from the states we arrived in Oran, where we spent only two or three days. The first thing told us at our camp in Oran was that American officers were not safe in the streets at night. They really put the fear of God and the Arabs in us. Too late we learned our concerned informants hadn't bothered to put in the word 'white'; white American officers, it seems, had done nothing to endear themselves to the Arabs. They had so thoroughly antagonized the Arabs the streets were unsafe at night for *them*.

"We went to Naples on an Indian freighter. Naples was in the throes of liberation when we arrived; the people were adjusting to their freedom. The black flyers' rest home was in Naples so we stayed there and spent our time sight-seeing. I remember visiting Pompeii.

"Our final move was to Ramitelli, Italy, where the 332nd was stationed. The morning the truck carrying us pulled onto the base a guy spun in at the end of the runway. I am happy to say it was the last mission of the 332nd in the P-47 or if you prefer the Thunderbolt, with those wing tanks guaranteed to incinerate at the slightest misshap. I can still see that fellow as he took off down the runway. He got up about 30 or 40 feet and he nose-dived in. The result was just one massive ball of fire. That was our introduction to Ramitelli. I'm sure most of us on the truck thought, 'It's not going to happen to me.'

"We immediately began transition-training to the P-51, or the Mustang. There, lady, was a plane! The Mustang was the most beautiful thing to fly in the world. It had speed, range, maneuverability, everything; this baby was a sheer pleasure.

"At Ramitelli we lived in tents in twos. My roommate, when I got there was a guy name Dickerson or Dixon from Oklahoma. After about a week he spun in doing acrobatics upside down in a Mustang. He evidently hadn't

---

*The 477th Bombardier Group did not complete its training in time to serve overseas in World War II. See the interview with Major Richard Jennings of the 477th, included in chapter 1 for its perspectives on stateside racial discrimination.

read the rules on a Mustang or unwisely decided to disregard them. One of the hard-and-fast ones was don't do any upside-down flying in a P-51 with over a half-tank of gasoline; it upsets the equilibrium. My roommate had tried to do a slow roll over the tent area under the wrong fuel-supply conditions and he went in about a quarter of a mile from our tents. When they found him he was dead, burned, decapitated, footless, and handless but still sitting in the cockpit as if he were flying.

"I flew just about all of the missions to Ploesti, Rumania, and there were plenty of them. I am sure any bomber guy who flew these missions could tell you exactly how many there were because they were the ones who had to go into one of the most heavily fortified aerial targets in all of Europe.

"In answer to the question did we do any bombing there?—No. Now there was an earlier attempt to knock out Ploesti a couple of years prior to our flights. Fighters might have been involved but I would doubt it because of the range, although their take-off point was in North Africa. In 1944 when we flew escort to Ploesti our plane was the Mustang and it was strictly a long range fighter aircraft. I flew 32 missions before I was shot down; most of them were to Ploesti.

"What did I see at Ploesti? Oil fields! Ploesti was a series of huge oil complexes. It had a lot to do with keeping Hitler's mechanized and flying forces moving. Hence it was heavily guarded by the Germans and an essential target to the allies. The days we went there were so clear we could see if our bombers had hit their target by the smoke that started billowing skyward. If they missed, nothing. The ack-ack Jerry put up over this city was something else. It was up in the sky so thick it looked like a huge black doughnut suspended in air. You knew you were in the target area by this great black doughnut of smoke from 19,000 to 28,000 feet. Inside of that smoke the ack-ack was so damn thick you could damn near walk on the stuff.

"We would take our bombers to the turning point, which was a 90-degree turn, then we led them into the periphery of this smoke and those goddamn 88s would be just carrying on. At this point we veered off to the side and sat there and counted the bombers as they flew out, or fell out, of that doughnut. Most of those that got back to rendezvous were in a sorry condition.

"From watching the bottom of the grotesque doughnut we had a good idea of what to expect. Planes fell in flames, planes fell not in flames, an occasional one pulled out and crash-landed; sometimes successfully; sometimes they blew up. Men fell in flames, men fell safely in their parachutes, some candle-sticked. Pieces of men dropped through that hole, pieces of planes. The sights we saw at Ploesti would make an addict's hallucinations look good. Have you any idea what it is like to vomit in an oxygen mask? Some of the most battle-hardened of us did at the grisly sights we saw. Everytime we saw a plane plunging, out of control, earthward, mentally we would chalk off ten guys.

"At rendezvous time we'd gather up the remnants of our bombers and take them home. We didn't worry about the Luftwaffe. These guys had seen the inside of hell and if they could stay airborne we damned sure were going to take them back. I know the men inside those shot-up bombers were praying to stay up; they had our prayers going for them too. If prayers and fighting spirit meant anything they had it made. Many times we flew beyond our point of departure, meaning where we were supposed to leave the bombers, to make sure a few stray members of the Luftwaffe weren't planning anything cute.

"You have to understand, a large number of the bombers were totally unable to protect themselves on the return trip. To stay in the air they would jettison everything aboard but the men. Then there were those who had wounded aboard, a crew that couldn't effectively man their guns. Hell, the holes were so big in those planes sometimes we could see the interior and we knew what condition the crew was in. I give the bomber guys credit for two things: guts, of which they had a surplus, and their overwhelming appreciation of the fact that we did our jobs to the very best of our ability.

"What about those who could stay in the air but couldn't keep up? Some of us hung back and nursed them along. On occasion it would cause this escort to run low on fuel. The British still held the island of Vis off of Albania, and we would land there. If an American or allied base was closer than your own and you were running low, you refueled at this home away from home and went on your way. If your gauge happen to go on the blink and you got over the field and suddenly, like empty, you joined the butterfly club.

"Henry Peoples* ran out of fuel as he was coming in, and he was ordered out. It takes Peoples to tell it. He said those guys were out of their minds; he wasn't about to take to the air, he was allergic to heights, besides it didn't appeal to him. That fool cut off his radio and rode his plane down to a perfect landing. He said the tower sounded like the navy hollering, 'Abandon ship!'

"I have often wondered if any members of those bomber crews we flew escort for, ever remembered after they came home that black men who did their jobs, sometimes going beyond orders, are the reason they came back to enjoy the privileges of this country.

"Quite often we had to fly to Blechhamer, Poland, doing escort work. It was a rough trip for the fighters because we had to cross Flak Alley. The name comes from the fact that those goddamn 88s were there waiting, and deadly. Flak Alley was between Vienna and Trieste on our way up to Poland. We had to go this way to escort the bombers on their long range missions. Most of the bombers were located at Foggia, Italy, and they would fly straight up the Adriatic to Vienna and then straight across to Berlin. The escort had to go

---

*Interview with Peoples follows directly.

the way the bombers went so for us it meant crossing Flak Alley to the rendezvous.

"I made one escort mission to Berlin. Talk about a long ride; seven-and-a-half hours strapped in one position. I went to Budapest but was never on any mission to Greece. The 332nd took part in the southern invasion of France; as a matter of fact it was there that I got shot down.

"But before going into that, I think I should clarify something. There were blacks flying in the RAF and RCAF. They came from the West Indies, Africa, and Canada. The 332nd has mistakenly been placed in areas where they were not based. Corsica is an outstanding example. I make this point because some black American soldiers saw these men, spoke to them briefly, they then answered in English, naturally; and our soldiers thought they were members of the 332nd. The mistake is an understandable one. However, I think it should be noted that there were other blacks flying during the war. For them to be a part of either the RAF or the RCAF meant they were good. Taking the word of the British, the Battle of Britain belongs to the Royal Air Force.

"The day I was shot down we were strafing radar stations outside of Marseille and Toulon. Four of us got it that day: Daniels, who was in my flight, my buddy Dick Macon, Robert O'Neal, and me. O'Neal was the lucky one, I later learned. He crash-landed practically in the lap of members of the French underground. They had a new recruit until the allied troops began to drive the Germans out. O'Neal was then able to rejoin the 332nd. I did not know about Macon until some hours after my own little incident.

"We were about 800 or 900 feet above the ground, doing our thing as the kids would say, when I saw Daniels was hit and he was heading his aircraft toward the water. I'm firing away and saying to myself, 'Not the water, man, not the water. You can't ditch a Mustang, don't ditch it! Oops, Jeffie boy you are on fire!' Its funny how thorough training pays off. My plane had dropped lower when hit, my hands would have been burned but for my heavy flying gloves. Still, the rules for leaving a burning plane and parachuting were running clear as a picture through my mind. I pushed back my overhead shield, loosened my safety belt, pulled up and rolled over, and dropped out. My chute opened just before I hit the ground to give you an idea how low my squadron was flying on this strafing mission.

"As soon as I cleared the plane, my thoughts were like in the movies. When I land I'll gather up my chute, bury it, and find a friendly area. Only one thing went wrong. Upon landing when I came to my feet I was looking into the shooting end of a rifle held by a very business-like German soldier. Said I, 'Yeah man!' The soldier said something in German and with my eyes glued on his cannon—it was growing larger every minute—I said, 'Okay, okay, just get that damned thing out of my face.' Somehow we understood each other and we got along just fine. I didn't get scared until about eight hours later; then I could not stop shaking.

"The soldier marched me to the nearby town square, and who should be coming from the opposite direction, under an armed escort, but Daniels. He looked like a wet rat. Later, Daniels told me he ditched his Mustang because he was scared to bail out so decided to ride her down. Another big don't about the P-51 is don't ditch her. This plane has a huge air scoop underneath that rapidly fills with water and flips the plane over, trapping the pilot inside. Daniels said he out-flipped the flip. He did something, because he was very much alive, to my pleasure. At least I was not alone.

"That night they put us in a stable with some horses—who's complaining, it could have been pigs. It was pitch black inside and we were feeling our way around when we discovered there was someone else occupying our quarters, a two legged animal. It turned out to be Dick Macon. He had a broken neck; two vertebrae in his neck were cracked. This had been attended to but not well, and to this day Macon has trouble with his neck.

"Bidding our four-legged friends adieu the following morning we were put back of a truck heading east and finally transferred to the back of a train heading east. Do you know what it was carrying? Those goddamn 88s; 88s as far as we could see, going east to be set up for another go at us. I kept wondering where the hell was our air force; it was the kind of target pilots dream of. Why we weren't strafed or bombed I'll never understand.

"Our route was up the Rhone Valley to Avignon, to Valence, all the way to Mulhouse, Germany. Those goddamn 88s, with us along, arrived safely and we had had clear weather all of the way.

"The three of us were put in solitary confinement at Frankfurt-on-Main, with bread and water as our diet. Then we were interrogated.

"The interrogation took place in a neat office with an impressive officer to do the job. The first thing he did was to offer me a cigarette, which I accepted not having had one for three days. In the meantime he went into his drawer and pulled out a book. On the cover I could see 332nd Fighter Group, Red Tails. Behind the smoke my eyes got bigger as he stopped thumbing through the pages and turned the book toward me saying, "Lieutenant, that's you.' It was a picture of my cadet graduation class and there I was, so I said, 'Yeah, that's me.' Then he began to spiel off my whole history: birth date, where, parents' names, etc. He summarized it all saying my sister's marks in music had averaged a B. This was September '44 and they had her marks from June of that year; yet I didn't know them because there had been a mail foul-up and I hadn't had any letters from home in months. (When I returned to the states I found out the German officer was right; I hadn't really doubted him at the time.) I sat there smoking his cigarettes as he did a 'this is your life' on me. It kind of blows your mind when you've been taught to be careful, say nothing, big brother is listening. Well, big brother had done a whole lot of listening over a long period of time. He didn't need to ask me anything because he knew as much, or more, about Alexander Jefferson than I did. I got to thinking about all of the publicity given the 332nd and its personnel, and I concluded smugly that it didn't take a helluva spy to gather the rest.

"From Frankfurt-on-Main we were sent to Sagan, Silesia, across the Oder River, fifty miles east of Berlin near Posen. Our location was halfway between Warsaw and Berlin and there was our new home, Stalag 3. The place had 5,000 American flying personnel alone. Then there was the British and the French so the population of Stalag 3 was something like 12,000 men.

"Since the barracks were pretty crowded each room had to take an extra man. A delegate from the room was allowed to choose the new room-mate. A died-in-the-wool cracker with the deepest southern drawl imaginable walks up to me and says, 'Ah think I'll take this 'un.' I'm thinking fast and hard to myself, 'Now wait a minute, Jefferson, you didn't come all the way from the USA to be with a bunch of Tennessee hillbillies.' I hear the drawl again, 'Yeyah, ah still think ah'll take this 'un.' Very apprehensive I was led off to a room filled with about nine other guys, crackers from the top of their heads to the tips of their ever-loving toes. Would you believe that every state of the Confederacy was represented in that room?

"It took me exactly three days to find out why these redneck crackers had chosen me. This room happened to house all the escape material. They had to have a new man in with them so they chose a 'nigger' whose allegiance could not be doubted; if he were black he could not be a German plant or an American turncoat. Isn't it ironic, I'm in the room with the guns, passports, uniforms, *money,* everything for escape. What did they say when they knew I knew? 'We'all knew we could trust you.' I thought it then and have said it many times since, 'Ain't that a bitch!' At home black soldiers caught hell from s.o.b.'s just like this. All a black could do for them was get out of the way. Now five thousand miles from home they can trust a black man because they are scared to death of a strange white face. I repeat, 'Ain't that a bitch!'

"I spent nine months at Stalag 3. I helped dig escape routes for others, etc. but there wasn't any use of my thinking about escape; for once in my life I was the very visible American. A few escapees got away but most were returned to the area in a relatively short time.

"Come January, after the Russians' big push, they got us out on the road and told us to march or be shot. It was cold as all-get-out and we walked about thirty kilometers. We were put in boxcars on a train and ended up at Moosburg, about 20 miles north of Munich. We were freed by black tankers, what group I do not know.

"By the way I got to Dachau about six hours after the Americans got there; the ovens were still warm and we could smell roasted human flesh five miles before we reached the place. We saw the bones still in the warm ovens and the piles of gold knocked out of teeth. And those that were still alive in their striped uniforms were simply bags of bones. They were too weak to stand up, too weak to crawl, cry, or laugh. They were zombies.

"We had heard about this place at the stalag but we believed the stories to be exaggerated. We rushed right to it when freed to see for ourselves. In this instance, at least for me, seeing is not believing. The stories we had heard had been understated. The imagination could not conjure up this sickening reality. Some of the fellows went on to see some of the other camps in the area, but I had seen all I wanted to see. For the first time the doughnut of smoke over Ploesti didn't seem so bad. At least those guys died fighting back and their deaths were quick. But this, Dachau, men, women, children, unarmed, terrorized; herded together like sheep and exterminated like cockroaches. No, I didn't want to see the rest of man's ingenuity in mass murder and bestiality.

"When the Americans came in with a field kitchen and it being the first good food we POWs had eaten in a long time, we truly ate our selves sick. Then along came a money wagon and everyone was given eighty dollars. Since nobody seemed to pay any attention I got into the line four times; I didn't want to run it into the ground.

"Daniels, Macon, and I took a plane that was supposed to land at LeHavre but instead landed near Paris. I hung around there two weeks having a ball and believing myself AWOL the whole time. When I got back to the 332nd I could have shot myself when I learned they hadn't expected me back so soon. One day I must return to Paris and see the whole of it; I never got beyond Pigalle.

"By the time we were liberated from our stalag at Moosburg there were about twenty or thirty black pilots there. Hathcock will never live down the fact that he landed at a German air base in Italy due to a navigational error. Their base was 35 miles in one direction and ours 35 miles in the opposite direction. Was he surprised when his ground crew spoke German and had white faces!

"MacDaniels, a squadron leader, was shot down, and 'Mo' Downs, who was ready to go back to the states, stayed on as his replacement. I think Downs had more than two tours of duty chalked up when the war ended. Mac had been knocked down by a jet when he joined us at Stalag 3.

"I mentioned I was scared often and this was true. There are two kinds of fear; the kind that immobilizes you and the kind that makes you fight like hell and remember the rules. Beware of a man who knows no fear; he'll get you killed; he does erratic things. He strikes out on his own. The rules and fear say: 'Stay with your wing man, you do not have eyes in the back of your head;

you look out for each other. You play it by the book.' Me, I'm stupid, I followed the rules. It's the wiseacres that get killed fast, or get someone else killed.

"Once or twice when I first tangled with the Luftwaffe I am not positive I knew what I was doing. Hell, there were planes all over the sky. I stayed with my wing man; I followed the rules and I was never accused of goofing or endangering a teammate's life.

"There was only one guy in the whole outfit who nobody wanted to fly with because all thought he was a threat to their welfare. It was no problem of his being a hotshot pilot. He was strictly a look-out-for-number-one boy. I mean boy, he was not man enough to sink 'me' into 'we'.*

"Oh I didn't tell you about the first German officer I encountered about a mile from where I bailed out. Our planes had gone by then, and I was escorted to this magnificent home and here this resplendent German officer is having tea on the veranda. He smiles pleasantly and in perfect American English tells me to have a seat. I'm flabbergasted as I drop into a chair. He dismisses the guard and offers me a cigarette. My mind is racing over intelligence directions: name, rank, and serial number, yes, and no. The gentleman then asks me if I knew anything about New York, Chicago, several large cities and finally Detroit. I stopped saying no and said yes. He described the Valley in detail for me when I answered yes to his question of had I ever been there. He talked about the Forest Club, the Oakland busline which was necessary to take to get to the Cozy Corner cabaret. 'Here I am sitting sipping tea and smoking cigarettes with a German officer on the French Riviera at Toulon, a POW, and being royally entertained by this man with the details of the ghetto area of my home town. He said he had lived in Detroit five years and actually knew some of the bartenders' names in some of the places.

"And think today's youngsters tell me my generation hasn't been anywhere or done anything!

"As I disembarked stateside I knew good and well I was coming back to the same kind of racism I left, separate and unequal. There had been some changes, such as the black air force, but at that time I had no idea the U.S. Air Force would be integrated within a few years. At the age of 22 or 23 I was too busy living to meditate over tomorrow. I had no thoughts, nor did the other younger fellows, about our being an experiment which was making history. Very few of us were conscious of the implications of the events happening, of the sociological changes taking place around us.

"Today, there have been fantastic changes compared to the early '40s. Changes are happening much more rapidly due to technological advances

---

*Every member of the 332nd I talked to mentioned the same man as being one pilot they could have done without. M.P.M.

that have expedited sociological changes. Then too, in one's early fifties one is prone to be more philosophical and optimistic about the future."

Lieutenant Colonel Henry Peoples of the 332nd, DFC, was an air force pilot in World War II and in Korea, with experience of both a segregated and an integrated air force. On his return to the United States following the Korean War, he remained in the air force as an instructor until his retirement.

Henry Peoples: "In 1943 I was in Chicago working for a newspaper, happily minding my own business, when I was notified by my Uncle Sam to report to Keesler Field, near Biloxi, Mississippi.

"Biloxi!

"Mississippi!

"Me?

"So I did.

"There must have been somewhere between two or three hundred of us gathered in the sand of Mississippi with the luxury of tents to sleep in and other comparable accommodations. The men represented a large number of universities and colleges since each had a B.A., some their M.A., and several held Ph.D.s. If it took college degrees to fly, move over, eagles.

"We were not given the GI issue of clothing but we went through some form of basic training; at least they called it that. We drilled in our own clothing, which I guess was all right since we had no guns to drill with; they would have hardly matched our civvies.

"When we weren't drilling we were busy propping up our tents; the stakes were too short for the sand so the tents collapsed if the wind sneezed. Did I say our living area, our marching area, the whole damned area had the sands of the Sahara. My first expensive pair of shoes, well they were expensive to me, were a sorry sight after a week of being covered with sand and full of sand but I just crunched along.

"Two things I never figured out: whether or not the resurrection of the tents was a part of the training program, and exactly what purpose this safari to Mississippi was all about. We were told this little period was 'psycho-motor testing.' I guess, and I'm stretching for this, it was to see if we had the temperaments to be pilots. However, since then I have flown a lot of planes and a gang of hours; I still don't understand what part the sands of Mississippi played. Guys who came in later didn't have to go through this.

"The noncoms putting us through our paces were blacks. Anything beyond the signing of their names stumped them and they called us to attention with, 'Hey, you guys.' Now you must admit the high caliber of our cadre, the collapsing tents, the sand in our shoes, must have proved something, but with all that aggregation of brain power, including a few psychologists, we remained mystified. It was conforting to know I wasn't the only jerk in the bunch.

"Once during briefing by a white lieutenant, the very enthusiastic manner in which he presented his material lulled me to sleep. My next two weeks were spent on KP, in my civilian clothes! If I keep harping on clothes, you recall that in those days ma and pa were not handing them out, you earned them by the sweat of your little brow. Abusing hard-earned merchandise didn't add to one's peace of mind.

"Finally we got our uniforms and as was routine our street clothes were sent to our homes. Strange thing about that, none of them ever reached their destination.

"All things considered, the luxury of our surroundings, the dullness of the lectures we attended which they were sure we didn't understand, it wasn't too bad. After all they were going to put us in an airplane and we were going to make like a bird and *that*, lady, was all we cared about; black men up in that wide blue yonder.

"After this ingenious exercise in what I choose to call futility, something like sixty-five of us passed something—it was a secret—and we were sent to Tuskegee. The rest of the men went to Chanute Field. They had the distinction of becoming the highest 'degreed' airplane mechanics in the business. They had a graduate engineer working as a mechanic!

"At Tuskegee we were housed on the campus and spent about a month there. What did we do? We paraded up and down and we sang, then we sang and paraded up and down. Oh yes, we did attend a few classes there. Ernie Wilkins, a black mathematical genius from the University of Chicago, was one of our instructors. Our courses were mostly math, since flying deals with this to a great extent. But we still did a whole lot of parading up and down, and we sang.

"Our primary flying instructors—few people realize it even today— were black civilian pilots. We first flew Piper Cubs and than the Sternman, a bi-winged type. After this we went to Tuskegee Army Air Force Base and began what was called our basic training. Our instructors there were white commissioned officers. We started on A56s, which were called Texans. On completion of this training we were then commissioned.

"My feeling about these white officers is, and was, that the majority of them wanted us to make it, if for no other reason than failure was a reflection on their ability. I don't feel there was any hostility between the instructors and the cadets. There was more apprehension on their part about our ability to absorb what they were giving us. If they had looked at our 201 files they would have found their boys could probably have taught them a thing or two.

"The 99th Fighter Squadron was there at the base with B. O. Davis, Jr., and George ('Spanky') Roberts. They gave us something to aspire to.

"After our graduation we went to the P-40s, which we supposed had come from the Flying Tigers because they had the shark head with the jagged teeth painted on them, an omen of good luck I understand. Wherever they had come from, they were as old as Atlantis.

"Francis Peoples got killed in one of them. We were supposed to take it up 20,000 feet and dive at 400 miles and hour before completing our training. He did but couldn't pull out of it. He dug a crater large enough to put a huge downtown building in.

"There was no racial problem on the air base; everything there was black.

"Twenty of us were sent to Selfridge Field, Michigan, as pilot replacements and to get in more flying. The planes at Selfridge were P-39s and P-63s. Every time there was a break in that stinking Michigan weather they'd say, 'Go.' And up we went into that gray, dull, slight overcast. We lost several of the guys in the lake: Hill, Moore, Singh. A couple of our guys landed on the highway when they got in trouble. It was quite a surprise to some of the motorists in the area.

"We were sent up to Oscoda, Michigan, for gunnery practice. There we shot at what was called 'sleeves' for accuracy. But so much of anything is boring. We were ready, we knew we were ready, and they knew we were ready but they kept us shooting at those blasted targets. To break the monotony we found other little outlets; like the time we flew under the Ambassador Bridge. Why did we do it? I suppose it's like climbing Mount Everest: for those who climb, it is there. We knew we could do it and we did it. No problem, we just single filed it nice and neat, one behind the other.

"Of course the 'wheels' weren't exactly ecstatic about our letter-perfect performance. Never did figure out how newspapermen were present from all three daily papers 'cause we sure made all the papers. They should have seen us when we used to drag our wings in Martin Lake in Alabama. Oh we got chewed out about that, but it didn't stop us. The lake was there, the bridge was there, no sweat. As I said, we were bored. Here we were razor-sharp, combat-ready and they didn't have a place for us. A lot of things like the bridge were the direct result of men trained to do a job and not allowed to do it. We naturally wondered about the hanky-panky that was going on to keep us stateside. I think they finally sent us over because they needed pilots and they didn't have any other choice but us. You see the 99th, which was already overseas, was a fighter squadron. The 332nd was a fighter group; so many squadrons make a group and that was putting a helluva lot more black-pilots in the sky in combat zones.

"Inadvertently, a small group of us found out that in a pinch we had great potential for the infantry. From Oscoda I had been sent to Walterboro, South Carolina. After doing the same wasteful flying around we had already done innumerable times a number of us were told we were shipping out.

"A bus took us to some little whistle-stop to catch our train some twenty-odd miles away. There were about eighteen of us dropped off at the little shack of a depot to wait until train time. We had our packs on our backs and since it made easier carrying we had taken our 45s and Thompsons out of the cosmoline and cleaned them. The pistols were on our hips and the Thompsons slung over our shoulders. There was nothing unusual about this.

"After standing around the station for a while we happened to see a sign, 'Cold Beer,' just a short distance down the road. Now what could be better to pass the time than a cool brew? We walked on down to the beer pad, entered, and I said, 'I'd like some beer.' The lady, in quotes, at the counter said, 'We don't serve niggers in here.' And I said, 'We just want some beer, we plan to take it out.' And she said again, 'We don't serve niggers in here.' Now I'll admit, we didn't have on our dress uniforms, but this wasn't exactly the Ritz, either. So I said again, 'All we want is some beer.'

"There were two white sailors and a marine sitting at the counter. Like we aren't having enough of a problem the navy has to intrude. One of these bell-bottomed boys steps down from his stool and growls, 'Ya heard what the lady said.' Now while I'm thinking on the new turn of events, about a second, a fellow—I can't remember his name but he was from Mt. Clemens, Michigan—hit the navy blue. This guy was the last man in the world you would have expected to do such a thing. He was quiet, the gentle type; besides he was physically awkward, you know he wasn't exactly hung together right and looked clumsy. But he not only hit that cat, the power behind his punch knocked the navy clear over the counter. And I said, 'All we want is some beer.'

"This joker behind the counter sticks his head up and Mt. Clemens laid a right on him like Joe Louis. One of those straight boys, right from the shoulder. The navy had been sunk; he did not rise again.

"I said, 'All we want is some beer.'

"I guess you might say the fellows were getting impatient because Thompsons were becoming rapidly unslung. The woman then asks if we would leave if we got the beer. I said, 'Lady all we want is some beer.'

"We paid for our purchases and departed, leaving an unconscious big mouth on the floor behind the counter. Well that settled that, we thought.

"As we started back to the railroad station, we noticed all of these cars coming our way. It had gotten dark and there was just one solid stream of light.

"I said, 'Ole buddies, I think we have a problem.' No one was of a different opinion. I directed two of the fellows to go up and take over the control tower to make sure they could not stop the train or call in the whole state. The rest of us dropped our packs in front of the station and dispersed around it in a wide circle, for it was clear the depot was the caravan's destination.

"The cars pulled up, about thirty in all; they circled the station and played their lights upon it. We were well beyond their perimeter of light, however. From our positions we could see those crackers good; it was like *mad*. They were armed with everything from pitchforks, to blunderbusses, to modern high-powered rifles with telescopic sights. Talk about the movies, this was for real. Here was a live lynch mob ready to close in on its prey, United States Air Force pilots who only wanted a drink of beer. There was one thing a little different about this scene; the victims-to-be were not in the trap. Moreover, the whole communications system of that little ole town happened to be in the signal tower where the men in charge were unhappily looking into the talking end of a sub-Thompson so our would-be-lynchers had no means of calling for reenforcements. Hell, yes, we knew this when we decided to take over the tower. There were too many wires running into that tiny little depot's signal tower for just the trains that passed through this out-of-the-way place.

"One of our men had been left in front of the depot to negotiate with—but who else—the tobacco-chewing, pot-gutted sheriff. He was along to make everything nice and legal. He said, 'Tell them niggers to come on out. We have to take them in.'

"It was then our spokesman's turn and he informed him, 'The first one of you that tries to step out of your nice bright circle of light gets shot, like dead and I mean real dead.' He was talking loud and everybody could hear him. 'Now the gentlemen you are referring to, my friends, they are not inside the station. They happen to be behind you in a neat little circle. In short, you are surrounded. In case you have any doubts about anything, before you do anything foolish, I suggest you look up at the signal tower.' Talk about heads up; there they could see a black face smiling beatifically down over the barrel of a Thompson.

"Remember that song, 'Bewitched, Bothered and Bewildered'? It hardly describes that sweating slob of a sheriff. The others were looking meekly at him for guidance and he couldn't get up enough saliva to spit out his chaw.

"Our man explained patiently, carefully, and clearly (let's face it, they were the cream of the illiterati) that the train would soon be in and we were going to get aboard. To guarantee this, he explained that when the train arrived two men, from among them, would pick up our packs and place them on the train. Then we would board and be gone. He told them politely but emphatically that we were all fighter pilots on our way to our POE to go to fight a war. However, the odds on a fighter pilot's survival were very low and if they didn't want the war to start right there they had better stay in that circle of light until the train was out of sight.

"You could tell they were nervous but you could also tell they didn't think we were bluffing either; we weren't.

"The train arrived on time, and everything went like clock-work.

The guys in the tower escorted the two telegraphers from the tower down into the circle of light, and we all got aboard. As the train pulled out we looked at them, not big, bad, and bold but scared as hell. And they had reason to be. We hadn't the slightest intention of being hacked up, shot up, and strung up in some two-by-four town that's not even on the map.

"We were quite relaxed from a nice trip when the train pulled into Camp Patrick Henry, Virginia, our POE. As we stepped off of the train we were greeted by several men in Ivy League suits. One of them said, 'Which one of you is Henry Peoples?' "And I said, 'Who wants to know?' Then he said, 'The FBI.' And I said, 'Oh, I'm Peoples.'

"To make a long story short, I have on my file in the Pentagon on my record and at the Federal Bureau of Investigation that I started a *race riot*, if you please, in South Carolina.

"We never did join up with the rest of the group at Patrick Henry because they did the fastest processing job on record on us. We were checked in and out in eight hours and were on a ship heading overseas. They placed us in two stinking compartments, nine men in each one. We were locked in and given no food or water. When we were thirty miles at sea which was about thirty-two hours later they let us out. I said it then, I say it now, 'Ain't that some stinking nerve!' They kept us locked in those damned compartments, practically standing on each other's backs all that time; fighter pilots of the United States Army Air Force going forth to fight for their country!

"Well, we did get overseas, didn't we! Seriously though, in World War II they couldn't find anything better than the black fighter pilot. We were the best they had. I'm not saying this because I was one of them. We gave our job everything we had and those bomber guys loved to see us Red Tails, which says just what it means, up there with them.

"Once we got overseas, in short order, it was known by all the bomber groups that we were always on time for rendezvous. Understand this, we were fighter pilots, but many times our job was flying escort for bombers. Time is an important element on such missions. When we were to rendezvous to escort bombers into their targets and meet them again coming out, baby we were there. No ifs, ands, buts, and maybes, we were there on time.

"Now some slap happy air-jockeys stopped to engage the Luftwaffe on their way to rendezvous. This would throw them behind schedule on meeting their bombers, and bombers can't wait. To the fellows in the bombers it meant having to fight the Luftwaffe themselves going into the target and coming out, which was hell for them.

"Escort duty meant you cover the bombers no matter what. If the Luftwaffe attacked it was the fighter's job to take care of them and the bomber guys didn't have to worry. They could save themselves until they got on target. I should say 'into the area of the target', which was always guarded by ack-ack. They got it all the way in and all the way out, those that made it.

"A lot of bombers came out of their target area really flying on a wing and a prayer. They'd have so many holes in them you'd wonder what was keeping them in the air. This is when bombers are most vulnerable; they are shot up and they've often got wounded aboard. I believe we set some kind of record for being on time, going in and coming out. We only lost a handful of bombers to the Luftwaffe. If I recall it was less than ten. This even when the Germans threw their new jets at us. We knocked off three or four of those boys before they got started good, and they took off.

"Now you don't have the thrill of a good old dogfight on escort duty. However, we did have the satisfaction of being in demand by all the bomber groups in our range to fly escort for them. And don't you ever forget the 332nd was one of the first choices to fly escort for the first bombing of Berlin. We would loved to have had some head-and-head shoot-outs with the Luftwaffe because there wasn't a doubt in the Spookwaffe's head that we couldn't take them. We whipped their tails several times when we first started escort work but, and this is a big *but*, we never got so carried away with our kills that we went high-tailing after Jerry. We kept our bombers covered at all times. See, that was a trick, just get glory-happy and give chase. As soon as you were out of sight another group of the Luftwaffe which had been waiting out of sight moved in and cut your bombers to pieces.

"Though we are never mentioned, we flew escort missions regularly to Ploesti. We took those bomber guys in, and when they finally came out of that holocaust of black smoke they were in tough shape. Those that came out, and could stay in the air you can bet your boots and saddle we brought them back safely.

" 'Spookwaffe'? That was a name we hung on ourselves. The Germans were the Luftwaffe and the American whites thought they were better than anybody else and most certainly didn't count us, so I suppose we wanted our own identity, something that sets you apart, special, so we became the Spookwaffe.

"We also had our own jargon, which carred over on our radio. Foolishness, like I might say, 'Race base, this is race ace. Give me the word and I'll make like a bird.' Whatever we said, the guys in the tower understood and answered in kind. It was a fun thing, again being different. One might say these things were our hallmark. They became so much a part of us that we carried it overseas. I have to admit it was a bit confusing to the RAF when they were monitoring us. But the Luftwaffe, they were just plain shook; they never did figure out what we were talking about.

"I think in a way it did something for us; it made for a little more camaraderie.

"We had another thing going we started at Tuskegee, and in spite of the lectures we carried on anyway. I think the boss finally just tore his hair in silence behind closed doors. If a plane were a car you'd say we gunned our motors. The only thing, in a plane it sounds more like motor failure but we enjoyed this bit of tomfoolery and you could always tell we were coming with our motors hitting and missing so to speak.

"Overseas the infantry appreciated this particular difference on our part; it saved them running for cover unnecessarily. When they spotted approaching aircraft if they heard our unique sound they knew it was the Red Tails and they waved us on. If we were flying cover for them they were like hunting dogs on point in the direction of our objective.

"Next to the bombers, the infantry liked to have us around; we didn't bomb short and mess up some of them. And we didn't stay 40 miles up in the air; we came down and did our damnedest to cut a path for them. Actually, more of our guys got shot up and we lost more planes this way than flying bomber escort. The invasion of southern France is a good example of this. I can think of three guys off-hand that went down there in one day and all of them were hit by small-weapons fire.

"One time, several of us were on leave in Bari, Italy. Being the typical upright young Americans, the first place we hit in the town was a bar. We ordered our drinks. Sitting at the bar were a couple of bomber pilots and navigators. One of them noticed us and said, 'Pardon me but are you guys with the Red Tails?' We answered yes and before we knew what was happening we were surrounded and being kissed. If it was possible I was beet red, a man kissing me! Finally we got the situation under control and asked what the hell this was all about. They explained they were just using the continental method of showing their enthusiasm for the Red Tails.

"Naturally, this made us feel good and it happened many times, in various cities throughout Italy, to all of the fellows in our group, but I never got used to the kissing. And the damnedest thing, it always sounded like this, I mean when they got around to expressing themselves verbally. 'We's sho glad y'all is here.' Southerners! I swear I believed sometimes the whole damn bomber groups were made up of down-home southerners. Now those southern boys in spite of all their kissing, praise, and booze I just could not help thinking to myself, when I get back to the states I'll have to kill'em but here we are kissing kin. Why couldn't we have saved some nice northern liberals?

"I was shot down over Yugoslavia and spent two months with Tito and his partisans. I went on a couple of their raids and they were exciting, to put it mildly. They were fine people and their women, such women! You talk about amazons; those Yugoslavian female partisans, I swear they could outfight their men. They were strictly f. and f.; fearless and ferocious.

"The partisans somehow got hold of a P-38. I had never flown one but my bird wasn't going to fly any place so I took off homeward bound.

"Anzio a soft landing? Not from what I heard. The 99th Fighter Squadron which had gone over in 1943 took part in the Anzio landing. They were in the air daily, sometimes two and three times a day during the Anzio fiasco. I said 'fiasco' because the allies had landed without any opposition at

Anzio; the Germans were actually taken by surprise. In the two or three days it took the allied command to decide to exploit this fact the Germans were alerted and ready and it became a bloody mess.

"On January 27, 1944, a flight of a dozen planes from the 99th, led by Captain Clarence Jamison, knocked down five German planes and returned to base without any losses. The pilots credited with kills were: Willie Ashley, Leon Roberts, Bob Diez, Ed Toppins, and Howard Baugh. That same day the 99th chalked up three more kills credited to: Lemuel Custis, Charles Bailey, and Wilson Eagleson. Eagleson got his second kill in less than two weeks still flying at Anzio. If the fighting record of the 99th at Anzio is a fair assessment of the situation, Anzio was anything but soft.

"Cassino was another job the 99th was assigned to along with other fighter squadrons. Their orders were not to hit the famous abbey sitting on top of Monte Cassino. Everybody in Italy knew the abbey with its panoramic view for miles around was being used by the Germans as an observation post but 'don't bomb the abbey.' They had to skip-bomb around it hopefully, I guess, to shake its foundation so badly it would collapse of its own accord. The 'wheels' that had this bright idea forgot that when they built buildings in the days when they constructed the abbey, they were meant to stand forever. The guys bombed and the abbey stood. What made it a nasty job was once the pilots had dropped their bombs they had to come up out of a valley. You just don't fly all over the sky when mountains are involved. You have to come out of them where there is an opening. At the end of this valley was a damned 88 just sitting waiting. This called for evasive flying to stay out of the German gunner's sight and at the same time not to slam into the side of the mountain but the order remained, 'don't bomb the abbey.' Finally the 'brains' decided the abbey was not going to collapse of its own accord and they were losing a helluva lot of planes and men, so the order came down to bomb the abbey and that settled that.

"The 99th also took out a bridge that other squadrons kept missing. Admittedly when they returned they had holes in their fuselage, wings, tail, kind of all over; they said they didn't want the ground crews to get lazy. The problem was the other jokers wouldn't get down low enough because of the defensive fire protecting the bridge. Our fellows went in there and got with it. As they said, 'If whitey could not take it out we knew we would if we had to sit on the damn thing.'

"This was something all black pilots felt, we had to prove ourselves. We had to be good, no, we had to be better. Like the Nisei, well you know what a fantastic job they did to prove themselves. I guess we were in the same bag whether we admitted it or not.*

---

*See the introduction to chapter 5 for a summation of the war record of the 442nd (Nisei) Regimental Combat Team.

"This is our stinking mistake, even today. We are always proving ourselves and we are as good as the whites; so many times we are better.

"Our group flew as many as sixteen straight missions at a time. We just did not have the necessary pilot replacements so this meant the same men were flying each time. I feel a few of our men died because they were plain exhausted and were a split second off in the crucial. The white fighter pilots knew this and because they had no such shortage some of them offered to fly with us, but our commanding officer politely turned down the offer. Any member of the 332nd that was overseas any time had over sixty missions. We just didn't have replacements, and until someone came so we could put up a full group, guys who had done their time went. That's all there was to it.

"Hell, yes, the odds are greater against a pilot returning from combat after he gets so many missions under his belt. The guy needs an intermission, not just a week at a rest camp, he needs some real time off.

"I was in the service about four years. And no, I most certainly was not naive enough to believe there would be any racial changes for the better upon my return to the states, and I was right.

"I was in the reserve when I was called up for Korea. There was a quick brush-up deal and then overseas again. In Korea I was still a fighter pilot flying F-100s and F-86s. I was called in for 21 months and it was five years before I got out. There I flew 120 missions while in Europe I had flown 68.

"Integration had caught up with the air force during the Korean war. They really had no choice; there was nothing left with any experience to fly in combat but old black pilots and old white pilots. In Europe we damn sure flew together; we were just at separate bases so it was no big deal.

"There were youngsters available in Korea, I'm speaking of pilots, but they weren't where the action was because they needed guys with experience, like—*now*! They didn't have time to wait for the kids to gain experience, so we old men were the hot-shot pilots in the early days of the Korean war.

"As war progresses you lose the old pilots in a lot of ways; not nearly as many are shot down as people think. As the older guys decrease in numbers the kids take over because all the time they have been gaining experience. But pit a young combat pilot against an old one and that kid will get clobbered; experience makes the difference.

"When I returned from Korea to my surprise I found I was an instructor without even a by-your-leave. Experienced guys like myself were going to do for the youngsters coming up what the Flying Tigers did for the white American pilots of World War II: give them the benefit of their know-how. In the '40s black cadets didn't see an experienced combat pilot until fellows of the 99th were finally considered as having enough missions and rotated back to the states.

"I did expect some changes when I retired from the air force, not overnight, but gradual. But now sometimes I feel I might have made a mistake.

I look at people complaining about busing. Once they bussed black kids miles to keep them out of white schools and it didn't matter. Now the white community is in an uproar about busing kids to equalize education. Things like this make me wonder, maybe I made a mistake. There must be some shrunken thinking somewhere if we can't use whatever means we have at our command to make this a democracy. Look, I've got a kid, a small one. I don't want to bus him, *but*, if it will make democracy work, than I shall make the concession of busing him.

"I keep looking for the desire on the part of the people in this country to have or work at having a democracy and I don't see it. Maybe I've blown all those years I was fighting because I was gullible enough to believe in the Declaration of Independence and the Bill of Rights. If I have been had, all of that killing for nothing, I'm not going to like it and that's for damned sure."

Captain Charles A. Hill, Jr., of the 332nd Fighter Group, had mixed feelings when World War II broke out: "I can't say I was anxious to become personally involved, for a very good reason. My grandmother was German, and I loved her very much. My opinion of the German people was naturally formed by our relationship. She never mentioned the war, and when the day came that I knew I would enter the service when drafted, because this was my country, I felt somehow my grandmother would understand it."

Hill applied for aviation cadet training while still an undergraduate at college. He received civilian pilot training at Wayne City Airport, Hartong Field not being open to blacks. On completion of training he received a civilian license in single-engine planes. He was called up in March 1943, and eventually reached Tuskegee after procedural delays.

Charles A. Hill, Jr.: "One does not speak of segregation at Tuskegee Army Air Force Base, simply because it was all black. There was no one to segregate. The relatively few advanced flight instructors and the commander of the field did not live on the base.

"You cannot in honesty say the USAAF claimed us, and since there was the RAF, RCAF, and the Luftwaffe, someone had come up with the word "Spookwaffe," you know, the invisible pilots. This became our unofficial name much to the annoyance of the powers-that-be in the air force, but there wasn't much they could do about it. However, we got an immense pleasure out of our nickname.

"We had other touches of individuality, such as the victory roll. Whenever we returned from a mission, to let the ground crew know our tally, we would do our victory roll the exact number of kills we had made. The white pilots picked this up and few of them cracked up; an order was cut forbidding it at all air bases. We never stopped and we never lost a pilot doing the roll coming back from a mission.

"A group of us flew up to Rome for a special show. We were really dressed for the occasion. We had a few added touches to our dress uniforms: yellow scarves with "Spookwaffe" embroidered on them, and we wore matching yellow gloves. We were forced to circle the Rome airport because some VIP was landing. It turned out to be an air force general who had a message relayed to us to do the 'forbidden' victory roll, which we did with a gusto. When we landed he thanked us for what he termed 'a remarkable performance.' He was less than enthusiastic about our dress and suggested we return to our base immediately after the show was over, which we did. However, we kept our scarves and gloves.

"I know someone has mentioned the importance of being on time at a rendezvous with your bombers when on escort duty.* This is one instance I'll never forget. We arrived, as always, on schedule to pick up our bombers coming from their target. Another group of fighters, which should have been there earlier, arrived as well as a group due later. The result was like Grand Boulevard at Grand River, Detroit, at 4:00 P.M. It was pandemonium with planes ducking up and down. Those who went down had to dive through the bombers, and their gunners—not expecting American fighters in such a position—cut loose on them. You can't blame the bomber guys because they had just come from a target and the only planes they would expect to dive among them would be the Luftwaffe. The colonel was with us that day, and I have to give him credit. Somehow he got us together, picked up our bombers and we headed out while the others were still playing leap-frog.

"The pride the ground personnel took in its pilots was wonderful. When a pilot didn't return, even when they were told someone had seen him go down you would see them hanging around his stand every now and than sneaking a look at the horizon as if to will him back. When there was no confirmation as to a pilot's being shot down they stayed there for hours looking into the sky. Whenever one of the guys did come limping back on that well-known wing and a prayer, his crew began to live again.

"There is much less formality between a pilot and his ground crew. After all his life depends on his crew. They in turn take pride in his accomplishments and those of the whole group.

"My crew chief put his life in jeopardy for me. Twice I had been diagnosed as having acute indigestion. The third time the symptoms of it began to occur was just as we were to take off on a maximum-effort mission. The colonel had given us a pep talk, realizing we were tired as we had been flying practically every day because there were no replacements. He emphasized we should fly in our turn, so I decided that I could cover the mission, all right. I did, but coming back the lower the altitude the worse the pain. I radioed ahead for an emergency landing and got permission to break formation and with an escort headed in.

---

*See the interview with Henry Peoples.

"The closer I got to sea level the more acute the pain. I finally reached the stage where I was flying by ingrained training. I was semi-conscious, for every now and than I would hear words giving directions which would fade away in a haze of pain. I remember, 'Drop your wheels, drop your wheels.' Next in the distance I could hear, 'Your flaps man, drop your flaps, drop 'em, okay now cut back on your throttle, the throttle, cut back on it. The brakes, *brakes*, brake it baby, you'll kill him.' That roused me enough to see my crew chief. He was on the wing of my plane indicating a left turn into my parking area. Instead I was going around in a circle and he was doggedly hanging on. I was a mass of confusion and pain, when the voice cut in again, 'Cut your motor, cut your motor, *cut it off, the motor*! For a split second I cleared and realized what was happening. I was spinning toward other aircraft and my crew chief would most certainly be killed. My hand went towards the switch and that's all I recall until I came to, spread-eagled on the wing of my plane. I learned the chief had me out of the plane and stretched out before the doctor arrived.

"Rushing me to the hospital, they removed an appendix on the verge of bursting. Had it not been for the men in the tower, who did everything but use sign language to try and keep me conscious and get me down, my crew chief, and the doctor I wouldn't be here.

"When I returned to the states and was married, I decided to get out of the regular air force but stay in the reserves; I loved to fly. The air force, still segregated, created the Second Provisional Troop Training Carrier Squadron. We worked in this capacity from 1946 until the Korean War. All of this time we were asking when we would be on a paid status. We were always given a stock answer, 'When you get a TOE'; that meant when we had enough pilots and crew members to maintain a complete squadron. They knew it was impossible for us to get the necessary number of blacks in the whole state of Michigan. As it was, some of our men came from as far away as Battle Creek.

"Just before the Korean War there was a reduction on all the TOE units, and I suggested to the white fellows who would be dropped that they come into our unit so we would reach TOE qualifications. They had no objections as long as they could fly and get paid.

"At the next meeting with a general, officers, and squadron leaders I asked again about getting paid. The reply was the usual. I then said the problem had been solved, since enough of the white flyers were willing to make up our numerical difference. Talk about evasive action, the general turned a lovely strawberry red. He hedged, he ducked. Finally he said he would have to find out. This meeting took place in the summer. The Korean situation deteriorated and war broke out. I constantly contacted Selfridge Field's commander as to active duty. I could get no answer.

"Around the first of January I was sent a Special Delivery letter from the War Department. Instead of being a call to active duty, it was a statement charging that I was a Communist because my father was suspected of being one and my oldest sister, Roberta, had attended a few odd meetings. My resignation was demanded forthwith.

"The charges were vague and nebulous to the point that I could surmise I was being charged with being a Communist by relationship. My father, a Baptist minister, had dared to make unpopular statements. He wanted a true democracy in our country and in his way he fought for it. He was truly crucified for his love of country. I was now being found guilty of being my father's son and my sister's brother. Roberta's husband was in Korea fighting at the time. He had become a career army officer.*

"Many hectic days followed for I hadn't the slightest intention of resigning from the air force. I demanded a full hearing before a board of my peers. At the automobile plant where I worked, I was given a guard to make sure I was not harmed by the nuts who only need hear the word 'Communist' to judge, condemn, and act.

"The *Detroit Times*, a racist newspaper, got wind of my problem and, to make sure they did not smear me, I contacted the *Detroit Free Press*. They did an excellent job of stating the facts as they were.

"The Review Board refused my request for a public hearing. However, with the publicity in the the *Detroit Free Press*, the *Detroit News*, the *Michigan Chronicle*, the Detroit edition of the *Pittsburgh Courier*, and even the *Detroit Times*, plus public reaction in general, I received an apology from the Secretary of the Air Force, saying a mistake had been made and all charges were dropped. Since I had not resigned, my position in the reserve remained the same. But I was never called up for service in Korea, even though experienced fighter pilots were desperately needed.

"I believe that of all of the things done to my father, none of the lies, vilification, and smear tactics, really got through to him until they tried to destroy a member of his family. It did not stop him, but he was astonished at finding men he was forced to deal with were not merely 'white sick' but utterly vicious.

"All of this mudslinging was indirectly the result of my suggestion that the Second Provincial Troop Training Carrier Squadron fill the black quota with white pilots who had no objections. It never occurred to me by the farthest stretch of my imagination that the USAAF, which I had served to the best of my ability, would try to ruin me and break my Dad.

"When I entered the armed forces of my country I sincerely believed in my government as it is supposed to be; a democracy that protects all of its citizens. My beliefs haven't changed, but I do wonder now just what kind of government we *do* have, where it is leading us, and just what World War II was all about.

---

*Lieutenant Colonel Roger Walden, whose interview is included in chapter 1.

"Our government is supposed to represent all of the people and it is the government I killed—I repeat I *killed*—other men for in the name of democracy. Could the joke have been on me for being naive enough to believe in my government?"

Lieutenant Herbert Barland, a late-comer to the 332nd, arrived by way of the 184th Field Artillery, Fort Custer, Michigan, and OCS at Fort Sill, Oklahoma. After a stint with the 93rd Division at Fort Huachuca, including maneuvers with the division in Louisiana and in the Mohave Desert, he had an opportunity to transfer to the air force.

Herbert Barland: "I learned they were looking for applicants for the air force, so a friend and I asked to be transferred. At first our CO refused to let us go; for reasons unknown he later changed his mind. We were sent to a pilot's training center at Greensboro, South Carolina. If we passed the examination there we would go straight into pilot training. I passed but my friend, who passed the written part with flying colors, flunked the psychomotor test. Through some fluke they sent him on to Tuskegee anyhow. There must be something to that particular test, for he washed out in the primary course and his instructor told him he would never make a pilot. However he remained in the air force and walked through the navigation-bombardier courses. He was a born mathematician.

"One racial incident at Tuskegee that was quite amusing was when a white major crashed and was critically hurt. He needed an immediate transfusion and the only men on the base with his type blood were black. The major being from Mississippi protested as loudly as his condition would permit. Suddenly the message got through that he was going to die, like in dead, if he did not have some whole blood and fast. Somehow and quite legally he received the transfusion, but never let it be said that he had not registered a protest.*

"When my group was shipped out from our POE, Patrick Henry, we were replacements for the 99th Fighter Squadron; the oldest squadron of the 332nd Fighter Group. There were less than a half-dozen of us, to give you an idea of the inadequate number of replacements sent to the 332nd.

"In our first month overseas we flew 20 missions, which were mainly long-range escort jobs.

"I was the leader of the four pilots to fly the last mission of the 332nd, which I am proud to say. It was a photo recon escort mission. We were escorting a British Mosquito bomber which was stripped of weapons to carry cameras. At the time I did not know it would be the last time the 332nd would officially be in the air.

---

*This incident is also mentioned by Ambrose Nutt, whose interview follows.

"Being a late-comer to the group I had the pleasure of basking in the reflected glory the men of my group had earned. Everywhere we newcomers went we were recognized and toasted as members of the best escort group in the business, the Red Tails, as the 332nd was known throughout Italy.

"Naturally we were most esteemed by bomber crews. This was paradoxical because I never had a bomber guy stop me to shake my hand or buy me a drink who didn't have a southern drawl. All of the pilots of the 332nd were aware of this. It was probably the one time in American history our white southern brethren appreciated black men. They were damned glad to see our black faces up in that 'wild blue yonder.' "

Like Major Richard Jennings of the 477th Bombardier Group, whose interview appeared in chapter 1, Lieutenant Earl Kennedy arrived in the air force via a circuitous route and only after determined efforts. As a TAC officer at Tuskegee, assigned to the base, he watched many classes of cadets come and go, and his interview details stateside experiences of black air force men generally.

Earl Kennedy: "The day I went down to Michigan Central Depot to board a train for some unknown army post I was accompanied by my family. The occasion was a memorable one. There were about two hundred or more fellows there bidding their families goodbye. Why I was selected to lead this group, or to be in charge, I'll never know since I had not yet led myself. However, I was told to get them aboard and somehow or other I succeeded in getting the men onto the train. I had also been told to see that there was no gambling once we were aboard!

"Before the train was in motion a crap game started. Doing my duty, I climbed upon a seat and suggested that they cut it out. Someone threw a shoe at my head so hard Vida Blue could have taken lessons from him. I stepped down, deciding shooting crap wasn't a crime, besides keeping my head on my shoulders was the better part of valor.

"After a long, noisy, hilarious trip we arrived at Stockton, California, where we were immediately slapped into quarantine. I questioned this since I had been at Fort Custer right after my induction, was tested, stuck, quarantined and then sent back to Detroit for a few days before catching my train. My question was met with a studied silence, and I remained quarantined.

"The recruits on the base near Stockton were from all over the country. The particular group that was to be with us was from Fort Benning, Georgia. These fellows were the most backward people we had ever encountered. Most of them were from the rural south and though many of us had attended southern colleges we did not understand their dialect and they didn't understand us. Young men being what they are—you've heard of the riots in the camps—well, there was a minor war between the 'blue denim' boys and the 'herring bone tweed' boys. They thought we were wiseacres and were going to try and take over things, and they were probably right.

"To form the 55th Aviation Squadron—both groups were members— it was necessary to have someone above the rank of private. I was made acting corporal along with a 'blue denim' boy who, to my surprise, could barely write his name.

"Noticing the letters SEP after the words 55th Aviation Squadron we 'herring bone tweed' guys wanted to know just what SEP stood for. The commanding officer told us if we wanted to continue there, we, meaning me, had better stop asking so many questions.

"As acting corporal, my assignment was in the orderly room. It turned out the 55th had nothing to do with aviation; we were a work battalion. Our squadron built a large swimming pool on the base, but we were not allowed to use it. It was for white only. I raised the question why couldn't we use the swimming pool after we had built it. I was told by the commanding officer there was going to be a one-man shipment if certain people insisted on asking questions. No one had to say more; he was coming through loud and clear in my direction.

"In the orderly room I would discuss with my friends the SEP which we finally interpreted as separate squadron and labor battalion. On various inspections of our barracks we would have footlocker inspection. The sergeant would walk down the line like an inspection of the guards at Buckingham Palace. If you had in your locker a *Pittsburgh Courier*, which was the only way of knowing what was going on in the outer world, you would be singled out, pulled out of line and severely censured. The question was asked, 'What are you doing with that inflammatory material in your locker?' The *Courier* was not the only paper that created problems. Black newspapers in general were considered undesirable.

"A group of us 'herring bone tweed' guys got together and decided we had to get out of there. I concluded OCS was the answer. Though I had never seen a black officer in my life, I was tired of being a corporal; I was no longer just acting corporal, nor was the 'blue denim' fellow; he too was a corporal.

"Two things I learned while stationed there: how to build a swimming pool and what the word 'sanding' meant. My corporal counterpart had sanding down to a fine art. Right after we both became full corporals I noticed that every day when he would see the captain he would dust him off and wipe off the captain's boots. This he did even though there might not be a speck of dirt on them; after all the man had an orderly. I couldn't understand this so I said to him, 'Man why are you always dusting off the captain, he hasn't done a thing for you.' He gave me a stupid look saying, 'Can't let the captain go around with dirty shoes.' He may have looked dumb but I was the naive character. One day I found the 'blue denim' corporal was my sergeant. The fact that this man had to have a subordinate read and translate directives for him was immaterial. The captain's gesture was no more than the act of tossing a bone to a dog who wagged his tail when he passed by. The new sergeant's 'sanding' had gotten him another stripe and an increase in pay. The captain's means of selecting a man for promotion was not the exception but the rule. White officers were not in the least concerned about black enlisted men as far as I could see; blacks were a necessary evil that had to be endured. 'Sanding' NCOs made it easier for the officers by bolstering their ego and feelings of racial superiority.

"I saw my first black officer in San Francisco while on furlough. We were sharing a pool room, as hotel accommodations, with about forty other guys. Our beds were the pool tables and the benches along the wall. He told me to get a commission and get it in a hurry. I will always remember the man, Lieutenant Pitts. He admitted being an officer wasn't exactly heaven but at least it was one step out of hell.

"As soon as I returned to camp I submitted my papers for OCS. I made them out thirty-five times and was rejected. The members of my labor battalion unit were all laughing, but I was determined to get to OCS. Upon my return to Detroit on furlough I saw Charles Diggs, Sr., state senator, now deceased, and others who might have some pull. I told them what was really going on at my base and that I wanted to go to OCS but was being given the run-around. These people wrote to Truman Gibson, Negro civilian aide to the president. They sent me copies of their correspondence. My officers quickly became aware of my mail since a goodly portion of it was sent from Washington, D.C. I was called into the office and questioned by five colonels as to why I was criticizing the base. I denied this. It ended with my being told I had been accepted at OCS.

"Instead of being sent to OCS they sent me to gunnery school at Boca Raton, Florida. I was flown there and had scarcely touched ground when I was informed they did not take Negroes at the school. I was permitted to eat in a 'black' area and they made arrangements to fly me back to California that night, which they did.

"My squadron had a good laugh at my swift return. After some delay I was sent to OCS on Miami Beach. Many of the luxury hotels there had been taken over by the armed forces.

"When I fell out that first morning on the Beach it appeared that I was one black man among a sea of whites. We went out to the staging area, which was Bay Shore Golf Course. There must have been somewhere around 12,000 whites assembled. I finally spied a dark speck about a mile away. Later I found out it was Bill Womack. There was no way for me to get to my 'brother,' as we had begun to march. As we marched around I saw another black face: it turned out we would be roommates.

"The officers directly over me were all West Pointers and southerners. I had two roommates, both southerners. They had the faculty for getting along with these whites on white terms; I had to watch myself. My roommates were fine guys, but they knew how to handle themselves.

"Hazing was a part of the system and this 'damned Yankee,' as my officers called me, was their pet project in the deal. Every morning they took time to play horsey on my back until they were wearied or bored with their little game. My 'roomies' were not subject to this. However they shared the cotton-picking detail. We had to go up and down the lobby on our hands and knees equipped with tweezers picking the lint off of the rug. Having been through hazing in college when I joined a fraternity this did not annoy me as much as it could have. I assumed this foolishness was to see if you could take it.

"Bear in mind I had come from a base which I could not happily go back to so I played horsey with those crackers, picked cotton, and every morning hit the bracing line: chin resting on your chest, shoulders back, as officers walked along behind you and whispered all kinds of things in your ear. I lost forty pounds while I was there.

"The haircut formation was an unpleasant revelation. My first week when the bulletin was posted, it stated there would be such a formation every Thursday at 1400. On said day I lined up with my squadron and marched down to the barber shop in the lobby. When I got in the chair the white barber said, 'I'm certainly glad you came. This is the first time a Negro has ever had his hair cut in here.' At that exact moment I perceived three officers standing at the door. When I got outside they grabbed me saying, 'You black sonofabitch, what the hell were you doing in that barber shop?' You only have three answers when addressed in OCS, yes sir, no sir, and, I don't know sir. Since none of these seem appropriate I said, 'Yes sir.' One of them said, 'I don't want to catch you in there again.' I tried to explain and was told, 'No goddamn excuses, say any more and we'll wash your ass out.' They finally allowed me to stand at ease saying they would talk to my commanding officer, Lieutenant Arnett from Clemson College, South Carolina. I had no doubts as to what to expect from him.

"When I returned he was waiting. He said, 'You know, I'm sorry I didn't tell you there was a special haircut formation for all colored candidates.' I told him I had only followed the information on the bulletin.

"The next week when the formation was called the whites went in one direction and the blacks in another. About twenty Negro officer candidates met on Lincoln Avenue, where we were picked up by a truck which took us to Miami onto Second Avenue, the main drag of the colored section. We were dropped in front of a colored barber shop. Well at least we were all together and had a chance to compare notes.

"The day of our graduation the commanding officer, in his oration for the event said, 'Some of you men will perhaps command black troops. You are going to have a unique experience. Black troops often conduct themselves in such a way you will need all of your first aid knowledge. Saturday nights is 'cut up' night for black troops, you will be called upon at times to assist in the patch-up work.'

"Along with this dialog a manual was passed to each of us. It had on the cover, *How to Handle Black Troops.* I believe this was supposed to have been made up with the assistance of the civilian aide in Washington. It contained such things as blacks are very sensitive about their mothers, so don't talk about their mothers. Watch the use of the words, 'You people.' Other interesting little ditties cluttered up the pages.

"Every Negro in my class went to Tuskegee, home of the black air force. The 99th Fighter Squadron was there and so was B. O. Davis, Jr., who was called the 'whip' behind his back. While I was there I was a TAC officer; I was in charge of a hangar.

"The cadets who washed out at Tuskegee were head and shoulders above those graduated ninety miles down the road at Maxwell Field. There was no way the flying officers at Maxwell Field could touch the boot straps of the majority of the black 'cats' washed out at Tuskegee. An example of what I mean is Ambrose Nutt, aeronautical engineer graudate of the University of Michigan, civilian pilot, and designing aircraft when he was drafted. He was washed out at Tuskegee; it was absolutely ridiculous.*

"The Spookwaffe had Selfridge Field as a tactical base, Oscoda Air Base as a gunnery base, and Walterboro, South Carolina as POM. With the eventual development of the 477th Bomber Squadron, Godman Field, Kentucky, was added to the list. Tuskegee men were supposed to land at those fields designated for them. The guys didn't strictly adhere to the rules. Once a bomber of the 477th landed at the Mobile Supply base. White WACs drove out in a jeep to pick up the crew. When they saw they were black, the WACs whirled around and returned whence they had come. Shortly, a jeep arrived driven by a Negro. People came from all around to look at the black men who actually flew an 'aireyplane.'

"We had a college graduate trained as finance officer. He spent his time shooting pool after going into the finance office and looking around. Only white sergeants were allowed to handle the money. It was a *cause celébre* around the base that white sergeants were doing the work a black officer had been trained for.

"Our provost-marshal was an ex-sheriff with a big, bulging gut. He spent his time riding around town with friends pointing out various places where he had shot a big 'nigger' over there, or a little skinny 'nigger' there. His black driver asked that he be replaced before he was the first black soldier the ex-sheriff shot and for a damned good reason, like kicking his ass.

---

*See the interview with Ambrose Nutt, below.

"Our men had their own way of doing just about everything; they had a flair that was especially theirs, and I am here to tell you they were good. Those men could fly by the seats of their pants, as they saying goes.

"As for being a black officer in World War II, if all of the men in this category told you about the insults and humiliation they experienced while in the uniform of the United States military it would take at least a year of around the clock interviewing. Once I was spat upon by a white woman in Alabama for having my black skin in an officer's uniform. Another time I was almost arrested for impersonating an officer. As they say in Paris, *c'est la vie*. However it is not the kind of life black men liked. They didn't like it then, they don't like it now in new guises. The young black today is only displaying the implacable hatred of the system that has always existed among blacks, male and female. What amazes me is the surprise of the whites. We should be grateful for second class citizenship in our own country when a white immigrant gets first-class treatment the minute he steps off the boat?"

Corporal Ambrose B. Nutt holds a B.S. degree in aeronautical engineering from the University of Michigan (1939). Before entering the armed forces, he had worked as a designer for seating in the latest model planes. He is co-inventor of the high-speed aircraft ejection seat. These facts in themselves are an ironic comment on his experience, first in the 332nd at Tuskegee, and later at Chanute Field.

Ambrose B. Nutt: "Shortly after graduating from the University of Michigan, I acquired my civilian pilot's license under the civilian pilot program. In keeping with the times I had the normal, extreme difficulties of a Negro trying to get a job in my field, in industry, or with the government for that matter. As a matter of fact before my graduation from the university every one in my class had a job waiting for them upon receiving their degree; I did not. I might add I was far from the bottom of my class. This should clarify the chances of a black aeronautical engineer in his field in the years prior to World War II.

"For approximately a year-and-a-half I worked on the assembly line at the Ford factory. My aunt, who was quite active in politics, succeeded in getting me an appointment to West Point. Not having anything better to do I accepted this. I was exempt from the written exam because of my educational background and was only subject to the physical examination. I underwent the physical and was informed that I had a tooth that had come in at an angle; its removal would permit my admission to the Point.

"Dental techniques being what they were then made this a rather painful procedure with an orthodontist. After being unable to eat or talk for a few days, while my minor surgery was healing, I finally presented myself to the physician who had previously examined me for West Point. The extraction was satisfactory, but I was subsequently informed that I was not eligible due to a generally deficient physical make-up, whatever that meant. I cite this as indicating my initial impact with the armed forces was to me somewhat less than stimulating.

"In 1941 I at long last succeeded in getting a job with the government in Dayton, Ohio. I went to work for the air force as an aeronautical engineer. About two months after I arrived in Dayton, the decision was made to set up a black air force. I was asked if I was willing to accept being drafted into the interpilot training. By this time the general homefront situation as far as black people was concerned did not make me anxious to reliquish my civilian job so I said, 'Thanks, but no thanks.' Besides I felt I was doing more for my country where I was.

"In 1943 I was drafted under the provisions of the law that said everyone under the age of twenty-six was subject to the draft. I was inducted as an aviation cadet at Fort Benjamin Harrison and was sent in a three-man shipment to the training school at Biloxi, Mississippi. On the train I objected to the curtain in the dining car and all the other little incidentals that are a part of a black traveling in the south. My real introduction to southern customs took place at the conclusion of the trip.

"We had arrived at Biloxi on a hot July afternoon. We had called the base pursuant to the instructions on a sign at the station. While awaiting our transportation we decided to get something cool to drink. There was a drug store directly across the street from the station. Upon entering the store I saw a coke machine. As I reached into my pocket for some change I heard the clerk say, 'There's a cloud over that machine.' I really didn't pay much attention until he spoke in a louder voice, 'Niggers don't buy cokes in here.' Well, being fresh from the north we agreed that was probably true, and left. My view about being in the armed forces as a black certainly was not improving.

"At the base all black trainees were quartered at the edge of the base. There was one black officer there at this time, and he was separated from all of the other officers who were white. He could not go to the officers' club but then we couldn't go into the PX. The best we could do was stand at a window outside to be served.

"After our basic training at Biloxi we were sent to Tuskegee for advanced pilot training. Tuskegee was essentially an all-black set-up. Naturally there were white officers at the top and the advanced instructors were white. They had a very good group of black trainees there. They were the finest group of black men I have ever been associated with.

The attitude of the whites there is probably best shown by a true incident. One of the white instructors had been critically injured in a plane crash. He was conscious and very much aware of the fact that there was a 'black' blood bank there. He was insistent that none of this blood be used in him. His wife was told he would be dead by the time they could get his type blood from a white base; the major needed a transfusion then. She consented to using the blood there at Tuskegee. I just wonder to this day if he knows what he is carrying around in him.

"As to the air base itself I would say the training was probably as good as that received anywhere else. As to going to town, we were cautioned to be careful. It was the first time I heard about the decoration one got when one *served* in the southland. The medal for the southern field of operations was the only ribbon in the army that came in two parts: one black and the other white and you couldn't put them together.

"One thing that the black military man was continually confronted with is again best told by a story. James Mosely, a friend of mine, had been a brilliant high school student. He won the high school students' Higgenek scholarship to college; it was withdrawn when they learned he was a Negro. James was also drafted into the air force and volunteered for engineer officers' training school at Yale. He finished top of his class. The top men were all being sent to B-29 training for engineers, which was the new bomber of the air force. James was skipped over and sent south. He tells the story that he initially was sent to Tulsa, or something like that, in Alabama to be an engineer officer at the base. The white officer to whom he reported there was thunderstruck at seeing a black engineer officer. In spite of his amazement he managed to tell my friend he would be shipped out at once. James Mosely ended up at Tuskegee, the resting place for black engineer officers, since there was no place for them elsewhere. They merely did what at best could be called 'incidental' duty. James was very embittered by his treatment at the hands of his government in the armed forces. After the war he went to school in Sweden rather than stay in this country.

"I have to confess that although my stay in the south was longer than I anticipated, I never got used to southern customs. Reveille in the morning, your government's uniform, and the unceasing prejudice and discrimination were a nauseating and angering mixture.

"But on to my flying career. I went through my primary and pre-flight training at Tuskegee; I then entered lower-advanced. My classroom instructor was black, a rather taciturn type. In our initial contact he was asking the various fellows what they did before coming to the air force. I said I designed seats for some of the latest-model planes. He didn't really believe me, but in any event he proceeded to personally wash me out. My performance, judged by talking to my classmates, was as good as anyone else's. I do not know why he washed me out. However, there was in those days a self-image that blacks had about blacks and anybody going beyond the reservation, so to speak, was put down when and wherever possible; such a person had a lot of nerve trying to counteract the image. He really didn't have to believe me, since I would have incurred his wrath anyhow by daring to dream beyond my 'place.'

"I was given a choice of OCS for the infantry or going to gunnery school. By now I was really 'teed off' and I had no eyes for hand-to-hand combat for the 'man'; I went to gunnery school in Florida.

"At the end of the war in Europe they closed this school and I was transferred to Chanute Field, Illinois. Because I could keep double-entry books I was made secretary of the NCO club, even though I was only a temporary corporal. Before I became bookkeeper I was a classification specialist. This meant reviewing the qualifications of incoming black troops and deciding what kind of jobs they should go on. I was always looking for a kid who was well qualified for something other than shoveling coal. One such youngster, high school educated and smart, turned me down flat when I offered him one of the jobs *now* opening up to blacks. He was running a crap game, and it would interfer with his overseeing the game. This was the direct result of occupations being closed to blacks when they first entered the service, not yet disenchanted. I have often wondered what became of this particular young man with a spectacular IQ and a lot of know-how; he should have been an investment broker on Wall Street or its equivalent.

"My two years in the armed forces were frankly quite dull. As you can see, my assignments were somewhat less than challenging. Any idiot could see that I would have been of much more service back in Dayton or somewhere doing what I knew how to do well, designing aircraft for the future. This was not only true of me but of the overwhelming majority of men washed out at Tuskegee. They were talented and able, yet this highly skilled personnel was allowed to stagnate doing menial jobs. What they could have contributed to the war effort if they had been treated as men, fighting men of America, is incalcuable; that is assuming the country had an urgent desire to bring the war to an end as quickly as possible.

"I have often wondered about the highly intelligent black military people. They were very much aware of the racial problems stacking up in the country. This I can say, I never saw a really gung-ho guy at Tuskegee in my time spent there. Behind the façade of 'for God and country' was the definite recognition of the sham. There was always the knowledge that no matter what, you were strictly second-class. Whatever was being done for you was minimal and absolutely necessary. The whole situation was biased in sub-optimizing in the use of blacks in the armed forces. In essence they were saying racism was to prevail over the winning of the war."

Interviews with the flyers of the 332nd make frequent mention of escorting bombers that raided the Ploesti oil fields in 1944. Master Sergeant Warren Bryant, of the 812th Aviation Engineers, was part of an outfit that built an airfield the previous year in North Africa to serve as a take-off point for raids on Ploesti conducted by the 9th Air Force in 1943. An early inductee, Bryant had finished basic training at Fort Leonard Wood and was stationed at McDill Field, Florida, when the attack on Pearl Harbor came.

Bryant is the only one of the men interviewed who served for an extended time in Africa. The 812th's first African assignment, in 1942, was to build a hospital for evacuees from the then disastrous North African engagements. After the fall of Sicily to the Allied forces in the late summer of 1943, the 812th built airfields there, going—without respite—to Corsica in early 1944 to construct airfields in preparation for the Allied invasion of southern France in August 1944.

Comments on racial discrimination, and on race generally, in this interview include aspects that others could not touch upon: relationships between the British and the black Africans; the British and the black Americans; the black Americans and the black Africans. Bryant also describes a cultural confrontation: British whites versus Appalachian whites, Puerto Ricans, and Mexican Americans.

Warren Bryant: "I was born in Cincinnati and reared in Detroit, so overt segregation was a new experience to me as well as to a large number of the other fellows when I went into the servce in 1941. At Fort Leonard Wood segregation was so complete you were hardly aware that it existed. No racial problems arose while I was there simply because blacks and whites had no contact with each other, with the exception of our white officers, of course. I guess Fort Leonard Wood should have prepared us for another dose of absolute segregation at McDill Field. But at McDill it got under my skin; I resented it bitterly.

"When we got a chance to go to town we had to wait until all of the white soldiers who wished to go had been taken to their destinations; then we were crowded like sardines into a couple of buses and driven directly to the colored section of the nearby town. One of our officers tried to make them allow us to get on the bus with the white soldiers. For his trouble he was told, 'When in Rome you do as the Romans do.'

"We did have a little trouble there, but it was between my group and a black infantry group. They had returned from maneuvers; we all had to use the same inadequate black facilities; tempers flared. A few slugging and wrestling matches gained us nothing, so we tolerated each other.

"The PX there was a classic. If you wanted to buy a pair of shoes you had to know your exact size because you were not allowed to try on any wearing apparel. This was on a United States Army base. You could buy pop and sodas, various things of this nature but you had to take them outside to consume them since you were not allowed to sit down at the counter inside.

"When the Japanese bombed Pearl Harbor, that particular Sunday, all of the whites at McDill Field were running around with loaded guns. We had no guns and no idea as to what was going on, so you can imagine what was running through our minds until we learned of the Japanese attack. Even with this knowledge it was of no comfort to be practically penned in our area with armed patty boys all over everywhere. We trusted them just about as much as a coiled rattlesnake.

"Frankly, we were delighted when orders came for us to go to our POE. Anything was better than this hell hole. We departed for overseas from Charleston, South Carolina. All of the colored troops were put in the hold, below the waterline, and it was a dirty ship to boot. I was bunked up in the prow. I could clearly hear the anchor being pulled up. At night they let us up for fresh air.

"Our first stop was out from Bermuda, where we picked up a British escort. We then went to Freetown, Sierra Leone, where we stayed, with no shore leave, until a convoy was assembled. The white soldiers had no shore leave either, but at least they were topside where they could breathe fresh air.

"The first time we left the ship was when we arrived at Durban, South Africa. We soon found that the state of Mississippi looked good beside Durban. There the whites controlled everything and I do mean *everything*. I wondered just where their system differed from slavery excepting for the lack of visible chains. When one white snapped his fingers a hundred blacks jumped. That is one place blacks truly have nothing to lose but their lives. As I saw it, it would be worth it as long as they made sure they took a few of those arrogant, overbearing, white sons-of-bitches with them.

"As we were preparing to board a British ship in Durban one of the officer's wives asked, "Are those our natives?' One of the guys spoke up quickly, saying, 'No, we're Uncle Sam's natives!' The woman was amazed that we not only walked and talked, but we talked back!

"On the ship we were separated, strictly along lines of rank: sergeants with sergeants, corporals with corporals, officers of the same rank, etc. We got along just fine with the English Tommies.

"Because of fighting in the Straits of Mombasa, our ship had to go around Mombasa. Here we pulled away from the convoy, breaking up our battalion. When we finally managed to land at Mombasa there were about 280 men with 32 officers. The officers were all white; two were from the deep south. One was a typical cracker, while the other was a Regular Army man and a real soldier.

"From Mombasa we were sent to Kenya. En route, we rode on what I called a trolley. The British rode first-class and we were in the section of the trolley for the lowest class. Our officers were forced to ride with us because they did not match the rank of the British.

"When we arrived in Kenya, we bivouacked in the Royal Game Reserve. Now, the British didn't know why we were there or how we got there, so they contacted the American consul to come out and identify us. This he did and then got in touch with the United States Forces in the Middle East. A general and his entourage flew out and welcomed us. We were treated very nice while we were there; our supplies were flown in regularly. At night we had to patrol the area in jeeps because of the wild animals. Our purpose there, we finally learned, was to help build a hospital. The allies were expecting to lose North Africa, and this was the area they had chosen to pull back to, to evacuate their soldiers.

"When we first went into Nairobi we could go to the best places to eat and sleep: we were treated as Europeans. This lasted until our officers made their first trip to town. We were quarantined for a couple of weeks under some pretext. When we returned to Nairobi, all of the best places were now closed to us. The reason given was that if the natives saw us frequenting these spots they might get restless in the stables and want to do likewise. The racial lines as I saw them were white on top; further down were the East Indians, and on the bottom of the heap was the indigenous population, the black Africans.

"While I was supply sergeant in Kenya, I had native blacks working for me. I wondered at their backwardness. A white Salvation Army worker told me that they were forbidden to teach natives anything beyond the fifth-grade school level. If they did, the government would expel the Salvation Army workers and close their mission.

"We got along well with the black Kenyans. It wasn't, as some of the younger present day blacks think, the brother routine. This kind of thing just didn't come up. They were inquisitive about us, and we were equally curious about them. They were well aware of America's racial policies so we did not try telling them any fancy tales. I don't recall any of them suggesting we return there to live. We were friends. Culturally we differed, but we did not think we were superior to them nor did they think they were superior to us.

"My unit was returned to Mombasa, where we boarded a ship that took us through the Suez Canal and on to Cairo. There we had trouble with both black and white South African troops. The blacks hated our guts. They said we were too much like the white man and would call us 'nigger' and things like that. Our basic trouble with the white troops was we Americans made more money; where the money was so were the girls. Whenever we went in to a bar we ended up with the girls. The British answer was a free-for-all. It got to be a regular and expected thing, a good knock-down-drag-out. I suspect we both kind of looked forward to it.

"One particular night however, some men from our sister unit, the 811th, were with us. The 811th consisted mainly of Puerto Ricans, Appalachian whites, and there might have been a few Mexican-Americans in the group. Now it never occurred to us they fought a little differently, like for keeps. Anyway we entered a bar, the girls were soon with us, and the fight broke out. The ending was quite different; there were several very dead British soldiers. They had been stabbed to death. The members of the 812th were allowed to leave the area, but they held the 811th. It may sound odd, but those guys who did the knifing had responded in the only way they knew. It simply never occurred to them that two opposing factions could have a donnybrook with no thought of killing. Where they had come from, a fight was to the death or at least until someone was seriously wounded.

"The 812th, my unit, was attached to the British 8th Army. In Cairo we were given British uniforms excepting for caps and shoes. There were no American clothes available for the climate we would soon be in, that of the Sahara desert. As we learned it was hotter than hell in the day and damned cold at night.

"We left Cairo in convoy. We traveled about a hundred miles a day to reach our bivouac areas by night. At this time Rommel's forces were pulling back, with the British in hot pursuit, and we had to make time. Our destination was Benghazi. Some of our men went on to Tobruk, where they took part in the final driving out of Rommel's forces. Those of us who stayed at Benghazi were assigned to the 9th Air Force (American) under General Ent. With the Germans being pushed out of North Africa, the air force began to strike at Europe from North Africa.

"We built an airfield at Benghazi, whose purpose was to be a take-off field for the bombing of the Rumanian oil fields at Ploesti. It put the 9th Air Force much closer to Rumania than the 8th, which was based in England. The runways we constructed were built from a mixture of desert sand and tar. The field was built to accommodate B-24 bombers, though the 9th only had B-17s. Our group also had the job of building a model, mock city of Ploesti with refineries in and around it. This mock city with its mock refineries was built in the desert, and the bombers practiced bombing them with bags of sand. When not practicing for Ploesti, they were off on real missions in Italy around the Naples area.

"When the time came for the Ploesti deal, the 8th Air Force flew in just in time to be checked over and refueled. They had evidently done their practice work for Ploesti in England. As I understood it, these planes were to return to England after they hit Ploesti. I have often wondered how many, if any, of them made it because the 9th took one helluva beating.

"In this 1943 raid, the first one made on these oil refineries, the 9th lost a great many planes and a large number of men. Those that got back to Benghazi were just plain lucky. The planes returning looked like they had been through a shooting gallery. It had been a low-level mission, and I saw some of the pictures taken at Ploesti. The low-level flying had been practiced right there in the desert, but from the pictures those guys really carried it to the extreme. Some of the photographs were taken just above tree level to give you an idea how low they had gotten. From scuttlebutt I got the idea that there was a mix-up somewhere and squadrons found themselves coming in and meeting each other face to face. It must have been a bitch playing hop-skip-and-jump in a bomber.

"This Ploesti raid had no fighter escort. Some of the bombers were heavily armed for extra fighting and less bombing, but no fighter planes were on the first Ploesti raid, unfortunately. Judging by those planes that returned to Benghazi the German fighters must have had a field day. I still believe the raid was unsuccessful, and to my knowledge no further raids on Ploesti were made from that field.

"As to our officer leadership, we didn't have any. In plain English our officers, all white, were about as select a bunch of chickens to be found anywhere; one was a M.I.T. graduate. Death was one thing they simply refused to face up to even in war. Anything that smacked of danger, like patrols, was passed on to a sergeant, and the officers stayed put. Many of the men of the 812th went on bombing missions to Italy with the 9th; not one officer ever made such a trip. A strange thing was that white pilots believed it was good luck to have a Negro aboard.

"After our work was done, my group was pulled back to Cairo to regroup. We were still just two companies; we had lost no men in combat, but a few went to jail or were sick. Then we left Cairo and went to Sicily. Our arrival was just after the Normandy invasion.

"When we landed in Sicily we were given a canteen of water which we promptly poured out in front of the first wine shop and refilled with the fermented juice of the grape. When we reached our bivouac area, which we had been told was a very safe location, we found it was under water—it was safe if you were a duck. The wine in the meantime had done its job and the guys cut loose and told our officers, in language they clearly understood, just what they thought of them and the whole fucking army. Our officers, true to the wide yellow streak running down their backs, scared to death, politely disappeared. The colonel then arrived upon the scene and he said he was going to bust all of the NCOs. I suggested he need not wait, he could have my stripes right then. He didn't want this because he knew the others would follow suit and without us sergeants he would be in one helluva bind. I told him quite frankly, if he would take his 90-day wonders and ride herd on them we NCOs would handle the men; that is how it was settled.

"We stayed in the duck pond a week. We never saw the enemy, but we were in a rough air raid. The next move was to split us up, right down the line, officers and men. My new unit was so small that each of us had to do the work of three men. On New Year's Eve half of the unit was placed aboard one LST, while the other half was put on another. We spent the night going up and down because of the rough weather and in the morning we found we hadn't cleared the harbor. Later in the day we finally got clear and headed for Corsica. They said the water was so heavily mined around Corsica our unit had been split and put on different LSTs to assure one of the halves getting through; this bit of information really made us feel great!

"The reason for this brilliant maneuver was the 'brains' had decided to make the outer perimeter of Corsica into a land aircraft carrier. There were no Germans on Corsica but they held Elba, Napoleon's old stamping grounds.

We could see German planes taking off from their island. We built air strips all along the coast of Corsica for our fighter planes. It was from these fields that many of our planes later took off for the invasion of southern France.

"Just before the invasion I received my first furlough along with some other fellows and we headed for Rome. We hitched a plane ride back, and on board were some fighter pilots returning from furlough. They said they felt the invasion was imminent since they had been given time off.

"When we landed at one of our airfields in Corsica (we referred to them as 'ours' because we had constructed them), I never saw so many planes in my life. Bombers had been flown in and they were lined up almost wing tip to wing tip. In between these bombers I saw my first black fighter pilot.* He was sitting in a fighter plane underneath the wings of the bombers. We learned fighters were stationed throughout, ready to take off at the first signal to intercept any enemy with designs on the bombers. The field also had a large number of gliders. French troops were present and we understood they would man the gliders.

"We were awakened at the crack of dawn by the sound of all of those motors turning over at once. When we got up a little later there was not a plane in sight. The only reason we were not sent as combat troops in this landing was the medical officer said we were physically exhausted. I am glad he noticed because we had worked like dogs getting those airfields ready in time for the invasion. We had come from Benghazi to Sicily to Corsica with no time off.

"The closest we ever came to combat was the raids, where they did the dishing out and we did the taking.

"After the invasion, the Corsican fields were only used for emergency landings. Our job was finished here so it was not too long before we were sent to Naples for a much needed rest, followed by the usual regrouping. While we were in Naples we learned we were to be sent to the Far East. My unit pitched a bitch. We had spent a few years overseas and we felt we should at least be allowed to pass through the states so we could see our families. V-J Day came while the hell-raising was going on. It evidently did some good, for we were almost immediately flown home via Casablanca, the Azores, and Bermuda. The skyscrapers of New York looked mighty good to us. Thank the Lord I was mustered out of service without having to return to the southland!

"I have saved for my ending the most pleasing incident that happened to me during my time spent in the armed forces.

"Shortly after our arrival in Italy, about six or seven of us were walking along the road to a village about a mile from our camp. Some crackers stationed in the area appeared, and the usual name-calling started. American

---

*According to Alexander Jefferson, above, he could not have been a member of the 332nd. Most probably, he was with the Royal Air Force or Royal Canadian Air Force.

whites only get cute when they have you outnumbered. We reasoned, so we get whipped, we damn sure weren't going to run, and they would know they had been in one helluva fight. Man, we were fighting all over the road when a truck load of Japanese-Americans came along. The driver jammed on the brakes and they piled off of their truck. Numerically things were just about even, but hell those little Nisei didn't need us. They kinda gently pushed us aside and waded in; it was murder, they tore those patty boys up. Talk about know-how in contact fighting. They didn't use their fists often, they would slip in under a punch and grab, then they would either slam the guy down on the ground or literally throw him a country mile. It was beautiful. I must admit I felt a little sorry for the crackers who looked like a bulldozer had run over them. When the Nisei had cleaned house in what seemed like a few seconds, they leaped back aboard their truck, waved and said, 'Anytime.' Those were the only words they had spoken. Why they got into it I don't know. Maybe they were thinking about their folks back home in the internment camps. Anyhow, I made it my business to learn their regimental number and anything I could about them. I kept up with their movements through the army newspapers and magazines. To this day I am grateful to those Japanese-Americans for giving me one moment's pleasure while I was in service. Also I will always remember that I saw whites outclassed in all ways by people of color. This incident helped make up for the insults I had to endure while serving my country in its armed forces."

Chapter **5**

General Almond's 92nd Division

The interviews in this chapter return to the nagging question "who was the enemy?" openly or implicitly raised earlier. Dr. Rudolph Porter, a physician stationed at Fort Huachuca with the 92nd Infantry Division, answers it bluntly: "In less time than it takes to change into a uniform a black man knew who the real enemy was, the United States military." Some of the men whose war histories are recorded here would agree with Dr. Porter. Others see the problems plaguing the division as an inextricable part of the American experience.

Lieutenant General Mark Clark, commander of the 5th Army in Italy, judged the performance of the 92nd Division "bad," its record "less favorable than any of the white divisions." In the popular mind, the dubious distinction of being the worst infantry division in Europe has clung to the men of the 92nd, while the divisional commander, Major General Edward M. Almond, and his staff have quite escaped responsibility for that record. In 1950, several months before General Almond was under criticism for incompetency in the Korean War, "Time" ran a four-page spread lauding his accomplishments as commander of the 92nd Division in World War II:

World War II . . . tossed him the hottest potato in the U.S.A., command of the 92nd Infantry Division. The 92nd was mostly a Negro outfit and the cynosure of the sensitive Negro press. Its rank and file had the handicap of less-than-average literacy and more-than-average superstition*. The 92nd did not learn combat discipline easily. Almond handled his difficult assignment with determination and dogged persistence. He trained the 92nd hard, sought to give it esprit de corps through extracurricular activities (it had a championship basketball team, a topnotch band featuring Sergeant Bobby Platter who composed the Jersey Bounce. . . . ["Time," 23 October 1950, p. 29, emphasis added]*

On the occasion of the 92nd's twenty-fifth reunion held at Viareggio, Italy, "Newsweek" referred to the division as the "hapless 92nd," quoted

258

*Clark's estimate of it, phrased its own question, and implied its own negative
answer:*

> Given the racial climate of the time, the big question was: could the Negro
> make the grade as a fighting soldier? From their mountain fortress line,
> German forces moved down toward the west coast of Italy and hit the
> 92nd in a head-on collision. The black troops gave ground, then broke and
> fled the field. Defeat followed hard upon defeat as, two months later, the
> 92nd was routed again. ("Newsweek," 8 June 1970, p. 45]

*The reference to the reunion as a sentimental journey includes a significant
statement: "There was a bond between Italians and black GIs. The Italians
remember the 92nd as liberators and good samaritans. . . . The black remember
that unlike the American Army, the Italians were color blind."*

*Colonel Queen, commander of the black 366th Infantry Regiment,
serving with the 92nd Division, charges:*

> General Mark Clark was frustrated in his attempt to become a General
> Patton. He tried to make the Italian campaign more than it was intended
> to be: a secondary area in the overall picture. He lashed out at the 92nd
> Division . . . when his grandiose scheme failed. He called this division the
> worst in Europe and placed all the blame on the junior officers and
> enlisted personnel. The statement is unfair and untrue. . . . Whatever short-
> comings the 92nd had rested entirely on the shoulders of Major General
> Almond. His entire staff was incompetent excepting for Brigadier General
> Coburn, the artillery commander, whose artillery was rated among the best
> on the front. [Personal communication from Colonel Queen, 1972]

*In this chapter the reader encounters some of those junior officers
and enlisted personnel. Their story begins with their assignment to one of the
three regiments comprising the division: the 365th, which trained at Camp
Atterbury, Indiana; the 370th, which trained at Camp Robinson, Arkansas; and
the 371st, which trained at Fort McClellan, Alabama. After the 93rd Division
had departed for maneuvers and POE, the three regiments came together at
Fort Huachuca, Arizona, engaging in maneuvers there in the fall of 1943, and
in Louisiana, spring of 1944.*

*The overseas history of the men of the 92nd Division belongs to the
final ten months of the war in northwest Italy, and includes the history of
units that were attached to it: the 366th Infantry Regiment and the 442nd
Regimental Combat Team (Nisei).*

*The Nisei are frequently mentioned in the interviews. By inquiring, I
found that many people, particularly those under forty, are quite unaware of
the contribution made by the Nisei in the armed forces during World War II.
Briefly, the 442nd was the most decorated infantry unit in the United States
Army, winning 10 unit citations, 3,915 individual decorations, 47 of these
being the Distinquished Service Cross, 1 the Congressional Medal of Honor.*

(The present senator from Hawaii, Daniel Inouye, was recommended for the Medal of Honor but was awarded the DSC.)

Nisei losses were 700 dead, 1,700 critical casualties, and 3,000 casualties. Twelve thousand Nisei replacements were needed for their combat team of 4,500 men. The 100th Battalion, the first formed of Nisei, was known as the Purple Heart Battalion because it is said that almost every man in this unit received at least one Purple Heart.*

None of the few Nisei I was able to locate would discuss his experiences with the 92nd Division. One veteran, who offered technical information, mentioned that the Nisei had had no special training in mountain climbing. On being directed to take certain mountains during the Po Valley campaign, they climbed at night. Their having been together as a team for so long, knowing one another's every move, made it appear to the amateur's eye that they were skilled mountaineers. My informant said that his own thoughts, on being shown the mountain they were to take (Folgorito), were, "They've got to be kidding."

From men of the 366th Infantry Regiment I quickly learned that to refer to that regiment as "belonging to" the 92nd Division was to commit an unforgivable error. Yet any information I received from government agencies invariably linked the 366th to the 92nd division. After the regiment was attached to the division 15 November 1944, most of its battalions were put under the direct command of Major General Almond and his staff. The commanding officer of the 366th was bypassed when orders were given to units of this regiment. Hence the army ties the 366th directly into the 92nd Division, attached or not. Ironically, it is thanks to members of the 92nd Division that the reader will learn about the 366th and its problems.

The 366th entered the line of combat 30 November 1944, serving continuously until 25 March 1945. Its personnel won nine Silver Stars, eighteen Bronze Stars, and suffered over 1,300 casualties in dead, wounded, and missing in action. The regiment won two Battle Stars for its regimental colors. Company C was awarded a presidential citation for participating in the Southern France landing in 1944 (personal communication from Colonel Queen).

On an adjacent page the reader will find the capsule battle history of the division, as recorded by the United States Defense Department. I have arranged it in the form of a timetable, adding within brackets the names of interviewees who furnish information about events within the timetable, names of participating units, and names of personnel receiving citations. Citations are included in the text where events described by one of the men most clearly visualize the attending circumstances.

The reader's progress through the interviews will be assisted by frequent reference to the timetable and the map, and by keeping in mind that

---

*Statistics from Daniel K. Inouye, *Journey to Washington*, pp. 123, 163.

the 370th was the first regiment of the division to go overseas (July 1944) and the first to enter combat (August 1944). The 365th and 371st arrived in Italy in late October. In March 1945 the division was reconstituted from the 370th (with replacements from the 365th and 371st), the 442nd (Nisei), and the 473rd (white). Personnel of the division who did not serve as replacements acted as service troops until the war's end. By fortunate chance, some of the men interviewed participated in two actions that have made the division a subject of controversy: the retreat following the German surprise attack in the Serchio sector the day after Christmas 1944, and the failed attempt to capture the town of Massa in February 1945 (here referred to as the attempt to cross the Cinquale Canal).

Timetable

92nd Infantry Division (370th RCT; 365th and 371st Infantry Regiments)

70th RCT, attached to st Armored Division	Arrives Naples	1 August 1944
	Enters combat, participates in crossing of Arno, occupies Lucca, penetrates Gothic Line; enemy resistance "negligible" [Described by Charles Brown, noting 370th near Pistoia by end of Sept. 365th, 371st sail for Italy from U.S., early Oct.]	24 August
Task Force 92	"Elements of 92nd" attack on Ligurian coastal flank toward Massa.	5–12 October
	Slight gains lost to counterattacks by	12 October
	"Remainder of the Division" concentrates for patrol activities [Brown, Jordan describe 370th patrol and assault activities in Apennines] [365th, 371st arrive Italy end of October]	13 October
Elements of the 92nd	move to Serchio sector; advance in Serchio River Valley. Fail to capture Castelnuovo.	3 November
	Patrol activities until [Brown describes, part of tank-infantry team. 365th now in combat. McCree describes patrol at Cinquale Canal. 366th assigned to 5th Army 15 Nov.; Col. Queen ordered to report to Gen. Almond, arrives Po Valley 26 Nov. 366th enters battle line 30 Nov. Col. Ferguson replaces Queen 15 Dec.]	26 December

Timetable (Continued)

Units of the 92nd	Forced to withdraw by enemy attack beginning and ending [Lts. Fox, Jenkins, and 53 comrades killed at forward observation post. Private Trueheart Fogg, 366th, Silver Star.] [Withdrawal described by Jordan] Patrols and reconnaissance until	26 December 28 December 5 February 19
Units of the 92nd	Attack in Serchio sector; enemy counterattacks nullify advances [Staff Sgt. William Newmuis, 366th Silver Star] [Millender describes drive to take Massa by crossing Cinquale Canal, E Co., 370th wiped out. Tanks: 769th and 768th support; 597th FA attached. Details by Williams, 366th; Duplessis, 758th Tank Bn; Hargrove, 597th FA]	5—8 February
	[366th dissolved 28 March, personnel to service units. Millender: division reorganized. McCree: 365th and 371st raided for replacements to 370th, remaining personnel to service units. [442nd (Nisei) and 473rd (white) regts. now attached to 92nd]	[March 1945]
370th and attached 442nd (Nisei) regt.	Attack in Ligurian sector, drive north against light opposition [McCree includes 473rd (white) and gives date as 5 April, as does Wells] [5 April Lt. Vernon Baker, DSC]	1—18 April
370th	Takes over Serchio sector and pursues retreating enemy [George: partisan uprising]	18—25 April
Elements of the 92nd	Enter La Spezia and Genoa, taking over "selected towns" along Ligurian coast until [Details in Wells]	 27 April
The Division	Leaves for home Is deactivated	16 November 28 November

Source: Capsule history of the 92nd Division, Defense Department, United States Government. Bracket insertions are the editor's.

The 370th, 365th, and 371st Infantry Regiments

Staff Sergeant David Cason, Jr., went overseas as a member of the 370th Infantry Regiment, but was transferred to the 365th. As he observed, experienced, and acted out the morale problems of the 92nd Division, his interview serves as a preface to the others. Of one stateside incident he commented: "This was the only time in my life I was prepared to die and I went overseas afterward," A Michigan man, inducted in 1943, Cason was sent to Camp Gordon, near Augusta, Georgia, for basic training.

David Cason: "On arriving at Camp Gordon, the group I was with was informed by a white colonel that even though we were soldiers we were in the south and would be treated as the Negro civilian population living in the area. Since most of us were northern-born it was strike one against the army.

"Because I had had ROTC training in high school I soon had the rating of a staff sergeant. I was interviewed for OCS and ASTP and chose the latter for two good reasons. More education was given in the ASTP program over a longer period of time, which meant being stateside longer and when you finished you were a first lieutenant. I was quite practical in making this decision but at the same time I was a flaming super-patriot; 'my country right or wrong' and all that crap. I had just finished high school and three years of ROTC. Let's face it, the young are highly impressionable and I was no exception.

"While waiting to learn the outcome of my ASTP interview I was made a platoon sergeant at Camp Gordon in the Quartermasters. It occurred to me that every time my platoon was sent on a work detail on the other side of the camp I was assigned to teaching military tactics. At the same time my men began to complain about the white civilian workers they encountered whenever they went on these work details. I then asked my immediate superior why I was excluded from the work details of my platoon. He replied, 'Just what would you do if those construction workers over on the other side began to give your platoon a bad time and you were in charge?' I answered truthfully, 'Return to the post and make sure all things were equal than return and fight on any terms they chose.' 'That,' he injected, 'is why you stay here and one of the southern sergeants is sent in your place.' My superior had sure pegged me right; I was never sent on a work detail.

"I went to Augusta, Georgia, exactly five times: three times on army business, twice on pass. My reason for staying on the post was twofold. I had heard of the trouble black soldiers courted by going into town, and frankly, I was afraid of getting done up or done in with no recourse. The other reason was the Negro people of Augusta did not want us there. They said one day we would leave and they would still be there paying for our thoughtlessness. As they put it, 'We don't like the laws down here either, but we have to live with them, you don't!' I stayed on the post.

"My acceptance for ASTP finally arrived and I was sent to A and T College in Greensboro, North Carolina. The three weeks I spent there were almost like being in the north due to the many Negro colleges in the vicinity. Yet one night on a date I watched my company ask permission to use a public telephone. *C'est la south*.

"From Greensboro I was sent to Howard University in Washington, D.C. and there were no problems in this cosmopolitan city. Moreover, Mrs. Roosevelt liked us a lot, we formed her honor guard many times, and she came up to Howard often to talk to us. Our shoulder patches of the lamp and the sword stood us in good stead with the MPs. They thought of us as college boys and did not bother us. The few months I spent at Howard were the happiest days I spent in the United States Army.

"Unfortunately things changed. They broke up the ASTP and the group I was with was sent right to the swamps of Louisiana to join the 92nd Division there on maneuvers. This was the 92nd's maneuvers just before POE. Our reception was a deflating episode. We were told in so many words, school was out and we were in the army. They didn't tell us we were there because they needed our AGCTs to bring the division IQ level up so it could go overseas.

"Speaking of maneuvers, on them we got a full dose of the Louisiana cracker, and I think he got a few surprises. One incident was comical, at least to us, and I can't see chicken feathers without recalling it. A small group of us were walking along, making like soldiers, doing our thing, when this shot-gun-totin' cracker appeared, having come from a house not too far in the distance. He ordered us off of his property or else, and moved the gun menacingly. The radio man, with the permission of our officer, put in a call to the light tank unit in the area. A tank arrived promptly and without even stopping it ran right over Shotgun Joe's henhouse. Man, feathers were everywhere! Old Joe withdrew quietly to the rear. I suspect our 'Uncle' paid for a new chicken coop somewhere in the heart of Louisiana.

"The second encounter I had with the charming, hospitable, slobs of Louisiana was the only time during my time in service when I felt I would not get back home.

"We had a maneuver problem of defending a bridge, which was no big thing. When we had spent the designated time at this bridge we were picked up by a personnel carrier headed up by a jeep. It had been a hot, boring day, and one of the guys spotted a little place with an ice cream sign out front. We were all young and hot and wanted some ice cream. The jeep driver must have had the same idea for he turned in at the sign and our carrier followed. Jumping down we headed for the door. Just as the first fellows off of the truck reached the door somebody inside hooked the screen, stepped back, and stood looking at us. The usual shot-gun totin' cracker was suddenly standing in the back door. Not a word had been exchanged; silence was deafening! The fellows closest to the screen wheeled and headed back to the carrier. Others followed as a few climbed aboard and one pulled back the canvas covering the 50 mm machine gun it concealed. The team that operated the gun pulled a belt of ammunition out of its box, slapped it into place, and the trigger man swung that machine gun around to cover the doorway of the ice cream parlor. The only sound was the activities of the men, no words. When I heard the gunner slide the bolt into firing position, with the rest of the men, I stepped back to the carrier, picked up my rifle, removed the clip with soap in the shell, reached in my pocket and pulled out the real thing. All of our clips being slapped into place at the same time sounded like a cannon going off.

"At the moment I was thinking, better here than there. None of us had any illusions as to what would happen when that .50-caliber opened up on that ice cream shack. It would cut it and everybody in it in half. We knew every white regiment and division in the state, plus their police at every level would be called down upon our heads. Without a word we had decided to make our stand.

"Fortunately for all concerned, the crackers inside realized this was for real, these were not 'niggers' playing soldier, these were black men who planned to kill and die for that right. The cracker in the back door disappeared; we could see his hasty retreat. The figure which stood looking at us like we were a new species of animal reached out and unhooked the screen. As we filed in we learned the silent figure was a waitress. Tears were streaming down her face as she scooped up the ice cream with trembling hands. Sitting in a cluster not far away crying and shaking like leaves in a breeze were several other women and a couple of kids.

"The whole scene was like an old silent movie: not one word was spoken. When the last man got his ice cream we walked out, swung aboard our carrier, the jeep motor started and than the motor of the truck; the noise sounded like the end of the world had come. We pulled off and all of the normal sounds of a countryside were once more heard. Funny thing the cracker didn't even report us, not that he would have recognized us among all of the other men—the advantage of looking alike. My own opinion is he was so glad to be alive he decided to forget it happened. This incident was the only time in my life I was prepared to die and I went overseas *afterward*.

"When the 92nd was returned to Fort Huachuca I was sent to the 370th Infantry Regiment's service company. My CO had promised me a warrant officership for my work in ordering the equipment for the regiment's going overseas. General Marshall came down and even commented on the efficient job I had done. It turned out, however, that my CO could not keep his promise because the ever-elusive 'they' wanted an administrative man in the position. Whether his being white had anything to do with it I do not know but patty was in and I was out. This was strike two in my book on the army. My CO said the best he could do for me was a T4 rating or I could transfer out. I took the transfer, reporting to the 365th Infantry Regiment, 3rd Battalion headquarters. I was given a choice of what I wished to do, and because a friend from Howard days was in communications I chose radio work.

"By now my friend and I had no false ideas about the white man's army so it became a game of seeing just how much we could avoid doing. We found out one of the most effective little gimmicks was to take a clip board, pad, and pencil and go up to the headquarters area and just walk around. No one ever bothered to ask us what we were doing up there. If our IQs said we were pretty smart cookies you can be assured we put every bit of our brain power together in the art of evading, dodging, and lying if caught. However we were very careful to make sure the 'great white father' was unaware that we were goofing off three-quarters of the time. The other quarter 'they' didn't consider worth bothering about, besides they didn't quite dig us. I mean our IQs as stated in the files made us some kind of freaks to them. Black men with AGCTs 115 and up, talk about a credibility gap; they saw it but it was absolutely inconceivable to those ignorant hicks running the show.

"There was a group of fellows in the 92nd called the Casuals. Some of the guys in this unit were ASTP men. Now actually these guys were malingerers and there was nothing, I mean *nothing*, the army could do with them. They were actually an embarrassment to the military. Yet the 92nd had to carry them because they needed those high IQs for the division's files. That the command did not recognize a tremendous morale problem in the division with so many highly intelligent men in the Casual group gives you an idea of the brain power in charge of the 92nd Division. It seems that the whites were completely blind at this point in history. The only sickness those Casuals had was one of morale. If they had been treated as human beings, as soldiers in the United States Army, they would not have become a problem. Now my group of game players decided we would not get into the Casual group because we did not know what would eventually happen to them as they were continually being threatened with all kinds of dire things.

"The army struck out with me when I got my first furlough from the 365th. I was returning by way of El Paso, Texas, where the passengers had a lay-over. I was hungry and the only place I could find that would serve me was a dingy, dinky place near the station. The station restaurant was doing a rush business with white civilians and German prisoners of war. There sat the so-called enemy comfortably seated, laughing, talking, making friends, with the waitresses at their beck and call. If I had tried to enter that dining room the ever-present MPs would have busted my skull, a citizen-soldier of the United States. My morale, if I had any left, dipped well below zero. Nothing infuriated me as much as seeing those German prisoners of war receiving the warm hospitality of Texas. I played games with the man and I knew he played games with me; was it some kind of game he was playing with the enemy or just a ghastly joke? It really didn't matter, because any way I looked at it I was the loser and the butt of the joke and I didn't like it, not one damn bit.

"Shortly after my El Paso incident and my return to Huachuca the 365th entrained for POE. We were told en route that if we helped load material we were picking up along the way we would be given passes upon our arrival at our destination. We stevedored all the way and upon our arrival at our POE we learned we had been told a lie; such had never been the intention of those in charge. Our response to this was to go AWOL. We, four friends and myself, slipped out of camp undetected, secreted ourselves on the Howard campus where we knew they would never look for us, and returned at our leisure in the same manner in which we had left, undetected. However my outfit had already gone. We learned some 400 men had gone AWOL. The majority had returned in time to ship out with their units.

"There was a lot of gear that needed to be loaded aboard ship, and we were asked to volunteer again. We declined the job and turned ourselves in as having been AWOL. Without our self-incrimination they could not prove the charge, but we chose the stockade to another snow job. A summary court-martial sentenced us to ten days. The reason for the comparatively light sentence was all of the 92nd had not departed and we could still be sent on with them.

"While we were in the stockade, which really wasn't too bad, we were to be subjected to taking our shots all over again. Our guards, reenforced by more MPs, marched us over to the medical building. We waited and we waited. Even the guards got tired, and one of them went to see what the hold-up was. He was told that they couldn't possibly take care of us because they were much too busy; they had some bodies to post. Curiosity got the better of the guards and they found someone they knew to tell them what had happened. The night before there had been a riot between some white paratroopers and black tankers in another area of the camp. What precipitated the fight we did not find out but the bodies being posted were those of white paratroopers. This explained our extra guards on being escorted to the hospital. That we heard none of the commotion, which was a real shoot-out the night before, gives you an idea just how vast a place an army post, POE or otherwise, can be.

"We were shipped out at last and landed in Naples, Italy. I could have easily caught up with the 365th but I learned there was going to be a training group in Naples for three months so I decided to volunteer for it. The 365th was on the front line and I wasn't in a hurry to get there. My negative attitude was the result of all of the demoralizing things that had been piled upon me in large and small doses, in open and in subtle ways. Then too, one is kind of rootless in the army, couple all of this with intelligence and you get a professional goof-off—one smart enough not to get so uptight as to let his real feelings show through, for this could bring severe punishment. You don't break the hard and fast rules you just bend the hell out of them and if you get caught, by sheer accident, you are absolutely incredulous that any action on your part could be so misconstrued; it was simply a misunderstanding on your part as to the rule.

"Not for one minute did any of us think all of the white officers were complete fools, although I must admit they had a pretty good batting average. They reasoned that we weren't real troublemakers and we certainly weren't stupid, so we seldom got a reprimand. This just gave us license to do more of the same; a good example of the tail wagging the dog. We kept our hostility concealed to the point we were never suspect.

"I should mention I had never had black officers until I joined the 92nd; I exclude those at Howard since they were not real army officers. At Huachuca I was quickly aware of the continual movement of officers so that no black officer ever commanded a white officer. If the same skill and dedication had been used in building morale as exhibited in the shifting of officers, as in a shell game, the 92nd could have been a damn good division. Few blacks reached the rank of captain, but the mobility of white second lieutenants upward was a wonder to behold. I bet records were set at Huachuca for moving white 2nd looeys to 1st looeys.

"I rejoined the 365th, after three months of goofing-off in Naples, about the time the 366th was brought into the 92nd area as replacements for the division. When the 366th arrived, black from top to bottom, that wreaked havoc with the 92nd hierarchy. There are those who believe that command's answer to this intolerable situation was to throw the 366th into some highly untenable positions and wipe them out. The habits and customs of the white officer corps in the 92nd were secretly and openly resented by both black officers and enlisted men. The degree can be illustrated by the fact that some of us—I am speaking of a group I was with—would have killed a white officer had we had the opportunity, while on patrol or in a fire fight.

"During my short time on the line the unit next to us had been pretty badly mauled. A new, young, inexperienced white second lieutenant was joined to this group. Our officer, a black first lieutenant, made some suggestions to him which he patently ignored and got a few more of his men done in. The white lieutenant reported our lieutenant to a white captin, saying he had dared to give him an order. The white captain came out where we were and proceeded to 'read' our black lieutenant. In front of us and in no uncertain terms the captain told him not to ever give an order to a white officer. Now the captain's sole intent was to degrade and humiliate a black officer whom he felt had gotten out of his place. Yes, we would have killed him because he didn't give a damn about our black lives and we were in a combat zone. The only thing that saved him was we were moved out almost immediately after the incident and we never saw the captain again.

"It was after this I went into S-2 at Battalion Headquarters. When the real push came in the spring of '45, the 92nd was actually made into a service unit. Only the 370th, with its casualties replaced from her sister regiments, took part in the spring offensive. What was left of the 371st and the 365th carried supplies, stretchers, and so forth, for white outfits. It caused some trouble because whitey would get cute and fights would start. Our men reminded them in a practical fashion that they were infantrymen, not members of a damn service unit.

"Just as the 370th had a reputation for being a good fighting unit the 371st got to be known for running. Now how true this was I can't say, but I do know with a black outfit one mistake or act of cowardice, they—meaning whitey—put all black units in the same category. This did not affect the 370th as much as others because its reputation had been established before its sister units had arrived.

"This is neither an excuse nor an apology; it's a fact. When I stopped and questioned myself what the hell I was doing there while German war prisoners lived off of the fat of the land in my country and I couldn't, don't you think every black in the 92nd asked himself the same question? Every black in our division knew exactly where he stood with the United States Army: precisely nowhere.

"I will say if the 92nd, in the same geographical position, had been told those were southern crackers up in those mountains, 'get 'em,' they would have, myself included, clawed their way up if necessary. We would have waded in our own blood up to our elbows to take them because we would have had a reason: an enemy we knew, despised, and would have enjoyed destroying. The German, what could he mean to us? Nobody bothered to make him our real enemy.

"Look, if we walked out in clear sight on the front line Jerry would kill us. Not because we were black but because he had been taught we were the enemy. But all we had to do was enter a village, town, any place where there were American whites and they'd start something, even kill us! Yet we wore the same uniform and fought under the same flag.

"I do not think the 92nd could have possibly fought up to its capabilities under the existing circumstances. We were black men, not black gods, all-forgiving and understanding. Many times, stateside and overseas, groups of us talked about present and past happenings in the service. Our conclusion was the white was demented. He treated us like boys or animals and then expected us to make Leonidas at Thermopylae Pass.

"The tragedy of the war is that the men who wore their country's uniform and saw it besmirched returned home, married, and had children. Those children are the young people you see around you today, warped and twisted. This is what the white man does not comprehend, what he did to the black personality. There are thousands of black ex-GIs who will not talk about

World War II because for the black man it was humiliating, degrading, cruel—and not by accident. The treatment of the black was deliberate, contrived, and planned as well as the Normandy invasion, only the invasion is over but the wounds of the black are still raw.

"I cannot emphasize it enough, the real enemy to the black soldier during World War II was whitey: white American soldiers, white civilians, and the white civilian and military police. They didn't leave a stone unturned to keep blacks in their so-called place and to make sure they would not share in the glory and victory of the '40s.

"The whites have forgotten all about the little sadistic games they played with us at that time, the seeds of distrust and hatred they planted. We have not forgotten, we were the victims, and let us not speak of forgiveness. You can only forgive people who know the meaning of the word or have some knowledge of the meaning of Christianity."

As a 1st sergeant in the 370th Infantry Regiment, Charles Brown was in one of the first units of the 92nd Division to go into combat. His account pictures the situation of the noncommissioned officer who is with his men as they engage in assaults and patrols in the Apennines, in the fall and winter of 1944–45. His account begins stateside as the ASTP program has been closed down, and he has been sent to Fort Huachuca.

Charles Brown: "It was quite apparent at Huachuca that the 92nd had had a tremendous problem raising its AGCT in order to qualify for Preparation for Overseas Movement. I taught literacy school there, designed to raise the level of the AGCT. With these classes, switching personnel in and out of the 370th from her sister regiments, the 370th soon met POM demands for shipment overseas.

"I think it's interesting that my basic training was with coastal artillery and my infantry training with a pencil. I never trained with the infantry but I wasn't overseas five minutes before I was a sergeant. What they wanted overseas was an acceptable AGCT that only black ASTP men could furnish.

"I could shoot fairly well with an .03 but they gave me an M1 and I had had no practice with the weapon. This was typical; all the ASTP guys were sergeants shortly after going over. A large number ended up as officers. I can't say this was racial because I have talked to white fellows who were in the ASTP and they had had similar experiences.

"In terms of death, your qualifications for this cannot be trained into you. Obstacle courses can teach you to keep your head down so it won't be blown off but cannot train you for the mental shock the first time a dead body is laying next to you. In my instance I had to have some brains plucked from my ear that came from another man; these things you cannot be trained for. I think the biggest thing in war is to untrain you from the influences that say you don't kill, and train you to say death is attractive. I feel the men I was with did not become untrained from the civilization in which they grew up. It takes time to make a killer out of a man. Situations make you fire to defend yourself and orders make you fire to do those things you are supposed to do. We had some gung-ho guys but for the most part, every time you are involved in an act of violence you have to overcome something, and in this process there is less resistance the next time. The men in my outfit became much more systematic in their responsibilities the time I was away in the hospital but they were not like the marines who could lop off heads, or murder people at Mai Lai.*

"The only time I know of that our division commander, Major General Almond, stood up for the 92nd was when we returned to Viareggio and there was an off-limits sign posted. I understand he angrily tore it down saying, 'My men took this town and it will not be placed off-limits to them.' We ran into the usual white American and German propaganda in Italy, about having tails and all of that foolishness but there is a lot of gentility in the black soldier. They try to adjust to a country while whites try to make the country adjust to them. Whites wanted the Italians to speak English instead of trying to learn Italian. The white GIs treated the Italians with contempt.

"The people in the countryside and in the mountains were terrific to us. They cried tears of sorrow when we left for the front lines and cried tears of joy when we returned safely. This was particularly true of the peasants. I have to this day some of these people as my best friends.

"The 370th Regiment never lost a battle to the Germans, nor did the Germans ever lose one to us. We were never committed in an all out shoot-out with Jerry; it's that simple. When committed to what is called small fire-fights the 370th didn't lose.

"My company was committed August 20, 1944, on the south bank of the Arno River in Italy just east of Pisa. We were part of a tank-infantry team with the 1st Armored Division, element of Combat Command A. Moving across the Arno our advance included the capture of Lucca and the villages in the immediate vicinity of the north bank of the river. Upon leaving Lucca we entered the mountains. At one point we climbed seventeen miles into the Apennines for the first allied penetration of the Serchio Valley. We went as far as the mountains above the Serchio River.

"The 370th was withdrawn from the Serchio and sent to an area near Pistoia where we were told we were to rejoin the 92nd Division. This was near the end of September and the only person we saw from the 92nd was Deputy Division Commander, General Wood.

---

*A reference to the killing of unarmed civilians by Americans during the recent war in Viet Nam.

"We were trucked from Pistoia to the coastal plains in front of Viareggio. In a few days we were committed in an all-out assault above the plains. The overall objectives for the battalions of the 370th were hills Maine, Georgia, Alaska, and California, all major mountains in the Apennines overlooking the plains. The specific goal for my group, 1st Battalion, B Company, 1st Platoon was Hill California. Its real name is Monte Cauala but you know Americans, they Americanize everything. C Company had their work cut out for them. I believe they had Hill Georgia, But whatever it was it went straight up, with marble slabs covering its sides.

"The 1st Platoon was organized with the 2nd Platoon under the leadership of Lieutenant Moss; we were spearheading the assault. My platoon was right behind Lieutenant Moss's unit. We were moving along rather well when the lieutenant and his sergeant were severely wounded and his A and B scout killed. Though some yards behind the lieutenant, we too were pinned down flat on our bellies for eight hours in a downpour. When night came we were able to withdraw about twenty-five yards where there was some protection. We remained there until dawn and regrouped and reorganized. This day we were to assault with white tankers, and we started out again. German 88s (artillery field pieces) opened up on them and they were forced to withdraw so we couldn't move forward an inch and had to withdraw to a position of comparative safety.

"At night patrols went out on both sides, and it was on one of these patrols, the second or third night, they they succeeded in bringing back Lieutenant Moss and his sergeant. They had been chopped up badly in the legs but maggots had saved their lives.

"We learned something in those few days. The Germans had a fire protective line made up of mortars from the reverse side of the slope of this line, artillery firing upon us from down the coast, and a barbed wire barricade covered by dug-in machine gun emplacements. As long as you did not try to get through the barbed wire they left you alone but when you touched that wire they let you have it. Jerry didn't care if you dug in, brought up supplies, or did the Watutsi as long as you left his fire protective line alone; that is, excepting for an artillery barrage that came in regularly at 4:00 P.M. every day.

"At that time our officers were: regimental commander, Colonel Sherman, white; regimental exec., Colonel Phelan, white; battalion commander Major Herrera, Mexican-American; company commander Herlan Doolan, black; 1st lieutenant Bass, white. Our two 2nd lieutenants, Moss and West, were black. Remember them.

"After the second assault attempt, as one of the sergeants of the line, I was sent to regimental headquarters to discuss enemy machine gun nests. Artillery was called in on these positions and just as they got the range they ceased firing. Artillery shells were rationed!

"I've said all of this to try to establish a sense of timing. We made seven assaults in ten days before we were finally taken off of Hill California. During that period we were pretty well slaughtered and reduced to a fair-sized single platoon.

"An officer from headquarters visited us after about the third day of our assault attempts and all was quiet. We were not on, at, or near the barbed wire. He advanced no further than our position and decided we were exaggerating and the enemy was not that bad. By the time his report got back to command we had made our sixth assault. Number seven was ordered and Major Wren, the battalion exec., was going to lead the platoon with Lieutenant West and Lieutenant Garnet. Garnet had replaced Lieutenant Moss as our immediate officer in command.

"Interesting point: our battalion commander and our company commander had both been evacuated. Neither of the men had been hit, for they had not been in the vicinity of the fire protective line. Lieutenant Bass had also departed, and he had not been wounded either. Now why they departed or were evacuated I do not know, but I do know they didn't have a scratch on them. What was left in the way of leadership was Lieutenants West and Garnet and the NCOs.

"Major Wren came up to lead us on the seventh assault. When we got close to the barbed wire Lieutenant Garnet sent for the major and he joined us up front. That was the first time a regimental staff officer saw the real size of our obligation. Oh, they had it on maps on the wall of their offices, but for the first time one of them looked at our job with the objective in clear view and he could see all of the visible defenses. We all knew we were just seeing the top of the iceberg. It was at this point we were ordered out.

"Lieutenant Garnet insisted that another sergeant and myself escort the major back to the communication center to assure his safe arrival. The major phoned Colonel Sherman and told him Hill California was as formidable as was first reported by us; that it was a major obstacle which required coordinated support: planes, tanks, and artillery; and that an infantry company could not possibly take that mountain. Ten days and seven assaults later headquarters decided we were not lying and goofing off on the job.

"Subsequently we were ordered to attack Cauala again and Lieutenant Garnet took a patrol up the mountain; no trouble, the Germans had withdrawn. We occupied Hill California for two nights, and K Company of our sister regiment, the 371st, relieved us. This was their first time in a combat zone. I might add that Hill Alaska was still in enemy hands. It was right up above us. You might say we were leaning against it.

"Finished with Cauala we were withdrawn, given time to take a shower and change clothes. We were then shipped to a gap in the mountains in the coastal plains. There we entered more mountains and climbed to a village called Ruosina. From it you could get a good view of one of the highest peaks in the area, Castelnuovo, where the Germans had an observation post.

"At Ruosina we were to fill in a thirteen-kilometer gap in our lines. Forward of this gap was Mount Pania Secca with the town Fornovolasco at its base. Pania Secca looked like a stone spear thrust up into the sky. From Ruosina I had taken patrols into Fornovolasco and would be met by our patrol coming from the west. We learned the Germans also had a patrol coming there and an ammunition dump. An Italian partisan group took the sergeant of the west group and myself into the middle of the gap we were supposed to be filling in, and from there right back to the coast. They were showing us this was more than a gap in our line; it was a damned big hole and to expect any company of men to fill this hole was wishful thinking. (I am detailing this because I was not with my outfit when it joined the 366th in the Serchio. This is exactly where the German breakthrough took place, and the 366th was not there in regimental strength.)

"In about three weeks we were pulled off of this mountain and sent to the Serchio Valley to relieve some Brazilian troops. The Serchio Valley has mountains on its north and south sides overlooking the Serchio River. It took us half a day and a night to climb to the Brazilians' forward position. Once they left, we were ordered down and to climb the mountain across the valley from us. I do not remember the name of the mountain but I do remember Vergemoli and a village Piet* were near it. On the top was a town called Brucciano. These places were situated west of Gallicano where the Gallico River enters the Serchio.

"Now back to climbing down one mountain and crossing over to climb another one to the north where the peaks kept getting higher. Half-way up we rested at some village and then went on to Brucciano, which was, all things considered, a plush, Fascist town. It had been a precipitous and dangerous climb, as such paths were oftened mined and we had done most of our climbing when it was safest, at night. Several of the guys had to be grabbed to keep them from plunging over a precipice. Upon reaching the town we continued through it to the peaks on the north side. From our position beyond Brucciano, by looking over two little peaks we were staring right into the German position on another mountain. When Jerry came up their mountain to occupy this position, one of our guys, Sergeant Grici, wiped them out. He received the Silver Star for a job well done.

"We dug in places on those two peaks. There was a middle peak and two bluffs on each side; we were on a salient. Our support was on a ridge to our right and rear. The path from the German emplacement to us went down a hill, then up to us, so we had the advantage. We were holding a good defensive and defendable position; access to us was negligible.

"At Thanksgiving we were still at Brucciano and recently had patrolled to Fornovolasco.

_____

*Possibly Perchia, near Vergemoli.

"At Brucciano we alternated, one platoon back, two platoons forward. Our new company commander, Captain H., white, never came to our forward position. My squad leader, Clarence Taylor from Detroit, was wounded in an artillery barrage showered on us from our own artillery because the captain didn't know exactly where we were. His vantage point was the basement of a house far down below us. Some rear observers had seen movement on the mountain, and since our captain was sure we had not reached our destination, thought we were Germans and unloaded some 105mm shells on us. Clarence was only hit in the wrist but others were seriously wounded. This occurred not too long after we had settled down on our mountain top. Our officer personnel on the mountain was one black lieutenant. The next in rank were NCOs. Sometimes the fellows, frustrated and bored, would shoot off their weapons. The result would be an artillery barrage and heavy mortars. However, we were so close to the Germans in terms of trajectory arc that they could not hit us and they would shower the town down below where the captain was, and he would have a fit.

"One day we got orders from the captain that we were going to withdraw on battalion orders. According to directions this was to be done at night and the 1st platoon, which was to be the last off, was to set fire to anything they could not carry.

" 'Angry' could not begin to describe our feelings. All the time and effort spent getting up to this mountain top, being blasted by our own guns, and having a good defendable position for a change—it really got us! In the meantime one of our men went down to the aid station for something or other. He reported on his return that battalion did not plan to have us move. Someone had remarked that our illustrious company commander talked too much; there had never been an order of withdrawal from battalion! Our captain had evidently cooked this little scheme up himself. The fire was to show we were under heavy attack and therefore had to withdraw. However, when our wandering soldier wandered into the aid station and said he'd soon be down there with them, one word lead to another and battalion got the news; that ended that. A couple of days after this an attempt was made to bring up our flanks. This failed so we were told to withdraw to one flank. We moved and we were at a little village, Molazzana I believe, when the famous breakthrough came.

"As always, just as soon as we stopped we dug in, planted mines, and booby-trapped our approaches. To the west of us was the Brucciano area. The village was clear of all soldiers but us. We had been told there would be a major attack along the whole front, the main attack being in the Bologna area where the 88th Division, white, was located. The major diversionary in our area was to be made by the 366th, recently attached to the 92nd Division. We were to be a diversion for the 366th. Because of this another sergeant from C Company and myself were sent on a patrol to the town of Cascio, which had once been occupied by the Germans. They had withdrawn, and Cascio was now considered forward of the German lines. (I think I had better remind you that when you are speaking of the Po River Valley Campaign you are in territory that goes up and down. The towns and villages sit on the side of mountains, or on top, or in a valley. It is not flat by the farthest stretch of the imagination.) But back to Cascio—it was to be a diversionary objective. Cooks, bakers, the works were to get out there and make as much noise as possible so the Germans behind Cascio would think it was a real attack and stay put.

"On Christmas Eve the other sergeant and I went on patrol with a group that had been patrolling the town and area in front of it regularly. We crossed a 'no man's land' and were walking along an aqueduct when our forward scout alerted us to something ahead. We took positions, and the recon patrol with us, became involved in a fire fight with some Germans who just happened to have a bazooka. It was forty-five minutes at least before we got ourselves together and got out of there. The fight had taken place in advance of Cascio in territory where Germans had not been seen recently.

"Upon our return, Lieutenant Brown and I reported the incident to our battalion commander, who told us we were both liars and had been fighting among ourselves and it was a cover-up, that there were no Germans in front of Cascio, or in Cascio.

"The next day was Christmas and my platoon was bundled up in the basement of a big house eating and singing carols and spirituals when we received a message that a German combat patrol team was loose in the area. We were to take up security positions where we were since we were not specifically attached to any group. We could hear the big guns to the east quite clearly now.

"I described our position at Brucciano, good and defendable because the Germans had to come up to us. This was true of the position we now held and of every platoon and company in the battalion. Nobody on the 370th side of the river was in any real danger or an indefensible position. A couple of our platoons chopped up some Germans who had tried to take their high ground and they didn't try it again.

"We learned the Germans were assaulting—battering would be a better word—the 366th east of us. (We later learned that among the other problems of the 366th was that a German Tiger Tank, mounting its 88 mm artillery piece, had been dug in at Cascio and was firing point blank across the river into the 366th area. This was the same town where our patrol had the fire fight two days before. The 366th paid dearly for the colonel's blind, bigoted stupidity.)

"The first we knew of any decision to move the 1st Battalion of the 370th was when Colonel Eberman assembled the NCOs and told us to withdraw from our positions. Major Wren had already gone; he had pointed his jeep due south. We didn't like this at all. It had been a long time since Jerry had to climb to us and we had paid for this high ground and now we were being told to give it back. We were bitter, but we followed the colonel's orders and withdrew until we were told to climb a mountain at another point. We found it was the same one from which we had once relieved the Brazilians, only this time it was covered with something like fourteen inches of snow.

"My platoon leader sent me to find a company from the 371st whose flank would be exposed with our departure so they could pull back into some kind of position. I located them and a liaison was worked out between us and this company that had been forgotten by battalion headquarters.

"Upon the mountain in the snow we dug in, set up a perimeter, were in touch with the forgotten battalion, and fought and held our ground. The only relief we had was when a Polish Fighter squadron came in and shut off the enemy tanks that had joined in the attempt to dislocate us.

"We had not heard from battalion in some time. At no time were we endangered in our position in the Serchio Valley. Our greatest danger had been in withdrawing on command from one secure forward position and having to recross the river and climb a mountain in the dead of the winter to another secure place but to the rear.

"I had to leave my company for the hospital shortly after this, due to frostbitten feet. I cannot say what happened while I was away. I do know men died and were wounded in the mountains and Lieutenant Garnet was killed on patrol. There were too many deaths of this particular kind and the responsibility lay with S-2 and S-3 (S-3 maintained positions and S-2 was intelligence.) They had a very bad habit of not letting each other know what they were doing. Result, an unalerted position that should be on the lookout for one of our patrols and an off-guard patrol expecting no such position; box score a dead lieutenant or possibly a whole patrol.

"Now this kind of thing is not going to come out in war stories, black or white, unless you talk to the men who were in the dirt, rain, mud, snow, front lines, or mountains. These soldiers can't tell you what was going on on a map hanging in some office with little pins stuck all over it but they can tell you they killed their own right up front because of a lackadaisical command. They also can tell you about those killed and wounded by their own tanks, artillery, planes. No, they couldn't see the overall picture but they can tell you about the command officers who never came to the front lines yet knew there was no obstacle because these things weren't on their maps, or intelligence hadn't reported it. But the men looked into the muzzles of the enemies' 88s, so to speak, and the enemy looked awful real to them!

"The higher echelon is worth looking at. The captain who wanted to withdraw us, also wanted to save face so he cooked up his little plot. Even though the facts were found out he still remained our commanding officer. He finally got to the place where he believed the men were trying to kill him. Colonel Phelan happened to walk into his office one day as a sergeant was trying to convince the captain that a hole in the wall came from shrapnel and not from an M1. When the colonel recognized it as a shrapnel hole, the captain was relieved of duty and put in charge of a mule train. All this time we had had an incompetent and frightened man imposed upon us. Back in Louisiana on maneuvers he was inadequate; being white had nothing to do with it. I felt the 92nd was the dumping ground for this kind of officer.

"As to our officers of the lesser ranks, they were a mixed bag. Some of our black officers were good, some were bad. We had guys who stuck with you from beginning to end and there were those who couldn't take it and were evacuated out, but that's par for the course.

"As for discrimination in a battle zone, you can't say it's a personal thing for there is no sign saying 'blacks not allowed.' That was left for postwar Viareggio. For the most part one never knows when he is being discriminated against. When committed you look for supplies and support. When we were with the 1st Armored these things were never lacking; in the 92nd supplies and support weren't comparable. But was this discrimination or inadequacy on the part of the quartermasters? Race as a factor in a combat situation just doesn't show itself in that way.

"In my judgment the trouble with the 92nd Division was at the command level. The unwillingness of men to fight can be evinced by the number who survive. The 92nd Division had its share of casualties. In the instance of B Company's seven assaults on Hill California in ten days, in what was finally admitted to be an impossible situation, you did not have a failure of troops; you had men committed in a haphazard, stupid manner.

"I'm not a general, but there are those of us who wonder about Lieutenant General Clark's qualifications by the performance rendered. One thing is true: we could not break through the German defenses in the Apennines until they themselves withdrew from their high ground, partly because General Saunders, a Pole, managed to break through into the Po Valley up in a northern corner, and began cutting behind them. Until the Italian partisan uprising, throwing men up against those fortified positions in the mountains was ridiculous.

"Excellent or even good results were impossible for the 92nd Division, for the men were not used wisely or well. Those who paid for this are still in Italy, and the lucky survivors have General Clark's statement that we were the worst division in Europe written into history. Perhaps if we had gotten ourselves wiped out like the 36th Infantry Division at the Rapido River he might have had some praise for us. But does slaughter such as took place at the Rapido,* and to a lesser extent at the Cinquale Canal—is this kind of thing

---

*For three days in early 1944, the Americans tried to cross the Rapido River near Cassino. The attempts were ill-prepared and carried out under bad weather conditions, and against entrenched Germans. The 36th Division lost almost 2,000 men because the ill-fated

heroic? These soldiers didn't fight to the last man; *they didn't get a chance to engage the enemy*! They were systematically destroyed like fish in a pond, from fortified positions in the mountains that our artillery could not even reach nor our planes take out.

"One could not help but get the impression that Clark took the 92nd reluctantly. Now the psychology of the military man at the general's level is that he must feel superior, whether he is a Clark or a Patton. At combat level the soldiers must have a superior attitude as to their ability to destroy the enemy, so standards are drawn to reflect this pattern. When you tell the general he must take waiters, busboys and shoeshine boys, he doesn't want them to begin with. The social reflection of the Negro in the United States has some of its greatest effect on the military mind; they are used to the superior-inferior situation. They start out lacking any confidence in your ability. There are two ways they respond as I see it, either by giving you menial jobs or setting out to prove they are right, like 'climb that mountain' or 'cross the Cinquale Canal.' I believe both methods were used on the 92nd."

A quirk of fate assigned a very unprepared 2nd Lieutenant Jefferson L. Jordan to the 370th Infantry Regiment in the fall of 1944. Like Charles Brown, he shared the fortunes of men at the front, assigned to patrol and search for enemy activity as winter approached. The job to which he was assigned in early November of that year when he was transferred to the 371st made it possible for him to throw light on a puzzling occurrence—the deaths of Lieutenants John Fox and Graham Jenkins and fifty-three of their men during the German counterattack that began on the night after Christmas.

Jefferson Jordan: "Having just graduated from Wilberforce University with four years of ROTC Training, I was sent, on induction, to the Tank Destroyers School at Camp Hood, Texas. My introduction to Texas was occupying half of a boxcar alone while white fellows were practically standing on each other's backs in the other half. At Hood the training area was well disciplined and well run, and in spite of my ROTC background I had to take the regular three months at OCS.

"Racial problems at OCS had been kept at a minimum because the commanding officer, once a president at a western university, spoke to us on our second day there. He said, 'I am here to run a school for the United States

---

attacks were persisted in. Some blamed General Mark Clark and said he overrode his subordinates in demanding that repeated attempts be made despite repeated failures. After the war, the "alumni" association of the 36th, a Texas National Guard Division, charged that the Rapido failure was not a blot on their escutcheon but a deliberate attempt by Clark, a West Pointer, to destroy a National Guard unit and its commanders. An inquiry was made but no charges were ever laid against Clark. (See Martin Blumenson, *Bloody River*, for the full account.)

Army. I will tolerate no racial prejudice of any kind. The moment I hear of any, there will be no questions asked; the party can start packing his gear.' The colonel's speech checked all overt signs of discrimination and made life quite bearable. The strange thing was I had less trouble with the fellows from the deep south, it was the border state guys and some of the outright Yankees who just stayed within the limits of the colonel's ultimatum.

"From OCS I was sent to the 828th Tank Destroyer Unit in Needles, California, in the Mohave. The enlisted personnel was all-black and the officers were predominately white. The commanding officer was a West Pointer, and neither he nor his officers seemed to have any trouble accepting the few black officers in the group. The 828th was an excellent unit, but once General Rommel was back in Europe after his African defeat there was no further need for more tank destroyer units; the 828th was broken up.

"We black officers and enlisted men wondered where we would be sent and hoped it would not be to the 92nd Division at Fort Huachuca. The thought of being sent to that bigoted outfit was depressing, and we were assured that we would not be sent there right up until the day we were handed our orders assigning us to the 92nd.

"The 92nd was going on maneuvers the day of my arrival. It was a bitter cold morning, and the headquarters of the 371st Infantry Regiment, my new unit, was topsy turvy. I was told to get out to the maneuvers area and I'd be taken care of. I was taken care of all right; I almost froze to death!

"The maneuvers lasted forty miserable days. The weather was freezing, and no fires were allowed as we were under simulated battle conditions. I knew nothing about infantry tactics, and no effort was made to enlighten me. All they were doing was complying with whatever was necessary to get the 92nd overseas; that many of the officers and men were not really learning anything was irrelevant.

"Things got so tense at Huachuca one time that they brought in General B. O. Davis, Sr., to pour oil on the troubled waters. I did not attend the closed session of the general and the men, but it was the talk of the fort. They felt that he had not come down to hear about their problems but to give a biographical run-down on how he had made it and to tell us to turn the other cheek. After his visit, the name of B. O. Davis, Sr., was synonymous with 'yes-sirism' and 'Uncle Tomism.'

"The highest-ranking black officers in the 92nd were the division chaplain and his assistant. They had practically no contact with the enlisted men and associated only with officers of their own rank, which meant whites.

"From maneuvers at Huachuca we went for more in Louisiana. At about that time I was made motor officer. My knowledge of a motor vehicle consisted of knowing how to raise the hood; I think I could also change a tire. The sergeant in charge of the motor battalion ran it—including the black officers—with an iron fist, and the men were expert at their jobs. The sergeant was tight with the colonel. There was a school for motor officers, so I suggested to my commanding officer that I attend. He was furious that I should think of such a thing when we would be alerted for movement at any moment; I was stubborn. He granted my request with it understood I would return at once should the situation change.

"I was called back to Huachuca before finishing my course, three days before our departure for POE. To my surprise and dismay, the sergeant had been nailed as an active homosexual, and section 8s were the order of the day. When we left Huachuca, my battalion was pitiful, with an overwhelming number of new men. The remaining NCOs with any experience managed to transfer out at POE.

"After thirty-three days at sea we arrived at Leghorn, Italy, where we disembarked, and marched immediately to the staging area, only to learn that the former chief of staff of our division had been killed in action. The morning came when we moved up to the front line. I was part of the service company of the 371st. In terms of position it meant my unit was some yards behind regimental headquarters, which was several hundred yards behind the front line. We were just about parallel to the Cinquale Canal, but over in the mountainous section while it is in the coastal flatlands. It might help to further identify the area in that north of the Cinquale you have little coastal villages that have the same name as an older village back upon the mountain side. An example would be Pietrasanta in the mountains and Marina di Pietrasanta on the coast.

"I was made replacement company chief. This job was to give soldiers who had been fighting a long time a place to rest, send them to Rome or other places to rehabilitate themselves. When the time came for them to return they were to be reconditioned for the front. I had been led to believe I would occupy this position permanently, but a quirk of fate intervened. It seems a certain 'Lieutenant Jordan' had failed to make an inspection called by General Almond back at Huachuca. The general made no bones about the fact that at the first opportunity Lieutenant Jordan was going to pay dearly for what he considered a personal affront. The 370th had, in its months of action, lost many of its junior officers and was desperately in need of replacements. A large number of the 370th's units were functioning with NCOs in command. Lieutenant Jordan's name was just about the first name on the list to be transferred to the 370th for an active front-line position. It was my name that was on the list, the wrong Jordan. Though they tried to correct the error there was not enough time since all officer transfers were to report at the 370th Regimental Headquarters at 8:00 the next morning. Having no choice but to follow orders, it was goodbye 371st.

"The combat units of the 370th were the focal point of the entire battle line on mountain ridges above the Serchio Valley. We didn't ever get to the 370th regimental headquarters; a regimental adjutant met our jeeps at some little place on the eastern side of the Serchio River to explain the situation. To my surprise he was Captain Kelly of the old 828th. He told us the troops we would be commanding were tired from being in combat a long time; their officers were dead, sick, or wounded, or suffering from combat fatigue; it was imperative that someone take hold immediately. Captain Kelly recognized me and knew my infantry training, like his, was nil. We were both good tank-destroyer officers. He took me aside and said he would see what he could do about getting me something to do at regimental headquarters.

"Later that day we arrived at battalion headquarters, which was in such a state of confusion they hardly knew we were there. They did tell us that we would have to wait until twilight before a jeep could take us up the mountain to company headquarters. From there a soldier would guide us to our destinations.

"It was quite a ride up the mountain. The road had hardly a place intact from the bombing and shelling. We could barely see the road, but for newcomers like me it might have been better if it had been pitch black. I kept up a brave front but to say I wasn't scared would be the lie of the century. I prayed that we would arrive safely at our destination and that I would not be responsible for the death of any other soldier. I was hoping I would get shot first.

"Finally we arrived at company headquarters. I sacked in because I was to be on my way at 4:30 A.M. afoot with the messenger who went up daily at this hour. We left on time and I won't say our climb was perpendicular, it might have varied about ten to fifteen degrees. I walked and walked. Mind you, I had a full pack on my back. My guide knew the Germans fired at certain points. It wasn't that they necessarily saw you, but fired at the sound. I didn't know this, naturally. My non-enlightening guide really hustled when we hit these spots. Not having the slightest intention of losing sight of him and getting lost by taking a wrong path, I kept pace. At long last the end of the climb came into sight. Just as I reached the top of the mountain there was a typical mountain village house. I could see two soldiers looking down on me. They were right out of Bill Mauldin's sketches in *Stars and Stripes*. One, big, unkempt, and bearded, the other, scrawny, unkempt, and bearded. Both were quite nonchalant about it all. They were typical American soldiers who had seen a lot of combat, been on the line too long, and nothing impressed them. One leaned out of his window and spoke quite matter-of-factly, "Now who is that maroony motherfucker?" My exhaustion almost disappeared as I fought to restrain the laughter threatening to surface. I pretended like I hadn't heard the remark.

"The guys on top of the mountain, black enlisted personnel, were a fine group of men. They had been fairly well trained and had done every job assigned to them. Believe me there had been some 'beauts.' These men had hung on much too long without leadership. They were close to falling apart, but I learned that one person, overdue from leave at the time, had held them together, Sergeant Dawson.

"The men made my job easy for me. The moment they knew an officer was looking after them, all things considered, they were in good shape. We hit it off well at once and they laid it on the line, they would do their best for me. Can you ask more of anyone?

"One day General Wood, Deputy Commander of the division, came to our position. He was a walking criticism box, contentious and as belittling. One of my men eased up behind me and said, 'Suh, up here as far as we are concerned you are the general. You say the word and we'll run him off here."

"The man most respected by the men was Sergeant Dawson, still on leave. Actually Dawson was AWOL. He was a soldier's soldier. When he took leave and got with booze and the babes it took a whole company of MPs to get him back. Once back on the line you couldn't find six soldiers who could do the job of one Dawson. The sergeant was from Tennessee. Physically and mentally he personified what a soldier should be. He could and did, if displeased, pick up two soldiers, any size, unless restrained. He had courage, intelligence, and integrity. He understood and got along with the men. Here was a 'topkick' who made you realize what is meant by the statement that sergeants are the backbone of the army.

"I was unaware at this time of the kind of man Dawson was. I only knew he was a week overdue and I was going to really chew him out. He was reported back just before dinner one night. At this point, I must say the cooks with that unit could do wonders with army chow. Since the sergeant was obviously dodging me I would not let my blast prepared for him interfere with my dinner. Seating myself in my usual seat the most aromatic dish I had ever smelled was placed before me by a man I didn't recognize. He said, 'I just learned on my return we had a new officer and that you liked a certain dish. It happens to be my specialty so I stopped to prepare it for you.' Now how can you lambast a guy when every salivary gland you have is screaming for the food on the plate before you? So ended the lecture for Sergeant Dawson.

"Dawson was truly a remarkable man. I was the officer and he knew his superior ability and his hold on the men. Yet never did he display anything but his talent as the best sergeant in the business. He never tried to show me up, though I knew he had to be aware of my shortcomings, nor did he ever try to prop me up, which most certainly would have revealed my flaws to the men. I could not help but like and respect him, and I believe he respected me— possibly for effort—we got along fine.

"As to our situation on the mountain, it was as bad as it could be. Among our problems, besides the Germans, was every day somebody would call regularly from regimental headquarters, battalion headquarters, or company headquarters saying, 'Send out a patrol and bring back six German prisoners.'

"Our position on the mountain was exactly face-to-face with the Germans. The only thing separating us was a mound of rock. We could almost toss cigarettes back and forth, to give you an idea of the proximity. We knew their position and they knew ours. We knew exactly when their mortars were going to lay down a barrage and they knew when ours were going to do likewise. Our field radio was not to be used for business except in an extreme emergency because they could hear the reply just as well as we could hear theirs. We used field telephones for communication and I wouldn't have been surprised if they had managed to tap into them. We even had names for certain voices.

"Two paths led around the mound. One was convenient for us to get to their position and the other equally convenient for them to get to ours. Our artillery and mortars were zeroed in on their approach and theirs on ours. Nobody had ever gotten half way along that path without getting clobbered, and we had the casualty list to prove it. They, too, had learned a lesson the hard way. The Germans appeared to have settled for this Mexican stand-off. Not *our* command, they kept calling to throw us into that meatgrinder. The guys had tried at night, in the rain, in fog, and they had paid for it. Nevertheless these calls would come in regularly, like our probes and attempts had been howling successes.

"Beyond these paths were fields for a fair distance that the villagers had once tended. Now they were a mass of mines. To step two feet beyond the path was a guaranteed trip to your just deserts. Besides these minor details you were dealing with men who should have been pulled out for rest long ago. After much agonizing as to what to do about these calls, the men solved my problem. It seems that whenever there was a predominance of Italian soldiers opposite us they waited for dark and surrendered, bringing along the Germans with them. The fellows had stashed them in the basement of one of the houses. When so many calls had been made for prisoners they would count noses and send a batch down to headquarters. Amazement hardly describes my reaction to this bit of chicanery. One of the men was quite blunt. 'Sir, if you want to live a little longer you had better forget those patrol orders and do it our way. You pick a patrol and we'll go with you and the men left behind can look forward to a new officer eventually, that is when they can find time to send another up here.' Dawson added, 'And don't think we are unaware of a trick group coming over that path to infiltrate us. You can forget it, we have our own little setup called SD, sudden death, and it is in operation every night. Any false moves, anyone coming behind, they are all dead.' Headquarters got their prisoners but not quite in the way they were ordered.

"The other unit on top of the mountain which had its own officer was actually the center unit; we flanked it. One day the officer in charge locked himself and his men in one of the houses for three days. He then just walked off and left his men. If the Germans had known what was taking place they could have infiltrated the center and the top of the mountain would have been a bloody mess. When this officer didn't return, his men finally informed me. I ordered them not to fire unless I gave the order. My men had to pass by them from one flank to the other, and I didn't want one of them accidentally killed by jittery men who had every reason to be tense. The officer was found and court-martialed. He asked that I appear as a character witness for him, which I refused to do. None of his men had walked off the mountain, even after his unexpected departure, and the strain of being up there was just as hard on them as it had been on him. His desertion was indefensible.

"I mentioned we never used the radio for communication, but we often listened in to see what was going on elsewhere. One day I had an ear attuned to it when I heard the artillery command say, 'I've seen some Germans,' and he gave *my* position for artillery to fire on. I didn't have time for the field phone. I switched to transmit fast and said, 'Listen, that's my position, don't fire, don't fire!' In a jovial mood this fool answers, 'Oh I see your men, but I see some Germans.' I tried to calmly explain that we saw those Germans every day; we were practically on speaking terms with them and 'Don't fire!' I dropped the speaker and hit the steps to warn the men outside. I never made it; three rounds came in and hit the side of my headquarters. Thank the Lord for those old-fashioned, thick stone walls. A hole was torn in the side of the building but the shell had spent itself; none of the men were seriously hurt. We received several more rounds before someone was thoughtful enough to turn off the artillery. The men were really shaken by this experience. Talk about morale shattering, they kept talking about having a hard enough time trying to kill Germans without our own artillery aiming in the wrong direction.

"I later asked the artillery observer to apologize to my men. His facetious retort was, 'It was old ammunition.'

"The men's morale reached its lowest ebb at this time. Every morning I made it a point to go out and spend the day in their foxholes. The fact that I was out there sharing the danger instead of in the relative safety of my basement headquarters made them feel better; to me that's what being an officer is all about.

"Returning to the culinary expertise of our cook, the men often supplemented our rations with chickens that strayed out of the fields of the villages further down the mountain and climbèd up the mountain into our kitchen. So help me, I never observed one of the men leaving atop with a large empty bag over his shoulder. Nor did I hear the clucking and cackling in the same bag as our maurader returned. Occasionally I would receive a call from headquarters about a complaint registered there by some villager about stolen chickens. This I emphatically denied, quite indignant that anyone would dare to impugn the reputation of an American soldier, as I contentedly munched on a chicken bone and wondered when the next chicken safari would take place.

"It wasn't too long before headquarters people decided to send up a company of men to pass through our point to see if the Germans had weakened their positions or possibly withdrawn. That we had seen no such evidence was inconsequential. It happened that Lieutenant Felton, a friend from stateside, was commanding this company.

"I'll never forget the morning Felton and his men arrived; bright and shiny, one of the worst days possible. Felton led his men onto the path and some tried going over the mound; they took a terrific mauling. The Germans had not gone anywhere. What we had been trying to convince them of was now revealing itself in blood. There were tremendous casualties among Felton's men.

"At one time Lieutenant Felton called for greater artillery support and the colonel he was talking to was quite incensed because the lieutenant had overlooked the niceties of rank in his concentration on what was taking place. The colonel actually threatened to court-martial him then and there and proceeded to give him a lecture on protocol. This in the middle of an action where men were fighting for their lives and dying!

"Felton and his men stayed on the top of our mountain until recalled three days later. Nobody ran and they were fighting a losing battle the moment they passed through our lines. They took their casualties and they still fought. They were simply cut up from the dug-in positions Jerry held. Those of us who were forced to stand by and watch felt anger, compassion, and pride as we watched Felton and his men assault the German's positions so many times we lost count. Each time there were fewer of them but they'd regroup and charge from a new angle, all to no avail.

"Almost every day of my stay up top a sergeant of the artillery and I had words on the phone. My premise was whenever the Germans fired, return the fire otherwise they would lay down a heavy barrage. I also insisted he change the position of his gun regularly so they could not get a line on his gun. Begrudgingly, on a direct order, he would do as I insisted; he hated my guts, but artillery I knew because I had been trained in this while I was with the 828th.

"I was reaching the end of my rope. I didn't know how much longer I could keep up the façade of a knowledgeable infantry officer when an order came through for me to report to regimental headquarters; Captain Kelly had kept his word. Naturally I was glad to leave alive and in one piece but I knew I would miss the men. They were a compliment to the army and a credit to the officers they served under. The men were unhappy at my leaving and at Thanksgiving and Christmas I was invited up for dinner.

"My new assignment was one that most people would find repulsive. I became grave-registration officer for the regiment. Anyone killed, my crew and I would try and get the body back and send it to a central point for burial. We also saw that their families were properly notified. It might not have been a nice job, but nevertheless one that had to be done. I was lucky in that my crew were experts in their business. They were all medics. They were proficient and could process several hundred bodies in a relatively short time. Because of their ability we were often assigned to outside units. The other part of the job was going out under battlefield conditions to get the bodies.

"When I first took over we did not have too many casaulties so I had a chance to learn about the work. My first shock was in the first week. As I walked among the bodies brought in that day there was the artillery sergeant with whom I had had so many disputes. It seems he stopped moving his gun as I had insisted and the Germans got a 'bead' on it. I later learned that Sergeant Dawson had lost a hand.

"Regimental headquarters was very interesting, full of intrigue and rivalry. The commanding colonel was all army and had little time for administration. His exec. was therefore in charge by default. The exec., a Texan, though far from bright was smart enough to recognize black officers who had superior minds. He did not actually befriend them but he made a point of not alienating them, thus having a reservoir of brain power on which to draw. He rode roughshod over his white staff.

"Thanksgiving passed and Christmas Eve was upon us.* I dressed for dinner as usual and noticed the casualty list was on the upswing. The list was necessary so we could go out and get the bodies. A growth in numbers meant more intensive fighting somewhere in the area. I didn't pay too much attention to a couple of tanks I saw in the distance as I went into regimental head-quarters. The place was empty; everybody was gone bag and baggage!

"I managed to catch a truck and the men aboard said it appeared the Germans had started an offensive, and our regimental headquarters had gone south on the other side of the river. Quickly alerting the men, we made hasty preparations for getting out. I saw the tanks I had seen previously, rumbling down the street. Much further up, coming around a corner were two German Tiger Tanks.

"Our only means of transportation was my jeep and a three-quarter-ton truck. Bodies, equipment, everything was piled into these two vehicles and we headed south through Italians fleeing with their few possessions, troops going up the road, and troops coming down the road; it was pandemonium.

"Just at the break of day we caught up with half of the headquarters company. It had split up, one group being with the colonel, and nobody in this half knew where the colonel was. We decided we would travel with this partial unit, but we had a problem: how to dispossess ourselves of the bodies we had, the number having mounted with those acquired along the way. Just as we had completed setting up a tent to process them we looked up to see troops coming

---

*The timetable gives the date of the German counterattack as beginning on the 26th. See also other informants.

over the hill. Our unique little group contained everything but fighting men: cooks, clerks, grave registration, and so forth. Captain Kelly rushed into the tent where we had all gathered and told us to find some kind of weapon to defend regimental headquarters (which was us) with. Have you ever seen soldiers armed with cleavers, butcher knives, skillets? The officers had their side arms, but here was the wildest assortment of weapons you could possibly imagine. Fortunately the troops were Brazilian. Had they been Germans we just might have been victorious; they probably would have died laughing at their formidable opposition.

"I cannot vouch for the sequence or the time element of events I am now about to relate. Things had reached a pretty confused state; my men and I were being shifted almost daily. I do know that at some point in the headquarters withdrawal we settled in a place up between two mountains which was comparatively safe.

"Early one morning I was summoned to headquarters. There I was presented to an officer from Corps who immediately advised me that everything said and eventually done was to be an absolute secret. I was somewhat relieved by his words, for all the way over I had wondered what an officer from Corps could possibly want with me, a lieutenant and black too! He said something about investigating a massacre, then cut this off to tell me I was to take my crew, though they were to be told nothing, and go to a designated area. I don't remember the name of it. There I was to find what I could, check the bodies in this village, look for possible bullet holes at the base of the officer's skulls, note the position of the bodies, and draw a conclusion as to whether or not they had been killed by American artillery, American aircraft, or German artillery. I was given five or six days to complete this mission and I was to report back to him directly, no one else. Why me? Division, Corps, Army, all had investigating teams for incidents, why a black graves-registration officer? Why all of the hush-hush? I was vaguely uneasy about this job. I knew that I had only been given the scantiest of details, but after all orders are orders.

"The place to which I was to go was in or near the Serchio Valley. When I reached the section I was looking for, there were British troops at the bottom of the mountain we had to ascend. They were Gurkha soldiers with English officers. I must inject that all of our movements were done at night because the situation here was not considered stabilized. We had to pass through these troops to reach our destination, which was practically on top of the highest mountain I had ever climbed. At the place I was to conduct my investigation were British troops. There was an English major, East Indian officers, and East Indian soldiers, the ones with the turbanlike headgear. It was still dark when we got to the top.

"The major noted that the officers of the men whose bodies I was to check had called artillery and aerial bombardment in upon themselves and their men. We waited until dawn to begin our work. With the first crack of light I realized every one of these bodies were black men. I cannot tell you they were of the 366th Infantry Regiment but I think they were. My men went to work as I checked the area, staying out of the range of the Germans who I had been told still held the north side of the village which was farther up the mountain. They crew called me concerning the identification of one of the bodies. There was nothing on the body to use for identification, and they wanted to know how to list him. While I stood looking at the cadaver deciding what should be done, it occurred to me that I knew this man despite the fact his face was battered. I had them open his mouth on the left side and there it was, a wedge of gold between two of his teeth. It was John Fox! He was an officer in the ROTC when I was at Wilberforce and we had been good friends. That gold wedge was not like the usual filling and he had often laughed about it. I continued to investigate the area. Bodies were piled upon bodies, but a person experienced with fire power could tell what happened to cause death. They had been aerial-bombed, and artillery had been involved also; they were really messed up. However, I was not prepared to say which came first under what I considered to be the very peculiar circumstances surrounding this investigation. One of the peculiar things was my being assigned to the job. I just gathered facts. The bodies were stacked up in the approaches to the little mountain-top village and in the path of the village. Some were at the entrances from the houses. The British were walking over them so I had my men move them to the side.

"I returned to regimental headquarters determined to give the facts and draw no conclusions. It was becoming quite clear to me that an attempt was being made to shift the blame for what had happened onto the black officers of this group, daming them and their men, and I would have no part of it. I did not know who said what to whom about either aerial or artillery bombardment but I knew their regimental headquarters was a mass of confusion when I passed through it. They were in such a rush about everything I had difficulty getting directions to my appointed destination. If they were like that now what could they possibly have been like when the German attack came? Perhaps I was not supposed to think about these things, but I did.

"The Corps officers were not at all pleased with my report. I was questioned and requestioned and always with the purpose of resting the blame on the men at the top of the mountain. I now knew why I had had a disturbing feeling about this job in the beginning. They had reached down into the lower ranks of the division for a black officer who had held various positions, and was now with graves registration. I did not know why then and I don't know now, but they were running scared. I also knew I would never tell them my conclusion. They had picked the wrong man for their investigation. I was orderd with my crew back to the area to bring down those bodies that we could. It took us three nights to do this. I can't remember the exact body count, but it was at least thirty, probably more.

"Upon returning to the regular regimental duties I was attached to the 442nd Nisei Infantry Regiment for a short time. They were sent into the very same area where black troops had failed to make any headway. The Nisei didn't make any progress, either. I know this because there were no casualties at the time. One morning the Nisei started probing the area again, looking for a weak spot and they found many. The Germans had simply withdrawn. It was fascinating to watch the Nisei. They could get into positions and stay totally immobilized for what seemed like hours; the enemy, unless he could see them, would have believed they were gone. With this sector now in our hands the Nisei were withdrawn and sent to the coastal mountain area. I believe the place was Massa. My crew and I were detached from them and sent elsewhere.

"Though no longer with the 442nd, I can say many of them were wounded and killed in Italy in the final offensive by allied troops, and they deserve a fair share for the success of the 5th Army in Italy. I make this statement not from casualty lists but from visiting several hospitals for the American wounded. My convoy had been strafed by American planes. I shall never forget it because I saw the planes overhead and thought nothing of it since Italian skies were clear of all German aircraft. Suddenly as I was observing a mountain ahead a plane came over its top, diving down its side toward us with guns spitting. I rolled out of my vehicle faster than I thought humanly possible. My driver wasn't quite as lucky. One of his arms was badly shot up as he went out of the truck on his side. Had we not gotten out we would have been on some else's casualty list. The front seat of our truck was shot to pieces. I went to see him in the hospital and found it full of men from the 442nd. Their stoicism in suffering was remarkable. From the number there I could make a good guess as to their fatalities. Their record showed that they fought until immobilized or dead.

"As the battle scene shifted north of Viareggio, and La Spezia had fallen to us, I was assigned to clean up the area in between. It was than that I was able to climb up into the mountains overlooking the coastal plains. From where I stood on that clear day I could see all of the way down to Leghorn. The Cinquale Canal was clearly visible and when I heard about the Cinquale incident, involving the 366th Infantry Regiment, I knew why it was a senseless mission. Climbing around those mountains I saw concrete bunkers, every kind of dug-in gun pit one could conceive of and at every level. And there were booby traps, which we were always on the alert for everywhere. The Germans had evidently had plenty of time to prepare these defenses, the whole mountain range along there was a masterpiece of fortifying a natural fortification.

"One man who was something of a folk hero among the 370th and possibly the whole division was Captain Charles Gandy. A patrol lead by Gandy at the Arno River, when the 370th first went into combat, had destroyed a machine gun nest and captured two German prisoners; the first to be taken by black soldiers. Gandy had attained his captaincy just before this action had taken place. General Mark Clark, on an inspection tour of the

370th, spoke to Gandy and asked him if there was anything he could do for him. Gandy replied he would like a promotion. Clark borrowed the bars of one of his captains and granted his wish. It could not have happened to a more deserving or capable man. His company was one of the most, if not the most, dependable unit in the 370th. Wherever he led, his men followed without question or hesitation because he was always up front, always where the going was the roughest. If a man wanted to speak to him it meant going forward because that is where he was. Gandy was killed in action. His body was in one of the most inaccessible parts of a mountain. It was on a rocky crag. How he got there we could not figure out, and though we could see him we could not get to the body. Perhaps later, some Italians reared in the tradition of mountain climbing found his remains and buried them. I hope so.

"The story about Gandy's death is that he was in search of a way to knock out a machine gun nest on some high ground. The only approach not visible to the enemy was a narrow ledge around a sheer drop-off. Gandy was moving spread-eagle along this ledge to get behind Jerry and then climb to him. From where his body was he made it around the ledge all right. His men say he was wounded and died fighting back. Whatever the truth, Captain Gandy, an inexperienced mountain climber, had managed to get into an incredible position. He hadn't sent one of his men, he had gone himself.

"Truman Gibson's visit had a terribly demoralizing effect on the troops when the army newspapers quoted him as using the term 'melting away' in reference to black soldiers. The men considered him a traitor. I thought him a fool. He should have taken time to check the casualty lists for the 92nd.*

---

*Truman Gibson, Jr., became civilian aide to the president following the resignation of Judge William Hastie in 1943 (see intro. to chap. 4). Early in 1944, on behalf of the Advisory Committee for Special (Negro) Troop Policies (McCloy Committee), he asked Major Oscar J. Magee, Intelligence Division, Army Service Forces, then about to depart for Italy, if he would bring back data on the 92nd Division's progress. Magee reported that the division's work was satisfactory with the exception of "infantry patrol and assault," on which he commented: "Too frequently the infantry 'melts away' under fire and an abnormal number of men hide in cellars until they are routed out by their officers." (Magee, memo 6 Dec. 1944, quoted in Lee, p. 560.)

Magee's phrase, so appropriate in a war dispatch for describing enemy retreats as distinct from one's own, which are usually "strategic withdrawals," was evidently quoted by Gibson in the press conference held 14 March 1945, at the request of war correspondents in Italy, some of whom interpreted the phrase as his, not Magee's. The editorial response in the black press was immediate; some demanded Gibson's resignation. The *Norfolk Journal and Guide*, 14 April 1945, noted that "occasions arise when troops must withdraw but that army press releases usually refer to them with phrases like 'our troops withdrew to lines they could better defend' or something of that tactful nature" (quoted in Lee, p. 579).

The news of the interview and the reaction of the press back home "reached men of the 92nd just in time for their spring attack" (p. 579). For more on the Gibson episode, see the interview with Robert Millender and the comments of war correspondent Collins George, below. See also references in the interviews to the "strategic withdrawal" at the Yalu River, during the Korean War.

There is an interesting side-light to Jefferson Jordan's story of finding his friend's body on the mountain. The dead officer was Lieutenant John Fox, 366th Infantry Regiment, Cannon Company. The village where he and his men were killed was Sommocolonia. To this day the men of the 366th believe Lieutenant Fox called in artillery on his forward observation post to stop an enemy advance, and that as a result, he and Lieutenant Harvey Jenkins and fifty-three men died heroic deaths. The men of the 366th also believe that Fox was done out of a citation for his sacrifice because of his color.

As reported by Lee, in "The Employment of Negro Troops," the sequence of Fox's orders was first, "Bring it in sixty yards." He was reminded that he would be the target, which he said he understood. Next he asked for "smoke" so his men could get out (p. 564). I had been curious as to why Lieutenant Fox's sacrifice of himself and "a few" men had won no official recognition; they had surely acted above and beyond the call of duty.

Previous to his interview, Jefferson Jordan had not known the story of the 366th and its troubles in the 92nd Division, nor the story of Fox's death as recounted by Lee and believed by the members of the 366th. When I related to him all of my data on the Sommocolonia incident, he told me the conclusion he had drawn at the time but had refused to divulge because he was suspicious of the whole secret investigation. Jordan concluded that Fox and his men died from being dive-bombed, which meant they had been killed by American planes. There was evidence of artillery shelling also, but the evidence indicated that aerial bombardment rather than artillery had killed them. Questioning Mr. Jordan, this is what I found out.

Q: "You said you were asked to look for bullet holes at the base of the skull, Why?"

A: "I was to look for bullet holes, at the base of the officer's skull, fired at close range. This would of course indicate they had been shot by their men. I could find no such evidence even though the bodies were in bad shape. Fox's body was in among a pile of his men's bodies. Nobody was shooting anything, everything showed those men were trying to get off of that mountain top. The bodies of Fox, Jenkins, and the other men were on the southern perimeter leading away from Sommocolonia. An observation post would have been at the northern end near the German's front line. I was there; Mr. Lee's facts are wrong. I don't doubt that there might have been an observation post where Lee states and it probably was shelled by our artillery, but I repeat neither Fox nor any of the men were killed in or near it.

Q: "Can you really tell whether or not men have been killed by artillery fire or aerial bombardment?

A: "Definitely, when you have a group of bodies. Aerial bombardment is much more destructive. The bodies are more mutilated. Then too, aerial bombardment causes the stacking. When these bombs hit, things are thrown up into the air; as they come down they pile on top of each other. Artillery explosions, because the projectile from howitzers comes in on an arc, throw the bodies backward from the point of impact and they are scattered away from this point. Remember, I was asked to determine if it was American artillery, German artillery, or American planes (we controlled the sky). The way I would know which artillery had done the job would be the direction in which the bodies were thrown. I knew from which direction our artillery was firing. Don't forget the Corps man knew such a determination could be made or he would have not have asked."

Q: "When did you find Fox's body and those of his men? Lee states it was over a week later."

A: "Well, we agree on that point. I am almost positive it was right after the New Year I was called to meet with the Corps officer. If, as you said, they were killed on December 26th and I was sent out right after New Year's and it took us three days to get to the area and up that mountain, it was probably nine or ten days later. I repeat Fox was with his men in a pile on the southern perimeter of the village. As I said, we arrived on the mountain at night and we had stumbled over a number of them as we approached the little village. Fox was evidently trying to get his men out when they were cut down by dive bombers. It was a tragic mistake."

Q: "You said the bodies showed evidence of artillery and aerial bombing. How can you say which killed them?"

A: "The mutilation pinpointed aerial bombing, and once a man is dead other wounds inflicted are different. Circulation has ceased and there is no bleeding with new wounds. Remember I had a crew of medics. When casualties were light they posted the bodies for cause of death. Also, before I was sent out there, *they* knew—I'm speaking of Corps—the men had been killed by aircraft. From what I have just learned of the 366th, I can see why they wanted to shift the blame. From their question upon my return, they were hoping I would give them something to grab onto. The Corps officer was most unhappy with me.

Q: "Lee makes no mention of Fox asking for aerial bombardment, yet the British major did. Lee's book says Sommocolonia was dive-bombed December 27th, one day after the death of Fox and his men. That is hardly a question. Were there other grave-registration units closer to Sommocolonia?"

A: "Certainly, probably several of them closer than me and my crew."

Q: "Wouldn't the 366th have a grave registration set-up?"

A: "I can only hazard a guess. As a regiment I would think so. I was never in contact with this regiment except for their dead on the mountain, so I just can't say."

After my interview with Jefferson Jordan, I talked to three former artillery men, all from different groups. They were in accord that a call for artillery, then smoke, didn't make sense. "Smoke," each explained, means "Give me cover so I can get out." It would be asked for first, and then artillery. They agreed that should such a call come into fire-direction center in reverse, a correction would be demanded because it just isn't done that way. One fellow said, "I'll bet your man asked for smoke, then gave artillery directions and dropped that phone and ran like hell because he knew the mail would be coming in fast."

I spoke to a Regular Army man of many years' experience, and he said you definitely can tell whether men were killed by artillery or aerial bombardment.

I then called two ex-fighter pilots of World War II. They were in accord that dive bombing has a greater impact than an artillery shell. The nose of the plane is aimed at the target and the bomb is released before you pull out of the dive. The speed of the plane adds to the impact of the bomb, on release. Both thought that aerial bombs were also heavier than artillery shells, particularly howitzer shells.

The 366th put the names of both Lieutenants Fox and Jenkins in for awards; and, as one more said, they ended up in the wastebasket. The men of the 366th thought this was due to the hostility of the 92nd Division command toward them. It would seem that the army had an honest reason, but one too hot to tell at the time. These men had been accidentally killed by American aircraft. Lieutenant Fox was doing what any good officer would do in this instance, try and save his men. He knew artillery was coming in so he was in the front of his unit to face it if there should be any mistake, when death came from an unexpected source, the sky.

Lieutenant Wade McCree, Jr., 365th Infantry Regiment, had gradu-ated from Fisk University and had just begun his second year at Harvard Law School when he was drafted.

Wade McCree: "To attempt to compress in a short taped interview the number, variety, and intensity of my experiences during four years of active duty in World War II and my reactions to them, is an impossible undertaking since I haven't the time and resources to prepare a carefully edited and balanced narrative. What follows must of necessity be cursory, episodic, and impressionistic; also, the few conclusions I make will be tentative and certainly not exhaustive.

"We were in the 1st Army area, and Fort Devens, Massachusetts, was the reception center to which I was to report. The initial experience was somewhat traumatic because some of my classmates at law school were with me on a typical night-before-bash before entering the armed services. We all probably drank a little too much but we had a good time. The next morning, we all went down to the reception center in Boston, Massachusetts, cradle of American liberty, where we were required to stand in separate lines on the basis of race. Entering the induction center was the last time I had anything like an integrated military experience until I went to OCS.

"When I was assigned to a Fort Devens reception center casual barracks, there again was racial separation. We took the Army General Classification Test (AGCT). I was fortunate and pleased when I was selected to go to the 366th because I had many friends in the unit.

"The 366th was a separate regiment, not attached to any division. Its commanding officer was Colonel Howard D. Queen, who had been an officer in World War I, and his executive officer was Lieutenant Colonel Alonzo Ferguson, who also had been an officer in World War I. Almost all the initial officers of the 366th were Howard or Wilberforce ROTC men. Many of my contemporaries in the officer corps there were friends and I could see some off-post social problems arising because during the past few years we had often dated the same girls and attended the same parties. I was now an enlisted man and they were my superiors.

"I went into the Regimental Training Center run by Samuel Mc-Cottrey. He was very proud of his position and very efficient and was determined to see that the men under him were properly trained. His assistant, Lieutenant Dillion, had been a regular army enlisted man in the 25th Infantry and had gone to OCS. He was looked upon as being a little different by the ROTC people because he didn't have a college degree. But Dillon was every inch a soldier and an expert with every infantry weapon, and was thoroughly liked by the ROTC enlisted personnel. He and Lieutenant McCottrey complemented each other most effectively. The 366th also had a high percentage of college graduates among its enlisted men because its location at the reception center for Massachusetts permitted it to select the best inductees from an area with an educational achievement level above the national average.

"I spurned a desk job because I wanted to be outside. I love the outdoors, and I was glad when I was assigned to the antitank company. Three of the platoons of this unit were gun platoons and a new one formed at that time was the mine platoon. An examination was held for surveyor, and I jumped from private to sergeant after about four months because I stood first on this exam. However, the men didn't mind because they wanted someone who could make accurate maps to show where we laid the mines, and that was the assignment of the surveyor.

"Most of the openings at OCS allocated to Negroes were closed at that time. We were hoping for a reopening but in the meantime I attended our regimental school for NCOs. By achieving the top score there, I was assured the first chance at OCS when an opening came. Two openings were announced. I got one and the other went to a candidate of the 372nd Infantry Regiment (stationed at Fort Dix under Colonel Gourdine), a Massachusetts lawyer who had been an Olympic track star.*

"My OCS training was at Fort Benning, Georgia, where all the Negro candidates were initially placed in one squad room of the barracks. After the first examination, our numbers were reduced until there were only four black candidates left. Then we were assigned alphabetically, and I felt like a human being once more. Only two Negroes finished the course.** Upon completing the course, I was sent to the 365th Infantry Regiment 92nd Division, at Fort Huachuca, Arizona.

"Many persons did not like Huachuca. I did. I found it a beautiful place. I liked the desert and the surrounding mountains. I was undoubtedly the exception rather than the rule in enjoying the physical isolation of this post.

"There were other aspects I did not like. Having been with the 366th, I could appreciate its élan and admired its morale. The 92nd Division was an entirely different cup of tea. A substantial number of the men of the 366th had AGCT scores of classes one and two, but the majority of the men at Huachuca were in classes four and five, which put them well below average on standard I.Q. tests. Most of these young men were from the rural south. Southern communities had no difficulty drafting Negroes, although they apparently had considerable difficulty building schools for them. Many of the southern states were afraid not to draft them in large numbers because of the large numbers of white men being drafted. There was fear that failure to draft Negroes might create an unacceptable racial imbalance in the home front power structure.

"I do not mean to imply that these were not fine young men; most of them were. One of my jobs was to teach illiterates to read and write. However, even the illiterates were quite skilled in many particulars. In terms of skills required for infantry service they excelled. Almost all were familiar with firearms. Some were absolutely fantastic shots. They were to a great extent

---

*Wendell Imes, later killed in action in Italy.

**John Bailey, the other one, was from Baltimore, Maryland. A peerless troop leader, he was cut down by a machine gun while leading his troops in the last week of combat in Italy.

familiar with the outdoors and infantry warfare is outdoor activity, so they fitted in very well there.

"The big disappointment was in the officer corps. All staff officers and initially all company commanders were white. The vast majority of the Negro officers were 2nd lieutenants. If you saw a black captain or someone in field grade, you could be sure he was a doctor or chaplain, neither of which had command functions. There was no competition for assignments above company grade at the command level since all one had to do was to be white. Before a Negro officer would be promoted to the same rank as a white officer, the white would be immediately upgraded. I recall sometime later when I made 1st lieutenant, the few remaining white 2nd lieutenants in my unit had been upgraded the day before. Many of the company commanders were caricatures of officers, looking for a soft spot where there was no competing and no demand placed upon them for performance.

"Now this was not true of all of them. My battalion had three very competent white officers: Captain Raichle, Captain Matachinskas, and a Captain Doiran, who was killed leading his troops in the 370th's final drive up the Ligurian Coast.

"There were others, including the commanding officer of I Company who showed the white feather and left just as we were preparing for overseas duty. One of our battalion commanders was an absolute disgrace. Not our first one, who was a West Pointer and asked out because he saw the impossibility of the situation. There was another who had been a clerk in peacetime. He was not only the worst officer I had ever seen but also a pathological liar. Under his command, affairs just deteriorated and there was no one there to challenge him. This was true all the way up the line in our division. There was no sense of mission. I found that the cause was the absence of any identification between the officers and men. When I say 'officers' I am speaking of the white officers because I believe the original design for the 92nd had been the Regular Army pattern of white officers and black troops. However, with some black officers coming through Fort Benning there had to be a place for them, and this upset that design.

"There was no identification felt in either direction between white officers and black soldiers, and the enlisted men were aware of this. What was worse, there was no identification between white and black officers. For example we had two officers' clubs, Lakeside Officers' Club was the white and Mountain View Club was the black club. The money for the support of these clubs was taken out of your check without even a by-your-leave. This minimized any off-duty contact between white and colored officers. In the Bachelor Officers' Quarters there were discriminatory billeting practices. Even in the officers' mess, field grade officers and battalion staff officers sat on different sides from company grade officers, and this pretty effectively separated the mess racially. None of this was lost on the troops; they didn't identify at all with their superior white officers.

"Just before we left for overseas there was a mass exodus of almost all of the white officers: particularly the company grade officers, who had found a soft berth, and now realized that their life of ease was about to cease and they departed fast. Negro officers were immediately catapulted into command positions in which they had little or no experience. Many grew into the responsibility, but by this time others were utterly dispirited and felt that no one really expected anything of them. Many of them, as far as a combat mission was concerned, thought in terms of one thing only, to survive and to bring as many of their men home as possible. I don't think one can overstate this survival approach even though it might not have been recognized by those who practiced it. This was pretty clear to me because I was a staff officer on the one hand and thereby had a broader perspective, but more significantly, I had a natural identification with the company grade officers. I socialized with them and spent a lot of time talking with them.

"Just before going overseas we went to Louisiana on maneuvers. Many things occurred there but in this particular instance our company commander had succeeded in getting us lost. For a day-and-a-half, we had been wandering around in a swamp. I was a rifle platoon leader, and some of my men hadn't eaten in all of this time, so I decided to find out what was going on. I took a messenger with me and pushed along, down the line of dispirited, lost, struggling souls until I found the battalion commander, because my company commander was as uninformed as I. He was being chewed out royally by a ramrod-erect colonel, who was an umpire from director-headquarters of the maneuvers. This man was a wounded veteran of Kasserine pass where the United States had suffered heavy losses in the beginning of the North African invasion, and he knew the importance of troops being where they should be at the right time. I heard him for the fourth time ream out our Battalion CO. Finally, he asked the CO if he knew his way out of here and though he tried to bluff, the colonel was not buying. The castigating colonel looked around in utter dismay and asked if anyone in the unit could read a map. Having just come upon the scene and being a little less observant of military courtesy than usual I said, 'Yes, sir, I can read a map as well as anyone.' He asked who I was and I told him I was from I Company, Lieutenant McCree. He threw the map at me and asked, 'Where are we now?' I had just tramped all over this terrain so it was no problem to recognize that we were at coordinates so-and-so. He stated that that was the first correct answer he had received since he had been attached to this unfortunate battalion. He then asked if I knew where we were supposed to be, and I didn't, and said so. I explained that I had come there to find out where we were supposed to be. The colonel told our commander to give me his field order. I looked at it and showed the colonel on the map where we should have been, observing that we were due there yesterday. 'You are right again,' the colonel commented and then asked if I knew how to move the battalion there. I told him I could, and he directed me to write out a field order to accomplish this. It was one of the elementary things we had been taught at Fort Benning and I prepared an order with little difficulty. He gave this to my commander and told him to execute it. My CO at this point interjected, 'I want you to know colonel that I've been keeping my eye on this young officer for a long time; I've been giving him personal lessons in map reading; I,—, and the colonel cut him off and asked why then was I still a 2nd lieutenant if I had been doing all of that. My CO, never at a loss for words replied, 'We have been planning to promote him.' The colonel said, 'Promote him right now. I want to make sure his name goes on orders before I turn the report in on your battalion.' My CO said to me, 'You had better stay here,' he wasn't even sure of my name so I reminded him. He told me to stick around in case I was needed. This is how I attained the rank of 1st lieutenant. Just before going overseas I was made intelligence officer (S-2) and became a member of the battalion staff.

"We left Newport News, Virginia, for Italy, having been preceded by our sister regiment, the 370th Regimental Combat Team, some months earlier. Our other regiments had been depleted of manpower to fill the ranks of the 370th where there were gaps made by its men failing to meet overseas requirements. They had also experienced the shipping out of some white officers who sought to avoid overseas duty. We entered the Mediterranean and, after a stop at Oran, landed at Naples. We were transported in trucks to Leghorn and then to Pisa where we assembled in a staging area outside the city. We went through some training exercises and experienced our first casualties when some soldiers on a conditioning march left the road and activated some booby traps. I guessed we then realized we were actually in a war.

"I soon became aware of two interesting phenomena. First, that the Italian people had suffered a great deal and second, that our troops had a great empathy for them. The Italian people recognized this and there immediately developed a wonderful rapport which apparently did not exist in the same intensity between the Italians and our white troops.

"We moved north of Pisa into the line at a little place called Forte dei Marmi. It means 'the marble fort' and the area is the Massa-Carrara marble-producing community of Italy. Ours was a relatively quiet sector of the line and it was the first time we were really faced off opposite the Germans. The whole division was put in this sector. The real principal allied effort was to the east of us, south of Bologna, where the mountains had been penetrated almost to the Po Valley plain. In that sector, there were just two or three steep ridges between the 5th Army, of which we were a part, and the Po Valley. Our division had been put into a relatively quiet sector to conduct a holding oepration. This deployment is not unusual with new troops, or troops of questionable quality.

"The Italian people were very much in evidence around Forte dei Marmi. When there was shelling they'd disappear into shelters, but as soon as it stopped they'd return and try to salvage what they could of their homes.

"Some of our quasi-literate and illiterate troops showed an amazing capacity for learning to converse in Italian. I was completely inhibited about trying to speak it at first. Having read the army language instruction book and having undertaken to master the inflection of nouns, conjugation of verbs, etc., I was utterly tongue-tied. I could read it with comprehension but I could not bring myself to try to speak it. I think it was six months before I finally broke forth in proper Italian.

"The ordinary GI who didn't understand grammatical English was blissfully unaware of the rules of grammar and was henceforth uninhibited. He learned the infinitive form of the verb and used it for every purpose, indicating the number by a noun or prounoun and the tense by an adverb, today, tomorrow, yesterday, etc. The Italians understood him. I knew it was not grammatically right so I just could not open my mouth. The men who did not speak English well spoke excellent broken Italian and they were not only understood but also greatly appreciated for it. These men really related to, and in many ways identified with, the Italians; it was a two-way street. Both groups knew what it meant to suffer.

"We stayed in our appointed sector for a short while, doing patrol work and suffered very few casualties. Later we were given a mission, but in the end it turned out to be a mission for the 366th Infantry. Evidently someone had an idea that an end run could be made around the German line through the surf along the Ligurian Sea, avoiding mines that had been placed in the coastal plain from the Sea up to the mountains at a place called Seravezza. In order to accomplish this it was necessary to cross a canal which spilled out into the sea, the Cinquale Canal. The canal mouth had silted up and it was important to find out to what degree. Tanks were to participate in this flanking move and it was important to make certain that they could cross the canal mouth without flooding out. We sent patrols out several times to take soundings at different phases of the tide, and the Germans could not help but know what we were doing.

"It was there that we lost Lieutenant Robert L. Stanley. He was of my former I Company. A sergeant, one of the three-man patrol accompanying Stanley, said they had crossed the Cinquale and proceeded further north when they were ambushed. The lieutenant told the men to make a break for our lines. As he started to run he stepped on a mine and they did not know his fate. It had taken the sergeant two days to return. This was one of our first casualties, and because I had transmitted the order to send Stanley out I felt obliged to look for him.

"The sergeant, another man, and I set out on the route taken by Stanley that night, one I shall never forget. The password, another permanent memory, was jade necklace: necklace being the countersign. I also will never forget that the literary allusion was lost on most of our men, because in no time I was hearing it pronounced as everything but necklace. (Jane Nickles was a common rendition.) In any event, the three of us struck out to try to find Stanley. We crossed the canal mouth without any difficulty since it was then only armpit deep at its deepest point. The only arms we carried were trench knives, grenades, and 45s. We were discovered by a German patrol once we were beyond the canal. They opened fire on us with automatic weapons and we had to withdraw.

"Once back across the canal there was a path from the shore to our position through the mine field on the beach. As we were crawling along, I knew we had a machine gun emplacement sighted right along this path at a given point. I could finally see the silhouette of our gunner and when within about 25 yards of him I raised myself a little and called, 'jade.' Instead of hearing 'necklace,' or 'nickles,' or even 'nicholas,' I heard the bolt of the machine gun come back to half-load. I lifted myself ever so slightly again and repeated the word 'jade.' This time I heard the bolt go forward into full load position. The next thing, I was fearful, would burst of machine gun fire, so the others and I went back to the water and swam about a half mile down the coast. When we finally came ashore, no one was around anywhere to challenge us or to require the password. Of course when I reported this to the regimental S-3 he almost had apoplexy. A German raiding party could have had a field day if it had chosen to make a modest amphibious flanking assault.

"We never found Stanley until an abortive push was made by the 370th after we had moved into another sector. They made a push across the Cinquale, went up the coast a considerable distance, and then had to withdraw. They found Stanley's body, and he had apparently been killed by the mine explosion.

"A few weeks later, we were pulled out of the coastal sector and sent east where we were attached to the 88th Division, an outfit stretched out along highway 65. They had fought quite well advancing astride highway 65 and one of its regiments had been badly mauled. There were insufficient replacements in the theater repple depple to build it back up to regiment strength. The 365th was elated to be leaving a quiet sector to go into a busy one, although all of Italy was considered quiet compared to northern Europe. The role of the 5th and 8th Armies in Italy was essentially a holding, or defensive, action to keep the German command from being able to reinforce its troops in the north by men withdrawn from Italy. We had heard that the 366th was going to replace us in line.

"The 365th was supposed to take part in a surprise Christmas attack just south of Bologna. Our flank was tied in with the British. You know the British; they believed in fighting a civilized war. When our liaison patrols happened to meet we joined them for tea. Our area at this time was about the hottest spot in Italy. We took a lot of artillery fire every day and our patrols were running into real fire fights every night.

"I remember setting up my intelligence section in an observation post, and sending patrols out on a regular basis to discover the best route to use in leading the assault of the 88th Division. On one of these patrols, we lost a man I regarded as the best enlisted man in our battalion, Sergeant Sheaffer of L Company, a former Oberlin student in music, who had joined us when the ASTP closed down or drastically reduced its members. Roscoe Browne, the actor, and Harrison Dillard, later to become an Olympic champion, also came in this group.

"A few nights before we were to make the push, we went out on combat patrol to secure a few farm buildings we felt might stall our attack if they fell into hostile hands. The Germans had the same idea, and a fire fight was the result. Sheaffer was hit several times in the side by a machine gun. We carried him back to the aid station where he was pumped full of morphine so he could be put over a mule and taken down the mountain to the field hospital. He died before getting there.

"Our attack was cancelled because of the breakthrough in the Ardennes Forest, better known as the Battle of the Bulge, in northern Europe. A large part of our aircraft in Italy was flown north to help stop this threat. I personally felt a sense of relief because I knew we were going to lose a lot of men. I had no idea how our men would hold up in a large-scale push, but their spirits were never better. I think they felt they were with a *real* outfit. They felt this was a serious undertaking. They saw the British to the right and the 88th to the left so it just wasn't going to be something only for colored troops. I think we missed the only real chance to find out what kind of fighting men the 92nd Division had. The division officers of the 88th were very much in evidence. They would come crawling along our most forward positions and speak to the men to ascertain how they felt. On the day before the attack was to have taken place, they were very much in evidence. This was something we never saw from our top brass with few exceptions, one of which was General Almond, who, whatever were his other characteristics, was fearless for his own safety. The officers of the 88th were very serious about their mission. They hanged one of their boys for desertion under fire. And they were very receptive to the men of the 365th.

"Our attack was no sooner called off when we learned of an attack in our own backyard, so to speak. We called it the Little Battle of the Bulge because it had followed the other Bulge pattern by hitting the weakest and quietest sector in our line. The Germans smashed into the positions now held by the 366th Infantry in the Serchio Valley. They overran their positions at Sommocolonia. The 366th took a terrific mauling but there were many examples of individual heroism. Lieutenant John Fox directed our artillery fire right down upon himself when the German infantry had penetrated his position.

"The 366th was forced back to Barga. The 5th Army Reserve, East Indian, were sent to check the breakthrough, which they did without firing a shot. The Germans had withdrawn of their own accord. They obviously had no intention of trying to hold the ground they had seized.

"After we took over the Serchio Valley, we launched an attack in February 1945, but after limited gains including the Lama di Sotto and Mount Della Stella hill masses, fell back to the Sommocolonia-Gallicano line. Our initial advance had been creditable, but no one from regimental headquarters seemed to know that our leading elements had seized their initial objectives. The regimental CO and S-3 weren't physically in evidence to find out, and the early gains were lost because of the command failure to exploit them.

"In preparation for the final push, a patchwork division was assembled to attack towards Massa, La Spezia, and Genoa. Its supporting troops were all from the 92nd, whose artillery ranked with the best in Italy, but only one of its regiments was black. Again, the 370th Infantry, which probably had the best regimental commander in the division, was selected, and once again the 365th and 371st were raided for both officers and enlisted personnel to replace casualties in the 370th.

"After our regiment, the 365th, had been stripped to bring the 370th up to strength, we were separated from the division and were placed under IV Corps command in the mountains near San Marcello, south of Abetone to prevent any infiltration to upset the impending final attack.

"As allied troops broke into the Po Valley, German units surrendered in amazing numbers, and the 365th was rushed into the valley to handle the prisoner-of-war processing. We processed literally hundreds of thousands of POWs until permanent camps could be established for them.

"I think the criticism that was heaped upon the 92nd Division was unfair, because the 92nd was never employed as were other divisions. The Cinquale crossing, which was supposed to be a feint, was certainly a misadventure. It was not a fair test, nor was it well conceived, because the tanks so important to its success were sitting ducks for German artillery.

"Frankly, I don't think anyone really expected to use the 92nd Division in World War II. I think it and the 93rd were formed because a large number of Negro troops had been drafted, since the South certainly was not going to leave large numbers of black men home with their women. Politically, you could not leave Negroes home when white boys were going to war.

"I had absolutely no resect for the division officers, with a very few exceptions. I saw nothing about them to suggest that they were first-rate soldiers. Also, there was an impossible officer dichotomy based on race. Possibly the 92nd would have finished the war at Huachuca except for pressures to get them overseas, so we went and were put in an area where the war was going to be neither won nor lost.

"I have the firm conviction that many of our troops felt that what they did, didn't matter. They realized they had not been entrusted with a significant mission and they suspected it was because nobody had any confidence in their outfit. I think nobody respected its officers. I think even our enlisted personnel suspected the 5th Army people didn't think much of our command because they never gave us anything to do of consequence.

"Now the curious thing is that General Almond, the commanding general of the 92nd, had a great deal of political acceptance. Even when it was decided to reorganize the 92nd Division for the final push up the Ligurian Coast, Almond still retained command. They continued to use the 92nd Artillery units, which were first class. When the war broke out in Korea, Almond was given a command there and I understand he didn't do well there either. He was involved in MacArthur's retreat from the Yalu River. I don't believe I ever saw my regimental commander as far forward as a company command post. To imagine him being in a platoon or company area was unthinkable. Our battalion commander was an utter coward. I never saw him in a company area. In one skirmish around Bebbio he panicked, and this had a tremendous demoralizing impact on the black officers. The rumor was out that our executive officer shot himself in the foot. All of these things added to the distrust of the orders coming down from higher command. Many of these officers saw only a map concerning their men and anything they knew was second hand.

"On the other hand, we had many fine company grade officers in our battalion. Lt. Joseph Stephenson of Red Bank, New Jersey, was an outstanding troop leader. Lt. Montell Kyler was superb in his command of our heavy machine guns, and Lt. Jehu Hunter and Capt. Laler DeCosta were excellent communications officers. Captain Phillips of K Company had an utter disdain for death which I'm told he later met in Korea when his unit bore the brunt of the initial North Korean attack. My mentioning these few is not in derogation of others, but in fairness it should be clear that under other circumstances, these men might have been decorated lavishly for gallantry.

"I think the men of the 92nd Division, if asked, would have said they were in a pretty sorry outfit. It seems to me you cannot treat people as second-class citizens or second-class soldiers and expect them to behave in a first-class fashion, particularly when they are ambivalent about the mission they are called upon to perform and can't relate it to the success of the larger enterprise.

"I share Ralph Ellison's concept of the invisibility of America's black citizens.* Just as we are not consciously seen and hence are not considered when national domestic policy is made, neither were we seen or considered when the conduct of World War II was planned. National Guard and

---

*Ellison's novel *The Invisible Man* was first published by Random House, New York, in 1952; it is available in a Vintage paperback edition, 1972.

reserve units like the 366th and 372nd were automatically and invisibly activated with other Guard and Reserve units, but the decision to form and later to commit to action new units, like the 99th Pursuit Squadron and the 92nd and 93rd divisions, came only as the result of agitation and pressure from the Negro press. And, whenever the pressure subsided, the not-required-for-the-war-effort treatment was reapplied and obscure training locations and invisible assignments resulted.

"My four-year military stint was an horizon-expanding experience, and not just in a geographical sense. To see how different personalties react under stress was enlightening and sometimes frightening. And to witness what happens to spirited men who are forced to accommodate the unacceptable is soul-rending."

Sergeant Eugene Lester, a medic with the 365th Infantry Regiment, was fortunate in being assigned to a job that he was trained for.

Eugene Lester: "Medics work as a unit supporting the regiment of which they are a part. They fall into three different categories: first, those who go up to the front line and stay there acting as first aid men; second, the liaison group, called 'litter bearers,' who transport the wounded to the aid stations; third, the medics at the aid station who assist the surgeon. I belonged to group three. It was my job along with the other medics at the aid station to keep a record of every man coming through. All data gathered was done in duplicate form, one copy being put on a tag tied to the wounded person's garment. Among those things included were all treatment and medication the patient had been given at the aid station. The aid station is usually near company headquarters, which is not too far from the front line. We were a link between the line and the hospital which was some distance back.

"Although in the army a good cook would often be made a mechanic and vice versa, I do believe they sifted out those people with any medical background and placed them in the medics. I had a pre-med background and most of the medics I knew had some experience along these lines: hospital workers, pharmacists, therapists, and so forth.

"After my induction in 1942, I was sent to Camp Atterbury to become a part of the medics with the 365th Infantry Regiment. From there I moved to Fort Huachuca with the 365th to become a part of the 92nd Division. There I was a part of the 1416th Medical Service Unit, which included the hospital. I had worked with nothing but white doctors at Atterbury. This was also true at Huachuca until just before the Louisiana maneuvers when black doctors began coming in.

"On post the medics assisted the surgeon with the daily calls of the personnel. It is at this time we got to know the surgeon and the men. Stateside the men resented us slightly because we had, comparatively speaking, bankers' hours and missed the hard dirty work. Overseas they forgave us because we were needed.

"My personal impression of the black-white relationship at Huachuca? When the regiments constituting the 92nd Division first arrived, I found then and have had no reason to think otherwise, the black soldiers as a whole were quite willing to accept the white officers they found at Huachuca in the positions they occupied. These soldiers were led to believe that this was a white officer cadre of experienced men with but one purpose, to build the division into a functioning unit. After all, this made sense since the three major elements of the 92nd had met at Fort Huachuca for the first time. The soldiers were told these positions would eventually be filled by qualified Negroes. All of us anticipated some of the junior officers coming from our own ranks.

"Not having been an officer I could only guess as to the relationship between black and white officers at Huachuca. The transition period of our medical set-up from white to black, as far as the doctors were concerned, went smoothly. There was no socializing between the two groups, but there appeared to be no medical problems.

"I can say that the black officers who came to the fort came from different units. This was somewhat of a disappointment to our men. There were men in the three regiments who were definitely qualified for OCS. This I know because the first two weeks of the medics' time at Fort Huachuca was spent straightening out the 201-files of the 92nd Division besides assisting in the daily sick calls. Somehow or other they had gotten all mixed up alphabetically. One could not miss the AGCT scores; high scores caught your eye immediately. A number of the men who had OCS or ASTP intelligent quotients had been told they would go to OCS. For some unknown reason not one of these men were ever sent. I have often wondered just what was the motive behind having no officers who originally came from the 92nd Division. I am speaking of having qualified enlisted men from this unit attending OCS. Even if qualified men had gone to OCS and been lost to our division it would have been different. Not to have any of them go did not add to the morale of the division.

"When we learned we would soon be going overseas they brought in more black officers, all from other units. Our black doctors were among those who came at this time. By the way, let's get this straight once and for all, many people have the mistaken notion the officers in the 92nd Division were predominately black when in fact the reverse is true and was true at all times.

"I repeat, the greatest influx of black officers came when we were POM. For the medics it was our first opportunity to work with the doctors who would be going overseas with us. I considered this a waste of valuable time. Working together builds a team, and practically at the last moment we had to learn new methods and new techniques, and try to rebuild our team. The army never intimated these would not be the men we would work with under combat conditions.

"I know the enlisted men did not resent their new black officers but there was a resentment against the idea of bringing in men totally strange at the time it was done. This meant adjusting to new leadership just as they were reaching the 'crucial.' The men at Huachuca were proud of their black officers but not of the fact that these officers had to catch up under the pressure of preparing to go overseas. They felt both the officers and they themselves had been given a raw deal.

"The result of this stupidity showed itself once we were overseas. The field soldiers, particularly those on working patrols, sometimes got really uptight because ofttimes the leadership was frightened and uncertain. Bad judgment or bad treatment in this kind of situation just might get an officer killed. This certainly did not add to the peace of mind of those officers who weren't 'together.' I say this because there is not doubt that a few officers passed through our aid station who had been taken out of the ball game by their own men.

"Men and officers have to rely on each other; it is of the utmost importance that they get to know each other. I think I could go so far as to say a poor officer whose men known him, and they haven't misjudged him, and he knows them, does not have to fear his men. If it happens he is a good guy but just lacks leadership ability his sergeants will go out of their way to cover for him. But—and this is the more common deal—a poor officer whom the men have begun to recognize as such will transfer out even before he gets the message. Oh yes, the men let it be known that once overseas they were going to be in need of a new officer fast. An officer who continues to antagonize his men is not going into a battle zone with them. When our POM time came white officers were transferring out like crazy. Black officers know when they, themselves, have gotten too far out of line and they understand the slang expressions of the 'brothers' or songs like 'Straighten Up and Fly Right' are warnings, not a vocal exercise so they 'cool it.'

"Now there were white officers who had gotten the message all right but in their white arrogance they did not believe a Negro would actually kill them given the chance, I should say 'in those days' since fragging is a common thing in the 'Nam.' From what I gather there was such an officer in the 92nd Engineers Unit, a real high-handed character with no respect for the black soldiers under him. He got the message about his longevity once overseas and laughed it off. Now these men were not on the front line but that officer was dead three days after they bivouacked. They never found out who killed him, but there was no doubt as to why he was killed.

"One of the hardest things for men drafted into the armed services to learn is discipline. By the same token the leadership has to see that discipline is extended to all of the men, not skipping over favorites. Teaching discipline to grown men can get a little tricky if you take anything for granted; good leadership would be aware of this. Poor leadership is oblivious to such trivia until it blows up in their faces.

"I said there was no problem between white and black doctors in the transitional stage of blacks replacing whites. This is true, but black doctors had to go through a whole lot of things the whites didn't. Whites were appointed to positions while black doctors were not even considered for them. All black doctors came in as captains but the white captains felt their word carried more weight than the blacks'. Strange as it may seem black and white respected each other professionally in spite of these obvious difficulties.

"Getting back to me, I think we began to feel like we were really a part of the war when we passed Gibraltar en route to our ultimate destination, Viareggio, Italy; however, we disembarked before reaching it and spent the night in an open field. We noticed for the first time the sound of muffled gun fire.

"There were men returning from the front, and naturally we plied them with questions. As we moved forward we had a chance to see the devastation being wreaked upon Italy. The old Italian houses are stone and solidly built. They take a lot of killing; though battle-scarred, many of them were still standing and in pretty good shape, all things considered.

"A couple of days after we arrived in Viareggio the 365th Regiment was ordered onto the front line as a replacement unit. Generally one unit moves up as another is pulled back to give the men some rest. As we moved forward we soon discovered our arrival was no secret from the Germans. Our medical group had hardly begun to set up shop when we were on the receiving end of a mortar barrage that scared the devil out of us. It went on for hours.

"If I recall correctly the 365th had relatively heavy casualties, dead and wounded, the first few days up front. I suspect this was due to the enthusiastic welcome the Jerries were giving to these new, green troops. If Jerry's intent was to make us uncomfortable I assure you he succeeded all too well the first day or so.

"The 92nd Division, as far as I could determine, was supposed to be in a holding position. The idea was that our very presence made it impossible for the Germans to pull out troops and send them to northern Europe where the main fighting was going on.

"My unit was at one time stationed on the mountain overlooking Bologna. I must state our supply and communication system was unique for modern warfare. Donkeys were the means of transporting supplies, wounded men, and the dead. Men carried the messages many times. I learned while I was at this particular spot looking down on Bologna that there was a water hole, the only one in the vicinity for good distance, and it was shared by American and German soldiers. I had fellows tell me on occasion they would arrive with their water kegs and canteens at the same time Jerry did. Each pretended they did not see the other, filled their containers, and returned to their respective positions. Once there they started shooting at each other with a vengeance but nobody ever shot at anyone while they were at the water hole. There was one neutral place in all of Europe, the waterhole. I don't know if the 'wheels' knew about this but the men in the area had made their own rules.

"As you know, medics with their visible red crosses were not supposed to be fired on. This was all well and good until some dimwit German got the bright idea of putting soldiers in medic gear; the arm band with the red cross and the helmet with the same marking. When we caught on we started firing on all guys wearing this insignia and naturally the Germans answered in kind. Medics became fair game on both sides in this sector, so being a medic or a litter-bearer was far from a safe job.

"Viareggio in one way was almost as isolated as Fort Huachuca; the soldiers there were all black. This is one of the reasons the town is referred to as the home of the 92nd Division. When we entered other towns or cities we always got strange looks from the indigenous population if our fellow white Americans had been there first. It is still beyond my comprehension that men on passes or furloughs from combat had the time or the desire to sit down and tell outrageous lies on men that the majority of them did not know even on a casual 'hello' basis. To attempt to undermine the enemy is one thing, but to do this to men wearing the same uniform and fighting for the same cause is quite different. Funny, no psychologist that I know of has found this a subject worthy of study.

"A point of interest to me was a lot of the men we spent evenings with at Fort Huachuca teaching to read and write might not know how to dot an *i* with a pencil but they could do Morse Code with a rifle or a sub-Thompson. They were simply terrific with weaponry.

"A Sergeant Sheaffer was one of the men who passed through our aid station. I knew him, and he was probably one of the best-liked soldiers in the regiment. Sheaffer was one of those qualified for OCS. He had been a student at Oberlin. He had gunshot wounds in the abdomen. I had high hopes about his recovery. I knew he would be all right because he was clear in his thinking and told us what had happened when he was hit. We repacked his wound and gave him more morphine. When he left, laying over a mule, I mentioned that from his behavior he would be stateside soon recovering. Captain Madison, our surgeon, shook his head saying, 'It's too bad, but he'll be dead before he reaches the bottom of the mountain.' I was somewhat shaken by this information. It wasn't long before I realized our doctor could size up the cases quite accurately. Often troops or Italian peasants—men, women, and children—were brought in after being caught in an artillery barrage. They would have a limb or two mangled and be a bloody mess. We knew they had bought it. Dr. Madison said after attending them, 'an amputation, possibly two, and treatment for the superficial damage and they'll be in good shape in a month or so.' We medics learned those who from all appearances were horribly mutilated ofttimes survived while those who superficially appeared to have everything going for them were dying.

"Our unit never serviced a white soldier. However, I have talked to black on-the-field medics who in emergencies worked with white soldiers. Because their lives had been saved by a Negro many vowed about their regeneration racially. Of course, home was far from the front line and the pressure of racism though seldom found on the front line was still deeply imbedded in white America. I don't doubt that these men meant what they said at the time but reverted to type once they got home.*

"The Italians, given a chance at all, were most hospitable. On a moment's notice they would have a little party with dancing and wine. We had to learn their way of waltzing, which was fun, and how to drink their wine all night without getting drunk. The secret was to sip it because the minute your glass was empty they refilled it. The Italians' curiosity about the black-white situation was insatiable. They wanted answers they couldn't find in books. One's rotation back to Viareggio was always looked forward to with a great deal of pleasure. The citizens of the town went out of their way to make our stay pleasant as possible under war conditions. I am sure the fondest memories the men of the 92nd Division have of the whole war are of Italy and its people."

Sergeant E. J. Wells, 365th Infantry Regiment, entered the U.S. Army from Decatur, Illinois, and was sent for basic training to Camp Atterbury. Here he ran into his old friend Kenneth Hines who, when Wells confided his surprise at segregation and prejudice in the army, observed, "You know the saying, you can't teach an old dog new tricks. Well, believe me, the army is a mangy old dog." Wells noticed that almost all the commissioned officers were white and southern-born. "A few Negro officers arrived while we were still in Indiana," he said, "and we were glad to see them." Wells's first comments deal with segregation on the post in Indiana. Later, at Fort Huachuca, as company clerk at headquarters, he was in a position to see aspects of the situation not mentioned in the other interviews.

E. J. Wells: "Our area was at the lower end of the post away from everything. There were two service clubs. Number two was for black servicemen and we were told to stay at two. Once we decided to visit number one to see what would happen. They served us, but let it emphatically be known that we *must* use club two.

"On pass in Indianapolis, the better-class Negro places of entertainment were off limits to us and, of course, white places were out of the question. Hotels, both black and white, would not accommodate Negro service-

---

*The unit in which Technical Sergeant Lathaniel Wilson was a medical corpsman attended both black and white troops in Algeria, where he was stationed more than a year. Sent to France, his unit attended white troops thereafter. He reported no racial problems: "Since we dispensed the medicine, we were just one big happy family."

men. Indianapolis could hardly be called a soldier's paradise, with only ghetto dives open to them.

"The 365th finally made its way to Fort Huachuca to join its sister regiments. I had become a company clerk under all white officers. When General B. O. Davis, Sr.,* came to Huachuca to inspect the troops, both black and white officers were jumping and being oh, so polite, but when he left I heard one of the white officers, Lieutenant Benson, saying, 'That nigger didn't look so big even with that star on his shoulder.' He and his friends thought this was a big joke. They were aware of my presence but as always when a black is in the subservient position he is invisible to whites and they say anything they please.

"More black officers came to Fort Huachuca and suddenly all of the white officers who had been 2nd lieutenants became first looeys; they were not going to have any black rank a white officer. I watched a white 2nd lieutenant go to captain in eight months while a large number of Negro officers never got above a 2nd lieutenancy. One thing, morale seemed to go up consistently with the arrival of more black officers.

"The division went on maneuvers in Louisiana. There were three towns near our camp area: Marysville, Alexandria, and Lake Charles. In Marysville a soldier going on an emergency leave struck the station master for calling him a nigger and a few added attractions. MPs called to the scene beat the devil out of the soldier. When they finished I am sure he was in worse shape than his sick mother he was supposed to go and see. That night other soldiers planned to return to Marysville and destroy the station, but the town, expecting trouble, had been surrounded by more military police.

"In Alexandria a bus driver was about to brain a black soldier with a gun for not moving back in the bus, which he couldn't do because the vehicle was jammed to capacity. When the driver reached for his gun under his seat another soldier hit him and the riot was on. Lee Street, which runs the length of the town with blacks on one end and whites on the other, was a shambles as those guys turned the town upside down. It was placed off limits to us for a week.

"Lake Charles was quite different. It had a white Catholic church that went out of its way to be nice to us. It was a totally unsegregated set-up and we could have a real good time. A number of white soldiers came to the church affairs. I never figured out whether they were guys stationed there or fellows home on furlough who went to the church.

"A great deal has been made out of the high illiteracy rate among those in the 92nd Division. No one would deny this since a large portion of our men were from the backwoods of the south. But the thing that positively

---

*General Davis was a member of The Advisory Committee on Special (Negro) Troop Policies.

astonished me was some of the poorest English, grammatically speaking, I have ever heard came from the lips of a great many of those southern white officers! It was not just carelessness on their part, for a lot of their memorandums came across my desk. They had no conception of English grammar and their spelling was atrocious. It struck me as ludicrous that they made jokes about illiterate blacks' English when theirs in many instances was so much worse. I often wondered what military academies they finished in or how on earth they succeeded in getting through OCS. The black officers, comparatively speaking, sounded like English professors, unless they were deliberately using what is now referred to as 'ghetto language.'

"A black officer got drunk in Tuscon one night and resisted MPs when they tried to pick him up. A free-for-all was the result, and in it he struck an officer who just happened to be with the MPs. The black officer was a captain and many of the men at the post couldn't understand how a major (the captain had to be outranked to be picked up by MPs) happened to be riding around with the military police. Anyway they put this officer in the stockade like an ordinary soldier and kept him there. A white officer, not drunk, struck his commanding officer at the fort. He spent about thirty-six hours in the stockade and was then transferred. The post paper said they were trying to railroad this colored officer out of the army. It seems he had become a one-officer army fighting the system and was under continual surveillance for a misstep.*

In June 1944 the 370th shipped out, and in September, when the 365th and 371st left Huachuca, battalion after battalion, it began to look like a ghost town. There were about two thousand men there when I left with the last group. Several blacks were made captains at the time of our departure. We sailed from Hampton Roads in October and arrived in Leghorn the 29th of the month. We disembarked at Pisa, where we spent one night in a field sleeping in a downpour. After five days we moved up to Viareggio and there, for the first time since June, the 92nd Division was all together again.

"The Italians were a little sceptical of us at first, because among other things they had been told we were cannibals by our fellow white Americans who preceded us.

"Now we as a people have been poor all of our lives, but I had never seen people eating out of the garbage cans until there in Italy. Old women and children would fight for the scraps we were throwing away. This really bothered our guys and their appetites increased tremendously, to the point that they always had enough on their tins for themselves and someone else. The cooks 'never' saw some of the fellows passing through the chow line two

---

*Wells did not know at the time that the officer, Dr. Rudolph Porter, was railroaded straight into Leavenworth Disciplinary Barracks.

and three times. The Italians found we were easy to get to and we got along fine. All of us made good friends in Viareggio and even today it is called the home of the 92nd Division.

"The front was about twenty miles from us and at night the town would be shelled. The 365th moved onto the front line in total the last of November, on the flank of the 370th. I believe the 371st was held in reserve for a while. On February 8, 1945, a large part of the division was committed to battle for the first time. I remember the date well because a lot of men were killed and wounded that day; it kept us clerks busy three days and nights writing up notifications for the next of kin.

"Companies of the 366th and 370th tried to make an assault across the Cinquale Canal. They were murdered. Tanks were supposed to spearhead the drive but got in trouble before they could get started good. Tanks aren't much good in water and mountainous terrain.

"At this time, our guys were getting worked over pretty good by the German veterans up in those mountains as our patrols were going out regularly. If I recall once the 370th was pulled back because they were stalled, and replaced by a white infantry unit from Texas. Being white and Texan didn't change one thing. They couldn't move either; it was simple, we were stalled. We were in this position until March, and it was then decided that a black division couldn't do the job. With the exception of a few companies from the 370th all three of the regiments of the 92nd were made into service units.

"Now some guys don't like to admit this, but we sure weren't fighting and we were packing supplies up and down the mountains to white troops and sustaining casualties just the same. Moreover, just typing up the memorandums and listening to the officers running off at the mouth at my company headquarters gave me the impression that there was a lack of replacements, trained or otherwise, as well as a lack of troops in reserve, when needed. Also they were shifting officers from one group to another so often that I wondered at times if the men knew who was commanding them. They spoke of a morale problem. From where I sat I can't recall the senior officers doing one thing to correct this; all they ever did was talk.

"April 3rd in Porte Domesta, where we had a big factory for our office, I was laying out on a big hill half asleep when it suddenly turned quite dark. This awakened me fully and then I heard the noise. I never saw so many planes in my life; there was a never-ending of them. They bombed all day and night and they were bombing in the area near our front lines.

"April 5th the big push was on. The little Nisei, men of iron, had been called down from France. The 370th was put back on the line with the white infantry group from Texas. Things began to move for the first time. The Nisei and the black soldiers got along fine when they had any contact.

"With the 442nd and the 370th leading in their own sectors we were soon in Genoa. There we found the Germans had done a hatchet job on the black soldiers. The Italians were too tired to care by the time of our arrival, and their children swarmed around us.

"I feel the 92nd was given a black eye unjustly. This in turn damaged the reputation of all black troops in Europe, as for their ability to fight. We were not trained together from the very beginning, as were white divisions. We were never totally committed as a division. We were not given the chance to learn from experience, as were white units. Overseas we didn't have the time together that other units had, for we were continually being split up into service outfits, or one regiment lost men to another as replacements. I sometimes wondered if the 92nd command had any real knowledge of warfare. Our stay at Huachuca certainly demonstrated that they did not know how to treat black men. What was so confounding to me was the they didn't make the slightest effort to profit by their mistakes; they just kept on doggedly repeating them.

"I felt then, and I still do, that the military did not want black combat units, particularly one as large as a division. They most certainly did not want black officers. Everything was done to divide us rather than to unify us into a cohesive fighting unit. During the war only black infantry was made to 'tote that barge, lift that bale,' many times without every having the chance to win or lose a battle of any size.

"On returning to the states all of us hoped that some changes had been initiated. Arriving back home in Decatur, I found nothing had changed. We blacks still had to sit upstairs in the theaters; we were still refused service in many places. It made me wonder what the war was all about. I had served my country to the best of my ability, and my country would and does deny me. The only answer is color!"

Warrant Officer Robert Millender, 371st Infantry Regiment (after March 1945, assistant regimental adjutant, 370th) kept a diary of his war experiences and made frequent notes covering the history of the 92nd Division from the time that its three regiments met for the first time at Fort Huachuca in 1943. His overseas records report his immediate reaction at the time of the actual events affecting the fortunes of the 92nd, including the Cinquale Canal incident, 5–8 Feburary 1945.

Robert Millender: "When the 92nd Division first went into the line, in early November, I believe the 371st was held in reserve. The last of the 365th units did not come into the line until the latter part of November. This line stretched from Forte dei Marmi to, I believe it was, Seravezza. During this time our men were involved in patrolling, to a great extent, which occasioned some fire fights.

"Reading from my diary:

The division jumped off on a drive to take the town of Massa. However, to do this it was necessary to effect the crossing of the Cinquale Canal, harmless enough in appearance but in reality a trap waiting for its victims. By this time, February 1945, the all-Negro 366th Infantry Regiment had been attached to the 92nd Division, actually as replacements for some of our losses. Some of its units were to take part in the Cinquale Canal crossing, accompanied by at least one company from the 370th. They had fighter support and tanks, the 760th medium tanks and the 758th light tanks, to assist them; the tanks directly, the planes indirectly by attacking some of the enemy coastal artillery. The crossing of the Cinquale was comparatively easy for the infantrymen. Most of the men of the 366th and 370th crossed without too many difficulties. However, once the foot soldier traversed the canal, the tide must have come in fast because the tanks never made it. There were only a couple of places they could ford the canal and it appeared that every time a tank hit those fording places the German artillery on top of the mountains would knock it out. Frankly, they destroyed every tank that tried. Those that were not hit were drowned out. The infantrymen, with no tank support, were caught between the mountains around Massa and the Cinquale Canal behind them. The largest number of casualties of the 92nd Division was suffered at that time. E Company of the 370th was just about wiped out.

"I recall that one officer and six enlisted men of that entire company got back across the canal. The 366th had fared no better. Months later bodies were still floating down the Ligurian Sea, the result of the carnage at the Cinquale. One of them was Captain Overhall of the 366th, who died covering the withdrawal of his men.

"The report of the incident was, of course, the usual thing: 'black soldiers were not of the same caliber as their white counterpart,' and so forth. The real truth was some big brains higher up had not figured on the Germans so effectively zeroing in on our tanks at the fording place; tank support was an absolute necessity in an assault on a place like Massa.

"Another excerpt from my diary: 'On February 14, 1945, following the Cinquale disaster, *Stars and Stripes*, or one of those papers in circulation for servicemen, came out with the inane statement that the 92nd Division suffered "relatively high" casualties. Relatively high, my backside! We had a large number of casualties and nothing to back us up. We needed reserves desperately. If we had had them, many of the unfortunate stories about the 92nd would have had a different ending.'

"Continuing from my diary:

In March 1945 they decided upon the reorganization of the 92nd Division. Theoretically they were taking the best men out of other units and putting them into the 370th, making it an attack unit representing the 92nd Division. To my astonishment General Almond was left in command.

Actually, the military hierarchy would have preferred excluding the whole division but feared political repercussions so used the 370th as a front. The two new regiments brought into the 92nd were the 442nd (Nisei) and the 473rd. They had highly competent leadership; particularly was this true of the 442nd.

"In short, two regiments of the 92nd were relegated to carrying ammunition, being stretcher bearers, and gathering up the prisoners, once the big push began. I doubt if you will find this in any document open to the public. Such documents probably state the 442nd and 473rd were brought into the Po Valley campaign to back up, or build up, the 92nd Division. But there was a new 92nd and it consisted of the 370th, 442nd, and 473rd Infantry regiments.

"Reading a complete statement I have here in my diary:

As I see it, since the first of the year there has been one helluva smear job going on as far as the 92nd Division is concerned; the *Stars and Stripes* after the February attack, *Newsweek* a little later, and then the *Stars and Stripes* again with one, Mr. Truman Gibson's article. As often as possible they slam our outfit. One of those rags says it took the 442nd thirty minutes to take some high ground that the 92nd couldn't take in six months. There is only one thing wrong with this statement. Lieutenant Eaves was up on that particular bit of high ground exactly three days before the Nisei passed through. He reported seeing two Germans and believed he killed one of them. There was no sign of a build-up there. This was on March 3rd. How could it be so strongly fortified in that short spell, without our knowledge, that it would take these thoroughly professional troops a half an hour to seize it?

The Nisei say and believe they are being used also to further the glory of the general and his white 473rd. The Nisei are taking the high ground [mountains] and the 473rd is getting credit for taking the towns, which would be impossible if the high ground were not secure.

If this isn't a sweet racket I'd like to see one. I could go on all day writing about this rotten deal. The lily-white staff with their promotion racket, where the white is safe, comfortable, and secure. We had ten white lieutenants come into this outfit and only one was sent to a rifle company, but all black lieutenants go to rifle companies. Promotions! Colored lieutenants have remained so for two years and they will promote a white lieutenant who has only been in the ranks five months. Then they wonder why the fighting spirit and the morale in this division is so damned low. They can't be that damned blind or stupid as to think they are dealing with the same black of a hundred years ago. This is the story Truman Gibson should have told and didn't.

"I have just a notation here but it recalls an incident that was by no means atypical of events that took place in the 92nd Division. I was in regimental headquarters at the time. Charlie, for C, Company of the 370th had been assigned an objective on this particular morning [5 April 1945]. A couple of hours or more had passed since their departure when we received a call from them saying they had reached their objective, which was Castel Aghinolfi. The S-3 officer said he didn't believe them. Every time Charlie Company called in that they were sitting on top of their mountain and digging in, the S-3 officer insisted they were lying and cut off the conversation. When C Company came under enemy attack the S-3 decided maybe they weren't a bunch of liars after all and sent reinforcements, which were too late. C Company had been forced off the mountain and suffered high casualties. Eight men and two officers returned in one piece.

"One of those officers was 2nd Lieutenant Vernon Baker. As you know, he won the Distinguished Service Cross, and you asked why he did not receive the Congressional Medal of Honor. Let me tell you about Baker. The very morning that C Company had to fight in retreat from Castel Aghinolfi, he had destroyed an enemy observation post, a camouflaged machine-gun emplacement, and a German dugout, killing eight German soldiers. He then volunteered to cover the withdrawal of the group containing the walking wounded and assisted in the removal of those in critical condition. Several men volunteered to stay with him. He was the last to leave, destroying the equipment they had to leave behind and acting as rear guard. One in his group was killed and another injured by a sniper. A private who had remained behind was a BAR man, and he picked off that sniper. Baker's group ran into a machine gun nest and the lieutenant, covered by the BAR man, crawled up to the machine-gun emplacement and completely destroyed it with grenades.*

"Now I had personally written up the citation, the recommendation of our commanding officer, for a Congressional Medal of Honor. One never forgets a thing like that; at last a black man was going to receive the Medal of Honor in this war. But the higher-ups decreed otherwise and he ended up with the DSC. When a story appeared in *Stars and Stripes*, the caption above the picture of Lieutenant Baker read, 'Lieutenant Baker Given DSC.' On the same page, right across from him, was a picture of a white lieutenant. His caption read: 'Lieutenant Such-and-Such Wins the DSC.' To me, this goes back to the same theme I've always had that there was a design or plan—call it what you will—to belittle the men in the 92nd Division by slanting the news. This is a beautiful example of the clever use of words. Baker was *given* a medal; the white guy *won* his.**

"Our outfit went into a town; they met no resistance. Patrols were sent back several times to check the town. The Nisei passed through the town

---

*Order #7, from Headquarters, 5th Army, 10 June 1945, making the DSC award, adds to the facts mentioned in Millender's account that "on the following night, 2nd Lieutenant Baker voluntarily led an advance through enemy mine fields towards the division's objective." Baker entered the service from Cheyenne, Wyoming.

**See also Bill Stevens, chapter 2, on this point.

on their way to some objective; in a few days there was a press release saying they had taken this town after several days of hard fighting. With their fighting record, the Nisei didn't have to stoop to such, they weren't the source. Staff officers made the press release. The time would come when the Nisei would protest their work being credited to the all-white 473rd!

"I didn't mind that damned army paper not giving us credit, but to tell outright lies on us was too much. For instance, when the big offensive came, to say we followed the Nisei is a bunch of crap. We were in entirely different sectors. We cut our own path and they cut theirs. I'm sure the men of the 442nd would tell you the same thing.

"The 370th had originally gone overseas with 108 officers and about 3,000 enlisted men. At the end of the war there were less than a third of the original officers and less than a third of the original enlisted men.

"One of the basic faults in the creation of the 92nd—and this probably held true of the 93rd—was that there were three combat regiments necessary for a division but no regiment trained to replace their losses. Logic would dictate that some, many, all of the soldiers in a regiment could or would get killed, and trained soldiers should be ready to replace them. When we got overseas and sustained losses, they attempted to use the 366th as replacements. I do not say this in disparagement. The 366th, although originally a combat regiment, had been sent overseas as an airfield guard unit and had had no further combat training since its deployment around airfields on various islands near Italy. It takes more than a day to get men up to combat readiness. Another solution was to take men from the 365th as replacements for the 370th and 371st. This so decimated the ranks of the 365th that it could not act as an effective group. If a regiment is undermined, the division is no longer an integral unit. I am sure this is one of the elementary lessons taught at military academies, but our division staff seems to have forgotten it.

"In the three regiments that made up the 92nd, black officers seldom held the rank above 1st lieutenant. Whites held the ranks from there up and in most instances they were southerners. When the 370th was on the front line, the white staff officers always had a rest place. Colonel Sherman would usually take over some villa in the area for himself, and the white officers were invited to come up when free from duty. The four black staff officers were not included. Rapport between black and white officers was very poor. There was almost a race riot between them in Viareggio, about the usual thing, girls in the area.

"The relationship between the Negro soldier and the Italians was excellent. They said we were 'simpatico,' which they explained meant we understood their plight.* The whites did not understand and really didn't care.

---

*This theme appears repeatedly in the interviews. See above, the interviews with Charles Brown and Wade McCree; also Frank Penick, chapter 1.

"As I look back, I question whether there was ever the intention of sending the 92nd overseas. After it happened, I fell the intent was to see that the 92nd was put in the poorest light possible."

The 597th Field Artillery and 758th Tank Battalions

Captain Hondon Hargrove, C Battery, 597th Field Artillery Battalion, is one of the most completely and thoroughly trained officers the reader meets in the interviews. His account of stateside training makes evident why the artillery was usually exempt from the criticism heaped upon the 92nd Division. Captain Hargrove also furnishes information from the artillery man's point of view about the Cinquale Canal. It need not be emphasized that the German artillery man enjoyed a similar perspective.

Hondon Hargrove: "When I was called into the military service I had had four years of ROTC training and was commissioned a 2nd lieutenant in the infantry reserve upon my graduation from Wilberforce University in 1938. My training had included two summer encampments at Camp Mead, Maryland. It was then I had my first opportunity to see the large number of potential Negro officers. ROTC units from Howard, West Virginia, and Tuskegee joined us at Camp Mead.

"Incidentally during my last year at Wilberforce the instructor in military tactics was General B. O. Davis, Sr. It is interesting that at that time he was thought of with a great deal of respect because of his high rank and dignified appearance. Maybe he should have stayed at Wilberforce.

"My contact with the army ended upon graduation until March 1940 when I was called up for extended duty. I was ordered to report to Fort Devens, Massachusetts, to become a part of the newly organized 366th Infantry Regiment. We had a regimental group of black officers assigned to the 366th; almost all were Howard or Wilberforce ROTC graduates. A few came from what was called the Citizens Military Corps. A cadre of NCOs was assigned to us from Fort Benning, Georgia. They were all army regulars, top soldiers, and they knew infantry.

"Colonel West Hamilton, a Negro member of D.C.'s Board of Education and from Washington's upper-class Negro society, who had been an officer in World War I was, I guess you could say, a representative commanding officer. Colonel Edmund Andrews, white, really ran the regiment. There was also Colonel Hesse, white. These two were very strict, rigid, and good. However I don't think they had much confidence in our ability to learn; they taught us well in spite of this hang-up.

"In about a year I had a chance to transfer into field artillery and I took it. While I was with the 366th it developed into a very good infantry regiment. I believe had they been utilized at their peak of training, still highly motivated and ready, they would have had one of the best records in the war.

"In June 1942 I was transferred to the 184th Field Artillery Regiment, which was also an all-black unit. It was made up from one of the few black National Guard units in the country, originating in Chicago, Illinois. Colonel Pitts, white, was the commanding officer and I can't honestly say I thought much of his ability. The caliber of officers in this unit varied as to college training and ROTC backgrround. They had some outstanding people like Major Orion Page, black, and others of mediocre talent. Orion was a brilliant lawyer, with ten years of National Guard duty behind him, and was superior in military knowledge and the practical use of it. When we were finally sent to join the artillery of the 92nd Division Major Page's high rank and knowledge of strategy and tactics really shook those crackers up; they simply didn't know what to do with the man. Command, at division level, I believe, tried to play the game 'the little man who wasn't there' with the major. Fortunately the only civilized and able commander in the whole 92nd of any rank was the artillery officer and he respected Orion's ability.

"The officers in this unit, up to Colonel Pitts, were all black. Colonels Randall, Marcus Ray, and Wendell Darrick, black, were all excellent officers who knew their business. Ray wouldn't let anybody kick his men around. He went as far as he could to protect them without having his own head roll.

"Typical of the military mentality of the time, the army split up the 184th Artillery Regiment, sending one half to Camp Butner, North Carolina, and the other to Camp Forest, Tennessee. The Camp Butner unit to which I belonged became the 930th Field Artillery group. At Butner we remained a medium artillery unit with the 155mm howitzer, a very accurate gun built in World War I. The 930th remained unattached.

"At Butner our enlisted personnel was practically all northern-born so I cannot say all was sweetness and light, because our guys just would not knuckle under. But we didn't have any serious racial outbreaks. General Parker, commanding general of the 78th Division at Butner was, I believe, a New Yorker and he didn't want a lot of racial strife. When our men tipped over a couple of buses because they had to wait while whites loaded first, the general sat down with Colonel Darrick and worked the problem out. Henceforth whites had their buses and the blacks had theirs—not the ideal solution but at least guys got to town before it was time to return. I think we were grudgingly respected because the guys took certain stands and that was it.

"While I was at Butner they wanted to charge a group of us with mutiny because we took our wives to the post theater and sat in the officers' section. We refused to move and after a lot of threats the whole thing was dropped. Our sister unit, the 931st, was having a rough time at Camp Forest. They almost had a shoot-out over blacks wanting to go to the theater on the post. One thing that made life at Camp Butner bearable was the black people of Durham were most hospitable.

"I spoke of attending army schools. The first time was in December

1941. Dennis Harrod (who won a Silver Star in Italy) and I were the first Negro officers to go to the company commanders' school at Fort Benning, Georgia. We two had separate everything from the whites, yet there were people of color from other countries there who were not segregated. Harrod had a degree in engineering and like myself had four years of ROTC behind him. We were sleeping in our separate room, or just fooling around, while those white guys were burning light like mad. Soon our separate quarters were jammed at night with our unequals to be tutored by us in the book work. This broke down social segregation in our living quarters, because they needed us.

"What happened to us as an artillery regiment didn't happen to white regiments. The army had a time table and at the end of it you were shipped overseas. But they didn't know what in the hell to do with us, with all-black officers. I went to two service schools in artillery alone while in the army, while whites generally attended one. Most of our NCOs and enlisted men had attended two or three service schools also. We got so we could drive a nail at ten miles, and do you know somehow we always had trouble passing the tests. Naturally those who scored us were white and they would deny this vehemently but this was their way of keeping us from going overseas. They said we were not ready!

"I was in charge of the guns at the pits while I was at Butner. Using myself as an example, it is a little ridiculous to say a man who has a B.A. and M.A. and completed two artillery courses cannot produce a battery firing four guns to minimum requirement, but they said otherwise and we stayed at Butner.

"In the spring of 1944 the enlisted personnel of the 930th and the 931st were put in a general service unit, which was a criminal waste of manpower. Excellent artillery men were made into engineers. I never understood the reason for this. An artillery unit certainly would not present the problem of white thinking people that an infantry regiment would. Yet with the stroke of a pen the high and mighty army threw away several years of training. The powers-that-be claimed the group never qualified—that's a lot of crap. The very fact that they could take a 'peckerwood' off of the street and make an artillery officer out of him in ninety days lets you know the job is relatively simple, and they didn't make any Napoleons out of most of them. All they asked of them was to operate within a unit, battalion size. Every guy in the crew has a relatively simple task and it does not require a mathematician to do the job.

"The officers of the 930th and 931st were sent to Louisiana where they joined the 92nd Division on maneuvers. We took over two artillery battalions, replacing the white officers. I was now using light howitzers, 105s. We consisted of three light artillery units and one medium unit, which Colonel Ray commanded. I must admit the departing white artillery officers seemed reluctant to go.

"There was trouble in Louisiana between the troops and the white citizenry. I understand the 92nd's stay in Louisiana was cut short on the demand of the governor of the state. I suspect the guys didn't have the proper respect for southern tradition and it would have taken a little doing to put down a whole division of infantrymen.

"Anyhow the 92nd returned to Fort Huachuca and I saw the infamous place for the first time. The training facilities for the kind of warfare we were going to have to conduct were ideal. It had mountains, desert, everything. The objective in all this training is to close with the enemy to kill him to keep him from killing you. All of the various teams, infantry, artillery, and tanks had the terrain they required at Huachuca. However, for a place to put a large number of black soldiers, it was pretty bad. The commanding general and his staff were not prepared to do what they should do to contain 15,000 or more black men and keep their morale in keeping with the facilities. They made an awful lot of mistakes if well conceived and executed plans to keep blacks aware of their helpless and hopeless situation can be called mistakes.

"Major General Almond, the commanding officer at Fort Huachuca, was a southerner. He had the typical view of black capabilities. I don't think he believed any black, no matter what his file showed, or how much training he had, was able in an officer's position. I have always believed he had no doubts about the black enlisted man's ability to fight, but he firmly believed only white officers could get the best out of them. He could not see that by destroying his black officers, through various but not unusual methods, he automatically shattered the morale of the men. Naturally soldiers would identify with their own. I repeat, I honestly believe he had no doubts as to the ability of the black soldier to fight and to fight well. He just could not countenance black officers leading them.

"One of our main problems, after getting overseas, was replacements for black officers. I really don't think they ever planned for, or that it ever occurred to them, that some of these people were going to get killed or wounded and would have to be replaced. I don't think they realized there were going to be casualty lists and they would have to have black infantrymen to replace the men on the listings. This is saying in so many words I don't think the army really meant to send the 92nd Division overseas; they avoided doing so as long as possible. In this I am giving the army the benefit of the doubt. They couldn't have been idiotic enough not to be aware that black men have no special power against bullets.

"The Negro press played a large part in the movement of the 92nd overseas. Then too, General Almond was General Marshall's brother-in-law, and like all generals he couldn't wait to get into the action. I do believe however, it eventually came down to outright expediency. Mark Clark's little old 5th Army had been gutted for the Normandy invasion and the expected battle in Europe. He would have settled for an orangutan. The fact that the Russians were on the offensive in 1944 would also have carried considerable weight. Anyhow, one, or all of these things, upset the grand strategy of 'keep 'em penned up at Huachuca for the duration.'

"And as should have been anticipated, one of the things that really hurt us, was there were no black infantry replacements ready, trained, and waiting. They did a lot of scrounging around Paris to grab guys for the Battle of the Bulge. They weren't all willing volunteers, and it just might have been harder digging up black replacements only, for the Po Valley campaign. I had a friend who was on leave in Rome from some noncombat outfit when he was tapped on his shoulder and informed he was now a replacement for the 366th infantry regiment. All of the 'white' divisions had trained replacements waiting at a nearby repple depple in Italy.

"Now the 366th got into the act when the 92nd command, desperate for black replacements, suddenly remembered the 366th, which had been on airfield guard duty for almost a year. It had once been an infantry unit. That unit thrown on the front line with no preparation had been hit hard so my friend was a replacement for them. In less than twenty-four hours from the time they scooped him up in Rome he was on the front line trying to learn how to use a M1 and not shoot himself or one of the men around him. I assure you his opinion of the army is unprintable.

"We had our share of cowardice and anybody who tries to make us all heroes is crazy. I know some of us blacks, and I'm speaking of officers, who were responsible for getting their men killed. In this instance the white man didn't have a thing to do with it directly. They freaked out and I can understand why. Those officers were catching a lot of hell. There was lack of confidence in some of the missions to which they were assigned. Moreover, you cannot build up distrust in a man over a long period of time and when his life is involved, and others depending on him, expect him to believe in your sincerity or your competency. This becomes even more so when he has gone on a couple of designated missions and gotten the you-know-what shot out of his platoon each time.

"In any combat action where you have new men involved you don't know how they are going to perform. It's not like an opera when all of those killed get up for the curtain call. In battle you get real dead. Those who survive several battles may not always be the nicest people but they know how to stay alive. It takes a little blood-letting for this to happen. Every time we had a little patrol skirmish we were supposed to emerge unscathed and victorious. I mean in every damn one of them; this just didn't happen, evidently to the high command's surprise.

"Now the men of the 92nd had been this route when along comes the relatively unprepared 366th. This regiment was piece-mealed out among the 370th, and to some extent the 371st. They were expected to perform miracles as they were assigned some of the damndest missions ever conjured up. All things considered they didn't do as badly as has been often said. One thing—they crossed that goddamn Cinquale Canal and stayed across three days, with no tank support, being methodically cut to pieces until recalled. No one ran; they stayed and they died.

"As artillery officers we were often placed in positions in the mountains where we could observe what the men on the lower terrain could not see. Let me explain something, from an artillery man's viewpoint, about the Cinquale Canal. Our guns faced the mountain range called Cauala. Now we were up in the mountains but we were looking up at the Germans. We were always looking up at Jerry and he was always looking down at us. Cauala was a series of razorback mountains that got higher the further north you went. The Ligurian Sea was on our western side and the Cinquale empties into it at a low level. Directly left and in front of us was La Spezia, an Italian naval base. The naval guns there were still operating and they could bring fire to bear on the Cinquale but we damned sure couldn't reach them with our field pieces. There was other German artillery throughout these mountains; the Germans could bring tremendous fire power to bear upon that little canal. Jerry was looking right down on the damn thing; hell, from where I was, below Jerry, I could see it.

"Enemy observation there was similar to that at Monte Cassino and the Rapido River crossing, or should I say attempt. They talk about black failure at the Cinquale; hell, the had white failure at the Rapido because in both instances they were asking for the impossible. It's all right to talk about 'if our tanks had gotten over at the Cinquale' or 'if the English had been able to protect the 36th Division's flank at the Rapido' what would have happened. Hell, that's conjectural and the tanks didn't get over at the Cinquale and that't that. If I had been an artillery man up in those mountains like Jerry you can bet your boots those tanks wouldn't have gotten across, either. The set-up there was an artillery man's paradise and an infantry man's hell; it's just that simple.

"If you take the 92nd Division as a whole, the 366th did just about as well as the division. Of course division command couldn't say this because the 366th was an all-black outfit with all-black officers. Command tried to make the 366th and the junior officers of the 92nd the fall guys for their own shortcomings and unfortunately succeeded all too well.

"The 366th sustained heavy casualties. I daresay their losses were heavier than those suffered by the 92nd, comparatively speaking. Their casualties ran something like one-third to one-half of their regiment and no regiment in the 92nd, not even the 370th, which saw most of the action in that group had such losses. This happened to the 366th in less than three months.

"As to the mistrust of the 366th by the men of the 92nd, it must be remembered that everyone knew there were only two all-black outfits in Italy, the 332nd Fighter Group and the 366th Infantry Regiment. The men knew the

332nd was in combat just as they knew the 366th was on airfield guard duty scattered all over the islands of the Mediterranean. Since the allies controlled the skies of the Mediterranean the members of the 366th really had nothing to do. Let's face it, through no fault of their own they were often referred to as the playboys of the Italian area. Now the men of the 92nd had had someone shooting at their behinds everyday for months so were becoming seasoned veterans. The 366th hadn't climbed a mountain nor fired a shot so was entering the fray where the 92nd had originally started. It was only natural the men of the 92nd looked askance at these replacements. The men of the 92nd did know that the new men were infantry-trained and were willing to wait and see how they measured up.

"In the original planning the 366th was not supposed to be assigned missions at once, but they were; the bloody mess at Cinquale was one of them. The Cinquale incident put the 92nd solidly on the side of the men of the 366th. The men of the 92nd had had some raw deals but nothing like what was dished out to the 366th.

"You know it was really ridiculous, some of the assignments we were given. Any good second lieutenant would not have issued a goodly number of the orders that came down from command.

"So okay, you, meaning the 'brains' up top, tell me what to do, I do it and get my ass shot up and I holler and scream. Am I a coward because of this? I am out there, up there, or somewhere on orders and there is not a goddamn place to go; I am being annihilated so I try and crawl back. Am I a coward because of this? Let's face a hard truth, they all holler and scream when they get chopped up in totally intolerable and untenably positions: black, white, yellow, green, red, purple, it doesn't make any difference. A man screams when his guts are spilling out or he's trapped and he knows he's trapped and he knows he's going to get killed. 'Coward' is an easy word to toss around but I don't recall many of the division-level officers going on any of the designated missions. Please don't give me that crap about 'they aren't supposed to.' Patton wasn't *supposed* to be in his lead tank but he *was*. I understand several of the 'wheels' in the air force went on bombing missions so they could see what was going on for themselves.

"When the Nisei came into the Po Valley the push had already started in some parts of the line. They were a regimental combat team, not a division, so they could not possibly cover the whole front. Now this irks me a bit, not the Nisei but our commander. He bent over backwards praising them. However, before the Nisei returned to Italy from France, the Germans were beginning to have to make adjustments in their lines because of the sacrificial lambs of the 92nd. The Nisei were good—they were damned good. When they moved out in their sector they made one of the most beautiful flanking moves I've ever seen executed, and those coming behind broke through. But they were only a part of the victory in the Po Valley campaign.

"When they saved the Lost Battalion in the Vosges Mountains in France, that was truly their success. Nobody could get those Texans out, but the Nisei did. It cost them over five hundred of their men to save something like three hundred Texas. This was probably the most outstanding accomplishment of any single unit in the war and all praise and glory should go to them for it.

"I have spent considerable time in Washington researching the archives on the 92nd. Referring to the division command, German generals whose forces opposed the 92nd have flatly stated that it was the most misled division they ever encountered."

Technical Sergeant Richard Carter's brief interview pictures the situation of the noncommissioned officer in the 597th Field Artillery Battalion.

Richard Carter: "Being in the United States Army was not one of the high points of my life. After induction in 1942, I went the usual route through Fort Custer and then to points south.

"I was sent to OCS, but along with a patty boy got kicked out for fighting. Looking back on it I guess it was a case of frayed nerves. At OCS you were on the go every minute but the five hours you were allowed to sleep. The patty named me and I 'teed off' on him and the fight was on. Fighting was forbidden among officer candidates so we were both bounced.

"I don't remember the name of the camp I was sent to from OCS but it really doesn't matter since I had hardly checked in when I was transferred to Fort Huachuca, Arizona. I took this in stride but I wasn't exactly thrilled to be going to Texas or Huachuca.

"En route to Huachuca I had a lay-over in some Texas town. It was stifling hot so when I hit the station which was cooled by fans I stretched out on a bench to get some sleep. I was awakened by someone hitting me on the soles of my shoes with a stick. The stick was a billy club and on the other end was the typical southern cracker cop: big hat, red face, Sam Browne belt, pot gut, and a big shiny pistol on his hip. He exuded arrogance and ignorance. 'You niggahs cain't sleep in heah,' he said. 'You bettah git on ovah in the niggah section befoh yuh git in a lot uh trouble.'

"You could have cooked a whole meal on me, I was so hot, but I wasn't a kid and I wasn't about to die at the hands of the likes of him. I moved. There were MPs all over the place but I hadn't the slightest doubt where they stood. As I walked in the direction of a sign marked *Colored,* I passed the station dining room. Would you believe that American MPs and some of Hitler's bully boys, now prisoners of war, were having a ball together, wining and dining! It was sickening.

"I finally found 'my place' under the watchful eye of the Texas

Gestapo. How they managed it I don't know but there was not a bit of air in the small colored section; not one fan anywhere. Sleep was out of the question because the room was stifling. I just sat there with rivulets of water pouring off me until my train finally arrived.

"Fort Huachuca was something else again. It seemed as if it spread over half the state of Arizona. There were some of the most educated blacks there and many who could neither read nor write. And then there were those who fell somewhere in between these two extremes.

"Here was a big sprawling camp containing somewhere between 17,000 to 20,000 black men with a small percentage of white officers (though they far outnumbered the black officers and held all of the staff posititions) who enforced the strictest segregation possible between themselves and the black officers. There only contact was strictly in relation to military activities; social contact was out. How they could possibly function together in combat was a question that had to pass through many a black officer's mind, not to mention the minds of enlisted men.

"Fights were a regular occurrence on the post between the enlisted personnel. When men are stuck out literally a hundred miles from nowhere, only so much baseball or basketball can be played. Tempers flared and fights resulted.

"I soon found out I had been sent to Huachuca because of my IQ. All of the black men they could round up who had been bounced from OCS plus those who were released by the closing down of the ASTP program were up for grabs by the 92nd. The division needed these high IQs to raise the over-all level of the 92nd.

"I was placed in the field artillery unit. If I had had a choice I could not have done better because the commanding officer of artillery was a fair man and a damn good officer. He was a career army man with no racial hang-ups. We respected him and he respected us. Our artillery group did a good job and was not included in the general down-grading of the 92nd. Our commanding officer can take a considerable amount of credit for that.

"There is not much I can say about the performance of the 92nd infantry regiments in Italy from actual experience. My artillery unit was placed on the side of a mountain and there we stayed. There was not a lot the enlisted personnel could see beside more mountains. We'd receive firing orders, do our job, and wait for the next orders. Of course now and then we'd pack up and move to another mountainside. Naturally we heard rumors about what was happening to the 92nd infantry and it was getting a bad name. Whether or not it was deserved I don't know but one thing is certain, only a fool, if he had seen what had gone on at Huachuca, would have thought the 92nd Division was 'together.' "

As a 2nd lieutenant in the 758th Tank Battalion, Harry Duplessis, like many of the other men interviewed, had a taste of combat before going overseas. After the war he remained in the Reserves. He served in Korea, and retired in 1970 with the rank of colonel.

Harry Duplessis: "Entering the army as a volunteer officer candidate in December of 1942, I had to take basic training at an NCO school at night in my home town, Philadelphia. We were taught tactics, armament, map reading, the fundamentals required of an officer. At the end of this period the volunteers for officer candidate were sent to Fort Knox, Kentucky, for a board hearing. There were four Negroes and we successfully passed the board only to lose one member on the physical examination. We were then split up, one man going to the infantry, another to the engineers and I was placed in tanks. I did not have to change locale since Fort Knox is the home of tankers. I retrained in tanks, which took fifteen days. When I finished I was made a corporal and placed on a team teaching the handling of machine guns. Forty-five days later I was admitted to the armored forces for officer-candidate training. I simply had to transfer across the area from my new assignment.

"Fort Knox, Kentucky, was quite different from Philadelphia, racially speaking. But once you have made it as a tanker the problems are comparatively minimal. There are two reasons for this: first, tankers think of themselves as a cut above the average and second, of 11,000 tank officers there were only 63 blacks; we did not constitute a problem. In OCS, where I ended up leading my class of fifty, I was the only black in my class.

"During my training period I encountered the notorious army prejudice. There were small, petty things. A rumpled bed that had been perfect when you left it. Everything you did had to be just a little bit better than the whites. Now, some harassment was to see if you could stay cool under pressure and it was applied to whites also. During this period you are perfectly automated in the sense that everything is done by time. Your sleeping period is exactly five-and-a-half hours. Men who were failing were removed at night to avoid embarrassment of having their classmates see their exit.

"Once my training was completed I was sent to Camp Hood, Texas, to join the 758th Tank Battalion. These were light tanks. The 758th was the first black tank outfit. It was the result of a determined campaign by the *Pittsburgh Courier* to see that black soldiers served in combat units.

"The prejudice and discrimination at Camp Hood made Fort Knox seem ultraliberal in its attitude. Camp Hood was frightening and made you wonder if you were still in the same army. Segregation there was so complete I even saw outhouses marked *White, Colored*, and *Mexican*; this was on federal property.

"The three black tank units: 758th, 761st, and 784th were supposed to be joined together but the idea of all of that fire power in an all-black group was just too much for the 'man' to bear so it never came about. A determining factor in this was blacks turned out to be exceptionally good with those little mechanical devices they couldn't possibly learn to handle, like tanks and automatic weapons. A close watch was kept on black combat units' attitudes at all times.

"Our commanding officer, Lieutenant Colonel Steele, was over age and under grade. It seems that he had been in a brawl in the Philippines and lost seventy slots toward promotion. The men called him 'the bull.' In one sense, to whip these black soldiers into line was a challenge to him. I understand that upon his arrival at Hood he called the men together and told them, 'It is traditional at West Point that black soldiers can't handle mechanical equipment and can't soldier. I want you to make a goddamn lie out of that tradition and I am here to help you.' There were mixed feelings about the colonel until his leadership began to pull the group together. When promoted to a full colonel he was transferred, and the men really hated to see him go.

"I must say the officer replacing 'the bull' was a sad specimen, also out of Louisiana. Our officer complement was five white officers and 33 blacks, five of whom were black captains, and they actually ran the unit. We were considered most unusual because of the number of black officers in our group.

"At Fort Knox I had not been segregated from my classmates. At Camp Hood they shifted white officers in order to place me in C Company, 3rd Platoon; 3rd Platoon was the ragtail platoon of all the outfits, the end of the line. Black officers were segregated in every respect at Camp Hood. My captain was an ROTC man from Louisiana. He was an excellent officer and made a point of never referring to the men as 'boys.' He was transferred later to command the 784th. I believed then and I believe now that the captain was one of our 'lost boundaries.'

"The 758th was often employed as school troops for tank destroyer units to see if they could take us out of play. It was fun in some respects and hard work in others. In the tank corps you never leave anything dirty; before retiring you clean your tank.

"I was returned to Fort Knox to study tank maintenance and after Hood I had a vague notion of how the slaves felt on Emancipation Day. When I returned to my unit ten weeks later we had moved to Fort Huachuca, Arizona, and were training with the 92nd Division. The only difference between Camp Hood and Fort Huachuca was in the latter you seldom got to town. On occasion we did cross the Mexican border. There again American race prejudice awaited us. However the Mexicans had a way of dealing with gringos; they saw to it that we got whatever we wanted.

"The racial cause célébre at Huachuca was Jackie Robinson's encounter with a cracker bus driver.* Jackie was already beginning to have

---

*See also the interview with Ivan Harrison, chapter 3.

trouble with his legs. He was taking the bus to go up to the hospital for x-rays. On board was the wife of a friend. She looked like white so was sitting up front. Jackie sat down beside her and the bus driver just about frothed at the mouth. The driver ordered Jackie to the rear, which was purely an exercise in rhetoric as far as Jackie was concerned. There are several versions as to what transpired, from Jackie knocking the driver from one end of the bus to the other to his making fun of a ranking officer who had come with the MPs to arrest him. Whatever happened he was court-martialed and acquitted. Subsequently he was discharged from the army because of his legs—the ones he became famous for stealing bases with.

"That old cliché that 'black troops just don't measure up' is just so much bunk. On the Louisiana maneuvers the 758th technically destroyed the 4th Army. Though the 758th would have been destroyed themselves in a real battle they would have killed more than four times their number. We crossed a river the 4th never dreamed could be forded. It was simple. The fellows took gravel from the river bank and built up the bottom until we had a fording spot and wiped them out, on paper.

"Our shipping orders were an open secret, so many men wanted passes to see their wives and sweethearts before shipping out. The white major was sure that these soldiers would not return in time to make the train. The black captains assured him the men would come back and he reluctantly granted passes. The following morning 22 men missed roll call. Just as I was about to turn in the roster a sergeant ran up and said, 'They are coming sir!' Twenty-one of the missing men were running across the field. Due to the rule that whites were allowed to board the bus first these men had been unable to get seats even though they explained their predicament. Having no other choice and determined not to fail their black captains they had jogged and walked all of the way back. The only guy who hadn't appeared was the 'lover' of the battalion. Everybody knew where he was and nobody worried. He made the train with a flying leap just as it was getting started. We put him in fatigues, which was the identical way he had arrived. The man was a good soldier but a natural lover on the side.

"Our train stopped in Memphis, Tennessee, and serious trouble was barely averted. The CO had given orders for the platoon sergeants to have the men make lists of what they wanted to purchase in the station. As soon as we stopped the sergeants lined up at the station counter. The first man was served at once but then a white man came up. Though there were two men working the counter one got very busy doing nothing while the other served 'whitey.' All hell was about to break lose. There were two white MPs nearby and one of the sergeants told them about their problem. The MPs told them they were in the south now and they would have to wait until they were served. The sergeant told them there were over five hundred men on that train who wanted some treats and they meant to have them one way or another.

"In the meantime another sergeant had rushed back to the coaches carrying the officers and told us trouble was on its way. Captain Morgan, who had more sense than most of us, went to the station master. The sergeants were ordered back on the train and that cigar counter was brought to the train in carts and the men could make their puchases from the side of the train. We didn't like it because it was a cop-out but that was that.

"One of the most amusing things I ever witnessed was an American Indian who had been assigned to our outfit. Now Indians usually serve with white units; in wartime they are equal, but this fellow was quite dark. He went haywire on the train, en route to our POE, and was running up and down the aisle shouting, 'Me no "nigger," me Indian!' They got him off of that train like lightning. The men did not find it funny and his problem would have been solved tragically if he hadn't been removed fast.

"We finally arrived at Newport News, Virginia, a staging area. The camp, Patrick Henry, was divided into eight sections; area eight, the bottom of the barrel, was for us. Fifty-odd AWOLs from the 92nd Division, which had departed a month before, were attached to us for transit overseas. Now infantrymen and tankers don't get along too well; frankly they fight at the drop of a hat, officers included, meaning me too, but we were stuck with these guys.

"We had reached our destination about 5:00 P.M. and settled down. Around 8:00 P.M. we heard a bunch of guys singing as they went by and we noted they were paratroopers from Fort Benning. Late that evening we heard a lot of commotion, swearing, and an occaional use of the word 'Geronimo.' Knowing that was a partrooper expression we split for the enlisted men's quarters. Upon our arrival the CO of the paratroopers was gathering up his men and ordering them back to their own area. They left with the parting remark, 'Niggers, we'll be back.' One of our sergeants was sporting a hicky the size of a egg on the side of his head. Instead of being furious and full of invectives he kind of smiled as the crackers left.

"The following morning a battalion of Puerto Rican engineers arrived to occupy area seven. Throughout the day I had noticed that our tankers were mighty tight with the attached infantrymen. I chalked it up to good sportsmanship or something since they, the infantry guys, were outnumbered. That night the men were given permission to go to the show. A few stayed behind but it appeared that the majority had gone off for some entertainment. We officers were in our quarters yakking, playing cards, relaxing, the usual routine, when at 8:30 a call came for our commanding officer, who had gone off to visit friends in the white area. The exec. ordered all of the officers up to the enlisted men's area on the double; we took off!

"We covered that block in record time. To our surprise it was apparent few if any of our tankers had gone to the show. Our guys were standing at our area entrance watching the paratroopers giving the Puerto

Ricans a fit. They had run the poor guys out of their barracks and were beating them with all kinds of clubs or substitutes; it was like a witch hunt. The tankers' attitude was it was their fight, let'em fight it.

"It finally occurred to those poor devils that the only place they could escape to was area eight. They cut for our section. The tankers let them through but when the paratroopers tried to follow it was a brand new ballgame. You could actually feel the earth tremble when our black tankers and those white paratroopers collided. Just as this very real no-holds-or-weapons-barred encounter swung into action the lights went out. I mean all over the camp. They stayed out for approximately three hours and during that time I fought harder than I did the whole time I was in Italy.

"We had a very dark officer who was a giant of a man. There was a tree behind the arms room and that guy took a running leap, grabbed a tree limb and plunged through a window into the building. The door was opened and we proceeded to arm ourselves with Thompsons, rifles, and side arms. Theoretically we didn't have any ammunition, but like magic our men furnished us with all the ammo we needed. It seems that those infantry guys knew where the bullets were buried, so to speak, and that was why the sudden friendship had blossomed between them and our men. Together they had carried out a combined operation of preparing for war. Not for one moment had the men doubted that those 'crackers' would return and they meant to be prepared for all eventualities.

"As the battle progressed several of the officers got their heads together and discussed strategy. It was agreed that the enemy would undoubtedly attempt to infiltrate our lines. Where? The logical place would be the drainage ditch that ran alongside the barracks. One of our recon scouts, 6' 4" and an ex-football star, got a trench tool and stood right at the corner above the ditch. The first white face that came up got his features flattened like a pancake. With his screams of pain those behind scurried out of there like rats only to be greeted by men who had been sent to cover their retreat. The lights came on as suddenly as they went off and the battle ended. The tally was three dead paratroopers and one black tanker shot in the foot while loading his weapon. He was furious because he could not go overseas because of his wound.

"The Puerto Ricans did not fight. They had run into our barracks and that's where they stayed. I can understand this. They had just come into the camp and the attack upon them was sudden, with no warning; they were just plain bewildered.

"The next day when I was receiving several stitches in the back of my head I was happy to note that the paratroopers being stitched and bandaged outnumbered us considerably. One thing certain, they didn't say anything about returning for a rematch, nor was the word 'nigger' being bandied about.

"We shipped out in October, and after thirty-five days at sea we arrived in Naples. Dreaming of things being much better overseas, our first few days there put us in doubt. It was Thanksgiving Day when we dropped anchor but we were not allowed to go ashore; our Thanksgiving dinners were sent out to us. When we finally got ashore we were put in some woods near Pisa. Though we had been told that there was race prejudice in Italy, particularly in the rural areas, we found the Italians to be very friendly. They were desperately poor and hungry and we were soon giving them half of our food.

"The great day came when we were to go down to tank ordnance and pick up our tanks. We had checked out on every tank in the army so we were ready. As we walked along we could see row upon row of brand new tanks and could hardly restrain ourselves in getting through the proper procedure and secure the tanks assigned to us. Our joy quickly turned to disappointment with the realization that the army transported its separate and unequal ideas wherever it went. The equipment given us had been used in the African campaign. The tanks were covered with layers of dust, full of sand, and corroded in every possible crevice. Our mechanics worked night and day, draining and cleaning gas tanks, removing sand from every conceivable and inconceivable place, to mention a few of the problems confronting them, in order to get these beat-up hulks into a usable condition. We watched white units come in and leave with brand-new equipment of all kinds. We inquired about the new tanks just standing there and were told they were not available for us. It was heartbreaking to see our guys working like dogs without let-up and those brand new beauties just sitting there.

"My tank, which was a light tank, had a gun on it that you might say just about spit its projectile out. I actually watched the projectile hit the stone wall of an Italian house and bounce off. We certainly were no threat to the Germans inside of that house. Infantrymen often told us to take our pea-shooter and beat it because we attracted fire which they didn't need. You couldn't blame them since our mighty weapons were practically useless.

"While the mechanics were still trying to get our tanks into shape an order came through for us to move them, on the double, up to the Cinquale Canal sector. Infantrymen of the 366th and 370th were to make an assault across this canal. We could only put five tanks on the road because of the terrible condition of our assigned equipment. We arrived at the canal and had to walk out into it to see about the footing; it was in February. Tanks will sink without a solid base. We asked for a load of gravel or anything to assure our being able to make it to the other side. We had found places, especially on the other bank that once wet could cause sliding, thus holding up those behind and causing them to drown out. We were told, 'To get those damned tanks across the canal.'

"Captain Morgan got out of his tank and walked so the tanks could follow his for a sound bottom. Just as he reached the other side he stepped on a mine and got a back full of fragments. There was a group of medium tanks, white, behind us and every one of us that managed to get across slipped and slid around that opposite bank and got the hell shot out of us, rendering our tanks absolutely useless. The others, backed up in the canal, just as we had predicted, drowned out. You had some pretty angry tankers, black and white; the utter waste because of rank stupidity. We lost one officer, who covered his men so they could escape. The infantrymen we were supposed to cover had waded on across, when I say waded I mean waist-high on the average man; they got the hell shot out of them once they moved up from that north bank of the canal.

"In April we were attached to the 442nd, Nisei. Our biggest problem with the little Japanese-Americans was keeping up with them; they moved like greased lighting. Instead of following the paths, which tanks have to do, they went up and across those mountains like crazy. We worked out a system. As they took out across the mountains we'd wind our way along until we received a signal from them. Than we would lay down a barrage as a diversionary. Jerry would be concerned about us and the Nisei would move in swiftly from the rear and mop up. I do mean mop; they turned those Germans every way but loose. We soon ended up in Genoa sitting out the rest of the war.

"The aftermath of the war was that the army experimented by putting a white and black platoon in the same company. They found that each platoon improved; the name of the game was competiveness. Another very important little detail was the American public had no idea how its manpower had been decimated; a lot of young men were dead or permanently disabled. The army knew and decided the black was needed to make up for this lack. Then too, the military realized that by integrating the armed forces they broke up black combat units and the threat they might become.

"As to the nonsense about Negro troops will not follow black officers, that's white propaganda. A black soldier will follow a black officer through fire and brimstone if he is treated right and he will support him when he thinks that officer is being oppressed. Negro officers might be a little tougher on their men sometimes because ofttimes they get caught up in that having-to-prove-themselves plague. But Negroes can communicate with each other. The Negro soldiers will often let you know just what he is feeling through songs he makes up, but the 'man' does not dig what he is saying. That was a big mistake in the Nam; many a white officer got 'fragged' because he didn't understand the warning signals that he had gone too far.

"The 758th had an exceptionally fine group of officers. They were intelligent, courageous, and respected their men. It was reciprocated by an outstanding group of tankers. By this I mean our guys always did their best and this is an enlisted man's way of letting an officer know how he feels about him."

The 366th Infantry Regiment

To this point the interviews have recorded the experiences of black soldiers and junior officers. The one departure is the following account by

Colonel Queen, commanding officer of the 366th Infantry Regiment, who was continually forced to do battle with members of the military establishment to insure fair and equal treatment for his men.

Colonel Queen: "The original 366th Infantry Regiment organized at Camp Grant, Illinois, 1917, was a part of the 92nd Division in World War I. It participated in the Meuse-Argonne offensive. The 366th was reactivated at Fort Devens, Massachusetts, in 1941. Its first commanding officer was white. All other officers were Negro, principally from Howard and Wilberforce ROTC units. Of these 132 officers, 128 were college graduates. Several held their master's degree and two were Ph.Ds. No man in the enlisted ranks had less than an eighth-grade education. The vast majority of those were in the cadre that had come from Fort Benning, Georgia, to help whip the 366th into shape. may have lacked education but they had experience and they knew their jobs well.

"One of our officers, Lieutenant Morrison, formerly of the 25th Infantry Regiment, Fort Huachuca, Arizona, had, comparatively speaking, little education. He came to Fort Devens a 2nd lieutenant and I promoted him to first by virtue of the fact he had fifteen years' experience in automatic weapons and was an expert in their handling and a skillful teacher in their use. While he sometimes murdered the king's English explaining the weapons he always got his program across. The men understood him, and in action they followed him without question. No higher compliment can be paid an officer.

"Directly after the bombing of Pearl Harbor, the 366th took over all essential installations from the Canadian border to Cape Cod, Massachusetts. The people of the state were most kind and always cooperated with the 366th. They knew we had a job to do and the inconvenience it caused them at times was accepted graciously. Our time spent at Fort Devens was a happy time.

"In January 1943 I was appointed commanding officer of the 366th, giving it an all-colored personnel. The original intent had been to replace the departing commanding officer with another white officer. Civic groups, political groups, the Negro press, and members of the 366th raised such a ruckus that the army changed its mind. For eight years I had been fully qualified for such a position but had been overlooked. To be given the 366th was a dream realized.

"In the fall of '43 the 366th was ordered to Camp Atterbury, Indiana. General Charles L. Ferber, commanding officer of Fort Devens wrote Washington a letter and sent me a copy. It commended the 366th on its splendid record while there and wished it well.

"First we were to report to Camp A.P. Hill in Virginia. The vehicles in which we traveled to Camp A.P. Hill were in first-class condition. These were changed at A.P. Hill and we were given sorely battered and worn trucks. It ended up with our being towed by wreckers in the bitter winter through the hills of West Virginia on our way to Atterbury. It was quite a trip for 3,232 men and officers.

"Upon our arrival at Atterbury I reported to Colonel Marquzette, the commanding officer, in accordance with regulations. He cordially welcomed me and my men to the installation. The colonel's warmth at our arrival was purely superficial. We were restricted to attending the theater at a certain hour and were not allowed to enter the Post Exchange. I protested and was informed he felt due to the presence of white troops it was for the best. Little rules kept popping up that curtailed the activities of the regiment.

"It was most interesting to note that German prisoners of war were granted privileges denied to colored soldiers. I entered a complaint with the Inspector-General and this situation was rectified at once. However Colonel Marquzette was a busy little fellow, trying to find new ways to discomfit us.

"It was brought to my attention that restaurants in nearby towns were refusing to serve colored officers. We found that certain staff members from Camp Atterbury had informed the owners that it was the desire of the post commander that they discriminate against Negro soldiers. The colonel vehemently denied any knowledge of such a thing so the problem was resolved; no objection from the base commander, the doors of the towns eateries were wide open.

"We survived many such petty schemes but were happy when our stay at Atterbury ended with an overseas assignment.

"The transport *General Mitchell* was the ship which took us to Africa. There were some 5,000 people aboard. Two white lieutenant colonels commanding a black antiaircraft unit were given staterooms. I shared a bunk with two of my officers in an entirely different section of the ship; I was the highest ranking officer aboard ship.

"Captain Fredrick E. Davidson, commanding officer of the 366th antitank company, brought it to my attention that an enlisted man from his unit had been confined to the brig on orders of a white lieutenant colonel for his disobedience to one of the white officers in his outfit. Disturbed by this usurpation of my authority I summoned the young gentleman to report to me at once. I asked him by what army regulation had he dared to assume authority over my men. He admitted he had no authority. My instructions to him were not to repeat the same offense or I would prefer charges against him.

"When we disembarked at Oran, Africa, April 1944, I received a copy of a letter sent to Washington, D.C. and the Port of Debarkation Authorities by Joseph W. Sensing, commander of the transport, USS *General Mitchell*. This part of the letter I shall always remember, 'Your unit has set an example of discipline and attention to duty while on this ship. The morale of your unit has been higher than any similar unit observed by me in the past.' Need I say I was very proud of the men of the 366th?

"Shortly after we landed in Oran, Colonel George W. Pense, a native of Alabama, and commanding officer of the base at Oran, called me to his headquarters for a conference. I was told to bring two of my senior officers. I reported with Lieutenant Colonel Oscar Randall and Lieutenant Colonel Alonzo Ferguson. Colored officers of a port battalion there, I believe it was the 484th, had warned me that Pense was up to no good; he was seeking my consent to a separate officers' club.

"After the formalities of introductions had been made Colonel Pense got down to the root of things. He said, 'I sent for you to talk about a separate club for these people.' Naturally I couldn't imagine who he was referring to so asked, 'What people?' He was not to be put off, he replied, 'Colored officers.' I told him the 366th had been stationed for two years and three months at Fort Devens, Massachusetts, and to my knowledge none of their black had rubbed off and no one had been contaminated by using the same facilities at the officers' club there. I stated quite emphatically, 'I am not a "colored officer" but a colonel in the United States Army. My answer to your request is absolutely, irrefutably no. I cannot and will not accept anything so degrading and still expect to be called a commanding officer of a regiment.'

"Pense was checkmated for the moment, but he came up with an answer. He issued an order that all dancing in Oran's officers' clubs would be discontinued until further notice. (Three weeks later, I am sure to Colonel Pense's delight, we were on our way to Italy.)

"While in Oran I made a 165-mile inspection trip to find out why I receiving so many delinquency reports at my headquarters about Charlie Company, commanded by Captain Charles Clark. It appears it was about soldiers not having their sleeves rolled down and failing to salute white officers. I found white officers had the habit of tapping colored soldiers on the shoulder while they were window shopping and telling them they had failed to salute. Every day in the week I had a two-and-a-half ton truck, equipped with seats, follow me to the military police station in Oran to obtain the release of my enlisted men that had been jailed. Major George T. Lawrence, regimental intelligence officer, now deceased, always went along to enter the establishment, gather up the men, and ask that my headquarters be furnished with the charges. There were 150 charges submitted to me in three weeks. Here was an outfit that even under the adverse circumstances of Camp Atterbury had never been a problem and now suddenly it was inundated with charges.

"Some of the men were even charged for doing what was correct. An example, two of the soldiers left their vehicle in the street unattended. They had removed the rotor distributor, immobilizing the vehicle according to army regulations, but off they went to jail. Since it was up to me to press charges none of the men were court-martialed; some of the charges were beyond the absurd.

"All of the harassment of the enlisted men of the 366th stemmed from the fact that black officers were taking French women to the officers' club. The old saying 'water seeks its level'—well the 366th officers were escorting French ladies who behaved and acted like ladies. The white officers were bringing women from the streets and gutters into the club. The contrast between the two sets of women was quite apparent and it didn't make the situation any better.

"Lieutenant Zachary went to the officers' club and as he pulled out his chair to sit down a white lieutenant kicked him on the hand. I instructed Lieutenant Zachary to press charges against his assailant. The white officer was brought to trial before a general court-martial. During the precedings the judge advocate asked Zachary about the incident. He explained that as he attempted to sit down he noticed a note on the table. It said if any nigger attempts to sit down take care of him. The white lieutenant was found guilty and fined $100.00. I wonder what the sentence would have been had it been a black officer on trial.

"From Oran my headquarters became San Severo, Italy. In no time I learned colored officers were not admitted to the officers' club there. I asked for a meeting with Colonel Polifica, commanding officer of the Photo-Reconaissance Wing, who had the say in such matters. I stated I wanted to know why colored officers could not be admitted to the officers' club. The colonel said the club was restricted because there were so many southern officers stationed in the town. I asked him if the club was to be run by the feelings of southern officers or according to army regulations. He replied, 'By army regulations.' He said colored officers would be admitted henceforth. I learned two weeks later colored officers were still barred. I wrote the commanding officer of the area through military channels and informed him that information had been received by me that this officers' club was restricted. Lieutenant General Dellers, commanding general of the Allied Air Force in Italy ordered Colonel Polifica to open the club or close it; it was closed.

"A letter was sent to me from the headquarters of the 15th Air Force that had originated with Lieutenant Colonel B. O. Davis, Jr., commanding officer of the 332nd Fighter Group. In the letter he suggested that the 15th Air Force establish a colored enlisted men's rest camp in Naples and that we send a representative from the 366th to accompany his two representatives to Naples. There was Captain Letcher and Major Percy Jones from the 332nd. I sent Major George T. Lawrence from the 366th. Before his departure I instructed Major Lawrence what my attitude on this matter was: it was not necessary and I questioned the advisability of establishing a separate colored enlisted man's rest camp in Naples when as a matter of fact all of these men went to the rest camp in Rome. The measure was defeated.

"B. O. Davis, Jr., did succeed in establishing a separate rest camp for his officers at Naples with a Lieutenant William Womack in charge. The Air Force rest camp for its officers was on the beautiful Isle of Capri. I thought this separation most unfortunate because the pilots of the 332nd were highly respected by white airmen, particularly by bomber pilots and their crews.

"In Italy the regiment was still intact as such and under my command, though individual units were scattered throughout the Mediterranean area guarding airfields. A combat-ready infantry regiment that had an excellent rating was put out to pasture, so to speak. When morale was high and we were in peak condition for combat they could find no combat position for us. When the situation reversed itself they threw the 366th into battle.

"In October 1944 I went down with typhus. I had just gotten back on my feet when I received word to gather up the units of the 366th and report to General Almond of the 92nd Division in the Po Valley.

"The 366th Infantry Regiment was brought into the Po Valley fray because the army had failed to have replacements ready and available for the 92nd Division, the only division in Europe that did not have a repple depple. One person who hastened the assignment of the 366th to the 92nd was Brigadier General B. O. Davis, Sr. The general visited me at my headquarters in San Severo. He said, 'When the war is over white people will say Negroes did not do any fighting. You are not sent over here to guard airbases.' I reminded the general that I could not order the movement of my troops.

"I submitted a statement to him that the regiment should be withdrawn from guard duty and given several weeks of intensive training. I had also informed General Jacob L. Davis, commanding general, ground forces, June 1944, that such was essential for the general welfare of the regiment. No action was taken on my suggestion.

"Upon our arrival in the battle area of the Po Valley, November 25, I requested thirty days in which to give the regiment intensive training to assure its readiness for battle. General Almond assured me of fifteen days, yet within five days, November 30, 1944, the 366th began entering the battle line. The period from November 25th to November 30th was filled with constant inspections, fault-finding, and changing equipment. On December 2 I was informed by Major Arnold of staff command that my regiment would occupy the line, quote, 'equipped or not equipped.'

"General Almond was living up to the unpleasant words he had greeted the 366th with: 'I did not send for you. Your Negro newspapers, Negro politicians, and white friends have insisted on your seeing combat and I shall see that you get combat and your share of the casualties.' He most certainly kept his word.

"Most of the 366th was placed under staff command and it was piecemealed out in battalions and companies. It was not committed as a regiment. I asked to be relieved of my command, giving the exact specifics of why I felt I had no other recourse. I was relieved in mid-December and Lieutenant Colonel Ferguson was my replacement. I was not in Italy when the 366th was thoroughly thumped by the Germans so I will leave this to those who were there, though I know the details well from the surviving men and officers of the 366th as well as from men of the 92nd Division.

"General Almond may have succeeded in decimating the ranks of the 366th and wounding their pride, but he never destroyed their self-respect. The 366th has an organization of its members that started with the war's end and continues to function. Among the members of the 366th were: Senator Edward Brooke; General Frederick E. Davidson; Judge Wade McCree,* Circuit Court of Appeals; Colonel John T. Martin (ret.), director of the Selective Service Bureau, District of Columbia; Judge Lett, Lansing, Michigan; Judge Blount, Phildelphia, Pa.; Dr. Lorenzo Nelson, for some years the only doctor in Lake County, Michigan, serving a community of 50,000 people.

Sergeant Willard A. Williams, 366th Infantry Regiment, was one of the men interviewed who had kept notes of his experiences during his four years in the army.

Willard A. Williams: "My name came up for the draft January 1941. However, I was not immediately inducted. I was told they did not have enough camps for colored soldiers so I was not taken into the service until June '41. I was sent to the 366th at Fort Devens.

"During our early training days at Devens we used wooden guns. Even our artillery pieces were made of wood. We were told to pretend they were the real thing. Members of the Negro press visited our camp and when they saw the wooden arsenal they raised quite a stink.

"At this time we were not at all sure just how serious our country was about having Negro combat soldiers. It was the general consensus that our outfit would never be allowed to engage the enemy because of its unique composition, all black excepting for the commanding officer, Colonel Edmund Andrews. Eventually this was changed, with Colonel Howard Donovan Queen occupying the position vacated by Colonel Andrews, making the 366th black from top to bottom.

"After continuous harassment of the government by civic organizations, the colored press, and some politicians, the 366th was finally committed to battle in northern Italy after a period of airfield guard duty in southern Italy.

"I don't think any member of the 366th will forget our arrival in northern Italy in the Po Valley sector where we were attached to the 92nd Division.

"General Almond, the 92nd's commanding officer, a real homegrown redneck, called us together.** In lieu of the customary battle-orientation talk of what we were fighting for, he chose to tell us that we were not there at

---

*First assigned to the 366th before transfer to the 365th Infantry Regiment. See interview with Wade McCree, above.

**Major General Almond was from South Carolina. See also the reference to him in the publisher's intro., note 12.

his request but because of outside pressure. He let us know he didn't give a hoot about having us but since we were there he would make use of us. He did, as cannon fodder. The general said we'd have our share of the casualties; he wasn't kidding. General Almond had his own sarcastic way of reminding this green combat unit that they had better make good because of the folks back home. You can imagine from this what the atmosphere was like upon our entry on the front line. We were an all-black regiment attached to three black regiments that had predominantly white officers. There is a great misunderstanding on the part of the general population thinking that the majority of the officers of the 92nd were black, with white staff officers. This is not so. There were white officers in the 92nd from the rank of lieutenant up. I would guess the officer ratio was between 60 to 70 percent white. To try and blame the weakness of this division on its black officers who were mostly 2nd lieutenants is just too ridiculous to contemplate.

"Shortly after entering the combat zone, Colonel Queen was relieved of duty because of illness and was succeeded by Lieutenant Colonel Alonzo Ferguson. Rumors were rife that Colonel Queen was forced out. We do know there was a hospital wagon in which they kept Colonel Queen several days. The colonel was a man who did not take any guff off of anybody. He was a Regular Army man and he knew the book forwards and backwards, word by word. He was a hard-nose type of man who had the respect of all of the enlisted men. He was tough but he was fair.

"My personal feeling, and that of many others of the 366th, was Colonel Queen was too strong a man to head up an all-Negro unit as far as the whites were concerned. He kept their feet to the fire from the time we left Fort Devens until we arrived in the Po Valley. There he was up against General Marshall's brother-in-law.

"Hell, they—meaning the whites—didn't want us to succeed anyway. Let's look at a brutal truth. We had suddenly been taken off air base guard duty, which entailed walking around airfields to keep out saboteurs and paratroopers. Neither were to be found since the allies controlled the skies over Italy. The fact is we had no job at all, more of a 'keep-them-occupied' thing. After months of this we were tossed on the front line. We were like a great golfer or pool player who has not picked up his club or cue stick for almost a year. The know-how is there but it takes a little practice to get back into form. The one thing we had going for us was that we were proud of our outfit and we were going to do our best. But we knew some of us were going to die relearning infantry tactics. Some of us would have died if we had been committed when we were combat ready; that's war. No one can convince me as many would have died so unnecessarily in General Almond's game of charades if Colonel Queen's request for a month of intensive retraining had been granted. The clincher was to replace Colonel Queen with Lieutenant Colonel Ferguson. With all due respect to Colonel Ferguson, he could not be compared to Colonel

Queen, he was too agreeable, too easy-going; he'd never rock a ship or raise his voice in protest.

"I was a platoon sergeant in my company, which was an antitank unit. We had been given orders to make an attack upon what they called a hill outside of the town of Gallicano. It was more like a mountain. Anyway, we attacked as soon as the order came down. We were to have artillery and air cover.

"When we hit that 'hill' the Germans mowed us down like clay pigeons. I recall twelve or thirteen of us made it to the top uninjured. There was no doubt that we were pretty well mangled. The real horrifying thing was our radio had been hit by shrapnel so we could not direct the artillery. They were zeroing in on us and the enemy, just below on the other side of the 'hill,' protected by a knoll, were lobbing mortar fire into our midst, so we were catching hell from both sides. We were pinned down there for several hours. I had resigned myself to dying because in the cross-fire the shrapnel sounded like bees around a hive.

"Fortunately the aircraft that had gone on before us to strafe saw our predicament on returning and took out the German mortars. (It might interest you to know the 332nd Fighter Group flew air cover for us, I should say for the 92nd Division, many times. When it was strafing missions they were generally the boys.) The men who had not reached the top came up and helped bring down those critically wounded. We withdrew a distance to regroup.

"We dug in that night, expecting a counterattack in the morning. Only one thing, the attack came sooner than we anticipated. I was sitting on the edge of my foxhole when a burst of gunfire cut into the area. This was followed by mortar fire. Again we were in a rough spot, but we fought our way out in retreat, though a number of men were killed as they climbed out of their fox holes. This whole incident was our first time under fire and we learned the hard way. Jerry pushed us right back to where we had started from and that is where we remained the rest of the winter.

"I wondered then and I have wondered since just where were our back-up troops. If they were there they were invisible because we certainly didn't see any. Now staff can say anything they want. They may have had some back-up troops on paper but they damn sure weren't there the whole time we were on the line. I ask the question about back-up troops because we got kicked off of that mountain, period. We held the line where we were but the Germans really didn't care because they had the top of the mountain and they could see us. All we could see was our own feet. We sent out patrols at night but that was the extent of our activities.

"Oh, the mountain was eventually taken but by then we had been removed. Fresh troops, not green troops, were brought in and there were back-up groups to spare. You see it wasn't really important whether or not the mountain was taken when they wasted us. The big offensive was planned for the spring after northern Europe was just about secure. We later learned ours was to have been a holding action until spring; you could have fooled us at the time.

"During the Italian campaign companies and battalions of the 366th—and this was possibly true of the units of the 92nd Division—were given frontage to cover which according to military science would require a division or at least a regiment intact. The 366th was never used as a regiment; yet we were given frontage beyond our capacity to cover consistently. We were assigned what was tantamount to suicide missions to carry out. One of these missions wiped out an entire company. The company commander's body was found floating down the river. Despite these inequities many of the men performed far above and beyond the call of duty but did not meet the super-standards set for the 366th Infantry Regiment to get official recognition.

"A few of our men did win citations for heroism. During the German counterattack that began the night after Christmas, Private Trueheart Fogg—that's his name honest—saw enemy soldiers approaching his platoon area. As they started to set up a machine-gun nest, he moved out under heavy fire and killed the four members of the gun crew. Another enemy machine gun on his opposing flank pinned him down. A squad of enemy soldiers advanced on his position. He stood up and completley destroyed the second gun position; he saved his platoon from complete annihilation. For that he received the Silver Star.*

"I was not in the companies committed to the crossing of the Cinquale Canal, but Staff Sergeant William Newmuis was in the first wave of troops in the attack. After leading his platoon across the canal and three hundred yards into enemy territory, he noticed an enemy 88mm gun crew firing at friendly tanks about 150 yards away. He maneuvered alone, under hostile mortar and small-arms fire, into a position where he picked off the five-man enemy gun crew. He then covered his platoon's advance, killing three snipers in the process. He led his men across the Margo canal and single-handedly captured thirteen enemy soldiers in a mortar emplacement.**

"If I recall correctly, Colonel Ferguson received a Silver Star for giving leadership to the 366th. I am sure the colonel would be the first to tell you most of the 366th was taken from under his command and was com-

---

*Williams's notes here summarize the official citation, which also describes the enemy soldiers as a "raiding party of twenty-five . . . armed with hand grenades, machine guns, and burp guns," and concludes with a mention of Fogg's "intrepid daring and fearlessness." Fogg entered the service from Newark, New Jersey. (Circular No. 89, Headquarters, Mediterranean Theater of Operations, 10 July 1944.)

**Williams's notes summarize the official citation, which mentioned that Newmuis entered the service from Pennsburg, Pennsylvania. (General Order No. 30, Headquarters 92nd Infantry Division, 23 May 1945.)

manded directly by staff. I do not question the colonel's medal, but knowing that the Silver Star and the Bronze Star are literally given to officers for running up to the front line and staying an hour, it would seem that Private Fogg and Sergeant Newmuis deserved higher awards. Newmuis's job was to lead his platoon; he didn't have to save those tanks. The snipers were attacking his platoon, so you could say picking them off was part of his job. However, when he left his platoon in a protected area and captured thirteen German soldiers, all mortar men, he was looking out for everyone. Nothing is more deadly to infantry than mortar fire. I have often asked myself just what constitutes 'above and beyond the call of duty' for a black soldier.

"When winter was over and the weather had cleared, all kinds of assistance was brought forth for the final push. The 366th had paid a high price but not high enough to be allowed to participate in the last and victorious chapters of the Po Valley campaign. More than half of the men of the 366th had been killed or wounded in action, but the fighting of our regiment was discredited so miserably that on March 14, 1945, at Bottinaccio, Italy, it was deactivated as a combat regiment and converted into two service units.* A more devastating blow could not have been dealt this group of soldiers who were proud of their outfit and their contribution to winning the war. Battle-hardened officers and enlisted men, who had seen their friends killed and mutilated and had taken the carnage as part and parcel of war, cried when they heard of this ultimate humiliation. We were completely shattered. As far as I was concerned, this ended the history of the 366th, which had been written in blood across the mountains of northern Italy.

"In my opinion, to come to some conclusion about whether colored soldiers are poor soldiers, or victims of unfortunate circumstances, it might be feasible to analyze the thinking of our military leaders. I quote an article carried in a postwar issue of *Time*:

> A former Japanese-American chaplain of the 442nd Nisei Regiment stated recently at a gathering of veterans of World War II, that after combat duty in France the 442nd was once more assigned to combat duty in northern Italy. The commanding general told their officers, before entering battle, that having done some commendable fighting they would no longer be sacrificial troops.

The Nisei fought under the same commanding general in northern Italy as did the 366th. Men of the 366th have good reason to believe that they were used as 'sacrificial troops.'"

Collins George was war correspondent for the Pittsburgh Courier. *He*

---

*General Order No. 32, Headquarters, 5th Army, gives the official date as 28 March. The two service units were the 224th and the 226th Engineer General Service regiments.

arrived in Italy in mid-March 1945 and reports first-hand on Truman Gibson's visit, on segregation in Viareggio, and on the fate of the 366th Infantry Regiment.

Collins George: "I was assigned to cover the 92nd Division and the 332nd Fighter Group in Italy by the *Courier*. My arrival in Italy coincided with the breaking up of the 366th Infantry Reiment. The regiment was being turned into two service units. Have you ever seen grown men cry? I witnessed officers and enlisted men alike crying over what was being done to their regiment, of which they were so proud. All of the men I talked to, whatever their rank, felt the 366th had been given a raw deal from beginning to end, once they were sent overseas. The reason, they were an all-black outfit. The commander of the 366th at that time was Colonel Alonzo Ferguson. I sincerely regret I did not arrive earlier so that I might have been in a position to report first hand what had happened to the 366th. I was several months too late.

"I should say at once that I was not a favorite of the commander of the 92nd Division, General Almond. He had allowed an officers' club to operate in Viareggio that black officers could not attend. As soon as I learned of this I got a friend who was an officer with the 332nd to come to Viareggio and try to enter the club. My photograph of this officer being expelled by the whites at the club was perfect and the general was furious because, of course, there was no denying the evidence. That picture closed down his club; General Almond himself had attended the club on occasion so he was very much aware of the policies under which it functioned. The all-white officers' club program died hard. They would open a new one elsewhere but as soon as I got wind of it I succeeded in closing their new venture down. General Almond could not keep me from attending his press conferences, so his childish revenge was not to speak to me. It was rather amusing to see a so-called big man his true size.

"You know there is a lot of talk about the final big push in the Po Valley by allied troops in the spring of '45. Now I don't want to take anything away from anybody but the big drive that ended at Genoa would not have gotten off of the ground if there had not been the Italian partisan uprising. The Italian underground came out in the open at that time and they were cutting the Germans up from the rear. This is what made it possible for the allied troops in the Po Valley to go forward. The Germans still held the high ground and it was strongly fortified. They would have been there a long, long time had not the Italian partisans hit them from the rear.

"I arrived in Genoa ahead of our troops and there was fighting going on; it was the Italian partisans cleaning up Genoa. The Italian Fascists were happy to see our troops because the partisans were working them over right along with the Germans.

"I was at the press conference where Truman Gibson was supposed to have used the term 'melting away' in reference to the troops of the 92nd

Division. This whole unfortunate thing came about because *Stars and Stripes* regular reporter was not there. They had some little pipsqueak in his place. To illustrate his ability, or more to the point his lack of ability, their representative had to ask who Truman Gibson was.

"Immediately after the press conference I filed my story. If one cares to look it up in the *Courier* they will find Mr. Gibson's words, and there is no such terminology credited to him. The *Afro-American* representative had also been present at the conference, but he waited to send in his story, unfortunately. When he did it was too late, the damage had already been done by *Stars and Stripes*. That little obnoxious dimwit had written what he had wanted to write, not what had transpired. The wire services picked up his story and it was spread around the world as the gospel. The black men of the 92nd were having a hard enough time without having this devastating blow to their morale, which was already low. General Almond most certainly could have made some attempt to defend his men and blunt some of the sharp criticism of them; it would have done wonders for his troops, but the general was a prejudiced man.

Perhaps the closest we can get to an unbiased report on the 92nd division comes from German officers captured during the Italian campaign. From them, Special Investigation and Intelligence learned that:

> *the 92nd Division forces were plan-bound. They would adhere strictly to plans formulated before the attack, never deviating from them. The Germans found that the scout and shock undertakings of the division were well prepared and carried out. . . . The front line troops of the 92nd were vigilant and in readiness for defense, but the German command considered the division, whose combat efficiency and training it judged inferior to that of other American divisions, to have made poor use of terrain, to have irresolute command, and to lack tenacity. [Quoted in Lee, p. 55]*

Lieutenant Colonel Marcus Ray, commander, 600th Field Artillery, 92nd Division, said in a letter to Truman Gibson:

> *the 92nd was doomed to a mediocre performance of combat duty from its inception. . . . I do not believe enough thought was given to the selection of white officers to serve with the 92nd, and further, the common American error was made of assuming that Southern white men understand Negroes.*
>
> > *In white officered units those men who fit the Southern pattern are pushed and promoted regardless of capabilities and those Negroes who exhibit manliness and self-reliance and self-respect are humiliated and disgraced. I was astounded by the willingness of the white officers who preceded us to place their own lives in hazardous positions in order to have tractable Negroes around them. [Emphasis added]*
>
> > *In the main I don't believe the junior officers guilty of faulty judgment or responsible for tactical failure. Soldiers do as ordered, but*

when plans sent to them for execution from headquarters are incomplete, inaccurate, and unintelligible there is inevitable confusion.

Racially we have been the victims of an unfortunate chain of circumstances backgrounded by the unchanged attitude as regards the proper "place" of the Negro. . . . I do not believe the 92nd a complete failure as a combat unit, but when I think of what it might have been I am heartsick. [Quoted in Lee, p. 589]

AFTERWORD

The history of the black soldier in World War II will some day be written. This book has recorded the recollected feelings of the black GI, part of the basic data the future historian will need to write that history. The future historian will have the factual army reports, archival materials, and Lee's "official" history among his sources, but how will he assay what went on in the guts and minds of the black GI? When we write of Caesar's soldiers or Charlemagne's troops we literally hunger for any scrap of chance evidence of what the soldiers thought and felt; the chance find of a *graffito* of a Roman legionnaire is pounced upon by the historian and sucked dry of any possible insight it may give into the humanity of the man who served. In later wars, letters could be used to reveal what the soldier thought and felt. Recording the actual speech of the men, this book cuts our guessing down to a minimum.

The author has let the GI speak for himself. He may be telling the absolute truth, the truth colored by twenty-five years of recollection, or he may tell less than the truth, deliberately or unconsciously. What is of most crucial importance is not exact correspondence of the report with the event—impossible even for the most carefully researched historical account—but how the actors in this World War II drama reacted, how they remember, what they choose to remember or forget, what they understood about their experience. There is no question that the twenty-five or more intervening years provide a view for the ex-GI quite different from the one he held when he left the army for civilian life in 1945. But it is better to record the past in reflection than to forget it altogether. And it is important to know what memories have stayed strong over intervening years, for that indicates the depth of the experience and the impression it made.

In quite another connection, a recent reviewer spoke of books that are both windows on the past and mirrors of the present.* The intensity and

---

*Rabbi Jack Riemer, review of *The German Church Struggle and the Holocaust* (ed. Franklin H. Littell and Hubert G. Locke, Detroit: Wayne State University Press, 1974), in *America*, 5 April 1975.

vividness with which the soldier recalls his abysmal situation during World War II reminds us how much there is left to do before an open society is achieved in this country. That the stories seem so shocking today indicates some progress in the social thinking of white Americans. We are also reminded that, just as prejudice did not begin in 1965, the fight against it was not born just a decade ago.

The Publisher

APPENDIX

Table of Organization, Infantry Division

Major-General, CO

3 Regiments
Colonel, CO

Regiment	Regiment	Regiment

(Each regiment has a Cannon Company,
an Intelligence and Reconaissance Platoon.)

3 Battalions
Lt. Colonel, CO

1st Bn	1st Bn	1st Bn
2nd Bn	2nd Bn	2nd Bn
3rd Bn	3rd Bn	3rd Bn

(Each Bn has Antitank Platoon
and medical detachment.)

4 Companies
Captain, CO

A Company	E Company	I Company
B Company	F Company	K Company
C Company	G Company	L Company
D Company	H Company	M Company
		(There is no J designation.)

Table of Organization, Infantry Division (Continued)

(D, H, and M are Headquarters Companies,
and Heavy Weapons Companies—
mortars, 81mm, 30mm machine guns.)

---

3 Rifle Platoons and 1 Weapons Platoon commanded by a 1st lieutenant make a company.
3 Squads make up a platoon, commanded by a 2nd lieutenant.

Division also has:
Division Engineers, Bn, Lt. Colonel, CO
Medical Detachment, Major, CO
Division Artillery, 3 Bns, 155mm Howitzers, Lt. Colonel, CO
Quartermasters Bn
Signal Bn
MP Company
These units are directly attached to Division headquarters. A Division has approximately 8,000 men normally; it can have more.

GLOSSARY

AGCT	Army General Classification Test; a measure of literacy and general education
ASTP	Army Student Training Program
AWOL	Absent without leave
BAR	Browning automatic rifle
Base	Used informally to refer to the airfield, camp, or fort where the person speaking is stationed.
CBI	China-Burma-India theater of war
CO	Commanding officer
Cracker	Any white southerner
DFC	Distinguished Flying Cross
ETO	European theater of war
Exec.	Executive officer (second in command)
FA	Field Artillery
G-1	Personnel section of division and upper staff
G-2	Intelligence section of division and upper staff
G-3	Operations section of division and upper staff
G-4	Supply section of division
LCT	Landing craft, tank
LST	Landing ship, tank
M1	Garand Model 1 semiautomatic rifle
MP	Military police
NCO	Noncommissioned officer
OCS	Officers Candidate School
OD	Officer of the day

Patty	Slang term for white person
POE	Port of Embarkation
POM	Preparatory for movement
POW	Prisoner of War
PX	Post exchange (supply store)
RCT	Regimental combat team
Recon	Reconnaissance
ROTC	Reserve Officers Training Corps
Repple depple	Replacement depot
Section 8	Discharge from the service for psychological unfitness.
SP	Shore Patrol
S-2	Intelligence section of regiment and lower staff
S-3	Operations section of a regiment and lower staff
Spookwaffe	Name adopted by personnel of 332nd Fighter Group, by analogy with *Luftwaffe*
Sub Thompson	Light, portable automatic weapon also referred to as a Thompson
TAC Officer	Officer in charge of a hangar
TDU	Tank Destroyer Unit
TOE	Table of Organization and Equipment
.03	Springfield Armory 1903 bolt-action rifle
201-file	Personal record file

BIBLIOGRAPHY

(Includes literature cited in Colonel Queen's foreword and in the publisher's introduction, as well as supplementary reading.)

Anderson, Trezzvant W. *Come Out Fighting: The Epic of the 761st Tank Battalion, 1942–1945*. Privately printed, 1945.
Assuring Freedom to the Free: A Century of Emancipation in the USA. Ed. Arnold M. Rose. Detroit: Wayne State University Press, 1964.
Blumenson, Martin. *Bloody River: The Real Tragedy of the Rapido*. Boston: Houghton, Mifflin & Co., 1970.
Bogart, Leo, ed. *Social Research and the Desegregation of the U.S. Army*. Chicago: Markham Publishing Co., 1969 ("Markham Series in Public Policy Analysis.")
Blacks in White America Since 1865: Issues and Interpretations. Ed. Robert C. Twombly. New York: David MacKay, 1971.
Butler, Broadus N. "The City of Detroit and the Emancipation Proclamations." *Assuring Freedom to the Free*. Ed. Arnold M. Rose, Detroit: Wayne State University Press, 1964.
Burton, Hal. *Ski Troops*. New York: Simon & Schuster, 1971.
Cardoso, Jack. "The Black Man as Soldier." *The Negro Impact on Western Civilization*. Ed. Joseph Roucek. New York: Philosophical Library, 1970.
Carisella, P. J., and Ryan, James. *The Black Swallow of Death*. New York: Marlborough House, Inc., 1972.
Catton, Bruce. *This Hallowed Ground*. New York: Doubleday & Co., 1956.
_____. *A Stillness at Appomattox*. New York: Doubleday & Co., 1953.
_____. *Grant Moves South*. Boston: Little Brown & Co., 1960.
Dalfiume, Richard M. *Desegregation of the U.S. Armed Forces: Fighting on Two Fronts, 1939–1953*. Columbia, Mo.: University of Missouri Press, 1969.
Drotning, Philip T. *Black Heroes in Our Nation*. New York: Cowles Book Co., 1966.
Dugan, James, and Stewart, Carroll. *Ploesti*. New York: Random House, 1962.
Elstob, Peter. *Hitler's Last Offensive*. London: Secker & Warburg, 1971.
Emilio, Luis F. *A Brave Black Regiment*. Boston: Boston Book Co., 1894.
Fall, Cyril. *The Great War*. New York: Putnam, 1933.
Farago, Ladislas. *Patton: Ordeal and Triumph*. New York: Dell, 1970.
Finkle, Lee. "The Conservative Aims of Militant Rhetoric: Black Protest during World War II." *Journal of American History*, 60 (1973): 692–713.
Fishel, Leslie H., and Quarles, Benjamin. *The Negro American: A Documentary History*. Chicago: Scott Foresman, 1967.
Fletcher, Marvin. *The Black Soldier and Officer in the United States Army, 1891–1917*. Columbia, Mo.: University of Missouri Press, 1974.

Franklin, John Hope. *From Slavery to Freedom*. 3d rev. ed. New York: Knopf, 1967.

Francis, Charles E. *Tuskegee Airmen: The Story of the Negro in the ASAAF*. Boston: Bruce Humphries, 1955.

Garfinkel, Herbert. "Negroes in the Defense Emergency," *Blacks in White America Since 1865: Issues and Interpretations*. Ed. Herbert C. Twombly, New York: David McKay, 1971.

Gatewood, Willard, Jr., *Smoked Yankees*. Urbana, Ill.: University of Illinois Press, 1970.

Ginzburg, Ralph. *100 Years of Lynching*. New York: Lancer Books, 1962.

Hastie, William H. "On Clipped Wings." *Crisis*, separate issue, October 1943.

Higgins, Trumbull. *Soft Underbelly*. New York & London: Macmillan, 1968.

Higginson, Wentworth. *Army Life in a Black Regiment*. Boston: Beacon Press, 1962.

Inouye, Daniel K. *Journey to Washington*. Englewood Cliffs, N.J.: Prentice Hall, 1967.

Landis, Arthur H. *The Abraham Lincoln Brigade*. New York: Citadel Press, 1968.

Leckie, William. *Buffalo Soldier*. Norman, Okla.: University of Oklahoma Press, 1963.

Lee, Irvin. *Negro Medal of Honor Men*. New York: Dodd Mead, 1967.

Lee, Ulysses. *U.S. Army in World War II: Special Studies: The Employment of Negro Troops*. Washington, D.C.: Office of the Chief of Military History, 1966.

Lincoln, C. Eric. "The Black Muslims as a Protest Movement." *Assuring Freedom to the Free*. Ed. Arnold M. Rose. Detroit: Wayne State University Press, 1964.

Logan, Rayford W., and Cohen, Irving S. *The American Negro*. Boston: Houghton Mifflin, 1967.

Miller, Donald M. *An Album of Black Americans in the Armed Forces*. New York: Watts, 1969.

Marshall, S. L. A. *Bastogne*. Washington, D.C.: Infantry Journal Press, 1946.

Motley, Mary P. "Charles Andrew Hill" (unpublished).

The Negro Soldier: A Select Compilation. Boston: R. F. Walcutt, 1861. Rpt. Westport, Conn.: Negro Universities Press, 1970.

Neil, William. *Colored Patriots of the American Revolution*. New York: Arno Press, 1968.

Nobecourt, Jacques. *Hitler's Last Gamble*. London: Chatto & Windus, 1969.

Otley, Roi. *Black Odyssey*. New York: Charles Scribner & Son, 1948.

Pritchard, Frank S. *Seek, Strike and Destroy*. Privately printed, 1946.

Redding, J. Saunders. *The Lonesome Road*. New York: Doubleday, 1958.

Romanus, Charles F., and Sunderland, Riley. *Stilwell's Command Problems*. Washington, D.C.: Office of the Chief of Military History, 1956.

Schoenman, Seymour. *Negroes in the Armed Forces*. Washington, D.C.: Associated Publishers, 1945.

Scott, Emmett. *The American Negro in World War I*. Washington, D.C., 1919. ("The Official History.")

Sitkoff, Harvard. "The Detroit Race Riot of 1943." *Blacks in White America Since 1865: Issues and Interpretations*. Ed. Robert C. Twombly. New York: David McKay, 1971.

____. "Racial Militancy and Interracial Violence." *Journal of American History*, 58 (1971): 661–81.

Spear, Allan H. "From the South to the South Side." *Blacks in White America Since 1865: Issues and Interpretations*. Ed. Robert C. Twombly. New York: David McKay, 1971.

Whitehouse, Arch. *Tank*. New York: Modern Literary Editions, 1960.

____. *Heroes and Legends of World War I*. New York: Modern Literary Editions, 1964.

CONTRIBUTORS

Note: An asterisk indicates that although the contributor furnished information used in the book, the full interview was not included.

Herbert Barland recently retired as Supervisor of Incentive Awards, U.S. Post Office, Detroit.

Clyde Blue is Union Representative for Postal Employees, U.S. Post Office, Detroit.

Charles Brown is an attorney living in Detroit, with offices in Washington, D.C.

Warren Bryant is a general clerk at the Detroit Post Office, with a sideline of bookkeeping and accounting.

Gilbert Cargill is a Federal Aviation administrator and a pilot examiner for the state of Michigan.

Ray Carter, of Altadena, California, is a private investigator.

Richard Carter is a clerk at the U.S. Post Office, Detroit.

Warren Carter is a clerk at the U.S. Post Office, Detroit.

David Cason, Jr., teaches sociology at the University of Michigan, Ann Arbor, where he is working on his doctoral dissertation.

*Bernard Coker is assistant superintendent, Division of School Housing, Detroit Board of Education.

Jesse Cummings works at Staley Corp., Decatur, Illinois.

Edward Donald is a supervisor in the Welfare Department, investigating welfare fraud cases, Lansing, Michigan.

Walter Downs teaches digital electronics and communications, Cass Technical High School, Detroit.

Harry Duplessis is a court administrator, Detroit.

Albert Evans, now living in Mexico, is a former commander, Detroit Police Department.

Horace Evans is a custodian for the Detroit Board of Education.

Samuel Fuller is a medical social worker in Detroit.

356

Eugene Gaillard is a musician and a custodian for the Detroit Board of Education.

*Wadye Gallant is a musician and part-time bus driver.

Collins George is music critic for the *Detroit Free Press.*

Walter Greene is a vice-president, National Bank of Detroit.

Hondon Hargrove is a permanent member of the Michigan Parole Board, Lansing, Michigan.

Ivan Harrison recently retired as a career officer in the Regular Army. He is now budget officer, Army Tank Automotive Command.

*Warren Harris is a custodian for the Detroit Board of Education.

Charles A. Hill, Jr., Detroit, is an instructor in mathematics at Oakland Community College.

*Kenneth Hines is a retired shipping clerk, living in Decatur, Illinois.

Alexander Jefferson is an assistant principal in the Detroit public school system.

*Edmon Jennings is a mail carrier in Detroit.

Richard Jennings is an auditor and IBM specialist, Detroit.

Chester Jones is warehouse manager, U.S. Post Office, Detroit.

Floyd Jones, Detroit, is Investigating Supervisor for Mental Care, Wayne County, Michigan.

Horace Jones, Detroit, is a retired Ford plant worker.

Jeffries Bassett Jones works in Supervision, U.S. Post Office, Detroit.

Ralph Jones is a contract and procurement specialist, U.S. Post Office, Detroit.

Jefferson L. Jordan is an attorney, Detroit.

Earl Kennedy owns and operates the Kennedy Tourist Agency, Detroit.

Willie Lawton is Superintendent of Maintenance, Detroit Police Department.

Eugene Lester is a teacher in the Detroit public school system.

John D. Long, an attorney in Detroit for many years, died June 10, 1975.

George Looney, Phoenix, Arizona, is a retired Army officer.

Wade McCree, Jr., Detroit, is a Judge of the United States Circuit Court of Appeals.

*Norman McRae is assistant director, Staff Development and Teacher Training, Detroit Board of Education.

Ambrose B. Nutt, Yellow Springs, Ohio, is chief of the Staff Plans Group, Air Force Dynamics Laboratory, Wright-Patterson Air Force Base, Ohio.

Eddie Oldham is a mechanic at Wagner's Casting Co., Decatur, Illinois.

Henry Peoples is a linotype operator and photo compositor for the *Detroit News.*

Frank Penick is a retired bus driver. He lives in Chicago.

Charles Pittman, Decatur, Illinois, was a detective with the Police Department, Decatur, until his retirement. He is now a Juvenile Probation officer.

Major Robert Pitts, Detroit, is a career officer with the Michigan National Guard.

Rudolph Porter, M.D., Detroit physician, died August 29, 1975.

William Price, Detroit, is an attorney.

Thomas Pruitt is storekeeper for the Detroit Board of Education.

Colonel Howard Donovan Queen. (See biographical note at the conclusion of the Foreword.)

Claude Ramsey, Detroit, is a retired postal employee.

Eddie Will Robinson is Engineer, Bell Telephone, Southfield office. He lives in Detroit.

William Purnell Shelton, Detroit, is Insurance Representative for League General and League Life of the Michigan Credit Union League.

Lester Duane Simons, Masury, Ohio, is a night watchman.

Bill Stevens works at Wagner's Casting Co., Decatur, Illinois.

Christopher Sturkey, retired mail carrier, now lives in Guadalajara, Mexico.

Douglas Tibbs is a custodian for the Detroit Board of Education.

Charles L. Thomas, Detroit, works for the Internal Revenue Service. He was partially disabled by wounds received during the war.

Roger Walden is a retired army officer and at present is supervisor of the Virginia Park Relocation, Detroit.

E. J. Wells is a committeeman of the Allied Industrial Workers Union, Decatur, Illinois.

Willard Williams is assistant to the General Secretary, Board of Education, United Methodist Church, Nashville, Tennessee.

Lacey Wilson is a police officer in Detroit.

Lathaniel Wilson, R.N., Dixon, Illinois, works at the Illinois State Institution for the Mentally Retarded at Dixon.

INDEX

Mary Penick Motley was born and raised in Detroit.
She attended the University of Michigan as an undergraduate, 1937–38, 1943–44, until forced to withdraw by ill health. Her *Africa: Its Empires, Nations,
and People* was published by the Wayne State University Press in 1969.

The manuscript was prepared for publication by
Barbara C. Woodward, who wrote the introduction.
The afterword was contributed by Bernard M. Goldman,
director, Wayne State University Press.

The book was designed by Richard Kinney. The type-
face for the text is Times Roman and italic designed
under the supervision of Stanley Morison about 1932.
The display face is Times Roman, with Stencil chapter numbers.

The text is printed on Natral white antique paper,
and the book is bound in Permalin's Buckram finish
cloth over binders boards. Manufactured in the
United States of America.